Gender and Mission Encounters in Korea

Gender and Mission Encounters in Korea

New Women, Old Ways

HYAEWEOL CHOI

Global, Area, and International Archive
University of California Press

BERKELEY   LOS ANGELES   LONDON

The Global, Area, and International Archive (GAIA) is an initiative of International and Area Studies, University of California, Berkeley, in partnership with the University of California Press, the California Digital Library, and international research programs across the UC system. GAIA volumes, which are published in both print and open-access digital editions, represent the best traditions of regional studies, reconfigured through fresh global, transnational, and thematic perspectives.

University of California Press, one of the most distinguished university presses in the United States, enriches lives around the world by advancing scholarship in the humanities, social sciences, and natural sciences. Its activities are supported by the UC Press Foundation and by philanthropic contributions from individuals and institutions. For more information, visit www.ucpress.edu.

University of California Press
Berkeley and Los Angeles, California

University of California Press, Ltd.
London, England

Library of Congress Cataloging-in-Publication Data

Choi, Hyaeweol.
    Gender and mission encounters in Korea : new women, old ways / Hyaeweol Choi.
        p.   cm.
    Includes bibliographical references and index.
    ISBN: 978-0-520-09869-5 (pbk. : alk. paper)
    1. Women—Korea—History.   2. Women missionaries—Korea—History.   3. Women in missionary work—Korea—History.   I. Title.

HQ1765.5.C445   2009
305.43'266023730519—dc22   2009023256

Manufactured in the United States of America

18   17   16   15   14   13   12   11   10   09
10   9   8   7   6   5   4   3   2   1

The paper used in this publication meets the minimum requirements of ANSI/NISO Z39.48 – 1992 (R 1997) (Permanence of Paper).

For Dan

Contents

Preface and Acknowledgments

This book started with a most serendipitous accident. While teaching at Smith College, I visited the Sophia Smith Collection, an excellent archive for women's history on that campus. There I read some private letters written in the late nineteenth century by American women corresponding with their families from overseas. I was immediately curious about the experiences of those women who ventured into foreign lands more than a century ago, and I could not help but to compare the experiences they described with my own experiences as an international student in the United States in the late twentieth century. I thought my solo journey to the United States as a graduate student was quite an adventure; however, the half-day flight across the Pacific Ocean paled next to the two-month ocean voyage from San Francisco to East Asia that these women took a century ago. I knew that the first girls' school in Korea was founded by an American missionary woman. Intending to prepare a single journal article on the history of that mission school, I visited major mission archives in the United States, and I gradually came to the realization that I had just uncovered a gold mine, and a very long but enjoyable process of discovery began.

The historian Martina Deuchler notes that "women do not figure prominently in Korean historiography past or present."[1] Such a long "tradition" is not likely to change any time soon. Yet there have been slow but encouraging signs of change in recent years. A growing interest in the proactive and even subversive power of women in the Confucian Chosŏn dynasty, an attempt to bring out a more dynamic and complex picture of the New Woman [sin yŏsŏng] phenomenon of the 1920s and 1930s, and a rigorous investigation of the oppressive nature of the predominant ideologies of modernization and nationalism in shaping and understanding women's lives signal a more comprehensive approach to history, taking gender as a legitimate and indeed a powerful category of analysis in comprehending history and culture.

In line with these ongoing endeavors in Korean gender studies, this book adds one more critical site for investigation: the West. The image of the West, more precisely that of the United States, has been closely tied with Korea's gendered experiences of the modern in the hierarchical world order since the late nineteenth century. To be sure, the enhanced status of South Korea in the contemporary world economy and the increasingly cosmopolitan experience of its citizens have begun to stimulate a much more complex understanding of the West. Yet the habitual perception of the West as "advanced" and "progressive," especially in the realm of gender relations, remains unchanged. Starting with the prevailing notion in Korean historiography that American women missionaries were the pioneers who acted as catalysts for Korean modern womanhood, this book examines the genealogies of the "modern" woman among Korean intellectuals and American women missionaries within the context of Korea's colonization by Japan at the turn of the twentieth century. Focusing on some of the major issues of modern womanhood, such as gender equality, access to institutionalized education, participation in the public realm, and representations of gender in the print media, the book investigates the dynamic interplay between the Confucian-prescribed gender ideology of Korea, the nationalistic desires for nation-building among Korean intellectuals, and the Christian gender ethics of American women missionaries. The analysis emphasizes both the institutional and discursive endeavors among both Koreans and Americans in fashioning modern womanhood in accord with their own mandates—either nationalist, Christian, or secular modern. In so doing, the book sheds light on the ways in which competing narratives on modern womanhood reconfigured Confucian gender ideology for the modern era and also reveals the tensions that women experienced between their newly-found space for emancipation and other forms of social and political control over their bodies and subjectivities.

I have been very fortunate to have many friends and colleagues who have offered invaluable comments and moral support that have helped to make what could have been an arduous task very fulfilling. When I first began this project, Donald Clark introduced me to key literature and offered continual support. Namhee Lee has been unstinting with her time and thoughtful insights. She read the entire draft, providing constructive comments and warm encouragement. Discussions with Hwasook Nam, Sun Joo Kim, Seungsook Moon, Theodore Jun Yoo, and Robert Eskildsen at different stages of the project helped to clarify a variety of issues. Ellen Widmer and Daniel Bays graciously lent their expertise in Chinese literature and history, and Jan Bardsley shared her knowledge of Japanese New Women through cheerful e-mail messages. I am also greatly indebted to Timothy Lee, Kenneth Wells, and Sung-Deuk Oak, whose comments pointed to some of the most important conceptual and empirical issues and helped me to go deeper in my analysis. I am grateful to a number of institutions for offering me the opportunity to present my research: the University of California at Los Angeles, the University of British Columbia, Yale University, the University of Utah, Amherst College, Harvard University, the University of Washington, the University of Southern California, the University of Minnesota, Smith College, the University of Texas at Austin, and Seoul National University. I benefited tremendously from the questions and comments from the audiences at these presentations. I would especially like to express my thanks to John Duncan, Namhee Lee, Robert Buswell, Sung-Deuk Oak, Jennifer Jung-Kim, Ann Choi, Bruce Fulton, Ross King, Donald Baker, Nam-lin Hur, John Treat, Janet Theiss, Paola Zamperini, Sun Joo Kim, Carter Eckert, Ian Miller, Ellen Widmer, Hwasook Nam, Clark Sorenson, Anand Yang, Kyung Moon Hwang, Ji-Eun Lee, Robert Oppenheim, Robert Eskildsen, Dan Horowitz, Helen Horowitz, Yung-Sik Kim, Chung Hyung Min, Mun Chung-yang, and the many graduate and undergraduate students who made insightful remarks and observations that prompted me to revisit a number of issues. At various panels and conferences, I greatly benefited from discussions with Laurel Kendall, Mark Peterson, Haesook Kim, Sheila Jager, Koen De Ceuster, Wayne Patterson, Vladimir Tikhonov, Elizabeth Underwood, Chong Bum Kim, Ruth Brouwer, and Margo Gewurtz. I would like to express my special thanks to two external reviewers who provided comments and valuable suggestions that greatly helped me to expand my perspective and sharpen my thesis. Needless to say, all errors or shortcomings are entirely my own.

I have enjoyed visiting mission archives over the years, in large part because of the generous support from the archivists I met. Margery Sly at the Presbyterian Historical Society in Philadelphia guided me with patience and moral support. Dale Patterson and Mark Shenise at the General Commission on Archives and History, the United Methodist Church at Drew University, helped me uncover some of the hidden treasures in their archive. Like many others who have been working on foreign missions, I feel lucky to have had assistance from Martha Smalley at the Yale Divinity School Library. I also greatly benefited from a number of librarians in the Korean book collections at various universities: Mikyung Kang at the University of California at Los Angeles, Choongnam Yoon at the Harvard-Yenching Library, Hyokyong Lee at the University of Washington, and Joy Kim at the University of Southern California. The generosity and able assistance of all of these people was truly invaluable.

Many grants enabled me to travel to archives or secure time for writing. They included the National Endowment for the Humanities Summer Stipend, the Korea Foundation's Advanced Research Grant, the Northeast Asia Council Research Grant of the Association for Asian Studies, the Academy of Korean Studies' Research Grant, Seoul National University's Kyujanggak Travel Grant, and a Smith College Faculty Research Grant. Arizona State University also offered assistance through several internal grant programs, including the Women and Gender Studies Summer Research Grant, the A. T. Steele Grant of the Center for Asian Research, and the College of Liberal Arts and Sciences Research Grant.

My home institution, Arizona State University, has been a collegial and intellectually stimulating place to work. I am particularly indebted to Karen Leong, Ann Koblitz, Margaret Knapp, Debby Losse, Tony Chambers, Tracy Fessenden, James Foard, Eugene Clay, Hava Samuelson, Susan Gray, Gayle Gullett, Andrew Barnes, and George Thomas for their comments on parts of the manuscript. Weekly Sunday walks with a group of amazing women friends—Gail, Debby, Helene, Isabelle, Bobbie, and Judith—introduced me to the charm and beauty of the southwestern desert (except for the coyotes) and kept me balanced and happy with delightful conversations at the breakfasts afterwards.

I am very grateful to John Lie, who took an interest in my work for this series and offered invaluable support. I am also indebted to my editor, Nathan MacBrien, who was always supportive, especially in my most anxious times. I feel lucky to have had his insights, advice, and encouragement throughout the process.

One of the delightful moments in the process of preparing the manuscript was when, out of the blue, I heard from descendants of the American missionaries whose lives and work in Korea are the topic of my book. Eric Garwood, a relative of Ellasue Wagner, whose unpublished novel is one of the topics of this study, generously shared several photos of Wagner. I also got connected with Sylvia Noble Tesh and Patricia Noble Sullivan, granddaughters of W. Arthur and Mattie Noble, who also kindly donated family photos to be used in the book. I am thankful to the General Commission on Archives and History, the United Methodist Church at Drew University; the Presbyterian History Society; and the Na Hye-sŏk Memorial Foundation for granting me the use of photographs included in this book.

I would like to express my gratitude to those journals that have allowed me to employ elements of previously published articles in chapters 4 and 5: "Women's Work for 'Heathen Sisters': American Women Missionaries and their Educational Work in Korea," *Acta Koreana* 2 (July 1999): 1–22; "Women's Literacy and New Womanhood in Late Choson Korea," *The Asian Journal of Women's Studies* 6, no. 1 (2000): 88–115; "Missionary Zeal in a Transformed Melodrama: Gendered Evangelicalism in Korea," *The Asian Journal of Women's Studies* 7, no. 1 (2001): 7–39; "An American Concubine in Old Korea: Missionary Discourse on Gender, Race, and Modernity," *Frontiers: A Journal of Women Studies* 25, no. 3 (2004): 134–161; "Christian Modernity in Missionary Discourse from Korea, 1905–1910," *East Asian History* 29 (June 2005): 39–68; "(En)Gendering a New Nation in Missionary Discourse: An Analysis of W. Arthur Noble's Ewa," *Korea Journal* 46, no. 1 (Spring 2006): 139–169.

I have always felt that I have the best possible parents-in-law. My mother-in-law's love and relentless support for me sometimes makes my husband envious. My father-in-law sadly passed away, but the trees he planted in our backyard provide a happy reminder of his love. I also lost my own father, whose passion for learning had long been a source of inspiration. I only wish he could celebrate the publication of this book with us just as we used to celebrate his publications. As always, my mother and my sister and her family in Korea have been more than ready to cheer me up and offer wisdom in life and work, and they are now wondering how much longer my next book might take to complete.

This book is dedicated to Dan, my soul mate, better half, and companion with whom I have discovered the beauty and joy of life. No words would be sufficient to express my deepest gratitude to him; I would simply sing "*Uri nŭn*" (We) for him.

A Note on Romanization and Translation

Korean words in the text are rendered using the McCune-Reischauer system, with the exception of proper names for whom alternative spellings are well established. Korean names follow the standard order—family name first—unless a particular name is traditionally rendered in Western order. Unless a source is specified, all translations of Korean texts are mine.

1. Re-Orienting Gender

In 1938, to celebrate the fiftieth year of the Korea mission, the Woman's Foreign Missionary Society of the Methodist Episcopal Church published a book entitled *Fifty Years of Light*. J. S. Ryang, the Korean general superintendent of the Korean Methodist Church, contributed the foreword, in which he stated:

> It was Mrs. Scranton's pleasure to establish the first modern school for girls in all Korea. It was the pleasure of her followers to establish the first school for the blind, the first kindergarten for children, and the first women's hospital. It was the Woman's Foreign Missionary Society that gave to Korea the first Korean woman M.D., the first Korean woman Ph.D.; as well as the first trained nurse and the first trained kindergarten teacher. . . . The work of the ladies of the Missionary Society over a period of fifty years has helped to bring Korean womanhood into a new world. It has dignified the wife and raised the mother to a higher plane. Personality has been liberated and womanhood has been permitted to look out upon a new world. And best of all we are permitted to see the establishment of true Christian homes.[1]

Ryang, as a male leader in the Korean church, congratulates the women missionaries for bringing Korean women to "a new world," noting that Korean women were able to pursue higher education and professional careers in the public realm because of the missionaries' efforts. His praise, together with the metaphor of light used in the book's title, represents the public image of American women missionaries as pioneers of Korean *modern* womanhood. Significantly, his foreword is accompanied by a painting of a Korean woman dressed in traditional clothes *[hanbok]* holding her child to her bosom, standing next to a beautiful garden with trees and flowers and a Korean-style pavilion in the background (figure 1). This

1

carefully chosen picture of a happy mother and her baby in the peaceful garden of a Christian family is Ryang's ultimate point; he concludes that "the establishment of true Christian homes" was the best achievement of women missionaries. In the end, Korean women's advancement in the public domain is secondary to the Christian domestic sphere.

Echoing Ryang's sentiments, the American women missionaries, largely Methodists and Presbyterians,[2] promoted themselves as agents that brought light to the presumed darkness of Korea, where women had lived a "life of want, vice and ignorance."[3] Under the guidance of American missionaries, Korean women "have begun to rouse up from a state of utter mental inertness, and are looking about hungrily for something wherewith to train and occupy their growing powers."[4] The metaphorical contrast between the "utter degradation of a Christless world,"[5] dark, ignorant and impure, and the Christian world, bright, pure and peaceful, is a recurring motif in emancipatory missionary discourse. However, although they introduced new ideas and encouraged Korean women to take part in modern education, medicine, sports, and professions, which had previously been unimaginable,[6] women missionaries still firmly believed that a "woman's most important place will always be the home."[7] This potential contradiction between the new public opportunities for women and their idealized role in the private domain of the family is the focus of this book: the multiple and conflicting meanings of modern womanhood in transcultural and religious encounters between Koreans and American missionaries in Korea at the turn of the twentieth century.

Korean historiography has often portrayed Christianity as a positive force in shaping modern womanhood, echoing some of the Western scholarship that has portrayed the women's foreign mission as the "first feminist movement" in North America and a contributor to "the liberation of women in Asia and Africa."[8] It generally cites two factors to support this view. One is the Christian notion of equality for women and men under God, a major shift in perspective from the hierarchical Confucian gender relations in which women had been regarded as inferior to men.[9] Coupled with Korean reformers' desire for *munmyŏng kaehwa* (civilization and enlightenment) from the late nineteenth century, the gender equality presumed in Christian doctrines has been thought to have been the foundation of modern womanhood. However, this largely laudatory evaluation has recently been challenged by a group of scholars who scrutinize both the doctrinal nature of Christianity and the persistent patriarchal structures of churches that have tended to oppress rather than liberate women.[10] Indeed, two prominent Christian women of that time,

Kim Maria (1892–1944) and Kim Hwal-lan (a.k.a Helen Kim, 1899–1970), were already vocal about the gender discrimination within the Christian community in the early twentieth century.[11] Similarly, while Korean historiography has portrayed women missionaries as modern and liberated, in actuality they assumed unequal, subordinate positions within the larger church organizations.[12] In line with the prevailing gender ideology based on the Victorian notion of "separate spheres,"[13] women missionaries were channeled into the "feminine" domestic arena, while men held leadership roles in the religious, evangelical domain through preaching and organizational supervision. Further, women missionaries themselves firmly believed the domestic sphere to be the ideal province for women, whose moral and spiritual strength was expected to nurture the family and the community.

The other, perhaps more important factor that associates missionary women with modern womanhood has to do with the missionaries' contribution to institutional reforms. In particular, the establishment of mission schools for girls is used as a prime example of how Christianity helped Korean women develop a desire for liberation from patriarchal Confucian norms and put forward new modern agendas to enhance women's rights. Some feminist scholars on Korea consider the first mission school for girls, *Ewha haktang*, to be the incubator for gender equality and emancipation and assert that Christianity was a central mover in facilitating the early feminist movements in Korea.[14] However, as I discuss in chapter 4, one cannot readily assume that the simple presence of schools is in itself a sign of modernity. To do so would be to overlook the role of institutionalized education as a site for "symbolic reproduction" that "comprises the socialization of the young, the cementing of group solidarity, and the transmission and extension of cultural tradition" through its curricular and disciplining rituals.[15]

What has been conspicuously missing in the aforementioned debates is the question of what constituted *modern* womanhood in the minds of the Koreans and the American missionary women. In what ways did both Korean and American gender ideologies collide and converge with relation to newly defined roles for women in the family and society? In what aspects was discourse on modern womanhood integral to or in tension with the emerging nationalism in Korea in the face of Japanese colonial rule (1910–45)? How does the early formation of modern womanhood closely associated with American Protestant missionaries affect the subsequent evolution of modern gender ideology in Korea? And what implications and relevance does the critical analysis of these transcultural encounters have for postcolonial feminist scholarship? To be sure, the historical and local meanings of the modern are extremely diverse and dynamic, manifested in such terms as *colonial modernity, translated modernity, alternative/multiple modernities,* or *gendered modernity.*[16] Naturally, the relationship between Christianity and modernity is a complex one.[17] The tensions between spirit and reason, religion and science, and religiosity and secularity prompted numerous debates that continue to the present.[18] Moreover, if we add gender as the main category of analysis to the already complex relationship between Christianity and modernity and the particular historical circumstances of Korea on the eve of Japanese colonialism, we face an extraordinarily complex phenomenon that defies any simple binary understanding.

In her study of the gender of modernity, Rita Felski argues that "the history of the modern needs to be rethought in terms of the various subaltern identities" that had long been suppressed, and "the history of the modern is thus not yet over; in a very real sense, it has yet to be written."[19] Recent feminist scholarship in Korea has rekindled interest in "the gender of modernity" as part of the effort to rewrite women's history from women's point of view, and in so doing, to restore women as historical agents rather than as merely the object of representation by men. Their special attention to *sin yŏsŏng* (New Women) during the Japanese colonial era has been strategic, in order to demonstrate how male intellectuals' hypermasculine discourse of modernity relegated New Women to the status of deviant and selfish individuals or tragic heroines, thus obscuring the dynamics and complexity of women's experience. Repositioning New Women as a political and sexual group rather than as scattered individuals, feminist scholars argue that New Women signified modernity by challenging Confucian patriarchal gender relations and by emphasizing women's own subjectivities.[20] Pointing out Korea's unique historical experience among colonized countries, they also call attention to how the Japanese colonial condition and the demand for activities for national independence intersected with the formation of modern female subjectivities.[21] As the feminist journal *Yŏsŏng kwa sahoe* (Women and Society) rightly puts it, the phenomenon of New Women should be understood within the intersection of modernity, colonialism, patriarchy, and Korean nationalism. Further scrutiny of the gendered modern experience has made some scholars cast rhetorical doubt on the relationship between gender and modernity. The title of an anthology, *"Kŭndae," yŏsŏng i kaji anŭn kil* ("Modernity," A Path Not Open to Women),[22] captures not only the strong sense of deprivation among women from the lively experience and adequate representation of the modern in Korean history but also the continuing power of the patriarchal family and the state in controlling women's bodies and lives.[23]

The majority of studies on modern womanhood tend to center on the period around the 1920s, which was surely the highlight of modern womanhood in Korea represented by New Women. However, I argue that a fuller understanding of the evolution of modern womanhood in Korea requires an examination of the era leading up to the 1920s. The decades immediately after Korea opened its door in 1876 shed light on the ways in which various social groups, including missionaries, competed for a hegemonic role in shaping modern womanhood while laying the foundation for their mandates in the form of particular discourse and institutional reforms. This period is also fundamental to our understanding of the root cause of the rather fixed and homogeneous image of American women missionaries, offering insights into the constant negotiations between various social groups in articulating and asserting what modern womanhood should be. In this sense, it is highly useful to adopt a Foucauldian genealogical method in order to bring out multiple representations, perceptions, and memories about the "modern" woman that are neither fixed nor homogeneous. As Foucault notes, genealogy helps us understand multiple deviations that do not exactly fit into the dominant discourse. Those deviations have been overlooked or ignored, but they are crucial to revealing the complex power relations in representing events and people in a certain way.[24] This book questions the conventional historiography that contributed to the production of certain reality and ways of thinking about modern womanhood. At the same time, it excavates oddities and deviations that were an important part of everyday life and constituted other layers that help us come to a fuller understanding of the meaning of the modern.

The book builds on previous studies of the American Protestant mission to Korea and East Asia, but it opens up a new area of research. First, much research on the Korea mission has tended to focus on its theological or political, especially nationalist, characteristics, paying little attention to gender.[25] Only in recent years have studies appeared that examine more complex cultural aspects of the Korea mission, with a subset that focuses on women missionaries.[26] This study takes gender as the primary category of analysis, critiquing the dominant forms of historical writing, which have largely marginalized women.[27] The book incorporates recent scholarship in colonial studies that reveals a more complicated picture of the mission field in which the experience of women missionaries was colored by their status as the subordinate gender but the "superior" race.[28] Centering on women missionaries' perspectives and their experience with Koreans, the book intends to untangle the complex web of ideas and activities that missionaries put forward in imagining "modern" Korea and modern womanhood within the particular historical circumstances of Korea at the turn of the twentieth century. In order to bring out more complex desires and diverse experiences of missionaries, I analyze not only official missionary records but also "missionary fiction" and personal diaries. Missionary fiction, in particular, is an important genre that blurs the boundaries between the public and the private, shedding light on the spoken and unspoken desires of missionaries in their observations of "the Other" and interactions with the local people and culture.

Second, previous research on gender and the foreign missionary enterprise has largely been carried out from the perspectives of Western women.[29] This study emphasizes interactions between Koreans and American missionaries by drawing on both Korean and American archival sources.[30] In so doing, it examines the intersections of their discourses and activities in order to understand the everyday experience of Korean and American missionary women, who tried to cope with the tensions between the old and the new and brought about new ways of life that were both liberating and oppressive.[31] As Donald Baker notes in his analysis of the role of Christianity in the construction of Korean identity, there has been overemphasis on the influence of missionaries and lack of attention to the ways in which Koreans "responded" to the new religion.[32] The mandate and evangelical strategies of the foreign missionary enterprise show remarkable similarities across the globe. However, distinctive features of the foreign mission emerged in the different responses that local people had toward the newly introduced religion, depending on their specific goals and agendas within the particular historical circumstances.[33] Thus, incorporating the voices of Koreans into the analysis of this transcultural experience is crucial in hashing out some of the local characteristics of the foreign mission.

Third, the book focuses on the interplay between the discursive formation of the modern in which it was imagined and represented by competing narratives and the institutional endeavors of different agencies. The public image of American women missionaries as pioneers of *modern* womanhood in Korea largely has to do with an "acultural" approach to modernity (in Charles Taylor's term) that focuses on societal modernization in the form of institutional changes and pays little attention to the discursive construction of meanings that are culturally coded within the unbalanced power relations that existed between missionaries and Koreans. Further, such an acultural approach fails to understand the complex life experiences of women, which cannot be separated from textually mediated discourses.[34] As Antoinette Burton argues, feminist historiography can greatly benefit from "a cultural reading of 'the social' or a social reading of 'the cultural'" that underscores the dialectical relationship between discourse and reality.[35] In an attempt to unravel the fluid and multiple meanings of modern womanhood, this book pays attention to the interplay between institutional/political changes and discursive formation.[36] In so doing, it brings out the ways in which both missionaries and Koreans acted from their own subject positions in the specific historical circumstances and participated in institutional reforms and the production of particular knowledge about the modern.

Finally, the book intends to offer some comparative insights into the legacy of American Protestant missionary work in the formation of early modern womanhood in East Asia. Unlike in China and Japan, the relationship between Christianity and modern womanhood was exceptionally close in Korea. To be sure, many modern women in China and Japan were influenced by Christianity, largely through their education at mission schools;[37] however, the majority of feminists in China and Japan were non-Christians, and in the discourse of Chinese and Japanese feminists, Christianity was sometimes referred to as a conservative force that hampered feminist causes.[38] In contrast, the majority of New Women in Korea were educated at Christian mission schools and formed the first cadre of professional women in Korea, becoming the symbol of modern womanhood. An insightful comment made in 1933 by Hwang Sin-dŏk, one of the New Women of the time, is revealing. She noted that since the opening of Korea in the late nineteenth century, "almost all women over thirty who were educated and had worked in society had been exposed to Christianity, even if it was only minor contact."[39] In his discussion of the unique contribution of Christianity in introducing "Western civilization, that is new knowledge" to Korean society, Yi Man-gyu, a prominent male educator, asserted in 1934 that "Christian-influenced women have near complete hegemony in the women's world" in Korea.[40] In this way, Christian-educated women often took center stage in setting the agendas and activities for the women's movement in Korea, and thus Christianity became an integral part of the idea of modern womanhood in Korea.

One of the main factors that set the Korean experience apart from that of the Chinese and the Japanese is Korea's colonization by Japan—a non-Western and non-Christian imperial power. While Protestantism was often associated with Western imperialism in China and Japan, American Protestant missionaries were perceived by Koreans rather positively because they were not associated with an encroaching colonial power and also because their work in medicine and education was instrumental to Korea's modernization project.[41] Negative perceptions of Western missionaries in China and Japan resulted in a series of acrimonious incidents, such as the Boxer Rebellion in China in 1900.[42] In contrast, the largely positive image of American missionaries led to the remarkable success of Christian evangelical movements in Korea.[43] More important, the diametrically opposed images of American missionaries, who were seen as bearers of Western civilization and potential allies for the Koreans in their anti-Japanese movements, and the Japanese colonial power, which was viewed as an oppressor of the Korean nation, had a significant impact on the discourse of modern womanhood in Korea. Using the concept of "Christian modernity" (as antithetical to secular modernity), I will elaborate on how Japanese colonial powers provided American missionaries with a unique platform to inculcate a variety of *modern* womanhood defined by religious devotion, domesticity, and social service.[44]

The other distinguishing factor was the state of women's education. Before missionaries arrived in China and Japan, there had been a sizable class of educated women engaging in publishing literature in China, and Japanese girls and women were educated at local schools during the Tokugawa era.[45] However, in Korea during the Chosŏn dynasty (1392–1910), while a small number of women, largely from the upper class, engaged in writing, the number of educated women never approached a level that could be said to sustain a community outside home or family, nor was there any formal educational system for girls and women.[46] Protestant mission schools offered formal education to girls and women in the late nineteenth century for the first time in Korean history, and, more important, they continued to play a key role in women's education through the first half of the twentieth century. In addition, while China and Japan had a relatively critical mass of educated women who were prepared to take part in public discourse and other national activities by the early twentieth century, the number of educated women in Korea remained very small throughout the colonial era; thus, there was an insufficient sociopolitical base to put forward critical agendas for women.[47] This contrast further affected the range and intensity of the discussion of modern womanhood in East Asia.

In this book, I focus on three major groups that played central roles in shaping public discourse on modern womanhood and pioneering institutional reforms: (1) American Protestant missionaries who first came to Korea in the late nineteenth century, (2) Enlightenment-oriented Korean male intellectuals, and (3) the Korean women themselves. Here the term *Enlightenment [kaehwa]* differs slightly from the Western notion that bloomed in the eighteenth century or the "Chinese Enlightenment," which often refers to the May Fourth Era in the early twentieth century (1915–1925). In Korea, while historians trace the root of the Enlightenment movement to the *Sirhak* (School of Practical Learning) of the seventeenth and eighteenth centuries, the term began to be deployed in connection with the development of a modern nation-state after Korea opened its doors to other countries starting in 1876. By the 1890s, "Enlightenment" and "civilization and enlightenment" became slogans used to promote the maintenance of national sovereignty, the overhauling of social structures, and civil rights.[48] The arrival of American Protestant missionaries coincided with Korea's Enlightenment period, and interactions between missionaries and Enlightenment-oriented Korean intellectuals were crucial in fashioning a certain mode of discourse on modern womanhood and introducing institutional reforms for women in the areas of education, work, and the family. This study largely focuses on the period that starts with the arrival of American women missionaries in Korea in 1885 and continues until the eve of Korea's colonization by Japan in 1910. However, it also draws on archival materials that stretch to 1945, the year Korea was liberated from Japanese colonialism, in order to show concrete examples from the lives of Korean Christian women that reveal the fluid and complex nature of modern womanhood.

It is appropriate here to point out some of the particular historical circumstances that significantly distinguish gender and mission encounters in Korea from those elsewhere. At the core is the desire for modern reforms in Korea that accompanied the critical examination of long-standing Chinese influence and emerging nationalist consciousness in the face of power struggles between imperial Japan and Western countries. When the first group of American missionaries arrived in Korea in the mid-1880s, Korea was being rapidly integrated into the global capitalist system after having been forced by Japan to open its doors. An influx of new ideas, customs, products, and institutional forms overwhelmed the society. While the government and Enlightenment-oriented Korean intellectuals were exploring reform models from Japan and the West in order to establish a modern nation-state, Korea became a site of contest among imperial powers. Competition among neighboring powers resulted in two major wars on the Korean peninsula— the Sino-Japanese War (1894–95) and the Russo-Japanese War (1904–5)— that radically changed regional geopolitics by upsetting the China-centered power dynamics that had existed for centuries. The Russo-Japanese War, in particular, was (in Peter Duus's words) the "takeoff point of Japanese imperialism," and eventually led to Korea's colonization by Japan in 1910.[49]

The first twenty-five years of the American Protestant mission in Korea coincided with a period of great political turbulence and sociocultural uncertainty. The threat of colonization by Japan in particular posed a unique political challenge for missionaries as they laid the foundation for evangelical activities.[50] This reality offered missionaries both advantages and disadvantages. The fact that American missionaries were not associated with the colonial authority provided them with exceptional advantages in gaining the favor of the Koreans. In his first annual report in August 1885, Henry Appenzeller, a Methodist missionary, already noted that the "American stands very high with the Koreans. We care nothing for their land and are anxious only to do them good, both of which they seem to recognize."[51] The fact that the American missionaries were not affiliated with a colonizing threat and that the Koreans tended to view them as potential allies in the anti-Japanese movement offered missionaries special opportunities for their evangelical work.

Although American missionaries were largely dissociated from imperialism in the eyes of Koreans, they made concerted efforts to gain the trust of the Japanese colonial authorities in order to maintain and expand their mission goals.[52] Further, the U.S. government strategically negotiated with Japan in mapping out colonial territories, as evidenced in the 1905 Taft-Katsura Agreement, in which the United States acknowledged Japan's interest in Korea, and this acknowledgment was reciprocated with Japan's support of U.S. colonial interests in the Philippines. Under these circumstances, missionaries were implicated in a tripartite power split in which Japan was the colonizer, Korea the colonized, and the United States (and the West more broadly) a competing imperial power. At a spiritual and religious level, American missionaries saw a binary division between the Christian West and the non-Christian East. Although Japan deeply impressed the West with its military-imperial power, the Western opinion of Japanese morality and spirituality remained unflattering, with a stubbornly lingering view that "modern civilization was synonymous with whiteness and Christianity."[53] This distinction between secular/political and spiritual/religious domains was strategically deployed by missionaries as a way to tackle politically precarious situations.

Given this unique political and cultural situation, I argue that American missionary discourse from the Korea mission field can be characterized by the notion of *Christian modernity*, more precisely Protestant Christian modernity, which served as a key foundation for the modern gender ideology advocated by missionaries.[54] By "Christian modernity" I mean an ideology that advocates the idea of an inevitable historical movement toward material and technological modernity and places the moral, cultural, and spiritual role of Christianity at the core of that enterprise. As Prasenjit Duara points out, during the nineteenth century "the singular conception of Civilization based originally upon Christian and Enlightenment values came not only to be dominant but to be the only criterion where sovereignty could be claimed in the world."[55] The notion of Christian modernity needs to be understood in the context of the dominance of Western modernity and the claim that Christian civilization is superior to all others.[56] The notion of Christian modernity emerged as a powerful way for missionaries to resolve the tensions caused by the intertwining of political turmoil with conflicting racial, cultural, and gender ideologies. Caught between a "heathen" Korea and a modern but non-Christian Japan, missionaries tried to locate and articulate "the Others" with relation to their presumably superior Christian civilization. In so doing, missionaries, either intentionally or unwittingly, tended to contribute to the justification of both Western and Japanese imperialism not by taking a position of outright support for any imperial project, but rather by putting forth the idea that true modernity needed to be centered on spiritual values, and moral superiority was the quality that missions could provide. I further argue that despite Japan's relative success as a modern imperial power, it was an expedient symbol for missionaries to use to point out the limits of *secular* modernity and the superiority of Christian ethics as the principal element of true modernity.

In addition, the idea of Christian modernity captures the dilemma of the modern as it was felt by Westerners in the nineteenth and early twentieth centuries. On the one hand, modernity seemed to offer unlimited possibilities in economic development, the rationalization of political organizations, and more democratic human relations. On the other hand, they witnessed its "negative" results in a lack of moral restraint and a pervasive sense of alienation and despair.[57] For religiously committed people, the "modern" weakening of moral restraint and growing challenges to religious establishments were urgent issues to be addressed, and they felt obliged to offer their own ideal version of true modernity. Arthur Brown, one of the most powerful spokesmen for the American foreign mission, stated in 1904 that a "Christless civilization is always and everywhere a curse rather than a blessing . . . No evolution is stable which neglects the moral factor or seeks to shake itself free from the eternal duties of obedience and of faith. . . . What is civilization without the gospel? The essential elements of our civilization are the fruits of Christianity."[58] While privileging Christian spirituality over material, secular progress, Brown was also keenly aware of the potential "yellow peril," referring to the potent military power of Chinese soldiers *if* they were "properly armed, disciplined and led," and more importantly to the soaring power of imperial Japan, especially after its victory over Russia in the Russo-Japanese War. He concluded that "Christendom has too long regarded heathen nations with a pity not unmingled with contempt. It is now beginning to regard them with a respect not unmingled with fear."[59] Brown's perceptive comments on China and Japan in the midst of imperial competitions around the world precisely points to the growing tensions between secular modernity and religious commitment. In the debate about religion's location in modernity, there has been a consensus that modernity does not necessarily mean secularization. In Talal Asad's words, "a single straightforward narrative of progress from the religious to the secular is no longer acceptable."[60] José Casanova also argues that in the context of the violent and calculated encounter between the West and the East in the era of Western imperialism, the important question is not the shift from the religious to the secular but the ways in which various religions respond to "the imposition of the new global worldly regime of Western modernity. . . . It is our tendency to link processes of secularization to processes of modernization, rather than to the patterns of fusion and dissolution of religious, political and societal communities, that is of churches, states and nations."[61] It is in this process of fusion and dissolution that the ideology of Christian modernity is articulated through negotiation, persuasion, and dissonance with competing social and political forces in the Korean context.

The gendered form of Christian modernity is prominently displayed in the missionary discourse on modern womanhood in Korea. It privileges the spiritual over the secular and the political in defining true womanhood.[62] From the standpoint of women missionaries, who believed that Christianity was a major reason for the "advanced" status of women in the West, the life of "heathen" Korean women was deplorable. Harsh critiques of the miserable and "backward" life of women in Korea came one after another, focusing on the denial of educational opportunities, the low respect from men and society in general, and the lack of hygiene. However, what deserves special attention is that women missionaries' critique of "heathen" womanhood did not necessarily come from any "feminist" consciousness. To the contrary, they were more conservative and traditional than the liberal groups among relatively well-educated working women in the West at the time.[63] As Kwok Pui-lan aptly points out, their role model was "Frances Willard, a Methodist woman who tried to save the home through the temperance movement, rather than Susan B. Anthony or Elizabeth Cady Stanton, the leaders of the suffrage movement."[64] As I will demonstrate throughout the book, women missionaries cherished the Victorian notion of true womanhood that valued religious piety and domesticity and held unfavorable perceptions of the suffrage movement and the phenomenon of New Women in the West.[65] Despite many obvious differences between Korean and American women in terms of their role and status in the family and society, the missionaries' conservative views on gender relations unexpectedly found a tangible alliance, when necessary, with Confucian-prescribed gender ideology in Korea, where the emphasis on domesticity and the socially subordinated role of women was in line with what Barbara Welter calls "the cult of true womanhood" of the Victorian era.[66] The interface of missionary gender ideology with traditional ideas of Korean womanhood was strategically beneficial in gaining trust and support from the Korean public, who were afraid that missionaries might Westernize Korean girls, who would then in turn ignore native customs. This shared gender ideology also persistently impeded the efforts of Korean women, notably New Women of the 1920s, to break away from traditional gender norms. As I show in chapters 4 and 6, this seemingly harmonious coexistence of Confucian and Victorian gender ideologies began to face serious challenges from the 1910s, when a sizable group of educated Korean women emerged and put forward their new agendas for modern womanhood by utilizing their broader exposure to the modern that went beyond the ideology of Christian modernity.

While it remains true that missionaries greatly contributed to the production of the first generation of educated women in Korea, I argue that the homogenized image of missionaries as "modern" ignores a complex set of tensions these missionary women felt between the putative images of the premodern and the modern, the East and the West, their racial superiority and gender inferiority, and their lack of authority within patriarchal mission organizations and the unprecedented authority in their own "women's work for women." I further argue that the perception of "modern womanhood" among missionary women was cultivated *through* their encounters with Korean women, who were presumed to be premodern, backward, and oppressed.[67] These encounters prompted women missionaries to feel more liberated and progressive than their Korean charges. Yet, despite their sense of freedom and gender equality vis-à-vis the oppressed status of Korean women, American women missionaries often felt tensions with "modern" or New Women in the United States at the time. Nonetheless, the hierarchical relationship between women missionaries and Korean women in terms of class and race in the West-dominant world order was an important backdrop for the rather simplified understanding of women missionaries as "modern." This understanding largely stemmed from the prominent image of the West as the central power in the modern era.

Another distinct aspect of Korean modern womanhood is its relation with the emerging movement of Korean nationalism. To be sure, the close ties between nationalism and modern womanhood are found elsewhere in the world.[68] However, in Korea the complex relationship between nationalism and modern womanhood was shaped within the context of the declining influence of China and the ascending power of Japan and the West. The supremacy of Chinese civilization began to crumble in the eyes of Koreans, especially after China was defeated by Japan in the Sino-Japanese War and co-signed the Treaty of Shimonoseki, which officially ended the tributary relationship between China and Korea that had existed for centuries. A series of political and cultural movements, including *Kabo kyŏngjang* (the Reform of 1894) and the proliferation of the print media, expedited what Andre Schmid calls the "decentering" of China.[69] Despite a tone of empathy for China's fate in some print media, it was often represented as "a nation lacking civilization" and "the object of the world's ridicule and humiliation," while the West emerged as the new center of civilization.[70]

Decentering China at this particular historical moment has significant implications for old and new gender relations. In their initial effort to modernize Korea, Korean intellectuals criticized Korea's dependence on Chinese social and cultural practices, including Confucian-prescribed gender ideology. As chapter 2 shows, within the larger national modernization project, the woman question emerged as one of the central issues demanding major reform. Starting with Pak Yŏng-hyo's memorial to the King in 1888, Confucian-prescribed gender relations were repeatedly challenged.[71] The Reform of 1894 was one of the first legal attempts to accommodate the new status and enhanced roles for women in modern times.[72] In his 1895 book, *Sŏyu kyŏnmun* (Observations from My Travels in the West), Yu Kil-chun observed that Westerners treated their women fairly well because they believed that "woman is the foundation of human society and the girder of the house, and thus if she is weak or ignorant, she would not be able to fulfill her central role."[73] The print media played a major role in reexamining the philosophically sanctioned notions of *namnyŏ yubyŏl* (the distinction between men and women) or *namjon yŏbi* (men honored, women despised). Gradually ideas about gender equality, women's education, and the role of women in society beyond the family started to gain currency as a new moral order in public discourse and literature. However, one of the arguments I make in this book is that, while their critique created significant cleavage in the centuries-long gender ideology and thus opened up new experiences and possibilities for women, it ended up recon-figuring Confucian gender roles through the evocation of another modern metanarrative: nationalism.

The discussion of nationalism that began in the late nineteenth century is of key relevance to Korean women's experience of modernity. Arguably, nationalism has been the most powerful frame of reference for sociopoliti-cal issues, not only in scholarly work but in basic ways of thinking among Koreans in modern times. In his discussion of nationalism, Craig Calhoun argues that it is one of the definitive features of the modern era and is "a way of constructing identity that does not address such variation so much as it simply posits temporal depth and internal integration."[74] Thus, a sig-nificant factor in nationalism is this definitional feature, which suppresses individuality and essentializes group membership. As a consequence, dif-ferent identities and subject positions, including gender, tend to be ignored. In addition, nationalism is not simply a political doctrine but rather a "basic way of talking, thinking and acting."[75] Here two key elements emerge as relevant to the Korean experience. One is that this organizing principle of nationalism often resulted in male-dominant societal and cultural arrange-ments and continued to demand women's subordination to men. The other is what Kim Tong-ch'un calls *chŏngsŏjŏk minjokchuŭi* (heart-warming nationalism),[76] a deeply rooted attitude toward the nation in which the col-lective as sacred is taken for granted and no other agenda can demand more privileged treatment. The idea that nationalism should be the central con-sideration for Koreans has been so widely accepted that privileging other sociocultural agendas has been unthinkable. That is why nationalism in Korea has rarely been critically scrutinized. It is only in recent years that historians, feminists, and literary scholars have begun to engage in critical examination of the nationalist discourse and its implications for gender.[77]

In a debate on the relationship between Korean nationalism and femi-nism, Kim Ŭn-sil and Yun T'aeng-nim scrutinize the ways in which Korean nationalism as a metanarrative has silenced women's voices. They argue that it would be impossible to see any serious progress in the emancipation of women without rejecting nationalism altogether.[78] In his analysis of Kŭnuhoe (Friends of the Rose Sharon, 1927–31), with a central focus on the promise and reality of nationalist claims for women, Kenneth Wells poses an important question—"what happens when one takes the position of women as one's starting point?" Critiquing the "central claim of nation-alism, namely, that nationalism works on behalf of all and therefore it is in everyone's interest to work on behalf of nationalism," he argues that women's experience in the 1920s and 1930s undermines this claim, and indeed women were hindered in seeking their own independent agendas.[79] Conversely, Chŏng Chin-sŏng and Chŏng Hyŏn-baek stress the positive impact of Korean nationalist consciousness and activities on the progress of the women's movement. Echoing the historical examples of women in former colonies, they argue that women's participation in nationalist movements and women's awareness of the Korean national situation helped them develop unique strategies that not only were appropriate to the Korean context but enabled them to expand the gendered domain.[80] What runs through in these various arguments is the almost immeasurable degree to which nationalist discourse and activities have been an integral part of the reconfiguration of gender ideology since Korea embarked on modern nation building.

The prominence of nationalist discourse in modern womanhood, however, does not mean that all gender issues were subsumed under the rubric of nationalism. To the contrary, women's everyday life and their subjectivities were far more complex and dynamic than what Korean historiography has portrayed with its central focus on nationalism. As Rita Felski points out, using Ernest Bloch's idea of synchronous nonsynchronicity, "individuals coexist at the same historical moment, yet often make sense of this moment in strikingly disparate ways."[81] The significance of the notion of synchronous nonsynchronicity here lies in the revelation of different realities experienced by diverse groups. It is these different realities experienced by women and men that help us go beyond the boundaries of metanarratives such as nationalism. In so doing, we can uncover not only gender-specific experiences of the modern but also patriarchal strategies of gendering the modern.

Throughout the book, I emphasize the *transcultural* context as a key element in our understanding of the gender of modernity in Korea. This is in part because in the late nineteenth century, the Western idea of modernity first reached Korea via Japan in conjunction with the discourse of "civilization and enlightenment" as a new mandate in the competitive global capitalist system.[82] It is also because the West, especially the United States, began to be represented among Koreans as *the* model to emulate in pursuit of modernity.[83] And the American Protestant missionaries were one of the most active groups in reinforcing the image of the West/United States as the bearer of advanced civilization and a benefactor willing to teach and share their civilization. Although much research now argues that the origin of modernity was not in the West but in the *interaction* between the West and its colonies, modernity has often been associated with the place—the West.[84] In this vein, Timothy Mitchell poses an important question: how was history staged to represent the West as the origin and dominant force of modernity?[85] In a similar context, Dipesh Chakrabarty investigates an image of Europe that "remains deeply embedded in *clichéd and shorthand forms* in some everyday habits of thought." These habits of thought both help and hinder the analysis of a complex historical process.[86] It is therefore critically important to understand the interactive and transcultural context in which American missionaries represented themselves and were represented by Koreans as modern, advanced, and progressive, a model to emulate in order to join the presumably singular path of history that positioned the West at the center and in the lead. In this reified and homogenized imaginary, the Christian, the modern, and the West are presumed to be a unitary system, which has been the basis of the image of missionary women as "modern."

The internal dynamics of the transcultural context can be best captured in Mary Louise Pratt's concepts "transculturation" and "contact zone." She introduces "transculturation" to explore "how subordinated or marginal groups select and invent from materials transmitted to them by a dominant or metropolitan culture. While subordinated peoples cannot readily control what emanates from the dominant culture, they do determine to varying extents what they absorb into their own, and what they use it for. Transculturation is a phenomenon of the contact zone." Then she defines the term "contact zone" as "the space of colonial encounters, the space in which peoples geographically and historically separated come into contact with each other and establish ongoing relations, usually involving conditions of coercion, radical inequality, and intractable conflict."[87] The contacts between Koreans and American missionaries were not "colonial encounters" in the traditional understanding of that term, and that fact significantly contributed to the mostly positive image of the United States.[88] However, it was in this contact zone that the initial imaginaries of modern Korean womanhood emerged in close association with the image of the West and American women missionaries. It is also in this contact zone that Korean intellectuals appropriated the image of the modern and the West for the purpose of subordinating gender to their mandate of nationalism and modernization.

In her seminal work, *The Gospel of Gentility*, Jane Hunter argues that women missionaries were not a mere part of the foreign mission enterprise but a powerful cultural force "in the crusade for American influence in China." She further points out the significant gap between the Chinese women and American missionaries in terms of their expectations of each other, arguing that "the key to the impact of missionary women on Chinese women's history lies less in their religious program than in the secular message transmitted by their lives."[89] The fact that Chinese women had a greater interest in the secular rather than the religious message is powerful evidence that they were not passive recipients of Western knowledge but active solicitors, choosing what they wanted to accept or ignore. In a similar context, Kwok Pui-lan advocates an approach that treats women converted to Christianity not as "missiological objects" but "historical subjects," bringing the voices of converted women as agents in shaping and reshaping their own lives.[90] The power of agency can also be found in the missionary women themselves. Ruth Brouwer demonstrates how some women missionaries wanted to go beyond the traditional "woman's work for woman" in pursuit of their own professional and social ambition.[91] The mission field uniquely provided these women with the opportunity to pursue their ambition and to exercise power and authority not readily available to them at home.

This study locates the emergence of modern womanhood within the matrix of the incessant social, cultural, and political changes in which Western modernity, Confucian gender ideology, Korean nationalism, and Japanese colonialism intersected. Examining the competing discourses of modern womanhood presented by American missionaries and Korean male and female intellectuals, the book traces the ways in which they embraced, collaborated, rejected, or appropriated each other's primary mandates— whether it was Christian, nationalist or secular modernity. In so doing, this book is an attempt to "re-orient gender" in two aspects. First, it critiques the hypermasculine historiography of modern Korea, investigating the ways in which a remarkably resilient patriarchal system has adjusted itself to the rapidly changing social and cultural milieu since the late nineteenth century by tempering women's voices and subjugating women to a male-centered national mandate. As chapter 3 demonstrates, despite the patriarchal constraints imposed on women in terms of what "proper" role they might have, women managed to find some ingenious ways to expand the scope of life into the public realm. Second, the book attempts to reconsider prevailing approaches to feminisms and to the West. I examine the multifaceted meanings of various representations—American missionaries' representations of Koreans, Koreans' representations of American missionaries, and the American missionaries' representations of themselves—with the aim to reveal the politics of gender and race within the historical context of these transcultural encounters. It is hoped that the work of "re-orienting gender" will shed light on the multitudinous nature of the modern woman and its far-reaching impact on contemporary gender relations in Korea and beyond.

Each chapter focuses on some of the major issues concerning gender and modernity in Korea. Chapter 2 focuses on gender equality as a new moral order, which was viewed in late-nineteenth-century Korea as a marker of civilization by both missionaries and Korean male intellectuals. Gender equality, and for that matter the equality of all human beings regardless of social class, began to be understood as a constitutive part of the new moral order in opposition to the prior one based on Confucian gender relations. I examine the ways in which missionary discourse and claims by Enlightenment-oriented Korean intellectuals addressed gender equality, and how they located the issue within the spectrum of their separate mandates, either the Christian modern or the nationalist modern.

The new movement for gender equality led to another noble development for women: women in the public domain. Chapter 3 focuses on the dynamic interfaces between the public and the private, considering them not as a clear-cut binary but as fluid, negotiated, and contradictory domains that women attempted to move between. To women missionaries, the foreign missionary enterprise allowed them to venture into the world, where they had unprecedented opportunities for power and authority. At the same time, they advocated the *domestic* ideals embodied in the Christian family. For Korean women, who were now deemed to have the same human rights as men, the physical engagement in the public space was a radical departure from the centuries-long *naeoebŏp* (inside-outside rule) that confined women to the inner chambers and, as a result, kept them out of public life. This transition, of course, was not immediate for Korean women. Residual forces of the inside-outside ideology doggedly remained. This tension between the public and the private, I will argue, ultimately culminated in the modern notion of the family as the central foundation for a modern nation-state, with women's roles reconfigured according to the ideology of *hyŏnmo yangch'ŏ* (wise mother, good wife).

One of the most direct and prominent experiences of public life was schooling outside the home. Chapter 4 examines the rapidly growing importance of education for women. Missionaries put a priority on educating girls and women as the fastest way to introduce the Bible and Christian teachings, while Korean intellectuals saw the importance of educating the future mothers of the male citizens who would lead the new Korea. I specifically analyze the overt and covert goals of education and the curriculum used at mission schools, examining how the idea of being educated in the modern era converged or diverged in the Korean and missionary minds.

Chapter 5 explores some literary representations of modern womanhood put forward by American missionaries. In contrast to newspapers and journals, literature offers a window into a more complex and fluid picture in imagining and representing the modern. Its "fictional" nature is not entirely bound by realistic or plausible situations or personae. Protagonists and their acts, feelings, and perceptions project a dynamic array of past and present, hopes and despairs, obligations to the collective and longing for the self, all of which underlie the complexity of modern experience. I examine missionary fiction, tracing the various images of modern woman that closely intersected with particular historical mandates—Christian, nationalist, or secular—and revealed the tensions between the old and the new, and the universal and the transient.

Korean male intellectuals' and American women missionaries' pursuit of nationalist or Christian modernity was never a one-sided enterprise. Chapter 6 focuses on specific examples of New Women who were educated at American mission schools and became symbols of "modern" women in Korea. The phenomenon of New Women from the 1920s embodied and simultaneously contradicted the Christian-centered or nationalist mandates driven by missionaries and Korean male intellectuals. Touching on a major shift in leadership in shaping new agendas for modern womanhood, the chapter analyzes key debates New Women brought to the public, including the importance of the self and a new outlook on working life, romance, marriage and motherhood. The proliferating print media constituted a vital site for women to contest traditional gender norms and engage in debates with male intellectuals. The public expressed both fascination with and relentless criticism of these New Women because of the challenges they presented to Confucian gender ideology through their desire for work, their scandalous love affairs, and their rejection of the sacred nature of motherhood. The lively debates in the media and portrayals of New Women as celebrities reveal the growing tensions between collective mandates—Christian or nationalist—and the New Women's own desire for selfhood.

In the last chapter, I discuss how and why the issue of gender and modernity is far from being resolved and continues to pose a number of questions about presumed "progress." I conclude that historically specific and textured analysis of the genealogies of American missionary knowledge and Korean intellectuals' ideas about the modern offers a strategic point for dissecting the multilayered realities and representations of the modern, critiquing the reified image of the West and the male-dominated historiography of modern Korea and heralding a new feminist scholarship.

2. Gender Equality, a New Moral Order

In his highly popular book entitled *Our Country*, prepared for the American Home Missionary Society in 1886, Josiah Strong confidently proclaimed that the Anglo-Saxon "is divinely commissioned" to lead the world. Strong based this claim on the argument that Anglo-Saxons were the best-qualified exponents of two great ideas: pure spiritual Christianity and civil liberty, both of which "have contributed most to the elevation of the human race."[1] The role of Christianity in advancing humanity was evident in the enhanced status of women. Strong noted that the idea of honoring womanhood has "its root in the teachings of Christ, and has grown up slowly through the ages to blossom in our own," resulting in the elevation of the status of women. This was great progress, considering the cruel history of women in the West, where "it was not very uncommon for an Englishman to sell his wife into servitude" as recently as the early nineteenth century.[2]

The improved status of women in the West was understood as one of the manifestations of Christian civilization's superiority and became one of the primary standards against which non-Western countries were measured. The image of "heathen" women as "the greatest sufferers from the horrors of Paganism" compelled many Western Christian women to feel obliged to engage in the foreign missionary enterprise to rescue their "unfortunate" sisters and to extend to them "the blessings of Christian civilization."[3] Equipped with the singular notion of civilization largely based on the doctrines of Christian and Western Enlightenment,[4] American missionaries actively participated in standardizing the world, and the status of women signified the level of civilization that a country had achieved.

At the same time that American missionaries were coming to Korea with this sense of moral obligation, many Korean intellectuals, influenced by Western Enlightenment doctrines as well as Christianity, were embracing a similar idea about gender and its relation to degree of civilization.[5] For these intellectuals, the degraded lives of Korean women simply proved Korea's backwardness—something to overcome in order for Korea to become a civilized modern nation-state. *Tongnip sinmun* (The Independent), a pioneering newspaper in late-nineteenth-century Korea, argued that the criteria for true civilization should be the ways in which the powerful treat those without power—i.e., the treatment of the young by their elders, of the weak by the strong, and of women by men.[6] It also identified the oppression of women in Korea as one of three evil customs, along with geomancy and idol worship, that needed to be eliminated in the march toward modernity.[7] If Korea wanted to become a civilized country, women as the weaker sex needed to be taken care of and treated gently. As part of the drive for "civilization and enlightenment," male intellectuals used newly emerging print media—newspapers, magazines, and *sin sosŏl* (new fiction)—as a vehicle for challenging Confucian-prescribed hierarchical gender relations and for advocating for the equal status for women in the new nation.[8]

To be sure, the turn of the twentieth century marked a critical point in which gender equality was spoken of as a new moral principle. However, at this time and in this transcultural context there were also oppressive elements in the discourse on gender equality. At its core was a radical shift in perspective from *hierarchical* complementary gender relations to *equal* complementary relations. This new moral principle undoubtedly served as a platform for women to gain unprecedented opportunities and to go beyond traditional gender roles. However, these opportunities were consistently promoted through Christian and nationalistic metanarratives that in reality continued to subordinate women and consign them primarily to the domestic or "women's sphere." Furthermore, the same discourse that required gender equality for true civilization foregrounded a linear, hierarchical path of history that was crosscut by racial discourse in which the Christian West was represented as superior and the pagan Other as inferior.[9] It was within this discourse of civilization that gender equality as a rhetorical trope served as justification for the respective mandates of the Christian mission and the Korean Enlightenment movements.

MISSIONARY RHETORIC OF GENDER EQUALITY

More than poverty or any other material gap, the degraded role and status of women served as proof of Korea's lack of civilization in the eyes of mis-

sionaries. Even Japan, whose military strength and imperial ambition garnered respect from the West, was not perceived by missionaries as a truly
civilized country partly because of the lower status of women.[10] The key
to true civilization was presumed to be morality rather than materiality,
and for the missionaries the core of morality was Christian ethics, which
allegedly promoted gender equality under God.[11] The missionaries considered the spread of the Gospel to be a moral and spiritual obligation that
would elevate the subhuman condition of heathen women who had been
"the slave, the dog, the toy, the chattel, the convenience of men, for all past
ages."[12] The tantalizing contrast between Christian womanhood and heathen womanhood filled the pages of mission journals and correspondences:

> [T]he Korean believes her destitute of moral existence, a being without
> a soul, unworthy of a name, a creature without rights or responsibili-
> ties, only a convenient adjunct to some man—his daughter, his wife,
> his mother! Ages of mental and moral degradation have, perhaps,
> taught the woman herself to believe what her lord believes, almost
> to be what she thinks herself. Verily, women should thank God for
> birth in a Christian land![13]

> The women as a rule are densely ignorant, vulgar, and overworked;
> their minds are filled only with prejudices, superstitions, and fears of
> the unseen; their subjects of conversation confined to gossip, scandal,
> and squabbling. What an unlovely picture! This is heathen womanhood.
> Is it any wonder that our physicians are many times called to try to
> relieve the suffering of some poor wretch who has tried to end her life
> because she could endure it no longer? Many times, as I look on this pic-
> ture of heathen womanhood, I return thanks to our Heavenly Father
> that I was born in Christian America, and that we realize that Christ
> our Lord is abundantly able to save unto the uttermost and does trans-
> form the lives of these unlovely creatures into the beautiful lives of
> the daughters of the King. We have seen it.[14]

The women missionaries described conditions so dire that the Americans
were compelled to express gratitude for the happy accident of being born
in the Christian West. Given the shockingly wretched condition of women
in "the land of the shadow of death," the missionaries imagined that it was
their role to heroically transform the lot of these Korean women through
Christian teachings.[15]

The missionaries identified Confucian philosophy and practices as the
root cause of the discriminatory treatment of women.[16] They studied Confucian texts about *oryun* (the Five Moral Imperatives), which included *pyŏl*
(the separation of functions) between husband and wife.[17] Understanding

Confucianism as a "dualistic philosophy," George Heber Jones, a Methodist missionary, elaborated on the philosophical rationale by which Confucianism relegated women to inferior status:

> All nature appears to consist of pairs of opposites, though he [the Korean man] does not hold with the Zoroastrian that these opposites are also antagonists. These categories run as follows: heaven and earth, light and darkness, strength and weakness, superiority and inferiority, virtue and iniquity, male and female, and so on. The first member of each couple is always superior, the second the inferior; as scientific categories they appear to be based in the very constitution of nature, and are thus necessarily correct. Nature having thus marked woman as inferior, a man-made philosophy hastens to ticket her to that effect, and the Korean is educated in the same from his earliest school days. . . . Woman is incapable of understanding a man's business, friendship, or life, and is continually exhorted to confine herself to "woman's sphere."[18]

To Jones, the Confucian rationalization of woman's inferiority was fundamentally contradicted by Christianity, and thus was evidence of a clash between the civilizations.[19] Quoting one of the Confucian texts, *Youth's Primer*, Jones described a worldview in which women were bound by *samjong* (three subjugations)—to father, husband, and son[20]—and *ch'ilgŏ chiak* (seven offenses)—disobeying parents-in-law, bearing no son, committing adultery, jealousy, carrying a hereditary disease, garrulousness, and larceny.[21] Missionaries believed that the introduction of Christianity would herald a turning point for Korean women, an opportunity to break away from oppressive gender relations and have equal companionship with men. In this discourse, the demonization of Confucian gender norms went hand in hand with the glorified ideal of Christian womanhood.

Newly converted Korean women further reinforced the stark contrast between heathen culture and Christian womanhood. In *Victorious Lives of Early Christians in Korea*, Korean women who had converted to Christianity reflected upon the impact of the new religion on their lives.[22] A theme throughout these testimonies is the sense of liberation from oppression associated with conversion. Kim Se-dǔi explicitly stated that Christianity meant a beginning of "women's freedom" and salvation.[23] Kim Syŏk'ŏsǔ said, "Korean women's freedom movement began only after the light of Christianity began to shine on the Korean peninsula."[24] To Yi Kyŏng-suk, who became the first Korean teacher at Ewha Girls' School, the moment she met Mary Scranton, Ewha's founder, and was introduced to Christianity was a turning point in her life "from old fashion to new way, from oppression to freedom, from sin-filled world to blessed world."[25]

For the first time these women felt that they had value. Kim Se-dŭi described herself as a "lowly thing" before her introduction to Christianity, which was for her an awakening moment. She felt that Christianity enabled her to see her own God-given value, which had been denied her by Korean custom. A particularly interesting illustration of this can be found in Kim Syŏk'ŏsŭ's reflection on her baptism. Women in traditional Korea were recognized only through their connection to the men in their lives—their fathers, husbands, and sons. Their lack of independent identity was meta-phorically expressed in the fact that most women had no name of their own. Mrs. J. T. Gracey reported with shock that the Korean woman "is absolutely nameless."[26] In this context, baptism came to be seen as a special rite of passage. Kim Syŏk'ŏsŭ wrote that "the day I was baptized was the happiest day in my life. We Chosŏn women lived under the oppression of men for thousands of years without having our own names. . . . For fifty years, I lived without a name. On the day of baptism I received the name, Syŏk'ŏsŭ, as my own."[27] The act of taking a baptismal name provided her with an independent identity. Baptism was seen as a symbolic act in which women were reborn as individuals, with their own wills, dreams, and identities.

For the missionaries, such testimonies provided a powerful validation of the missionary enterprise in that they could claim Christianity had raised these women from heathen status to Christian womanhood. For the Korean women, their conversions were associated with a newly found sense of freedom and independence. They described coming into a direct relationship with God without the mediation of patriarchal figures, and thus achieving a measure of equality.[28]

"EQUALITY OF PURPOSE" VERSUS EQUAL RIGHTS FOR WOMEN IN THE MISSION

While missionaries and converts portrayed Christian womanhood as a har-binger of gender equality, early feminists in the United States were posing critical questions about the gender inequality embedded in the interpreta-tions of the Bible and the Christian community at large.[29] Most notably, in 1895 Elizabeth Cady Stanton and her colleagues published *The Woman's Bible,* in which they critiqued culturally constructed, male-centered bibli-cal interpretation. At the core of the critique in *The Woman's Bible* was the fundamentally unequal status of American women within the church organizations and the political arena. They argued that clergymen believed that women "owed all the blessings and freedom they enjoyed to the Bible," but at the same time "the demands for political and civil rights were irreligious, dangerous to the stability of the home, the state and the church."[30] Thus the church took the paradoxical position that women were endowed with their freedoms by the Bible, but that demands for freedom were antithetical to the Bible. Focusing on this contradiction, they cast a straightforward question to men: "If the Bible teaches the equality of Woman, why does the church refuse to ordain women to preach the gospel, to fill the offices of deacons and elders, and to administer the Sacraments, or to admit them as delegates to the Synods, General Assemblies and Conferences of the different denominations?"[31] They further critiqued men's attempt to ostracize women who were demanding political and civil rights as antithetical to Christian feminine virtue.

While the women's suffrage movement was taking center stage in the United States during the late nineteenth and early twentieth centuries,[32] there was a contemporaneous debate on voting rights for women in the Korea mission field. The debate took place only in the Presbyterian mission and specifically centered on the voting rights of *married* women missionaries. No parallel debate took place in the Methodist mission. This contrast is a result of differences in how the two denominations appointed and organized women missionaries.[33] In the case of Methodists, women missionaries who were unmarried or widows were often appointed by the Woman's Foreign Missionary Society (hereafter WFMS),[34] which maintained significant autonomy and independence from the general church board in terms of personnel and finances. It was common to see men and women missionaries in the same stations "appointed and salaried by two different boards in America."[35] In each Methodist mission field, women missionaries sent by WFMS created a separate woman's conference and enjoyed considerable autonomy in administering women's work. Ultimately, the Korea Woman's Conference of the Methodist Episcopal Church was established in 1899.[36] Its Constitution stipulates: "All representatives of the WFMS and the women of the General Missionary Society may become members of this conference by signing the Constitution. Those who have passed the exam of the first year's studies in the Course of Study in the Korean Language laid down for missionaries and who are engaged in active work shall be entitled to a vote."[37] According to this Constitution, not only representatives of the WFMS but also women who were appointed by the General Missionary Society[38] were invited to participate in the woman's conference, and they all had voting rights within this woman's conference. Therefore, the venue of the woman's conference enabled all women missionaries, both single and married, to participate in the decision-making processes in the work to which they were assigned.[39]

Presbyterian women also organized separate women's boards of foreign missions. However, they neither administered funds that they raised in the United States nor had power to control personnel issues because they were "auxiliary to the General Assembly's Board."[40] This streamlined unitary structure resulted in different modes of participation for women in the mission field. While single women missionaries had full voting rights, equal to those of men, married women "have hitherto been denied a voice—avowedly because they would simply double their husbands' votes and make unfair majorities."[41] The rules and by-laws stipulate: "Members of the Mission shall be entitled to vote in both the Station and the Mission after one year of service in connection with the Mission and the passing of the language examinations appointed for the first year, *except that married ladies shall not vote*" [emphasis added].[42] In 1912 a resolution was put forward that married women be allowed to exercise a vote "on condition of their passing the third year language test." This was a much more rigorous requirement than the successful completion of the first-year language test, which is what was required of other missionaries. Two prominent married women missionaries of the Presbyterian Church, Lillias Underwood and Annie Baird, offered competing reactions to the resolution.

Lillias Underwood, who came to Korea as an unmarried medical missionary in 1888 and married Horace G. Underwood a year later (and did not leave Korea until 1921), felt the resolution deserved a "protest" from married women missionaries.[43] To her, the resolution was "a slur, both on the intelligence and devotion of the married ladies of the mission" because it assumed that married women "are either too dull to be trusted with a vote, before we have passed an unusual test required of no one else for a vote, or we are so callous and indifferent to the cause we came to serve, that while a poor petty chance to vote might spur us on, love of Christ and his poor could not."[44] She argued that "if the vote on passing of the third year language examination is offered as a bribe, a sort of sugar plum to the woman who has perfected herself in the native tongue in order to obtain this, and *who needed it to spur her flagging ambition on to the goal,* or whose fitness to vote could not be depended upon otherwise, we can only say that it were far better such women not only had no vote, but had never come to the field at all." Underwood observed that, despite the trials of housekeeping and child-rearing,[45] married women demonstrated "the courage and devotion with which they plodded on against a thousand odds." She further noted that "the majority [of married women] we believe do pass all 3 examinations in the end, and often do better than their husbands." Her protest of this "humiliating" resolution was thus not narrowly drawn, but rather castigated the general lack of acknowledgement of married women's capabilities and their invaluable contribution to the mission field.[46]

In a follow-up discussion, Annie Baird (in Korea 1891–1916), who came with her husband, William Baird, offered a more traditional view and proposed dropping the discussion of married women's voting rights altogether.[47] She considered voting to be a way to exercise *moral* power in the "warfare against organized vice," such as white slavery; therefore, she was not convinced that it was necessary to have voting rights within the missionary circle, where no vicious element existed to fight against. Furthermore, in her view, "as a sex we seem to [be] credited with being ruled largely by our sensibilities, and being consequently unable to take a purely impersonal view of debated questions." Women's fundamental emotionality (in opposition to male rationality), she feared, would prove detrimental to mission policies when expressed at the ballot box. At the familial level, she pictured a worst-case scenario in which a husband and wife differed on specific issues, asking the readers, "Are we to vote with them in spite of our convictions, or not vote at all, in either case nullifying ourselves, or are we to vote against them to our and their discomfiture and grief?" She concluded that "[t]he advantages of the proposition do not seem to me very evident. The possession or otherwise of a vote has no real bearing on our personal activity as missionaries. We are under Divine obligation to do all we can in any case, and if any of us are ever disturbed by a smothered sense of injustice, we may extract comfort from the thought that there are few lots in life, even among the dominant sex, that are absolutely just in every detail." Giving priority to their role in spreading the Gospel, Baird urged her fellow missionaries to put aside any secular or political interest including voting rights, echoing the message in the antisuffrage stance of many conservative church people. In the end, the debate over the voting rights of married women missionaries was dealt with in a motion in 1913 "to rescind the clause dealing with the right of women to vote on matters relating to women's work, and refer the matter to the Executive Committee who shall determine the attitude of the married women."[48] The issue was eventually resolved, with married women missionaries gaining limited voting rights "only in their respective Stations on questions relating to women's work,"[49] which still excluded them from decision making for the general mission.

Single women missionaries had roles and positions that were relatively more fulfilling in terms of their ambitions within the mission. Often with no plan to marry and sometimes insisting on remaining "permanent single" ladies,[50] unmarried women frequently assumed leadership positions in women's work for women. In the Methodist women's conference, the majority of officers were single women. They had more frequent opportunities to travel to the countryside for evangelical work and to mingle with Koreans. In fact, they sometimes preferred to be surrounded by Koreans instead of their fellow missionaries. In her trip to the countryside with Susan Doty, Ellen Strong wrote, "I am sitting on a pile of bedding as I write, because I have come down to our Korean house at Koa-no-mo Kol for a few days to get away from English speaking people, and to get acquainted with the women in the neighborhood. . . . I cannot stay away longer from the school, now, but would like to do this thing often."[51] Josephine Campbell, who was in charge of the Carolina Institute, a girls' school, thought the location of her school, "quite distant from any foreign resident," was an advantage because she had "real neighbors."[52] While male missionaries were concerned about the safety of single women missionaries, especially when they were beyond the supervision of their male colleagues, women missionaries tended to take it as a privilege and pleasure to be surrounded by Koreans only. When a discussion of relocation of a Presbyterian girls' school in Seoul came up, the Board opposed the move partly because the new location would not be safe for single women missionaries. However, Victoria Arbuckle, one of the three single missionary teachers at the school, wrote, "None of us three ladies have any fear in going to another part of the city."[53] Because single women missionaries had closer and more frequent contact with Koreans, they often became authorities in certain aspects of Korean life, and some even identified with the "life and people of Chosen [Korea]" more deeply than their own American culture and people.[54]

To be sure, single women missionaries enjoyed a degree of freedom and independence as equal participants in missionary matters. However, despite the exceptional satisfaction most single women expressed, there were areas where they were treated unequally, especially in the matter of salary.[55] For example, in the Presbyterian Church in 1902, a married male missionary earned $1,250 and a single male missionary earned $833.33. In comparison, a single woman missionary received $625. The Committee on Salary of Unmarried Men justified the gap by appealing to a man's "personal expenses being greater and his necessarily more public life involving greater expense."[56]

In a significant way, women missionaries, both single and married, were constrained by a patriarchal church structure that institutionalized gender inequality. Women complied with these strictures because in their view the adversary was not the patriarchal structure of their own church but rather the "heathen" practices that they found in the mission field.[57] What they ultimately emphasized was their service to God, spiritual devotion, and self-sacrifice, as the discourse of Lillias Underwood and Annie Baird above makes clear. Concerns about issues related to institutional inequality for women missionaries were regarded as secondary and even selfish. Ann White argues that woman's work "gave female missionaries an equality of purpose which transcended their shabby treatment as 'assistant' missionaries."[58] In other words, women missionaries could claim that the opportunity to serve in the mission, alongside men, all doing the work of God together, was the measure of their equality, and any issues of imbalance in terms of the structure of the mission or the practical benefits were unimportant. Therefore, it was rare to hear women missionaries publicly challenge the male-dominated mission organizations.[59] The majority eschewed an explicitly feminist agenda and often dissociated themselves from the women's rights crusade at home.[60] Nonetheless, work in the mission field offered women unexpected, albeit limited, opportunities to fulfill ambitions and participate in the governance of women's work.[61] Especially, the situation that they witnessed among Korean women allowed them to feel a sense of greater freedom and equality that they attributed to Christian tradition. The testimonies of early converts further convinced them that Christian teachings had actually liberated these women, thus confirming their sense of the priority of their spiritual endeavor and reinforcing their acceptance of institutionalized gender inequality.

GENDER EQUALITY FOR THE NEW NATION

When missionaries rebuked some aspects of Confucian-prescribed gender ideology as backward and oppressive, leading Korean intellectuals who had been influenced by Western learning and Christianity echoed the missionary critique. For these intellectuals, criticism of Confucianism went far beyond the realm of gender relations. It was an integral part of Korea's pursuit of status as an independent modern nation-state.[62] While Confucianism had been "the source of the civilizatory process" during the Chosŏn dynasty,[63] it now became the primary barrier to a newly defined "civilization" based on Western learning. China's privileged position as the center of civilization was undermined in the face of new challenges, especially from Japan and the West. In fact, China came to signify a *lack* of civilization.

It should be noted that the contrasting images of China as backward and the West as advanced did not mean that Confucianism was to be abandoned all together. Although the image of Confucian scholars in the late Chosŏn period is often that of ultra-conservative anachronisms, they were enormously diverse in their understanding of and responses to the rapidly changing circumstances, ranging from a group that advocated the doctrine of *wijŏng ch'ŏksa* (defending orthodoxy and rejecting heterodoxy) to those who favored reforming Confucianism by critically reevaluating its principles and practices and incorporating beneficial aspects of Western learning.[64] To be sure, the history of Confucianism is replete with reinterpretations in the face of sociopolitical changes, and the major challenges in the late nineteenth century were not exceptional in prompting scholars of Confucianism to reconfigure it to make it more appropriate for the new era.[65] As Andre Schmid points out, *Hwangsŏng sinmun* in particular actively represented Confucian morality as part of the definition of "Enlightenment," retrieving prominent examples of "advanced" civilizational accomplishments in the ancient times in an attempt to "displace the claim of the East's other, the West, as the sole locus of historical progress."[66] In this context, Kyung Moon Hwang argues that "the enlightenment project can be viewed as the latest in a long history of Confucian reform movements in Korea."[67] Thus, it is significant to examine the gender discourse led by prominent male intellectuals who had considerable exposure to Western learning and Christianity as well as Confucianism and played a key role in envisioning new womanhood as part of the project for "civilization and enlightenment." Situated in the contact zone between the Confucian-ruled late Chosŏn dynasty and the challenging new forces of Japan and the West, intellectuals like Yu Kil-chun, Pak Yŏng-hyo, Sŏ Chae-p'il, and Yun Ch'i-ho paved the way to reformulating Confucian moral principles as they were being influenced by Western political and sociocultural ideas and practices.

In his analysis of early Enlightenment intellectuals in the 1880s, Yi Kwang-nin argues that they were interested in adopting Western technology but still insisted on an Eastern way, represented by the phrase *tongdo sŏgi* (Eastern way, Western method).[68] Within this interface of the Eastern way and the Western method, Pak Yŏng-hyo's "Memorial on Domestic and Political Reforms" of 1888 represents the first manifestation of new gender relations put forward by an Enlightenment-oriented intellectual who attempted to use Confucian ethics while adopting Western ideas and institutions.[69] Pak submitted the memorial to the Korean king in 1888 while he was in exile in Japan after *Kapsin chŏngbyŏn*, the failed coup of

1884 that aimed to expedite modern social reforms. In the memorial, he urged the king to consider his reform ideas, comprising eight items ranging from political and economic matters to cultural domains. Likening the rapidly changing political milieu of the late nineteenth century to the Warring States period of China in which militarily powerful countries aggressively conquered weaker ones, Pak warned that Korea's national sovereignty would be at stake if Korea continued to remain complacent with the past.[70] He deplored the fact that Korea was "still in a state of unenlightenment, like an imbecile or fool, a drunkard or lunatic, and without knowledge of world affairs, thereby inviting insult from the rest of the world."[71] Given the imminent political crisis, he proposed that the king as ruler take a leadership role in putting forward and implementing drastic sociopolitical and economic reforms.

Within this broader national project, Pak proposed inalienable equal rights for women, whom he saw as an important segment of the people *[inmin]* whose happiness and stability was key to a strong nation. Pak argued that it was a universal justice that all people were entitled to pursue freedom and happiness. Aristocrats and men had created law and customs only to make their status superior and their lives privileged, while women and men of the lower classes suffered from a deprivation of opportunities in life. Only when everyone, regardless of gender or status, had equal rights to pursue happiness, could they play an optimal role in their proper place, which would make the nation healthy and strong. Pak reminded the king of the phrase in the Book of Documents that instructed "the people are the foundation of a country, and only when the foundation is strong, the country can be peaceful." In order to make the foundation strong, he argued, the king should make the people united, and unity would come from people's happiness and the stability that resulted from equal rights.

In his memorial, Pak maintained a strong allegiance to the king, but he hinted at a modern understanding of what Charles Taylor calls "sociality," defined as "the society of mutual benefit, whose functional differentiations are ultimately contingent and whose members are fundamentally equal."[72] He challenged the hierarchical order of human relations based on gender and class and emphasized complementary but equal relations governed by justice and fair treatment.[73] Although Pak drew wisdom for his reform ideas from the classical Confucian teachings, his acceptance of a social-Darwinian notion of an evolution toward modern society enabled him to advocate the equal status of women for the prosperity of the nation. In addition to the proclamation of gender equality at a philosophical level, he specifically proposed some practical changes such as equal education for girls and boys after age six, abolition of the concubine system, permitting widows to remarry, and the prohibition of early marriage, violence against wives, and drug-induced abortion.[74]

Since the 1884 manifesto for *Kapsin chŏngbyŏn* did not include any mention of gender equality, Pak's thoughts might have been developed during his intermittent exile in Japan through close contact with Japanese intellectuals like Fukuzawa Yukichi and Westerners, especially American missionaries. Inheriting some of the Korean intellectual tradition of *Sirhak* (practical learning), he later became a close associate of progressive intellectuals, including Kim Ok-kyun, Yu Hong-gi, Sŏ Kwang-bŏm, and Sŏ Chae-p'il, taking part in propagating rapid modern reforms in Korea.[75] In addition, during his exile in Japan, Pak met the first group of American Protestant missionaries heading to the Korea mission field, and served as a Korean language teacher for William Scranton and his mother, Mary F. Scranton, while learning English from them.

This brief but significant encounter with Mary F. Scranton is particularly noteworthy because in 1886 she founded Ewha Girls' School, the first girls' school in Korean history. (A statue in her honor remains on the campus of Ewha Womans University; see figure 2.) She firmly believed that "for the most speedy advancement of the country the women and girls must be educated,"[76] and that education would be a powerful means for reaching out to Korean girls and women to spread the Gospel.[77] It is very likely that Scranton shared with Pak her vision of opening a girls' school. Judging from Pak's keen interest in social reform, he must have welcomed Scranton's vision for women's education. Mary Scranton wrote on April 20, 1885, from Yokohama: "I wonder if you have heard about my teacher, Pak Young Hio [Pak Yŏng-hyo]. He is one of the refugees; the one highest in rank. He is a good teacher, and just as patient and persevering as a common mortal would be. We are becoming attached to him, and to the others as well. We have met them all; they are bright and intelligent. I wish they were back in power. They will be some day, I am sure, and that will be a good day for Korea."[78] In another letter, she spoke of Pak's plan to go to America. She offered all the support she could give.[79] These letters suggest that Pak had a close, friendly relationship with American missionaries residing in Japan and shared his vision for a new Korea with them. Impressed by Pak's royal status through marriage and by his enthusiasm for modern reforms in Korea, Korea-bound American missionaries in Japan held high hopes for his prospects as a leader in Korea. As Mary Scranton pointed out, Americans' support for him and his reform plans must have inspired him and his associates to venture to the United States

to learn and absorb modern knowledge. However, due to financial con-
straints and difficulty in communication, Pak left the United States after
only seven months and returned to Japan. He then attended Myŏngch'i
Hagwŏn (Meiji Gakuin), run by American Presbyterian missionaries in
Japan, where he would have further absorbed ideas about reform from the
West and Japan.

Despite the historical significance of Pak's memorial, it was not circulated for public discussion, and thus its reform ideas remained in obscurity.
However, like-minded associates, especially Sŏ Chae-p'il and Yun Ch'i-ho,
brought the issue of gender equality to prominence in public discourse
via the emerging print media, which was regarded as a catalyst for public
enlightenment.[80] Sŏ Chae-p'il was one of the key members of the 1884
coup, and along with Pak Yŏng-hyo and Sŏ Kwang-bŏm he was exiled to
Japan first and then moved to the United States. There he attended Harry
Hillman Academy and La Fayette College, and he eventually received a
medical degree from Columbian Medical School (now George Washington
University Medical School).[81] Sŏ returned to Korea in December 1895. Yun
Ch'i-ho did not endorse revolutionary actions and was not directly involved
in the 1884 coup; however, his association with the coup leaders led to his
exile. He first went to the Anglo-Chinese Southern Methodist Mission
School in Shanghai, and then pursued studies at Vanderbilt University and
Emory University. Upon completing his study in the United States, Yun
went back to China to teach at the Anglo-Chinese Southern Methodist
Mission School for several years, and then returned to Korea in February
1895.[82] In this politically turbulent span of ten years, both Sŏ and Yun
received significant exposure to Japanese and Western civilization as well
as Christianity, and they became two of the most prominent intellectuals
advocating the value of Western Christian modernity.

In 1896, a year after returning to Korea, Sŏ Chae-p'il founded *Tongnip
sinmun* (The Independent), the first Korean-language newspaper with an
English-language edition.[83] The editorial in the first edition declared that
Tongnip sinmun was designed to inform both Koreans and foreigners of
the news of the world and domestic affairs, and of new knowledge and
perspectives.[84] It also claimed that the newspaper intended to advocate for
"the most wretched, poor and ignorant population of Korea," adding that
Korean women were the most miserable of all because of their suppression
and mistreatment in the name of traditional customs.[85] It argued that the
backwardness of Korean womanhood was caused by such old customs as
the seclusion of women, the virtual prohibition of women from education,
early marriage, the concubine system, and son preference. These customs

deprived women of their dignity and their right to learn, move freely, and contribute to society.[86] From their leadership position in *Tongnip sinmun* and as the main contributors to the editorial page, Sŏ and Yun effectively used the newspaper as a medium to express their vision for the future of Korea while critically reflecting on traditional customs and ways of life. It is not an exaggeration to say that Sŏ and Yun shaped the content and perspectives of *Tongnip sinmun*. Their philosophical and sociopolitical vision was largely drawn from Western bourgeois ideas and Christian morality. Their exceptionally harsh critique of the Chinese influence on Korea was in keeping with their political stance against China and in favor of "civilized" Western societies. In his description of the goal of the Tongnip hyŏphoe (Independence Club), for which the *Tongnip sinmun* was the unofficial organ, Sŏ made it explicit that Tongnip hyŏphoe had helped Koreans "realize the superiority of western civilization over that of eastern civilization."[87] While Sŏ was clearly pro-Western in his opinions, it is noteworthy that he maintained a certain distance from Christianity in his personal and political activities. For example, during his study in the United States he was initially sponsored by William Hollenback, who later proposed that if Sŏ studied theology and became a pastor, he would be willing to support his college education. Sŏ declined the offer.[88]

In comparison, Yun Ch'i-ho was deeply influenced by Christianity and majored in theology during his study overseas. As a student at the Anglo-Chinese Southern Methodist Mission School in Shanghai, he absorbed the teachings of Christianity and Western civilization. His "confession" in 1887 was widely circulated among missionaries and mission journals.[89] After years of experience overseas with close contact with theologians and Christian acquaintances, he came to the conclusion that "[t]here was a time when the most enlightened nation of this age was as low-down as the Coreans; and there may come a time when the Coreans shall be as enlightened as any people. This is one comfort at least. Christianity is *the* salvation and hope of Korea."[90] He wrote in *Tongnip sinmun*, "History tells us that wherever Western civilization has made its appearance, the place was transformed into a new country altogether. . . . We hope the time will soon come when Western civilization will penetrate every corner of the Continent of Asia and make use of the Creator's beautiful soil for the good of His people the world over."[91] At the core of Yun's reform ideas and activities were the moral teachings of Western Christianity, which were presumed to lift the status of women to a higher level.

In their capacity as leaders of Korean Enlightenment, Sŏ Chae-p'il and Yun Ch'i-ho used *Tongnip sinmun* to put forward their vision of a new ideal for gender relations. As Yung-Hee Kim points out, Enlightenment-oriented gender discourse at the time was often "under the mandate of nationalism."[92] Sŏ and Yun's advocacy was not an exception to this trend, as they tended to highlight the role of women in building a strong modern nation-state. For example, Sŏ argued that a woman was the teacher of her sons and the adviser to her husband. But her respectable role as teacher and adviser gained currency only when she contributed to the well-being of the family by supporting them from the private sphere so that husbands and sons could optimally play their role in the public domain. The education, wisdom, and sacrifice of women was regarded as necessary to help their husbands and sons contribute to the prosperity of the nation.[93]

Yun Ch'i-ho noted that women in the West are treated gently and respectfully because women were perceived as the weaker sex.[94] The whole idea of a "woman's sphere" and the family as the safe haven in the West was closely related to ideologies of women's weakness, fragility, and dependency, which required their protection from the world. As noted earlier, an editorial in *Tongnip sinmun* suggested that the treatment of those without power, including how men treated women, was a qualification for an advanced civilization.[95] Therefore, Korea could only become a civilized country if it reformed itself to treat women with care. However, the same editorial warned that women should not abuse any rights given to them, know their proper place, and not oppose men's will. In the end, the phrase *puhwa pusun* (husband treats wife gently, wife obeys husband) was suggested as a general rule for this newly endowed right of women.

The norm of "husband treats wife gently, wife obeys husband" is found both in Confucianism and *Tonghak* (Eastern Learning) as basic ethics between a husband and wife.[96] The husband bore responsibility for treating his wife and children with generosity. In return, the wife would create a peaceful and harmonious family by following the husband's lead. Thus, the newspaper presented an ideal vision of the modern family that reproduced the traditional subordinate role for women. In the end, Sŏ and Yun tended to foreground their argument for gender equality on the premise that women as creatures of God should be treated equally, but women as the weaker sex needed to be protected. This protection involved relegating women to the safe domain of the domestic, familial arena. In turn, their wisdom, sacrifice, and industriousness in the home would eventually benefit the nation through their fulfillment of their duties in child-rearing and supportive companionship for their husbands.

It seems that there was a degree of anxiety among male intellectuals on the topic of gender equality. It is difficult to reconcile the bold statements identifying gender equality as a critical achievement for a truly civilized nation with the repeated warnings about the dangers of overly powerful, independent women. Especially when it came to the issue of political power, the rhetoric of gender equality tended to subside. Yun Ch'i-ho's views on women's suffrage are a case in point. Yun was a strong supporter of women's education and built solid partnerships with early women's organizations. However, his views on women's voting rights were in full agreement with the American male clergymen that Elizabeth Cady Stanton had criticized.

Yun had been exposed to the issues of gender equality and women's suffrage while he was studying overseas. During that period he had two influential teachers who served as his mentors: Young J. Allen and Warren Candler. Allen had founded the Anglo-Chinese Southern Methodist Mission School in Shanghai, where Yun studied from 1885 to 1888, and was a chief sponsor for his further study at Vanderbilt and Emory.[97] Allen influenced many Korean intellectuals of the time through his monthly magazine, *Wanguo gongbao* ("Review of the Times").[98] He is especially notable because of his progressive views on gender. He regarded "the status of women and their treatment in every country as the yardstick for judging the degree of civilization of each culture" and argued that "no country could ever hope to flourish without elevating and educating its women."[99] By contrast, Candler, who was Yun's professor during his study at Vanderbilt University from 1888 to 1891, was a vocal opponent of women's suffrage. Candler often "warned his students against the dangers of the 'ungodly politics of woman suffrage.'"[100]

The contradictory influence of these two teachers is evident in Yun's views. Like Allen, he acknowledged the enhanced status of women as a sign of enlightened civilization. He attributed the root cause of the crisis in Korea to Confucian philosophy, which he believed "contains the seeds of corruption in its doctrine of inferiority of women, of the absolute submission to kings, of its everlasting 'go backism'".[101] In this, he is in agreement with the general sentiment of the missionaries that was described in the earlier section. However, his endorsing the improved status of women did not extend to the issue of women's suffrage. He strongly echoed Candler and the majority of male clerics, who dismissed women's suffrage as antithetical to Christian feminine virtue. Yun deplored the politicization of the Woman's Christian Temperance Union, arguing that "the pro-suffrage American Women's Christian Temperance Union was unwisely confounding the proper moral influence of good women on a society with political voting rights."[102] He feared that the organization's main goal would be "crippled by fooling and being fooled with politics."[103] To Yun, politics was a decidedly male arena and a woman's virtue should be in her "feminine" role as good wife and wise mother.[104] Yun's view on women's voting rights and ideal womanhood encapsulated the overall culture of the Christian community, which heavily emphasized women's spirituality and domesticity but abhorred the idea of their political engagement.

Threatened by the political and cultural implications of gender equality, male intellectuals often used Korea's political crisis to justify caution over women's individual rights. The tension between national priorities and women's rights grew severe especially after Korea became Japan's colony in 1910. The head-on confrontations between vocal feminist women and male intellectuals were most visible beginning in the 1920s, when educated New Women began to participate actively in public discourse and complicated the previously male-dominant construction of ideal modern womanhood. I will return to this topic in chapter 6.

FROM WIFE AND MOTHER TO CITIZEN

The initial discourse on gender equality in the print media was largely led by male intellectuals.[105] However, a growing number of women readers came forward in public to express their points of view.[106] The epitome of the increasing awareness of the new gender ideology among Korean women was the distribution of *Yŏhakkyo sŏlsi t'ongmun* (Circular for the Establishment of a Girls' School; hereafter *T'ongmun*), which was composed and distributed by two women on September 1, 1898. Its main demand was the establishment of a school for girls and the equal treatment for women.[107] The *T'ongmun* stood as the first public demand for equal rights written *by women*, signaling the beginning of a women's rights movement in Korea. It marked a change in the role of women from passive beneficiaries of the Enlightenment discourse led by male intellectuals to that of women as the agents of social change. It reads in part:

> Is there any difference between men and women in their bodies and senses? How could women, like idiots, just sit and be fed by what men earned? How could women staying in the deep inner chambers just be restrained for life by others? If we look at those countries that were civilized earlier than ours, men and women have equal rights. Early on, they attend school, attain various learning, and expand their perspectives. . . . The reason why women in those countries are not oppressed but respected by their husbands is because women learn as much as men and both have equal rights. Isn't this beautiful? Alas, reflecting on the past, [Korean] men tried to oppress women in

the name of the so-called classics that teach women not to talk about the outside world and only to dedicate themselves to making food and drink. Why should women become almost lifeless and ignorant of world affairs due to their suppression by men when there is no difference in the bodies of men and women? It is time for us to eradicate old custom and to strive for enlightenment and progress. For this, we need to establish girls' schools to send our daughters so that they can become a group of talented women like in other countries.[108]

The *T'ongmun* was issued at the height of the Korean Enlightenment movement. Its message was clearly inspired by the vision of male intellectuals in their pursuit of a strong modern nation-state. It asserted that all people, regardless of gender, should abandon the old customs and learn the ways of the new Enlightenment. Similar to the discourse led by male intellectuals at the time, the *T'ongmun* made reference to women in the West as examples to follow. It portrayed the West as an ideal society in which women enjoyed complete equality in the family and society. The respect and rights Western women had were attributed to their education, and thus the *T'ongmun* urged the government to provide women with educational opportunities equal to those of men. Most newspapers expressed amazement at such a bold but welcome action on the part of women, and they took it as a sign of enlightenment, offering moral support to these women.

What draws special attention is that the writers of the *T'ongmun* specifically questioned the legitimacy of gender "differences" in both the physical and the mental sense, calling for *namnyŏ tongdŭngkwŏn* (equal rights of women and men). They challenged the essentialized language of "difference" or "distinction" embedded in Confucian cosmology based on the heaven-earth, yin-yang dualism. Although the complementary roles of binary opposites—women and men—were said to sustain the relationship in balance and harmony, the emphasis in the discourse on *differences* between the opposites actually justified and perpetuated gender inequality. In this vein, the key issue here is that, as Tetsuo Najita surmises in his analysis of Ando Shoeki's critique of Confucian philosophy, "the yin-yang dualism that serves as a metaphor for the equality of contraries was a falsehood, for rather than being two equal halves that became one, these were unequal portions in which the light, active, and masculine is preferred over the dark, passive, and feminine."[109] When the *T'ongmun* called for equal rights for all, it demanded a major epistemic shift from *hierarchical* complementary gender relations to *equal* complementary ones. This shift is sharply illustrated when one compares the *T'ongmun* with Queen Sohye's *Naehun* (Instructions for Women), which was published in

1475 and represents a traditional gender discourse informed by Confucian ethics.

In the *Naehun*, Queen Sohye stated that all human beings were equally endowed with the virtues of the Five Moral Imperatives. Being "endowed" meant that each person was born with the capacity to fulfill the *proper* role designated by the rule of virtuous conduct in the Five Moral Imperatives. Virtue was differentiated on the basis of gender, class, and seniority. Such differentiation inherently presumed an unequal, hierarchical, complementary relationship. Queen Sohye made abundantly clear that men as *yang* (heaven) were superior to women as *ŭm* (earth). She admonished readers that "men's virtue lies in strength, while women's beauty relies on gentleness,"[110] and that the "wife always has to submit herself to her husband even when he beats her. . . . What man does is inevitably honorable, and woman's action is contemptible."[111] She also emphasized the separation of genders in which women's sphere was firmly in the private and domestic, which was presumed to be inferior to the men's sphere, the public. Further, a virtuous woman's behavior was summarized in the four basics of womanly conduct: moral conduct, proper speech, proper appearance and the conduct of womanly tasks. A woman did not need to have exceptional intelligence, beauty, talent, or skill, but she should have a demure, chaste, modest, and disciplined attitude, all of which was designed not to violate the superior status of men.[112] Sohye commented that "All persons at birth receive the spirit of Heaven and Earth, and all are endowed with the virtues of the Five Relations. There is no difference in the principle of jade and stone, but yet how is it that orchids and mugwort differ? It depends on whether one has done one's utmost in fulfilling the Way of cultivating the self."[113] Although education could make people into "orchids" instead of "mugwort," a woman's capacity to become an orchid did not mean that she was equal to a man. Rather, it meant that education would enable her to fulfill her duty of "womanly conduct" that was appropriate for the subordinate gender. The "distinction between husband and wife" [*Pubu yubyŏl*], one of the Five Moral Imperatives, explained the differences between men and women in a literal sense, but its deeper message was to emphasize the complementary but hierarchical relations in which men and women should fulfill their different roles.[114]

In his analysis of Queen Sohye's *Naehun*, John Duncan explores the ways in which the elite women of the Chosŏn dynasty were able to exercise a certain level of agency despite the constraints of the Confucian-prescribed gender ideology and practice. He argues that Sohye's emphasis on the role of women as advisers to their husbands hints at an indirect way of exercising power in the political arena and thus going beyond the private and domestic sphere.[115] Indeed, as we discussed in the previous section, Sŏ Chae-p'il, a champion of gender equality, made a similar point by portraying women as teachers and advisers to men. Martina Deuchler also notes that *Naehun* emphasizes women's education because "a woman's 'goodness' influenced, beyond the domestic realm, the moral condition of public life."[116] Thus women were not merely passive and powerless beings confined to the inner chambers. In a similar vein, scholars of Confucianism have recently attempted to reinterpret Confucian texts and argue for a more proactive role for women within Confucian philosophy, critiquing the oversimplified understanding of the role and status of women as passive and powerless. They even try to find a point of contact between Confucianism and feminism.[117] Yi Sug-in, for example, emphasizes *kwangye chŏk chaa* (the relational self), which does not exist as an isolated individual but rather as a relational other vis-à-vis the family, society, and nation. While the relational self is dependent on others, Yi stresses the active role of the relational self in shaping those relations.[118] Dependence provides a means for creating an independent and proactive role for the relational self.

However, while we acknowledge some level of agency that women had within the constraints of Confucian gender ideology, it is still important to keep in mind the secondary and subordinate role of women that was firmly embedded in Confucian texts. It presumed the hierarchical differentiation of gender roles as a reflection of natural law. It is this subordinated and essentialized role of women that was being challenged in the late nineteenth century. Awareness of the inherent inequality in the dualistic Confucian gender ideology signaled the emergence of a new moral order that contested the hierarchical relationship and advocated equal endowment of human rights for all. In this new moral order, what changed was not the complementary, mutually beneficial aspect of gender relations but the hierarchical, essentialized order of things.[119] In this vein, late–nineteenth-century writing on gender distinguishes itself from its predecessors. It specifically focused on the cruelty and inhumanity of the hierarchy and called for the elimination of the idea of differences between men and women in terms of talents and potential for their role in society.

Not only did the *T'ongmun* signal a new voice for women, it led to the establishment of the first women's organization in Korean history, Ch'anyanghoe. After the distribution of the *T'ongmun*, women and men in Seoul gathered to discuss the founding of a girls' school, and soon decided on the name for the school, Sunsŏng yŏhakkyo (Sunsŏng Girls School). Ch'anyanghoe was founded in order to support this school.[120] *Tongnip sinmun* reported that the initial membership of Ch'anyanghoe was almost four hundred people. Some of the founding members took up leadership positions, while they invited men and foreign women to join. Yun Ch'i-ho was chosen as the president of men sponsors.[121] Some Western women and Chinese and Japanese women expressed their support; for example, Western women gave speeches at weekly meetings and volunteered to teach at the girls' school without pay, and a Japanese woman donated funds.[122] Encouraged by the overwhelming support, about one hundred members of the Ch'anyanghoe kneeled down in front of the royal palace, urging the government to start a public girls' school.[123] Their plea was eventually rejected by the government in 1900, citing a lack of funds. The historian Pak Yong-ok argues that one of the reasons for this outcome might be related to the close ties between Ch'anyanghoe and the Independence Club, the organization led by Sŏ Chae-p'il and Yun Ch'i-ho. The Independence Club was eventually charged with sedition, and it was disbanded in 1899. Members of Ch'anyanghoe had offered explicit support of the goals and activities of the Independence Club. Because of its support for the Independence Club, Ch'anyanghoe might have invited suspicion and disapproval from the government.[124] For all intents and purposes, Ch'anyanghoe had ceased to exist by 1901. However, its mission and weekly meetings to educate women left a significant mark in the women's movement.[125]

As the political situation of Korea grew more turbulent in the face of colonization by Japan, especially after Korea became Japan's protectorate in 1905, the discourse on women's equal rights rapidly extended to the new role of women as *kungmin* (citizens) in strengthening the nation. An article, entitled "A New World to Korean Women," published in *Taehan maeil sinbo* in 1908, argued that women should bear the full duties of citizenship.[126] Its female writer, Kim Song-jae, first delved into the past when women had been virtual slaves to men due to the "inside-outside rule."[127] She went on to argue that women now needed to realize that they should have *chayu* (freedom) and *tongdŭngkwŏn* (equal rights) and deserved equal access to education, art, and business. Only after women got equal education could they fulfill their duty to "serve the king loyally and love the country."[128] In *Yŏja chinam* (Guide for Women), the first women's magazine in Korea, founded in 1908, one contributor criticized Korean women for being entirely dependent on men and allowing themselves to be confined to the inner living quarters. She argued that if women, constituting half of the entire population, always relied on men, the nation was doomed to decline; therefore, women's freedom and independence was indispensable for the prosperity of the nation.[129] Women's equal rights were now closely linked to their civic duties, and by fulfilling those duties, they would strengthen the nation. Largely in line with various forms of *chagang undong* (self-strengthening movements) after the 1905 Protectorate Treaty, women writers urged their fellow women to free themselves from dependence on men and to prepare to take up new civic roles by acquiring modern knowledge.[130] Yun Chŏng-wŏn, the first Korean woman to go to Japan for study, envisioned woman as *kungmin chi mo* (mother of the nation), *sahoe chi hwa* (flower of society) and *illyu chi t'aeyang* (sun of humankind).[131] Extending the role of women from the family to the society and the world, Yun actively integrated women into the public, national and even world spheres. In his discussion of the unique and fluid nature of the public and the private in the Confucian Five Relationships, Fred Dallmayr proposes one more relationship—"between citizen and citizen in a shared public sphere and under a common rule of law."[132] In a significant way, this new category of relationship aptly captures the slowly changing nature of gender boundaries in which women began to be drawn to the public realm not simply as a moral force exercised from the domestic but a political force with direct participation in the public. Enthusiastically responding to male intellectuals' call for nation-building, women writers' discourse on gender equality was deeply rooted in the nation's self-strengthening movement and revealed a fledgling idea of citizenship extended to women.[133] It was significant progress for women to be integrated into the nationalist project, at least at the discursive level. However, the nation-centered outlook also paved the way for women's issues to be perpetually treated as a secondary consideration. More importantly, unlike the development of women's citizenship in the West, the link between nation-building and women's citizenship in Korea suppressed the idea of the individual.[134] Ultimately, the failure to incorporate the idea of individual rights into the new role envisioned for women in society resulted in the condemnation of New Women, whose advocacy of individual freedom was dismissed as selfish, bourgeois, and unpatriotic.

American missionaries and Korean intellectuals participated in the rhetoric of gender equality as a new moral principle for the modern era. They significantly differed in their ultimate reason for deploying such rhetoric. To missionaries, Christian morality provided a divine foundation for gender equality. The dramatic contrast between the life of women in the Christian West and that of Korean women allowed the missionaries to validate their mission to "rescue" Korean women and lift them to a higher place. In comparison, Korean intellectuals saw the enhanced role and status of women as a crucial factor in building a modern nation-state, especially in the face of Japanese encroachment on the Korean peninsula. These competing discourses on gender equality clearly led to a major shift in perspective on gender relations in Korea. Such a shift marked progress toward a new womanhood that emphasized equal standing for women and men. By the mid-1920s, the *idea* of gender equality was considered cliché as it had become so widespread and even taken for granted.[135]

However, the rhetoric of gender equality was often driven by either Christian or nationalist mandates, and both of these continued to relegate women to the domestic sphere as the subordinate gender. The underlying message in the Korean nationalist discourse of gender equality was not that women held an equal share of responsibility for strengthening the nation but that their role in nation-building was instrumental, taking the form of assisting male citizens as educated wives and mothers. The missionary discourse on gender equality was effectively deployed as part of the civilizing mission in its effort to standardize the world. Missionary women certainly enjoyed greater freedom and equality than Korean women, which gave them a sense of privilege and liberation. Yet they not only were bound by the male-dominant mission organizations that assigned women to the separate female sphere, but most women missionaries readily embraced the Victorian notion of true womanhood that valorized domesticity as well as religious piety.

The new moral principle of gender equality as a sign of civilization and modernity was crucial in challenging the conventional gender hierarchy. It provided a basis for new opportunities for women in the public realm that had been closed to them for centuries. However, this principle, advocated by both Koreans and missionaries, remained largely at the abstract level of belief rather than the practical level of implementation. Consequently, one finds contradictions between the rhetoric of gender equality and the practices which continued institutionalized gender inequality.

3. The Lure and Danger of the Public Sphere

One of the most shocking realities that early missionaries found in Korea was the seclusion of women. As Juldah Haening, a Methodist missionary, put it, "Korean young women are conspicuous by their *absence*" in the public space.[1] To American missionaries who were used to social gatherings and casual outings where women were free to participate without any special limitation or concession, the sequestered life of women was nothing less than a symbol of heathen oppression. More immediately, it presented a major "hindrance to the Gospel's progress" because the conventions of strict gender segregation prevented the male missionaries from having access to the Korean women.[2] The missionary zeal to bring Korean women to the public space was shared by Korean reformers, who assailed the longstanding practice of confining women to the inner quarters as a sign of backwardness and an obstacle to the modern project. Citing the cases of "enlightened" Western women who were seen as educated, well-versed in world affairs, and active in the economic domain, print media urged Korean women to leave the cloistered life of the past and prepare themselves to contribute to the prosperity of the society.[3]

Nothing could be more dramatic than the contrast between the public engagement in the global evangelical enterprise of American women missionaries and Korean women's confinement in the inner chambers of their own private homes. American women were allowed and, to some degree, encouraged to take on the duties of the mission within Christian and Victorian gender norms, while the cloistered life of Korean women was prescribed by Confucian gender ideology. This chapter examines the ways in which the different social and cultural norms about women's proper domain held by Koreans and American missionaries were challenged, negotiated, and reshaped through their transcultural encounters. In particular, it

45

traces the shifting and intersecting notions of the public and the private as a site of contest in refashioning gender ideology. Here the meaning of "the public" is different from what Habermas refers to as "the public sphere," which is based on the history of Western Europe and the experience of white, property-owning men.[4] Rather, I adhere to the ongoing discussion among feminist historians about the public/private divide as spatial and social realms to which men and women had been conventionally assigned. As Mary Ryan argues, the public/private category is an expedient analytical tool in investigating historically constructed, multidimensional gender boundaries. Recent studies challenge the "great divide" between public and private, arguing that the boundary between gender-specific public and private realms was never clear-cut but rather fluid.[5] For example, as I discussed in chapter 2, Martina Deuchler's and John Duncan's analyses of the influential *Naehun* (Instructions for Women) indicate that women's position in the domestic arena during the Chosŏn dynasty did not prevent them from having influence on the public domain through their wisdom, goodness, and morality.[6] In a similar vein, JaHyun Kim Haboush complicates the conventional binarism of gender role construction. In her analysis of the narratives in *Inhyŏn wanghu chŏn* (The True History of Queen Inhyŏn), Haboush demonstrates how the categories of public and private intersect, and how "woman" emerges as a superior moral being with autonomy and subjectivity.[7] Similarly, the history of women in other parts of the world provides ample evidence of the complex and dynamic meanings and practices of public and private.[8] For example, Leslie Peirce details how royal women in the Ottoman Empire, while physically confined to the harem, nonetheless shared remarkable power and sovereignty.[9] In her analysis of American women in late nineteenth and early twentieth centuries, Paula Baker argues that women's sense of moral superiority demanded they take a role beyond the private domain and they "used the idea of domesticity as a wedge to gain political influence usually accessible only to men."[10] Thus, as Leonore Davidoff aptly puts it, "public and private, with their multiple and shifting gender connotations, have to be recognized within particular contexts and particular times."[11]

The ideologically and historically constructed dichotomy between public and private loomed large with the advent of modernity and imperialism, as political, economic, and cultural landscapes were greatly transformed. In particular, transnational colonial encounters triggered and contributed to a major shift in perspectives on gender boundaries.[12] It is also important to note that the transcultural interaction was not a one-sided affair in which one society's cultural practice was imposed on the other. Rather both parties actively participated in redrawing the boundaries for the appropriate behaviors of the genders. It was within this dynamic contact zone of transcultural interaction that the missionary women's Victorian notion of a proper sphere for women and the Confucian idea of the "distinction of men and women" were first at odds but later came to be negotiated and reconfigured. I argue that the public presence and activities of women missionaries made inroads that led to, in Martha Vicinus's words, a "widening sphere" for women in Korea.[13] Seizing the opportunity provided by the missionaries, Korean women themselves were actively involved in expanding their realm of life and work into the public. However, the expanded sphere for women with some of their prominent public activities continued to converge into the domestic as an ideal sphere for women. Women's "public" engagement was justified as an expedient way to create a more essential sphere for women—a modern private sphere of Christian homes in which women could foster religious piety in tandem with hygienic and scientific homemaking.

INTERPRETING THE HIDDEN AND EXPOSED BODY

To missionaries, the widespread practice of the separation of genders was the central illustration of the shockingly oppressive lifestyle Korean women led. Upon arriving in Korea, Hattie Heron learned that "all Korean ladies (except dancing girls) are kept in the strictest seclusion. The '*aung paung*' [anpang], or women's apartments, are shut off from the front of the house, and have double shutters for the windows."[14] George Gilmore noted that no traveler or resident would ever see a family picnic or a family luncheon party in the woods or by the sea, as was commonly practiced in America. He further observed that Korean men and boys might be seen in the streets, but women and girls were nowhere to be found because social customs dictated that they had to stay within the confines of the inner chambers of the family home. Thus, "social evening gatherings where both sexes meet to chat, and sing, and play games, are entirely unknown."[15]

This custom of physically separated gender domains did not exist in Korea before the Chosŏn dynasty. For example, during the Koryŏ dynasty (918–1392), women were free to join seasonal outings, go to Buddhist temples, mingle with men in the streets, and even bathe naked in an open stream in the summer.[16] It was only from the Chosŏn dynasty that women's mobility was restricted and direct contact with men prohibited, except for family members. This newly constructed gender boundary was part of the "Confucian transformation of Korea" during the Chosŏn dynasty, which embraced and institutionalized neo-Confucianism as its state ideology.[17] Confucian philosophy propagated "the duality of female *[yin]* and male *[yang]*—with male ascendant—as the basis of the natural order and as the normative force for the social order. It subordinated women to men, assigned them to stereotypic social categories—chaste woman, devoted wife, dedicated mother—and confined them spatially to the inner rooms of the house."[18] This philosophically sanctioned distinction between men and women stipulated the proper domain of genders—the public/outer space for men and the private/inner space for women. The idea of the distinction between men and women led to a daily practice of the "inside-outside rule." It meant that women should not see or talk with men who were not family members and should stay in the inner chambers.

American missionaries were well aware that class and age made significant differences in the social life of women in Korea, especially in terms of the level of the observation of the inside-outside rule. Missionaries had learned that the rule was strictly applied to women of the upper class so that when they went out for a visit, they were carried in a palanquin by servants or they wore *changot* or *ssŭgae ch'ima*, special clothing designed to keep their faces and bodies covered (see figure 3).[19] In comparison, women of the commoner classes or those in the countryside were not expected to observe the rule fully.[20] However, as Ellen Strong, a Presbyterian missionary, stated, "the custom of seclusion extends pretty far down the scale of rank."[21] Young unmarried women especially had to hide their faces with "a long white cotton coat tightly wrapped around them, covering them from head to knees"[22] in order to protect themselves from "the vulgar gaze of man."[23] George Gilmore claimed that the only women who made no effort to cover themselves from the view of men were restaurant keepers, who were willing to be subjected to the men's prying gaze "for the sake of the 'mighty cash.'"[24] With the exception of *public* women in commerce and entertainment, who did not garner any respect from people, the invisibility of women in the public space was a point of culture shock for the Western missionaries.

If the physical seclusion of Korean women was tantamount to "pagan" oppression to American missionaries, American women missionaries' freedom in public spaces was nothing less than scandalous in the eyes of Koreans. The missionary women, who had left their own families to help set "heathen" women free,[25] evoked Koreans' contempt or pity. In her missionary novel, entitled *Daybreak in Korea*, Annie Baird described how Korean women, seeing a missionary wife walking together with her husband in her own garden, thought this was "no lady" because she was "out in the open like any other coolie woman, with nothing over her face, and her head in the air if she didn't care who looked at her. She can't be anything good."[26] A husband and wife strolling together in the garden would be a most natural and appropriate behavior for a woman in the American cultural context, but it was a sign of unladylike behavior and impropriety in Korea. Similarly, when the well-known world traveler Isabella Bird Bishop had a conversation with a Korean woman of the higher class, she asked how she felt about the freedom Western women enjoyed. The Korean woman's response was "we think that your husbands don't care for you very much,"[27] meaning that if a husband truly cared for his wife, he would not let her go out unprotected. This response clearly indicates an attitude among Koreans that staying in the inner chambers was a privilege rather than an oppression.

Some missionaries came to understand and appreciate this Korean view. They saw the Korean custom as something other than a sign of backwardness or gender oppression. Rather, they contemplated that the seclusion of women might be a precaution against the danger prevalent in the public space in modern times. Lillias Underwood commented that Korean girls were "terribly shut in, but I wonder if that is worse than the unshielded, unguided publicity of the lives of many of our girls."[28] Rosetta Sherwood Hall, a Methodist medical missionary, expressed the opinion that the custom was "rather a novel custom, but rather a good one."[29] In a similar context, a correspondent for the *New York World* wrote that Korean women's seclusion was "a blessing to them" because too much exposure often led to "the most demoralizing results."[30] These comments show that the Korean custom prompted some Westerners to question the openness of their own customs and to see the value in the so-called backwardness of "pagan" practices. In a significant way, their appreciation was also a reflection of their growing anxiety about the exposure of women in public without proper moral guidance. The great challenge for missionaries was how to bring Korean women into public spaces so that they could receive the Gospel while at the same time preserving the safety that had been afforded them in their seclusion.

It is somewhat ironic that in a context where missionaries represented Korean women as secluded, formless, and veiled, they also complained of the fact that some Korean women of the commoner classes occasionally appeared in public with their breasts partially or fully exposed (see figure 4). Korean women's dress in the late Chosŏn period typically included an extremely short jacket that reached down only as far as the armpit and a long skirt that was tied just above the breasts.[31] Sometimes the breasts became exposed, either accidently through simple exertion or deliberately in order to breastfeed, which caused Westerners to feel embarrassment and sometimes outrage. In the missionary collections and travelogues, there are numerous examples of pictures in which Korean women posed (or were posed) with their breasts showing and blank eyes or no expression at all, providing a stereotypical image of the heathen or uncivilized woman. Even those missionaries who actually admired the beauty of the Korean traditional dress could not help but to make a note of "marks of heathenism."[32] Annie Baird vividly portrayed the reaction of one particular Western woman:

> The exposure [of the breasts] that resulted was a never ending offense to a vigorous old lady from Kentucky who spent several years in Seoul. She used to descend bodily on women thus unattired whom she met on the street, and make energetic though futile attempts to pull their skirts and jackets together across the objectionable gap, scolding the meanwhile in good round English, not one word of which the victims could understand. I never had any reason to think that she accomplished anything beyond a strong impression on the mind of the assaulted one that this must be a foreign devil of a peculiarly violent type.[33]

One reason why the exposure might have caused such embarrassment to the American woman in the passage above was her particular perception of the body as a sexualized object and a sense of shame and propriety specifically informed by late-nineteenth-century Victorian Protestant culture.[34] It is very likely that those Korean women who were "exposed" typically came from the commoner class or lower. They might be merely carrying pots on their head or breastfeeding babies in the street as part of their normal, everyday life, and they probably did not have the foggiest idea why this foreign-looking woman was so upset. However, to the American sensibility, the intimate, private domain of the body should be adorned and covered in public, and thus the exposure of the breasts was simply a sign of backwardness. Interestingly, according to Leonore Davidoff, breastfeeding and sexual activities, including intercourse, along with other activities such as sleeping, spitting, urinating, defecating, and vomiting, were done in public during the Georgian era but later became withdrawn to the private, enclosed space as a vital component of modernity.[35] That is, the "embarrassing" scene of breastfeeding in Korea in the eyes of Western women was commonly practiced in public in Western societies just a century earlier. Nonetheless, the vision of a half-naked women's body in public was represented as a metonym of Korea's degraded culture.[36]

While most Westerners would have gasped at this sensational sight in the streets, seasoned missionaries, like Annie Baird, attributed "the objectionable gap" to motherhood, reasoning that "[t]o be a mother was their [women's] one claim to consideration, and they were accustomed to dress in a way to present the least possible obstruction to the frequent nourishment of their little ones."[37] Baird was acting as an interpreter in this culturally tangled zone, demonstrating a capacity to understand the culture-specific significance of the presentation of the body. Baird's interpretation emphasizes that the structure of Korean women's dress met a vital function in that it allowed the fulfillment of a woman's maternal duty to feed her child. While a publicly exposed breast might be seen as offensive, vulgar, or even barbaric from a Western point of view, it could also be seen as a natural part of motherly performance that simply defies the sexual connotations attached to women's body.[38] Recalling a typical evening dance party in the United States, Baird poses a rhetorical question for her American readers: "What explanation would they [Koreans] have regarded as sufficient to account for the unseemly lack of attire and the unheard of familiarity of the attitudes?"[39] In other words, Baird urges Western women to think about how *Korean* women might perceive the rather revealing evening dresses at Western-style social parties that bore no motherly function and thus would have hardly been justified by Korean standards.

The dynamic interpretations of what were "proper" bodily presentations in public led to negotiations, accommodations, or rejection of one form over the other. For example, girls' mission schools were well aware of the importance of accommodating Korean customs for the sake of gaining Koreans' trust, and thus they required girls to cover their faces and bodies when they went off campus. However, by 1908, the students of Ewha Girls' School did not have to cover their faces with *changot* when they went out. Yŏndong Girls' School (later Chŏngsin Girls' School in 1909) even prohibited students from wearing *changot*.[40]

Unlike the general trend moving away from the traditional body-covering practice, some mission schools insisted on the Korean traditional way. Even after 1910, students at Paehwa, founded by the U.S. Methodist Episcopal Church, South, were required to cover their faces when they attended their school chapel, which was located outside the campus.[41] Susanne Colton, a Southern Presbyterian missionary, was one of the prominent examples of missionaries who rigorously imposed the traditional way on their students. Colton was the principal of Kijŏn Girls School in Chŏnju, northern Chŏlla province, which was founded by the Southern Presbyterian Church in 1902. She was known among students as strict and conservative. She made a stringent rule that when students were on outings, they were required to wear *changot*. However, students were already being influenced by modern ideas about women's freedom and began to resist this requirement. In 1915, two students, Yim Yŏng-sin and O Cha-hyŏn, submitted a petition that the school abolish such practice, but the school rejected it. After this formal rejection, a few students protested by refusing to wear *changot*, and as a result, they were expelled. Angered students went on strike, demanding that those who had been expelled be allowed back. This student-led strike was resolved after three days through intensive negotiation between the school and the local community.[42]

The above-mentioned episodes are illustrative of the dynamics of the transcultural encounter in which the old practices of bodily presentation in public were challenged, justified, or embraced. To be sure, women missionaries contributed to the elimination of *changot*, which served as a symbol of the old, oppressive Confucian civilization. Yet, as shown in the incident at Kijŏn Girls School, there were some ironic situations in which it was American women missionaries who insisted on the traditional Korean ways, while young Korean women were eager to eliminate some of the traditional practices.[43] This conflicting situation reflects both the individual and collective desire of American and Korean women— whether it was Christian zeal or longing for modernity. Furthermore, their desires inevitably intersected with the prevailing cultural outlook as well as local and national particularities upon which these women acted. In the midst of these dynamic interactions, women's bodies, whether hidden or exposed, often served as a metonym for the heathen, uncivilized, backward condition of Korean women. By contrast, the transformation of the body through Christian modesty and restraint conjured up the exulted image of modern civilized Christian womanhood. The following section examines the ways in which the transcultural encounter specifically influenced American women missionaries and Korean women in refashioning new gender boundaries.

A SEPARATE GLOBAL FEMALE SPHERE

Women's engagement in the foreign mission field is best represented by the prevailing notion of "women's work for women" to save women and children in non-Christian countries. Enveloped in a "glamour of romance" in opening up "heathen lands" to the "full light of the Gospel of Jesus Christ,"[44] their voyage to the mission field was also characterized by the decidedly feminine and domestic virtues of love, giving, and self-sacrifice.

Women missionaries' zeal to spread their domestic and spiritual virtues to the world captures how the public, private, global, and local closely intersected. On the one hand, the catchphrase "women's work for women" was firmly grounded in the late-nineteenth-century Victorian notion of true womanhood.[45] The unique, separate sphere of women was located in the private and intimate domain of the home and family where the superior quality of women's morality and religious piety was presumed. On the other hand, the zeal to advocate true womanhood brought women out of the domestic sphere and ushered them to engage in various activities in the *public* and *global* domain. Reflecting the seamless linkage of the private (feminine) and the public (global), missionary training schools emphasized not only religious subjects but also the "divine art of homemaking," including such subjects as home economics, domestic science, and "gracious womanly arts," through which they aimed to enable women missionaries to "make the world more homelike wherever they go."[46] As Susan Thorne notes, "part of the transformative power of the missionary project was its sanctioning of transgressive behavior as religious exceptions to gender rules. It was, after all, the pious woman's 'duty' to overcome her 'natural diffidence' in order that she might better serve the mission cause."[47] Under the banner of Christian faith and its propagation on a global scale, traditional gender rules were bent as women missionaries actively engaged in public life as professionals.[48]

It was particularly crucial to have women joining in the foreign missionary enterprise in the regions where the separation of genders was strongly enforced by tradition. Dana Robert argues that the "strongest public justification for including women in the foreign mission enterprise at all was not to be companions and helpmates to their husbands, but rather to reach the otherwise unreachable women and children."[49] In the Korea mission field, the entrenched idea of the separation of genders in Chosŏn Korea made it difficult if not impossible for male missionaries to have any contact whatsoever with women whom they were hoping to convert. Henry Appenzeller, one of the first missionaries in Korea, said, "I preached to fourteen believers and seekers; this does not include women. These are taught by Mrs. M. F. Scranton in the Ladies' Home."[50] In his recollection of the strictly secluded life of Korean women, James Gale noted that when he stayed at a Korean home in Sorae, he never saw the woman who cooked for him for his entire stay of three months.[51] William Scranton, a medical missionary, was not allowed to treat women patients. His mother, Mary F. Scranton, mentioned that "the doctor [William Scranton] continued to have calls for medicine for women whom he has not seen and whom he cannot see; and he desires to place all such cases in the hands of some one who can come in contact with the patient."[52] In this context, George Gilmore emphatically stated that "lady missionaries are as absolute a necessity as the more usual men" in order to get access to half of the Korean population.[53]

A diversity of factors brought young, educated women to the foreign mission.[54] One of them was the Student Volunteer Movement from the last quarter of the nineteenth century, which brought about a shift in the emphasis of the foreign mission from saving individual souls to a social gospel "that patiently and thoroughly renovates heathen life in its personal, domestic, civic, tribal, national practices and tendencies—aiming to make the heathen commonwealth, as well as the heathen individual, a new creation in Christ Jesus."[55] As Jane Hunter points out, "Perhaps the single most influential catalyst to mission service in the lives of both young women and men was the evangelical, premillennialist Student Volunteer Movement. An offshoot of the YMCA, the Student Volunteer Movement was responsible for as many as half of the missionary volunteers of the early twentieth century."[56] North American missionaries who came to Korea were not an exception to this general pattern. Between 1884 and 1910, 247 women missionaries came to Korea. Among those, 107 were student volunteer missionaries, including some who would become among the most prominent women missionaries in Korea, such as Lillias Horton, Mary Cutler, Lulu Frey, Annie Adams Baird, Margo Lee Lewis, and Marjorie Lucy Hanson.[57] While in medical school at the University of Michigan at Ann Arbor, Mary Cutler was in the first group of student volunteers and served in the Korea mission field for forty-six years (1893–1939) as a medical missionary to women and children. Marjorie Lucy Hanson recalled the influence of a student volunteer for her decision to join the group. She wrote: "Near the close of my college days, I became acquainted with Miss Margo Lee Lewis, who at that time was preparing for the foreign field, and who at present is Principal of a Woman's College in Seoul, Korea. I recall how she especially enthused me with a strong desire to give my life in service on the foreign field. . . . I soon joined the Student Volunteer Band of the Oregon Agricultural College, a step that seemed to bring me nearer to the realization of my long-smoldering ambition."[58] Lulu Frey, another student volunteer, remembered the influence from her encounter with an article, "Why Should I Not Go?" written by Mrs. Lucy Ryder Meye in *Heathen Woman's Friend*. Intrigued and inspired by the question, she eventually chose to follow in the footsteps of other student volunteer missionaries who came before her.[59] Once arriving in the mission field, these student volunteer missionaries also served as an excellent tool for future recruitment of young college students. Jessie Marker, herself a student volunteer, expressed her satisfaction and reward from the work in Korea, saying, "I am so glad to be here. If more of our college young people had a real vision of missionary work, I am sure they would be willing to join our ranks."[60]

To many well-educated young women, Mary Lyon, who founded Mount Holyoke College, was an inspirational figure who prompted them to consider the foreign mission as a lifetime commitment. Rosetta Sherwood Hall, a prominent medical missionary, noted how one of Lyon's addresses to a graduating class had a profound influence on her. She wrote that Lyon's address "has ever influenced my whole life, and I would that it may thus be used to influence every girl and young woman who may read this. It is: 'If you want to serve your race, go where no one else will go, and do what no one else will do.'"[61] At Mount Holyoke, Lyon actively promoted the importance of missions among her students, ultimately turning the school into one of the primary institutions turning out female missionaries. Indeed, in the 1880s graduates of Mount Holyoke constituted more than 20 percent of the women missionaries connected to the American Board.[62] Her continuing influence was evident when women missionaries in Korea took Lyon and her college as a model in planning and executing women's work, especially in their educational endeavors, so that Lyon also became an inspirational figure to Korean girl students.[63]

Encounters with former and current missionaries were also an important venue for attracting young women to work for the foreign mission. After meeting a missionary from Persia, Annie Ellers "became wrapped up in the hope of being of service to the Persian women." But due to an urgent call for a woman physician in the Korean mission, Ellers went to Korea as a medical missionary. Aboard ship she captured the bursting excitement and ambition of fellow missionaries, enthusing "[w]hat vision, what longings, what hopes and what anticipations of great and wonderful deeds filled the minds and hearts of these simple, inexperienced venturing ones!"[64] Esther Shields, who became a medical missionary in Korea, had been deeply impressed by a woman who had served in the mission in Burma and developed an interest in such work. Shields came to believe that "a medical missionary has so much greater influence for doing good by being able to minister to the body as well as to the soul," so she "might be made use of especially in a country where women and girls are so downtrodden and cruelly treated."[65] Local churches at home often invited missionaries on furlough to share their experience in the mission field with church members and also to recruit prospective missionaries. The following experience of Nell Johnson Null is a classic example of the influence such an occasion made on prospective missionaries:

> A few evenings, after I had told the Lord of my willingness to do anything, I heard Mr. Nash—a well known, consecrated Bible reader. Such a missionary sermon, I had never heard! The story, of the millions of starving-dying souls, appealed to me. Their emaciated figures were before me. They held out their hands to me for bread. It was so real. Then Mr. Nash said "All those who will give up their lives to service in a foreign field, if God *should call them*, just stand." The congregation, of that First Pres. Church, were very earnest in their prayer. The silence and solemnity was intense. I did not think God would call *me*. I prayed as I never had before, then I stood with the eleven others who had arisen. Soon after the Rev. W. E. Parsons organized us into the Mission study class. God blessed me, answered my prayers very definitely and I was so happy.[66]

The missionary zeal to save heathen people was also fostered at home. Many women missionaries came from families with long histories of missionary service. Lillias Underwood, for example, was brought up in a family of devout Calvinists. Her mother had been deeply interested in going into the foreign field, a cousin of her father's was a "missionary to the Indians," and one of her mother's kinswomen "had endowed a hospital in China in the days when such an undertaking was most radical."[67] Discussing her father's encouragement, Esther Shields quoted one of his letters to her: "I am sure I have no greater desire than that all of you may be used of God to please His name and advance His kingdom."[68] In some cases, family members or relatives were already in the Korea mission field, and that became part of the incentive to serve. When Margo Lee Lewis applied for a position as a missionary, she indicated that her preferred location would be Korea in part because her uncle, Graham Lee, was already serving in Korea.[69]

After these women arrived in Korea, they engaged in three main types of work—educational, medical, and evangelical. To be sure, many women missionaries had had work experience before they came to the field. However, they had rarely gained that experience in large organizations, let alone ones in which they would have been allowed to take any leadership role. The mission field provided women missionaries with exceptional opportunities to discover and develop leadership skills. It is clear that the young women involved were experiencing a sense of both excitement and trepidation about participating in this new frontier of leadership. Edith

Blair expressed both anxiety and enthusiasm about the establishment of the Presbyterial Women's Missionary Societies, stating that "I am to go to Anju, in our Presbytery, the 19th of this month, to help the women organize. I feel so ignorant about it myself. I came to the field so young that I had no experience of such work at home. Of course the Korean women have no idea at all of organization, so we shall have to begin from the ground up!"[70] Maude Hemphill Cook talked about a shift in her life from being a passive follower to a leader of others. She wrote: "Strange all these years I was doing something which I never thought I would do—namely TEACH. I had not made any special preparations in this line, somehow I had always liked following rather than leading, but it seems to me God knew better than I did, and He led me on and on."[71] In this context, the prevailing tone of women missionaries was often filled with "much joy in the service" and the acknowledgement of the "privilege to work for Christ among a people so teachable and lovable as Koreans."[72] Their expanded and indispensable role in women's work for women often made them feel exhilarated and accomplished.

Women missionaries' dedication and accomplishments were recognized both inside and outside the field. They garnered significant respect from their male counterparts. Praising the "splendid progress" women missionaries made, E. M. Cable reported that "we feel proud of our able co-workers of W.F.M.S."[73] William Scranton believed that women's work was "deserving of special note and worthy of our emulation."[74] In the 1895 annual meeting, William Scranton praised the indispensable work that women missionaries did: "To close this report without direct reference to the ladies of the Women's Foreign Missionary Society would be a mistake. If your vision is as keen as it should be it will discover their touch and influence in nearly every department of our work mentioned. To be fair we must acknowledge that had it not been for their work along all lines much of our effort would not have had half its fruitage."[75] Scranton's tone and language suggest that the women's work had not been fully appreciated because it was regarded as a mere subsidiary unit of the parent boards. He reminded his fellow missionaries that in order "to be fair," they ought to recognize the contribution of women missionaries not only in "women's work for women" but also "for their work along all lines."

At the individual level, the distinguished career of women missionaries was prominently celebrated. For example, Margaret Best (in Korea 1897–1937), Presbyterian, was awarded a Doctor of Laws degree in 1934 by her alma mater, Park College, for her four decades of pioneering work in the Korea mission field. She was the first woman to be so honored by Park College.[76] Her colleague and housemate, Alice Butts, wrote that "[s]he was the one who made the plans and started things in the way they are still going today, and it was in recognition of this that her college gave her this degree at this time."[77] The missionary legacy of Margaret Best in the Christian community in P'yŏngyang, where she spent most of her career as the principal of the Woman's Bible Institute, was vividly manifested when she retired in 1937. The students and graduates of the Women's Bible Institute, the Women's Higher Bible School, the Women's Missionary Society of the P'yŏngyang Churches, and the Woman Workers' Organization erected a monumental tower in honor of her contribution. A huge crowd of women gathered to attend the dedication ceremony on May 4, 1936, where she was also honored with songs written for the occasion and a special acrostic poem.[78]

In addition to the prominence given to the accomplishments of women missionaries, there was the fact that in actuality women were the majority of missionaries in the Korea field. By 1890 the number of women missionaries worldwide had surpassed that of men.[79] Barbara Welter explains that the greater representation of women in the foreign missionary enterprise was in part because men were losing interest in mission work, which had been a prestigious profession but was now losing standing. While men were searching for more promising alternatives, women were filling the void and "achieving prominence in an institution which was itself declining in prestige."[80] In the Korea mission field, statistics indicate that in the period from 1884 to 1910, 419 American Protestant missionaries of all denominations arrived in Korea. Of them, 247 (59 percent) were women and 172 were men (41 percent). In addition, the number of unmarried women was greater than that of married women among women missionaries.[81] By 1936, women missionaries in Korea constituted 63 percent of Protestant missionaries.

The increasingly greater proportion of women missionaries in the field caused concerns among men missionaries. Facing the steady rise of women in its ranks, the mission began to call for "adequate male leadership."[82] The editorial page of *The Korea Mission Field* reasoned why this happened and warned about the lack of male leadership:

> The larger proportion of women missionaries is partially due to
> greater missionary activity of women in the churches from which
> the missionaries come. There are women's missionary societies
> in all the churches, and separate Women's Boards of Missions in
> some denominations. . . . It seems certain that both in the sending
> countries and on the mission field, the larger proportion of workers

and of Christians will be women. Women are better than men, more interested in religion, that's all. The Gospel message makes a stronger appeal to them. *Nevertheless to have missions and churches without adequate male leadership is not normal.* It is the part of the wisdom to make a persistent effort to secure and maintain a more balanced proportion as between men and women both in missions and the church. Not too many women in the church, of course, but a larger proportion of men is wanted.[83] [emphasis added]

While endorsing more participation of devoted women, the editorial above reveals male leaders' anxieties. Keenly aware of the growing concern about lack of male leadership, women missionaries tried to adopt strategies to realize their goals without offending their male colleagues. Helen McCune, a Presbyterian missionary, illustrated this strategy of "womanly politics" in pursuing women's causes. She wrote:

[T]here have been organizations to hold the women's local societies together and of late it has been felt that this method should be more general and so the church is in the throes of such organization. A group of missionary women got their heads together and then they chose some men and asked them to help them. *This was partly womanly modesty but largely womanly politics.* They knew that the best way to get the things done was to get some of the leading Korean men interested in forming it. So the committee last year asked the women of the several stations for any suggestions worked that they might have to make a tentative Constitution. Then it was worked over by the committee and laid before the General Assembly. Some of the brethren shied a little, just as men are prone to do, when women try "to take authority to themselves" but it finally passed and during this year in various places the Presbyterials are being organized where they have had nothing here-to-fore, or the new constitution considered where there is already an organization. I am sure that this is going to result in fine co-operation on the part of the women.[84] [emphasis added]

McCune's "feminine" strategy of modesty and subordination firmly grounded women's work in the traditionally acceptable arenas. Yet the strategy, or "womanly politics," was to avoid potential conflict with male counterparts but still enable women to take on more ambitious work of their own. Similarly, Annie Baird, one of the most prolific and influential women missionaries at the time,[85] made an impassioned argument about the ideal missionary wife, whose primary role was to take care of her husband and children, but whose "influence" on her husband was ultimately to enhance the evangelical work. She wrote:

> Are we [wives] a help or a hindrance to missionary work? . . . a good
> wife ought to influence a good husband and a good husband ought to
> be neither afraid nor ashamed to be influenced by a good wife; and by
> the use of this influence there are some ways, I am convinced, by which
> we may prove that we not only do not impede but do actually accelerate
> the promotion of the missionary enterprise. . . . One determination
> should be fixed in the head of every missionary wife and that is that
> her husband's service is for life. Whatever illness or family cares may
> come to her even to withdrawing her permanently from the field, the
> years of his service shall not be shortened.[86]

Baird firmly believed that the legitimate and ideal role for missionary
wives was to be supportive helpmates to their husbands, who had a lifetime commitment to the mission's work. Considering family to be a potential burden to male missionaries, she urged missionary wives to ensure
that their husbands could devote themselves entirely to their higher calling—allegiance to God—rather than being distracted by the need to give
comfort to their wives and children. Indeed, she set an example in her
own life, especially after she was diagnosed with cancer in 1908. She dealt
with the disease for several years, but in 1915, she was forced to return
to the United States for treatment. Her prognosis at that time was bleak,
and when she realized that her days were numbered, she chose to go "back
to her adopted home [Korea]"[87] because "to cause her husband [William
Baird] to leave the work, the Cause, the Crusade, which had given ultimate
meaning to both their lives, to return to the States to await her inevitable
end, was unthinkable."[88] She died in P'yŏngyang on June 9, 1916. In her
words and her deeds, she fulfilled the role of a "helpful wife and wise and
tender mother," as James Gale said at her memorial service.[89] At the same
time, her discourse ultimately pointed out that missionary wives joined
their husbands in the evangelical work and, through their wifely influence, contributed to and even accelerated the promotion of the missionary
enterprise. Furthermore, she asserted that male missionaries should feel
no shame or fear in accepting the advice of their wives.

In concert with the "womanly politics" of conforming to traditional
gender roles while exerting their independent domain, women missionaries used strategic discourse to portray themselves as ultimately triumph-
ing over the adversities that accompanied life in the mission field, such as
logistical and cultural difficulties in reaching out to the local people, frus-
tratingly slow progress in language learning, and the sheer struggle of living in a foreign land.[90] Missionary reports alluded to "difficulty and struggle," but missionaries, and especially women missionaries, were cautious

to avoid the possibility that their reporting about their struggles might be perceived as complaint. Thus, while sharing their hardship and limitations, they tended to use them as a way to justify and even glorify their noble calling as missionaries. Indeed, the title of an article, "Weakness Made Strong," in *Woman's Work* captures the contrast of women's delicacy with their fearlessness in their devotion to the mission's work:

> Most of the women missionaries whom we have met are quiet if
> not timid women who naturally shrink from adventure, danger and
> difficulty for its own sake. They would never stir from the seclusion
> of their quiet homes were they not lured by the love of Christ and pity
> for their poor darkened sisters, but that love leads many a delicate girl
> who never traveled across her own state line to cross wide seas, take up
> a home among alien people, and unshrinkingly meet hard conditions
> and danger.[91]

While portraying herself and her fellow women missionaries as delicate and timid, the anonymous missionary above amplified the power of Christ that prompted such a weak woman to take a dangerous voyage to a heathen country in order to save "poor darkened sisters." Leaving a comfortable home behind and coming to an unknown country was merely a beginning. Missionaries faced enormous difficulties in the field. For example, they were often required to make trips to remote villages to reach out to people. They would "go from one dreary and dirty little village to another, caring for diseased bodies and lost souls, sometimes crossing rough winter seas, or angry rivers filled with ice, or riding pack ponies or even oxen over indescribable roads, climbing tiger and wolf-haunted mountains . . . [,] eating and sleeping in little mud huts or cold, barn-like meeting houses warmed—if at all—with tiny, inadequate stoves whose most vigorous faculty is to throw out suffocating clouds of smoke." When they made these trips, they were sometimes carried on open sedans by coolies, who were often described as irresponsible people and heavy drinkers (see figure 5). One missionary noted that she traveled at midnight with "only worse than useless drunken" coolies, and she had to creep "on hands and knees over a dangerous icy pass to teach her women."[92] Some trips were fatal, as in the case of "Miss P.," who died after a fall from her horse while traversing a treacherous bridge on her way to a class.[93] In addition to the danger of travel, the missionaries were forced to deal with loneliness. They generally traveled in pairs, but when their partner was on furlough, solo journeys were inevitable. On one such journey to countryside villages, Henrietta Robbins reported how much she missed her co-worker, saying that "I spend nearly all of the time in the country, only returning for fresh supplies and a few days rest. I found it exceedingly lonely to visit the same villages where Miss Estey and I had gone so many times together."[94] To those who spent many years in the field and developed close ties with co-workers, the isolation they felt when a colleague was absent due to furloughs, illness or death was a recurring theme that was included in their reports.

In addition to difficulties during their travels, they expressed frustration with the struggle to acquire the Korean language. Florence Sherman conveyed a common exasperation of newcomers caused by lack of language skills. She said, "not being able to speak or understand the language, there has been little I could do to help these [Korean] women . . . the only way in which I could express my sympathy was by look, act, or by calling upon an interpreter. You all know this is not a very satisfactory way of expressing one's real feelings."[95] Especially in the beginning of the mission, it was particularly difficult to learn Korean because, as Mary Scranton put it, "there were no books, no teachers worthy of the name and no interpreters where knowledge went farther than the simplest forms of speech."[96]

Despite all these expected and unexpected adversities in the field, women missionaries concluded that "after all missionaries are certainly the happiest and best rewarded people in the world, and count any difficulties they meet as unworthy to be compared with the joy of blessing with hope these poor, hopeless women, the glory of the Vision and present crown, not to mention that which is to follow."[97] The discursive strategy is to present the difficulties and then reinforce the idea that these difficulties are no match for the joy experienced in doing the work of God. In doing so, women missionaries tended to remind the readers of the stereotype of feminine delicacy in order to ultimately highlight their transformation into strong, active women who had experienced the world to become indispensable agents for spreading "the glory of the Vision" to non-Christian societies.

Women's participation in the foreign missionary enterprise was primarily guided by the Victorian notion of true womanhood. The idealized women's sphere coupled with the desire to Christianize the world brought a large number of young, educated women to the foreign missionary enterprise who were channeled into separate "women's work for women." Although separated and excluded from clerical rights and decision making within general church organizations, women's engagement in the mission was decidedly public and global. In her argument for the strategic importance of *separate* women's organizations in putting forward feminist agendas, Estelle Freedman urges us to examine the implications of a "strong, public female sphere."[98] As much research demonstrates, while women's separate organizations in the mission field were clearly constrained by patriarchal church structure and norms, the very fact of a separate domain was the basis for the development of powerful women's organizations.[99] The separate women's domain was also a crucial platform for women to make major strides both in professional and personal growth.[100] As shown in the reports of women missionaries above, they did not publicly challenge traditional ideals of femininity. Rather, they wholeheartedly embraced the broadly accepted notions of feminine virtue. Crucially, it was that very feminine virtue that opened the door for women to engage in the global missionary enterprise. It was also the separate women's sphere that provided women missionaries with a fertile ground to exercise power and authority in strategic and ingenious ways and enabled them to assert their invaluable contribution to the mission.[101]

"HISTORY REPEATS ITSELF": KOREAN WOMEN MISSIONARIES

Given the prevailing custom of the inside-outside rule in Korea, the idea that women attended church meetings and engaged in church activities with male members was considered a significant violation of proper conduct. Those early Korean converts often had to endure insults and persecution for going to church. As William Scranton reported, these women's "husbands will hinder and forbid; their neighbors will look askance; and the baser sort will leer and pursue."[102] Kim Tŏk-sŏn, an early Christian, recalled her long struggle with her husband who opposed her going to church so strongly that he attempted to cut her wrist and hit her forehead with a lamp, leaving permanent scars on her body.[103] Even newly converted Christian men hesitated to bring their wives to church because the inside-outside rule was so deeply entrenched in Korea.[104]

In an effort to accommodate the strictures of the inside-outside rule, early missionaries created separate church meetings for women only. Mary Scranton wrote in 1888 that "I have had some difficulty in getting a teacher for the women and have adopted a new plan. I asked one of the colporteurs if he would come and talk for me, provided the women were willing to have him do so. They consented, provided he did not see them. So now I shut him up in a room by himself until they are seated and ready to listen. Then I arrange a screen between them and the place where he is to sit, and in this way the women's ideas of seclusion are held sacred, and the speaker's voice can be heard as distinctly as though he were visible."[105] In 1890, Scranton reported that "on account of the rigid seclusion of a large part of the women of this land, it has seemed necessary to organize our little band into a separate church, and at our recent annual meeting a pastor was assigned us (Rev. F. Ohlinger), who is to be with us one evening in three."[106] Eventually, when missionaries attempted to have men and women meet in the same church, they put a paper partition through the center of the room so that men occupied one side and women the other. Men and women entered the church through segregated gates and doors in order to avoid seeing each other.[107] While trying to accommodate the traditional rule of the separation of genders, missionaries felt that it was still a new experience for Korean women to come out of their houses and go to the public space, the church. In this sense, Margaret Best felt that one of the most important impacts that the Gospel had on the lives of Korean women was that it "broke the door that kept them in houses."[108]

The newly opened public space at church was dynamic culturally and socially. It brought Korean cultural norms into contact with American practices, which in turn opened some possibilities for Korean women, although it imposed new constraints as well. George Gilmore observed an intriguing but significant attitudinal difference among Korean women toward foreign and Korean men here. He wrote: "It is to be noted that women, after becoming acquainted with us and our ways, have shown no reluctance to meeting gentlemen, and are fond of paying visit to the wives of such foreigners as they know, often manifesting not the slightest embarrassment at being seen even for the first time by strange gentlemen. But were a male Korean visitor to enter the room, his entrance would be the signal for their instant withdrawal."[109] Gilmore observed that while Korean women were stringently bound by the Korean convention of the inside-outside rule in their interaction with other Koreans, they showed a surprising openness and willingness to interact with men of other cultures. One may infer that Korean women might have felt rather unconstrained in front of foreigners, largely because of the presumed differences in social norms. Indeed, the scenes of the church described earlier, in which a long screen prevented male and female participants from seeing each other but allowed everyone to see a foreign male pastor, reflects this selective application of the inside-outside rule. In a similar context, a reporter in *Taehan maeil sinbo* lamented that when some Korean women encountered foreigners, they were so glad to see them that they grabbed the hands of the foreigners as if they were in a loving relationship. In contrast, when they saw Koreans, they immediately turned around, hiding their faces in order to adhere to the inside-outside rule.[110] These episodes indicate that Korean women maintained a different mental and cultural space in their interaction with foreigners, and they even felt free to transgress the boundaries of gendered space, which would have been unthinkable in their interactions with Korean men. In addition, as Daniel Gifford observed, Korean women converts tended to enjoy the freedom of movement that they had when they attended church meetings.[111] From her own personal experience with Korean women who came to her Bible classes in P'yŏngyang, Margaret Best noted that for Korean women, coming to church or attending Bible classes was "a bright spot in an otherwise humdrum existence. Discouraged ones come for cheer and hope; persecuted ones for strength and the sympathy of fellowship."[112] Ch'a Mirisa (a.k.a. Kim Mirisa), a prominent Christian woman educator and founder of Kŭnhwa Girls' School in 1921, joined the Sangdong Church of the Methodist after she became a widow. She recalled what it meant for her to attend the church at the time: "Once I went to church and prayed to God, I was able to forget the agony and loneliness of the past and saw the hope and light of the future . . . While singing hymns and playing piano for fellow believers, all the troubles of life simply disappeared and I felt like I was living in a world of fantasy."[113] In this way, the Christian religious community provided some Korean women with a unique social space where they felt a sense of freedom, comfort, and solidarity. In a significant way the gap between Korean and foreign expectations of social life was a fertile ground in which Korean women began to juggle secluded, private life and open, public life.

If going to church was the first step for women to break the inside-outside rule, playing an active role in the church opened up unparalleled opportunities for Korean women to acquire new knowledge, organizational skills, and leadership within "women's work for women."[114] Their active involvement in "women's work for women" was inevitable because American missionaries often confronted various barriers in their work due to a lack of proficiency in the Korean language, insufficient cultural understanding, and "the suspicious attitude and the misunderstandings" of Koreans about foreign missionaries.[115] In addition, as Margaret Best noted, "it was manifestly impossible for the missionaries . . . to visit more than a very small proportion of the Christian women, in their home churches" largely because of lack of personnel and time.[116] Thus it was imperative for missionary women to work with newly converted Korean women who could serve as assistants and Bible women in order to reach out to a larger number of women in Korea.[117] In this context, as Lulu Frey put it, the Korean Bible women were "quite the most important factor in our work among the women of Korea."[118]

A "Bible woman" [*chŏndo puin*] was defined in various ways. In general, she was "a Christian woman employed in the distribution of Christian literature, and in biblical instruction"[119] and was "supported by foreign funds who is the personal helper of one of the foreign women, and works under her personal supervision."[120] Kate Cooper, a Methodist missionary, explained the evolution in the requirements for Bible women. In the beginning when the number of converted Korean women was tiny, "the first women believers were used in the capacity of Bible women, the only requisite being that they must learn to read." They were "women of no education, with no equipment,"[121] and were often hesitant to learn to read because they felt they "have no sense," meaning they did not have the intellectual capacity.[122] However, over time, with the growing number of eligible Christian women, the requirements to become a Bible woman became more rigorous. They specified that a candidate for Bible woman "must be without home responsibilities; widows are preferred. She must be able to give her whole time and service to the Lord's work; she must be a woman whose life has proven her to be a doer of the word and a follower of the Master not for any earthly gain but because of her love for the salvation of souls. She must be a graduate of a Bible Institute able to teach the home course for many of the country women are dependent almost entirely upon th Bible women for all their help in the study of this course."[123] With the expansion of the mission, the need for Bible women rapidly grew. Statistics show that the Methodists saw an increase in the number of Bible women from 17 in 1912 to 85 in 1917, and the Presbyterians had similar growth from 39 in 1907 to 114 in 1919.[124]

Although diverse in their background and motivation for joining the church, those Koreans who became Bible women tended to share a certain kind of life experience, which came out of economic hardship and the extremely patriarchal nature of the Korean family system.[125] Many of them were widows with little financial stability. Those who were married had to endure the pain and humiliation inflicted by unfaithful husbands or abusive in-laws. Incurable disease or sterility had also brought misery to their lives. A few Bible women came from the upper class, as exemplified by Chŏn Sam-dŏk and Kim Tŏk-sŏn, but the majority came from impoverished families.[126] Some of the graduates of mission schools also took up work as Bible women.[127] Another important commonality among the Bible women was that they were either trained in literacy or already had some basic literacy in vernacular Korean, which proved very useful in recruiting new converts.[128] Based on her observation in 1899 at the Woman's Dispensary of Extended Grace in P'yŏngyang, Rosetta Sherwood Hall estimated that only one out of forty women was able to read.[129] Given the low literacy rate among Korean women at the time, Bible women were in a situation in which they would have to teach newcomers how to read in order to introduce them to the Bible. This feature of the work of the Bible women itself became a powerful recruiting tool as many Korean women were attracted by the opportunity to gain literacy.[130] Mary Scranton explicitly referred to this aspect of the Bible women's work when she described how they endeavored "to awaken ambitions in the minds of the women in regard to learning to read, and in some instances [they] are succeeding."[131]

Bible women were trained by the women missionaries in explanations of the Bible that they could offer to non-believers (see figure 6). The Bible classes were held for one to two weeks on average. Given the limited resources, such classes were often held at the mission centers in the cities rather than in the countryside.[132] As a result, many participants had to walk long distances to attend the sessions. Some walked "three hundred *li*,[133] and not a few had burden of clothing, books and babies on their backs" with "no word of complaint that the way was too long, the roads too rough, or the burdens too heavy but with joyful faces and cheerful words of greeting."[134] Esther Shields was deeply impressed and inspired by the women's enthusiasm and wrote: "Think of a woman with rheumatism in her leg walking fifty-three miles in two days to attend three Bible studies! That is what Kim Que Pan Si—a consecrated evangelist, especially to the heathen women—did. Right royally does she adorn her profession; may some of us become more consecrated because we see her devotion."[135]

A more systematic curriculum for Bible women was established by 1904.[136] They learned not only religious texts but also practical knowledge, such as basic mathematics, writing, hygiene, physiology, cooking, and care of the sick.[137] They were also instructed in some principles of teaching and planning lessons, conveying what they knew and the value of questioning the potential converts.[138] Those who completed the curriculum successfully were awarded a diploma, which was an obvious lure to "inspire faithful attendance and enthusiasm to the end." As Olga Schaffer observed, "the Koreans 'love' diplomas, and their good prestige depends largely upon the possession of one or more—even our old Bible women feel the need of such a parchment sorely, if they would really accomplish great things among their people and be received well; and so it is a pleasure to give them one beautiful, satisfactorily worded certificate."[139] Upon completing their preparatory education, Bible women were assigned to lead small groups of women in the study of the Bible and the performance of other church activities under the guidance of the women missionaries.

Many women missionaries reported the positive impact of having Bible women around. Lura McLane Smith recalled how Korean "patients stared in blank amazement" when she made an earnest attempt to tell the Gospel story through the Korean Bible in her first year in Korea. Then there came to her rescue "a little deformed lady with a shining face" who "served as Hospital Bible woman all through the years making her presence felt throughout the length and breadth of Whanghai Province." [140] A medical missionary, Mary Cutler noted that her "attempts at teaching the Bible to native have been few and usually quite unintelligible so I have concluded that more good could be accomplished by calling in our Bible woman to do the teaching and exhorting to repentance whenever occasions develop." [141] Cutler provided a more detailed description of the routines the Bible women might have had. She wrote:

> [T]he most important work done at our Hospital and Dispensary would remain unreported were I not to tell what has been done by Mrs. Mary Whang, our Bible woman and head nurse. As nurse she takes and keeps record of the temperatures of the hospital patients, sees to giving their medicine, and dresses their wounds. As Bible woman she has held daily morning prayers and Bible readings with the hospital helpers and patients in the wards. Every noon she went to the Dispensary waiting room, to pray with and to read and expound the scriptures to those coming for medicines. 1,786 persons were reached in the Sunday afternoon services she held in the same room. . . . Mrs. Whang does not limit her Christian work to stated hours but loses no opportunity to do personal work with patients and visitors.[142]

Mrs. Whang's routine is just one classic example of the range of activities that the Bible women engaged in.[143] They were a critical workforce in the mission and developed indispensable working relationships with missionaries. N. M. S. Hall MacRae considered her Bible woman, Martha Pak, to be "truly my dear friend and fellow worker as if her skin had been white and her language my native tongue . . . I think of her earnestness, her charming personality, and untiring zeal in the Master's service."[144] The extent to which Bible women became indispensable to the work of the mission can be seen in the sheer number of church people who were under the guidance of Bible women. According to a report from P'yŏngyang in 1908, there were 89 Bible classes, and among these, 14 were run by missionaries with 721 students, while 75 classes were operated by Bible women with 2,248 students.[145] To this extent, the large scope of evangelical work was done by Bible women, although the missionaries felt that "constant teaching and supervision" on the part of the missionaries would still be necessary.[146]

Bible women did not restrict themselves to approaching those who came to mission hospitals and churches but also made house-to-house visits.

Being Korean certainly gave them easier access to other Korean women. Lulu Frey described the ways in which Bible women could effectively approach Korean women. She said that these Korean women might never have been interested in hearing about a foreign religion but became curious due to the stories told to them by the Bible women. She wrote:

> [A Korean woman's life] is spent largely within the walls of the house where she lives and works day by day. She welcomes the Bible woman; her visit affords a little diversion. The Bible woman sees her opportunity and tactfully makes the most of it. The Bible stories are interestingly told and she has no trouble in getting an invitation to come again. If we could look in upon them from time to time we would see the woman poring over her primer in her effort to learn to read as the Bible woman does. We would be delighted to hear her questions as she listens to the Old story and the light begins to dawn on her darkened mind. She finds she has a soul and that there is love for her in Christ, fellowship among other Christians and a hope of heaven which grows more precious to her every day.[147]

Bible women traveled extensively, visiting the most remote villages where missionary women could not go. Those trips were not easy for the Bible women, and they often had to endure physical hardship and hostile attitudes from Koreans. A Bible woman named Huldah reported on her extensive travel and physical hardship, saying that she "in one day waded thirteen streams nearly to her waist. She said that at last she was afraid to see water."[148] Chŏn Sam-dŏk, one of the pioneering Bible women, was ridiculed by people who wondered "what deceived her to do this crazy thing as a woman from a well-to-do family?"[149] They sometimes faced more than contempt. As Ella Lewis reported, "the Bible women who visit the country have by no means an easy time; one was detained in the street two hours by an intoxicated man, who held her tightly, until she was released by a passing soldier. Another one was struck with a piece of wood. Many have been driven away from houses they had entered uninvited."[150] Facing a variety of barriers, some Bible women came up with indirect and ingenious ways to gain access to nonbelievers. Cecilia, a Bible woman from Chemulp'o, went "from house to house as a peddler, taking care to sell her wares at prices which shall make the women desire to see her again, and never forgets to talk with them about the King's business."[151]

With the growing membership of the church, women missionaries and Korean women wanted to further develop "women's work for women" by creating a systematic platform to organize themselves and train the next generation. Mary Scranton organized the first Sunday School for women in January 1888, after repeated requests from Korean Christian men who asked, "we are being taught, why should not our wives learn the doctrine also."[152] Since then, a number of Sunday schools were organized in each church that became a site not only for religious teaching but other useful instructions on daily life. The Joyce Chapter was created in 1897 as part of the Epworth League, a national Methodist youth organization. Its membership was largely drawn from the students of Ewha Girls' School, but also included teachers of Ewha (both missionaries and Koreans) and members of the Chŏngdong Church.[153] The main activities of the Joyce Chapter, as well as other Epworth League organizations, centered on religious teaching; however, they also included diverse topics for discussion. A prominent example was the well-known public debate on whether women and men should receive equal education. The debate, jointly organized by the Joyce Chapter and the Warren Chapter, a young men's group largely composed of students from Paejae Boys' School, took place on December 31, 1897, and it drew significant attention from the print media at the time. The significance of the Joyce Chapter is that although women missionaries, such as Josephine Paine and Lulu Frey, acted as leaders in its formation, Korean women themselves began to play leadership roles in further developing the organization.

If the Joyce Chapter was designed for younger women, the Woman's Aid Society [*Pohoyŏhoe* or *Yŏbohohoe*], created in 1900, was for women older than thirty-five for the purpose of more proactive work for women by women. Its origin is found in the late nineteenth century, when American Methodist women organized a Woman's Aid Society largely in order to support traveling Bible women.[154] Lulu Frey explained the background of this organization in Korea:

> The women have always felt grieved that the age limit of 35 barred so many out of membership in the Epworth Leagues; so we talked over the plans together and decided on something similar in its working. The plans were laid before the women on Sunday the 9th month and 24th day, and 28 of them gave in their names and, on the 10th month and the 16th day, at the week-day prayer meeting it was formally organized . . . the membership has grown to forty-nine, all enthusiastic workers. You would be convinced that the women of Korea are deserving of a higher place than they now occupy . . . The meetings are orderly conducted. The roll is called, inquires made as to absent members, minutes interestingly written and well read, verbal reports of committees, short and to the point, giving incidents of work done and plans for the future. These meetings are held once a month after the regular weekly prayer service.[155]

As Frey indicates above, the Woman's Aid Society was run chiefly by Korean women with a decided focus on evangelical work and aid programs for poor women. Its monthly meetings were conducted where members participated in discussion and decision-making in a democratic fashion. One Bible woman expressed her amazement after observing a week-long meeting of Korean women. She said, "Oh, I just sat there so happy, thanking first God, and second the missionaries; for there was a Korean woman (Mrs. N. K. Hahr), who presided like a Bishop, Korean women read the Bible, Korean women sang, Korean women played the organ, Korean women prayed, and Korea women preached. I thanked God over and over again that afternoon for the privileges He is giving to the womanhood of Korea."[156] The previously secluded women of "old Korea" had been transformed into a "remarkable group of women" who presided over their own meetings with much grace, dignity and capability.[157]

The speedy and vigorous development of women's organizations within the church was most dramatically manifested in the journey of Korean women as foreign missionaries themselves starting in 1931. By 1931, Korea was already "the first country known as a 'foreign mission' to send out missionaries of her own to an alien people" when three Korean male pastors were sent to work in Shantung in 1913.[158] Almost within a generation after the introduction of Protestant Christianity, Korean women were themselves working as missionaries or Bible women in foreign lands. Margaret Best reflected upon the growth of Presbyterials of women's societies for home and foreign missions over the years as follows: "The first society of which the writer has any knowledge was formed in 1898 by the original women members of the first church established in Pyeng Yang [P'yŏngyang]. These women had already caught the vision of one of the central messages of the Bible and pledged themselves to contribute one cash each Sunday for sending two of their women to villages within a radius of five or six miles outside the city wall to preach the Gospel to other women. At that time to these new Christians, their decision gave the same thrill that sending one of their women as a foreign missionary to work among Chinese women in Shantung gave them at a later date."[159] Sponsoring Bible women to distant villages was the beginning of the efforts to distribute the Gospel beyond the vicinity of the home churches. It eventually evolved to the idea of sending Korean women evangelists to foreign lands.[160] In 1903 Esther Shields, a Presbyterian missionary, reported a spirited moment when Korean women already imagined themselves as missionaries emulating the model of American missionaries. She quoted a Korean woman's plea, "Those two American women were sent to school with their brothers, etc., what reason is there why the Korean girl cannot equally develop, and be sent to women in other countries where the gospel needs to be taught and preached?" Shields marveled at her comment and contemplated, "Surely if they would make as good evangelists in other countries as they do in their own and be guided only by the Holy Spirit in all their efforts they would be a power for good."[161] Sure enough, in 1908 the Presbyterian Church sent its first Korean woman evangelist, Yi Sŏn-gwang, to Quelpart (now Cheju Island), which was considered a "foreign field" to Koreans in the early twentieth century.[162] The Research Team in Women's History at the Research Institute of the History of Korean Christianity estimates that 164 Korean Bible women were sent to foreign lands between 1908 and 1945. Their major destinations were Manchuria (108), Siberia (22), Japan (17), China (8), Quelpart (7), and the United States (2).[163]

However, it was in 1931 that the first Korean woman missionary, Kim Sun-ho, was officially appointed and sent to Shantung, China, by the newly united body of the General Board—a union of the Presbyterial societies of Presbyterian U.S.A, the United Church of Canada, and the Australian territory.[164] Born to a Christian family in Hwanghae Province in 1902, Kim was educated at Chŏngsin Girls School in Seoul, the Women's Bible Institute in P'yŏngyang, and the Women's Theological Institute in Yokohama, Japan. She worked as a missionary until 1942.[165] Another woman missionary, Yun Chŏng-hŭi, was sent to Manchuria in 1933. No other details of her biography are known except for her years as a missionary, which ended in 1942 when she resigned for health reasons. These two pioneering women missionaries were unmarried, and their salaries came from the treasury of the General Society.[166]

Women of the Methodist Church had a similar history. In 1913, Korean women and American missionaries of the Methodist Episcopal Church, South, organized a Woman's Missionary Society in Wŏnsan for the purpose of "sending the gospel into the villages of their District by the lips of women whose salaries should be paid from their own funds and not with money sent out from America by the Woman's Council."[167] With these funds, in 1915 the Missionary Society chose two women as "their first missionaries" who "went into the neediest part of the District to preach the Gospel." Some of the funds were even sent to Africa to help out with women's work there.[168] This organization inspired many other districts to create similar societies. American missionaries helped develop the Missionary Society programs using "stories from Mexico, Brazil, China, India and Africa" and "sketches of notable lives such as David Livingstone in his early years, Florence Nightingale, Frances Willard, and Booker Washington."[169]

The first general meeting to which representatives of these organizations were sent was held in Seoul in 1920. The same body decided in its meeting in 1922 to send a Korean missionary to Siberia for the first time, and Naomi Ch'oe was selected to be the first woman missionary to that region. She was born in Kaesŏng in 1873 and was introduced to Christianity while she was suffering through the agony of infertility. Working as a Bible woman with Carroll Collyer, a southern Methodist missionary, Ch'oe began to engage in evangelical work largely in the Wŏnsan area. She was later educated at the Women's Bible Institute in Kaesŏng and also worked as an instructor there. She served in Siberia from 1923 to 1926.[170]

In the case of the Methodist Episcopal Church, it held its first General Executive meeting of the Woman's Missionary Society of the Korean Methodist Church in 1923. Mrs. Alice Kim-Jung, who was elected as its first president, and Mrs. Helen Choi, who was its first treasurer, "led the thinking and planning of the group along lines followed by the 'mother society,' the W.F.M.S. in America."[171] The Woman's Missionary Society chose India and Manchuria for the foreign mission field, supporting two Indian primary school teachers, and sending Rhoda Yang (a.k.a. Yang Wurodŏ) as the first Korean missionary woman to Manchuria to work with Korean migrants.[172] Marie Church recalled the inception of the Society: "The service of consecration, when an appropriation pledge was made, in this historic meeting, kindled a new the fires of missionary zeal in the hearts of all missionaries privileged to be present."[173] She further commented that "affiliation with the International Department of the Woman's Foreign Missionary Society makes the society in Korea a real part of a world sisterhood in the glorious task of Kingdom building."[174] By 1930, as the two branches of Methodism in Korea were united, the two separate women's missionary groups also converged into one "mighty group of Korean missionary women, who now carry on as only Oriental women can, when given an opportunity."[175]

In 1911, when Yi Sŏn-gwang returned to P'yŏngyang from her assignment as the first Korean woman evangelist to Quelpart, she spoke about her missionary experience to the large congregation. The event reminded American missionary women of one of the typical "Women's Missionary Meetings at home." That is, "the missionary was introduced in much the same way and everybody looked expectant and ready to listen to all the curious and wonderful news they knew must be in store."[176] The success of the first Korean woman evangelist prompted important questions for American women missionaries, who insisted on their role as "teachers" and thus showed what Yun Ch'i-ho called "the unintentional but the matter-of-fact 'bossism' of missionary superiors."[177] Given this overall hierarchical relationship between American missionary women and Korean women, Margaret Best in P'yŏngyang asked an important question—had American missionaries overlooked the fact that Korean women were "capable of conceiving, undertaking and successfully carrying out plans to teach with the Gospel message those whom they have never met but whom the love of Christ in the heart brings within the range of their interest and their desire is exemplified in various ways in every station."[178] She further asserted:

> The history of the Society shows that Korean women, given motive, are capable of doing much good for their own people. Is it not our part to help them and just as soon as they are ready for it (and perhaps a little sooner than they are ready for it in the minds of some of us careful ones) put responsibility upon them, not only in matters like this, but in teaching and in other ways that will suggest themselves. If we think the Korean woman is unfitted because she has not been educated, as we count education, we fail to do justice to native ability, and to what the Grace of God can do for heart, mind and character, and so lose much of the help in our efforts for woman that she might give us, and at the same time keep her from coming into her own. Let us help her to find herself, and when once she has done that, she will have no small part in raising the standard of Womanhood in the church, and in bringing Korean women to a knowledge of Christ.[179]

There are abundant missionary reports that praised the significant help missionary women received from Korean women, whose dedication, persistence, hard work, and self-sacrifice deeply impressed them. Yet in terms of their perception of Korean women, no activities other than Korean women's own missionary work left a lasting impact on American women. To be sure, American women missionaries and their "Women's Foreign Missionary Societies" served as a model, and this point was repeatedly emphasized in missionary writing. However, many women missionaries expressed their amazement at the remarkable success of Korean women missionaries. Impressed by Korean women's engagement in the mission's work, together with their demonstrated strength and resilience in the face of terrible conditions,[180] Edith Blair noted that "the outstanding thing in our women's work is the sending of a Korean woman missionary to the Korean mission in China and Manchuria, by the Korean Women's Missionary Societies. She is a fine young woman, well trained and full of enthusiasm for the work. All her salary, travel and equipment are furnished by the Korean women."[181] While observing Korean women's meetings and their missionary activities with the Chinese, Blair reminisced about the repeated history of women in the missionary enterprise. She wrote:

The real point of the meeting came with the reading of the reports of the two [Korean] women missionaries sent out by the Society, Min Sinho working among the Chinese in Shantung Province, China, and Yun Chung Hwi working among the Koreans in Manchuria. The work they had accomplished, their needs for the coming year, their earnest requests that the women at home should stand back of them in prayer— *how familiar it all sound to us foreign missionaries who were present. What woman of old Korea could have dreamed of women like these, forward looking, intelligent, efficient, devoted, eager and prepared to take their share in the work of the church in any capacity required.* I was amused to see in this gathering the same types we meet in Presbyterials at home; the woman who pops up to question every action, the woman who is self-appointed watch-dog of the treasury, the woman who is a stricter for rule, the pessimistic woman, and the woman with rosy spectacles who is sure there will be money enough to do everything any one wants. But through all this, was the evident desire that not only the delegates themselves, but all the women of the church in Korea, should be ready to do their part in fulfilling the Master's last command. [emphasis added][182]

The returned woman missionary from Shantung, Kim Ho Sun, had one evening in each class and gave most interesting addresses. As she spoke of some of her difficulties with the Chinese language, one old lady spoke up, "Why don't you teach them Korean?" feeling that it would be an easy solution. Surely, I thought, *history repeats itself.* [emphasis added][183]

To be sure, the history of Korean women during the Chosŏn dynasty shows the public engagement of certain groups of women in work outside the gendered boundaries of the "inside-outside rule." Female shamans, folk healers, and entertainers *[kisaeng]* were "lowborn women of influence" who transgressed the conventional perimeter drawn for women in the private sphere through their crucial role in religious, healing, and leisure activities.[184] However, the lives of the overwhelming majority of Korean women remained confined to the private domain. In this vein, Korean women's engagement in the foreign mission in the early twentieth century was an important juncture that signaled a major shift in perspective. The novel task of Korean women as foreign missionaries resulted from their extensive participation for decades in various church activities at the grassroots level. As Marie Church described it, "this most powerful force in the Korean Methodist Church, did not spring from a suddenly conceived meeting of a few women, but it was the breaking forth of long hidden forces."[185] Women were often key players in founding new churches. They donated rice or physical labor for the building of churches.[186] More important, when American missionaries suffered from personnel shortages in the face of rapidly growing demands for itinerating and country work, Korean women served as an indispensable work force. Some gave "a tenth of their time to the Lord— two weeks in preparation and three weeks in country work" and went wherever missionaries sent them.[187] As described earlier, the role of Bible women in particular was crucial in recruiting, organizing, and educating Korean women. Ranging from Sunday schools to the Joyce Chapter and the Woman's Aid Society, small- and large-scale women's groups and meetings prepared them for the expanded role in the public realm. Along with the increase in the number of educated women, Christian women's involvement in public arenas was further accelerated when they established the Korean Young Women's Christian Association (YWCA, Chosŏn kidokkyo yŏja ch'ŏngnyŏnhoe yŏnhaphoe) in 1923. As a nationwide and internationally affiliated organization, the main goal of the YWCA in Korea was no doubt to promote Christian spirituality. However, it became a major player among women's organizations in challenging traditional gender rules, promoting women's education, seeking women's economic independence and equal legal protection, and participating in the broader movement for national independence and reconstruction.[188]

Despite progress, Korean women were denied the opportunity to engage more fully in church activities by the male-dominant church organizations. As with the case of the American women missionaries in their own organizations, Korean women were prevented from becoming pastors and excluded from the general body of the church in decision-making. Women continued to suffer from a wide gap in salary vis-à-vis their male counterparts. It is argued that the process of institutionalization of Korean churches ironically led to the decline in the role of women as leaders, relegating them to the status of helpmates only. One male church leader specified the distinctive roles of men and women in the church, arguing that it was the duty of the male church leader "first, to teach truth, second, to govern the church and third, to administer church finances." In contrast, he advised that Bible women "should be neither proactive nor intervening" and advocated as their only duty "to pray for the betterment of church activities."[189] These sentiments precisely echoed a typical position of American clergymen in the late nineteenth century, who argued that women had "the right to membership, work, worship, protection and defense," but should keep out of "official business, governing, the exercise of discipline and maintenance of order."[190] This type of gender-specific hierarchy was prescribed in a context where women were participating in the activities of the church more enthusiastically than ever before. Just as American women missionaries represented the greater percentage of mission personnel, so Korean Bible women outnumbered Korean Bible men. The reality at the time was that there were few jobs for women, and Bible woman was one of the few professions available for an educated woman.[191] Thus, by the late 1920s there were twice as many Bible women as Bible men.[192] Yet the structure of the church hierarchy and religious training show that while women's participation was encouraged for the prosperity of churches, their official leadership was systematically precluded. Christian churches thus became a complex arena in which Korean women thrived with newly found roles and public engagement on the one hand, but continued to experience discrimination on the other. The historiography of Korean Christianity reflects such unequal gender dynamics. Despite the exceptional contribution of Korean Bible women and their missionary work at home and in foreign lands, it is hard to find any historical record of who they were and what they did. As the church historian Yang Mi-gang argues, there was no space for women to claim their place in history.[193]

THE MODERN PRIVATE SPHERE

Just as Korean women's involvement in church activities contributed to the changing role of women in the public arena, so it also had a significant impact on the nature of home and family. The traditional Korean norms included such notions as *samjong chido* (three subordinations of a woman) to the three male figures in her life—father, husband, and son—and *namjon yŏbi* (men revered, women despised), which was used to define overall family gender dynamics. From a missionary point of view, these practices simply reconfirmed the harm of pagan customs against women. Reporting their observations of women's low status in the family, women missionaries launched a long march to reform Korean domestic life. One caveat in this reform effort was that any major challenge to indigenous customs might alienate some Koreans and create antagonism toward Christianity. Thus, missionaries were very cautious in suggesting to Koreans what the ideal of a family should be and what role women should play in the Christian family.

Korea's custom of early marriage was one of the familial customs where missionaries made significant efforts to change the status quo. In 1894 the Korean government promulgated the legal age for marriage as twenty for men and sixteen for women, but the longstanding custom of early marriage continued to prevail. It was not uncommon for a twelve- or thirteen-year-old girl to be committed by her parents to marry a man whom she had neither known nor even seen before.[194] Mary Scranton expressed her concern about the impact of early marriage on the mission work: "I am greatly bothered these days in regard to the subject of early marriages. No less than three of my girls, who have just begun to learn, must soon go out from us, and as their husbands have been chosen by their friends they do not, of course, marry Christians, but God . . . will not let the labor expended on these girls come to naught."[195] A medical missionary, Rosetta Sherwood, had similar concerns, citing the case of "three of the girls in the school I am training to assist me in the drug room and dispensary. If it were not for the Korean custom of early marriage, we could depend upon the girls for pharmacuitical [sic] work and nursing, and in time for assistant physicians, but we cannot keep them beyond the age of sixteen."[196] The custom of early marriage arranged by parents caused serious problems for the success of the mission in that youngsters often quit school and never returned to church, which was seen as a serious detriment to the growth of the Christian community. Missionaries cautiously tried to discourage Korean believers from following the custom. In the beginning it was difficult to bring Korean girls to mission schools; however, it was even more difficult to keep them there until they finished their schooling. Although missionaries did not engage in any public campaign, they felt "very strongly that they [Korean girl students] should not be married until they are at least eighteen."[197] In the face of the reality in which missionary teachers lost many of their young students, they sometimes found ways to prevent early marriage. For instance, when one of the young students at Ewha Girls' School was arranged to be married, the missionary teachers would award her a scholarship, hoping that this would inspire her to continue her study.[198] In 1900 the missionaries made an official resolution in their own missionary circle to discourage early marriage and to actively try to use their influence to prevent their young students from being committed to marriage. The missionaries would take it upon themselves to "urge the education of the daughters in the church, pick out and send us your brightest girls, encouraging the parents to allow them to stay and finish the prescribed course."[199] Josephine Paine and Lulu Frey, teachers at Ewha Girls' School, proudly informed fellow missionaries in 1901 that "the last girl who a few months ago was married from the school was twenty one years old. She has acted as a pupil-teacher for the past two years, in this way receiving her training for the work she is now doing as day school teacher. The resolution adopted by the last Annual Conference discouraging early marriage is having effect."[200]

Another problem with the early marriage system was that it was the parents who had power to select a future spouse and not the girls themselves. This lack of freedom led to a problem for the missionaries in that the hard-won Christian girls and women might not be able to form Christian homes if they were arranged to marry "pagan" men. Having seen the dominant power of the husband in the patriarchal Korean family system, the missionaries understood that it would be very difficult for a wife to convert her husband to Christianity. For missionaries, expanding the Christian community was a central goal, and thus an ideal marriage was a union between a Christian man and a Christian woman, exemplified by the marriage between Esther Pak, one of the most prominent graduates of Ewha, and Pak Yu-san, an assistant to the medical missionary William Hall.[201] As William Scranton put it, "Our boys in the school marrying girls from the school are strengthened and every reinforcement of good against evil has a multiple power. Our Girls' School of today is a pattern that might well be copied by older institutions and its every effort seems directly effective to the very end we desire to reach."[202] In this context, discouraging early marriage and advocating the freedom to choose a marriage partner served as an expedient mission strategy on one hand and constituted a most important ideal in redefining modern family on the other. The 1912 edition of *The Korea Mission Field* applauded the "New Woman of the East," who strenuously objected to the marriage arranged for her by her parents, arguing that since the prospective groom was not a Christian, he would probably be a bad husband. To missionaries, what she did "sounds impossible to us who have lived long in the east and know its supposedly unchangeable customs." What was particularly surprising to the missionaries was that this Korean girl was "not from the capital, but from one of the country stations," which were generally more conservative. The missionaries held up this case as an example of fruit born from their reform efforts against early marriage and for the right to choose a spouse, which shed "light on the new Korea of 1911, as well on the life of the native Christians."[203]

In addition to the problems caused by early marriage, the concubine system, which some may call "polygamy," was also a topic of deep concern. William Baird, who opposed the custom of plural wives and the concubine system, made a comparison between Korea and other countries with respect to the custom of polygamy. He wrote:

[I]n savage countries where wives are simply bought and sold, or
exchanged, some arbitrary rules might be made, but in countries
like Korea, with an ancient civilization, he would be a rash man who
would run counter to all the best customs of the land . . . Marriage is
largely a social affair regulated but slightly by the state. Marriage law

is moral and social rather than legal and punitive . . . The question of concubinage is not so complicated in Korea as in India and many other countries. There real polygamy exists and is regarded as right. Not so in Korea. Though freely tolerated, the lightest standards of morals denounce both polygamy and concubinage as wrong.[204]

While Baird's understanding has some truth to it, the marriage system of the Chosŏn dynasty was more complex than that. The Chosŏn dynasty certainly denounced the plural marriage system of the Koryŏ dynasty, but it institutionalized the differentiated status of primary and secondary wives as part of an effort to create a Confucian patrilineal system. In her analysis of the impact of neo-Confucian legislation on women, Martina Deuchler argues that "the early Neo-Confucian legislators were preoccupied with the 'rectification of names' [*chŏngmyŏng*], that is, with determining and identifying social status. For this, only a clear line of descent would provide a criteria on the basis of which descent group membership and thus social status could be verified. The singling out of one wife and her children as a man's rightful spouse and legitimate heirs was therefore of paramount importance." In this context, the "ranking of these women as primary [*ch'ŏ*] and secondary or minor [*ch'ŏp*] wives was thus a fundamental task for stabilizing society."[205] The elaborate ranking system was mostly for the upper class. However, as long as they could afford, commoners also acquired concubines for the purpose of continuing the family line or sexual gratification.[206]

To the missionaries, the taking of concubines or secondary wives strictly contradicted the rule of monogamy that was in keeping with Christian ethics. In 1895 the Methodist Church made a unanimous resolution that men with plural wives could not be baptized, any church member who had concubines should be expelled from membership, and those who were involved in this custom should not be accepted into the church. In comparison, the Presbyterian missionaries were initially divided into several groups, taking different approaches to the issue of polygamy, but by 1897 the Presbyterian Church also resolved to prohibit the taking of plural wives or concubines.[207] However, because the custom was so widespread, it was important for missionaries to try to strike a balance between their desire to eradicate the custom and strategies to minimize the potentially negative impact of such effort on recruiting and maintaining church membership.[208] The real challenge for missionaries to tackle was what they should do with those church members who had already taken plural wives before becoming Christian. Missionaries reported many successful cases in which a Korean man gave up his second wife and in some cases even a third wife and returned to his primary wife. Similarly, concubines who became Christian gave up their bonds with men in order to become true Christian believers.[209] Despite those success stories, there were often difficult situations in which Korean Christian men continued to live with their secondary wives. Such situations are best exemplified by the case of Sŏ Sang-ryun, a prominent Korean leader in the Presbyterian Church. Sŏ had two wives—the first chosen for him by his parents and the second of his own choosing. He considered the second wife to be his true companion and refused to give her up, despite pressure to do so from the members of the mission. Since he would not cut off his relationship with his second wife, he was disqualified from consideration for becoming an elder or pastor even though he was widely viewed as one of the best-qualified individuals for such a role at the time.[210]

This long and difficult process of advancing the idea of monogamy, coupled with the policy of discouraging early marriage, marks a missionary effort in redefining the ideal home and family. Mattie Noble proudly presented how missionary work made an impact on the Korean home and family:

> We helped train in our home scores of scholarship boys from our Mission schools . . . They have watched us in the training of our children and have seen our companionship with them. Different ones have told me how wonderful it appeared to them to see a mother in her home, educated and capable, able to enter into the fuller life experiences with her husband, and to be a real companion, mentally and physically, with her children, even with the grown-up ones. This can better be understood when one remembers the place of inferiority that pagan religions impose upon women. Christ blessed the home, and lifted women in the home; he came that they as well as the men might have life "more abundantly." . . . the training of their children was better, the family life was sweeter, and that all the members of a Christian family began to study and to fill their hearts and minds with rich treasure . . . I would like to tell of the scores of things material that have been improved in and around the homes of this land, of which a great deal has been due to the precept and example of the members of the missionary home—father, mother and children, (missionaries' children have a great part also in this out-going influence.) . . . let me just say, that love through Christ gradually but surely brings cleanliness, purity and beauty. A missionary's home shows the plane to which Christ lifted women. The modern Korean woman, in many cases, is no longer the subservient one but the co-serving one; she no longer remains aside while her master, (the husband), and her sons eat; she no longer walks behind her husband with downcast eyes and covered by a cloak thrown over her head and held closely so as to nearly cover

her face and form; no longer does she have to give to the mother-in-law complete authority in the raising of her child; no longer does she have to show no outward affection for her husband; or to be a pathetic, servant-like member of the parents-in-law's home; or to suffer many other indignities because she was born a woman. No, for Christ has lifted women. She is learning, and she sees the bearing out of this truth in concrete, tangible form in the missionary home, by observing the wife and mother,—her freedom, her love, her authority . . . this missionary mother has met people who have told her how, in the raising of the children, they have taken pattern after some methods they had seen used in the raising of children in the missionary home.[211]

Noble's description of the ideal home and family starts with the idea that her home has been a site for the training of these converts, and she points out that the missionary family is a model for Koreans to look up to and emulate. (For a photo of the Noble family, see figure 7.) The relationship between the missionary husband and wife demonstrates the ideal of "companionship," in which the wife no longer has to be subservient but rather is "able to enter into the fuller life experiences with her husband." Even the children of missionaries play a great role in their "out-going influence." For instance, when a child from a missionary home refused to accept a piece of candy offered by Koreans until "he had asked his mother if he might accept it," such training of children by American missionaries inspired Koreans to train their own children in a similar fashion.[212] In this context, the "Korean modern woman" is someone who overcomes the inferior status of women in old Korea and becomes a real companion to her husband, an educated mother, and a practitioner of modern knowledge and more importantly, a woman of Christian faith that can serve as the foundation and spirit of the ideal home.

The new ideal of the educated wife and mother here goes beyond her role as a moral influence, which was firmly embedded in traditional womanhood. Her new and modern contribution to the family involves material improvement in such areas as hygiene, nutrition, and the raising of children (see figure 8). As Mattie Noble noted above, missionary work with women led to changes in "things material that have been improved in and around the homes of this land." Seeing is believing. Missionaries used their own homes as the model to teach new ways of housekeeping and cooking. In general, missionary homes, typically located in the "mission compound," were not open to the public for reasons of safety and hygiene,[213] or because missionaries believed that the "rude sightseeing and idle curiosity" on the part of Koreans might deter their evangelistic work.[214] Mattie Noble was one of the few women missionaries who was willing to show her mission home to Korean "sightseers." In the eyes of Koreans, those Western style mission houses were like a fancy "heaven" equipped with an organ, a clock, a sewing machine, rocking chairs, and imported kitchen facilities that they had never seen before.[215] Nellie Holdcroft demonstrated the typical method of missionary influence in helping Korean women improve their skills in housekeeping and raising babies. She wrote, "I invited the women of my cottage Bible class to meet here instead of in the Korean home where we usually meet. About twenty came and seemed to enjoy it so much. Most of them had never been in a foreign (American) home and our home is very attractive I think, and has just been freshly kalsomined. I served them tea and sponge cake after our Bible lesson."[216] While new methods and lifestyle were introduced, missionaries were keenly aware that Western ways could not be implanted due to vastly different material and cultural situations. For example, Susan Ross, a Presbyterian missionary, wrote in 1929 about the improved condition of raising children in a more hygienic and scientific way and yet noted that the material situation was still too poor for Korean mothers to implement newly learned methods. She reported that "[b]abies are very much better taken care of now than when we first came to town. Still, the most willing mother has so little with which to do that it is small wonder if she sometimes grows tired of hearing foreigners who can have all the milk, soap, clean clothes, mosquito nets, orange juice, big airy rooms, etc. they need for their babies tell her how to do things. She would be glad to do so also if only she could."[217] Within this context, missionary women and Korean women found some alternative means for providing "modern" ways of hygiene and nutrition. Nellie Holdcroft, for example, reported that "an interesting development of the work is the preparation of bean milk for infant feeding. It is much cheaper than cows milk and can be used very successfully."[218] In this way, Western forms of hygiene, health care and child rearing became an important part of creating the modern Christian family in Korea.[219]

Significantly, the newly emerging "modern" family and the role of women within it was in parallel with a major shift in perspective on ideal womanhood in the United States. That is, Victorian notions of true woman-hood was being replaced by what Sheila Rothman calls "educated mother-hood," which redefined the private sphere and expected women to have a systematic and scientific understanding of child development and household management.[220] In his analysis of New Women in colonial Korea, Theodore Jun Yoo similarly points out the changing nature of ideal womanhood from *hyŏnmo yangch'ŏ* (wise mother, good wife) to *hyŏnmyŏng chŏnŏp chubu* (wise and prudent professional housewife) equipped with "bourgeois norms of efficiency."[221] A number of national reformers and New Women proposed and advocated the efficient ways of housekeeping, children's education, dress code, hygiene, and time and budget management.[222] It became fashionable for educated women to be able to make Western food as a sign of being a modern woman. As chapter 5 shows, girl students learned how to cook crisp biscuits or broiled steak, skills that could be appreciated by future husbands who were most likely to be Western-educated. In this way, the idea of a "professional housewife" presented a "modern" form of domesticity that was informed by scientific knowledge and made efficient use of time and money. Given the higher level of knowledge and skills, a claim emerged that the work of a housewife ought to be paid like regular work outside the home.[223] This seemingly elevated status of "domestic" chores with a modern, Western flavor recentered the traditional roles of women in the private for which missionary homes and women missionaries as wives and mothers served as a model. However, as chapter 6 discusses, the modern construct of domesticity was sharply criticized by Korean liberal and socialist feminists, who interpreted it as a duplicitous patriarchal gender ideology or an expedient strategy used by capitalists and colonial authorities to turn Korean women into a yielding commodity to advance their scheme of assimilation and exploitation.[224]

The encounters between Korean women and American women missionaries shed light on the ways in which the notion of an ideal sphere for women was challenged and reshaped through competing interpretations of the proper place for women. Although women missionaries came to Korea to rescue "poor darkened sisters" who were leading lives of seclusion, they had to be cautious in how they interacted with Koreans in order to meet their evangelical goals. The cultural differences that they needed to navigate were evident, for example, in Korean attitudes, based on centuries-old gender practices, that led them to critique Western women's presence in public as improper, unladylike behavior. Similarly, Korean women were drawn to public spaces such as churches and schools not simply because of the missionary endeavor but also to advance their own agendas. Despite seemingly different gender practices upon first contact, the notion of "separate spheres," cherished by the women missionaries, and the Confucian idea of the "distinction between man and woman," held by the Korean women, greatly overlapped in that both recognized *different* roles for women and men and at the same time the *moral* influence women had on the family and the society. This nexus of ideas about the proper place and roles for women provided a favorable space for negotiations and accommodations. More important, it was in separate "women's work for women" that women missionaries and Korean women were able to expand significantly the scope of their lives and activities while conforming to the widely accepted role of women in the private sphere. In a significant way, both women missionaries and Korean women shifted from a life in the "seclusion of quiet homes" to that of the wide-open global mission field. In this transformation, they foregrounded their feminine virtues and employed "womanly politics" to cope with the patriarchal church organizations and to soothe male anxiety about women's emerging leadership.

FIGURE 1.   An ideal Christian woman (from *Fifty Years of Light*, 1938).

FIGURE 2.   The statue of Mary F. Scranton on the campus of Ewha
Womans University (photograph by the author).

FIGURE 3.   Korean women in full body-covering clothing on the street (courtesy of GCAH).

FIGURE 4.   A Korean woman on the street (courtesy of GCAH).

FIGURE 5.   Gertrude Snavely itinerating with Korean aids (courtesy of GCAH).

FIGURE 6.   Women's Bible Class, Taiku [Taegu], 1917 (courtesy of PHS).

FIGURE 7.   The W. Arthur and Mattie Noble Family (Photo courtesy of the Noble family).

FIGURE 8.   A missionary woman demonstrates how to change a diaper at a clinic (courtesy of GCAH).

FIGURE 9.   The first graduates of Ewha College in 1914 (courtesy of GCAH).

FIGURE 10. Annie Adams Baird (courtesy of PHS).

FIGURE 11. Ellasue Wagner (photo courtesy of the Garwood family).

FIGURE 12. Sue Wallace, an American woman who married a Korean man (photo courtesy of the Garwood family).

FIGURE 13.   Kim Hwal-lan (a.k.a. Helen Kim) with an Ewha College committee (courtesy of GCAH).

FIGURE 14.   Na Hye-sŏk (courtesy of Na Hye-sŏk Memorial Foundation, Seoul).

4. Disciplining the Modern Body and Mind

A Christian Korean intellectual and educator, Yun Ch'i-ho, stated in 1918 that "if the Christian missionaries had accomplished nothing else in Korea, the introduction of female education alone deserves our lasting gratitude."[1] This "lasting gratitude" shared by many Koreans has most significantly contributed to the image of American women missionaries as the pioneers of modern womanhood in Korea. Indeed, it was women missionaries who founded the first girls' schools in Korean history, at a time when neither the Korean government nor private citizens paid any attention to female education. Those schools offered literacy training in Chinese, Korean, and English as well as modern subjects such as geography, arithmetic, physiology, and music, producing the first cadre of professional women in the fields of medicine, education, art, and literature. The graduation ceremonies, art exhibits, and public field-day activities held by mission schools were a source of fascination among the public, who marveled at the girl students' intellectual and physical prowess.[2] Given the long history of women's seclusion and the absence of formal schooling for women in old Korea, mission schools undoubtedly served as a platform for unsettling the Confucian doctrine about women's inferiority in intelligence and heralding modern womanhood.[3]

However, the trajectory in the founding and development of mission schools for girls presents a more complex picture. Missionary teachers firmly believed that education in Christian ethics and ways of life was an expedient vehicle for "both evangelism and social uplift" for their "heathen" sisters.[4] The reason why the Woman's Foreign Missionary Society sponsored schools was because it believed that "no nation rises higher than its mothers, and that no nation can become Christian without Christian mothers."[5] In this context, female education was particularly crucial in cultivating future mothers who would build Christian homes, an ultimate goal of mission education. The high value that missionaries placed on education for women was wholeheartedly shared by many Korean male intellectuals, who advocated educated motherhood in their pursuit of national reformation. One can view the mission schools as a microcosm in which both Christian and nationalist goals were intensely pursued, negotiated, and challenged. Both seized on the opportunity to put forward their own goals. However, as the population of educated females grew larger and rapid cultural changes swept Korea, especially from the 1920s on, the differences between Western missionaries and Koreans in terms of their priorities for education increasingly induced tensions and conflicts. This chapter examines the ways in which the missionary desire to civilize and Christianize Korea was infused with Koreans' desire for modernization and nationalist agendas. Specifically focusing on the beginning of mission schools and their educational goals and curriculum, the chapter shows how missionaries made strategic changes in their educational policies in response to specific local demands by accentuating a "home-grown" variety of Christian character with special emphasis on domestic virtues.

A NEW BEGINNING:
THE ESTABLISHMENT OF EWHA GIRLS' SCHOOL

Ewha Girls' School was Korea's first school for girls, founded in 1886 by Mary F. Scranton, a Methodist missionary from the United States. The crucial background to its establishment was the opening of the Methodist mission in Korea, and particularly the role of John F. Goucher. In 1883 Goucher met a group of Korean emissaries to the United States by chance on the Union Pacific train.[6] After this encounter, he actively sought ways to send missionaries to Korea. He had been active not only in the Methodist Episcopal Church of Baltimore but also in world missions, from Asia to Africa, with particular interest in education. Baltimore was one of the most active and vibrant centers for Methodist women's organizations in the country, having already sent women missionaries to China to open several girls' schools.[7] During this time, Goucher laid the foundation for the establishment of Goucher Women's College in Baltimore, which opened in 1888. The college specifically trained women of the Methodist Episcopal Church and significantly contributed to training future women missionaries.[8] Because of Goucher's longstanding interest in the world mission and women's education, after his chance encounter with the Korean emissaries he urged R. S. Maclay of the Methodist Mission in Japan to pay a visit to

Korea to investigate the possibility of starting missionary work there. He also donated a significant amount of money to bring about the opening of the Korean mission field. With Goucher's sponsorship, Maclay made his first visit to Korea in 1884, and he obtained a "royal permit to Christianity" and successfully garnered considerable support from reform-oriented Korean politicians such as Kim Ok-kyun.[9] Maclay later received a letter from General Foote, the U.S. minister to Korea, who had gotten "renewed assurances from His Majesty that not only will no obstructions be thrown in your [Maclay's] way, but that you will be tacitly encouraged in founding a school and hospital at Seoul."[10] Clearly, what the Korean government was interested in was not the religious mission per se but the educational and medical institutions the missionaries were expected to bring.

After returning from Korea to Japan, Maclay hired a Christian Korean man, Yi Su-jŏng [a.k.a. Rijutei], who was residing in Tokyo, to serve as his translator. The connection between Maclay and Yi is an important one. Around the time their association began, Yi sent an appeal to churches in America through Henry Loomis of the American Bible Society urging them to send a woman missionary teacher to Korea as a matter of the greatest importance. Believing that "to elevate and reform a people, to educate children, to lead their husbands to virtue, are woman's mission," he regarded the establishment of a girls' school as an urgent matter.[11] It is not clear to what extent Maclay influenced Yi in sending the letter. However, Yi's intellectual background and his associations with many American missionaries and Japanese intellectuals suggest how he was led to the appeal. Intending to study agriculture, Yi went to Japan in 1882, accompanying the special envoy of the Korean government. While in Japan, he was influenced by Japanese intellectuals such as Tsuda Sen, a strong advocate of Western knowledge and Christianity,[12] as well as American missionaries. In turn, with his faith in Christianity and modern reforms, Yi was said to influence Korean intellectuals, including Yun Ch'i-ho.[13] It was within this context that Yi urged the American Bible Society to send a woman missionary teacher to educate Korean women, which he believed would result in an elevated Korea informed by the teachings of the Gospel.

Against this background, the first group of Methodist missionaries arrived in Korea in 1885. In the following year, Mary F. Scranton opened Ewha Girls' School with one student. Scranton was the first woman missionary sent to Korea by the Woman's Foreign Missionary Society (WFMS) of the Methodist Episcopal Church. Born in Belchertown, Massachusetts, in 1832, Scranton grew up in a very religious community. She was the daughter of a Methodist minister, Rev. Erastus Benton, and many of her relatives were active in the church. She married a manufacturer, William T. Scranton of New Haven, and was widowed at the age of forty. They had only one child, William B. Scranton, who graduated from Yale College and studied medicine in New York. After finishing his study, William Scranton moved with his family, including his mother, to Cleveland, Ohio, to practice medicine. In fall 1884 William Scranton was appointed to the Korea mission field, and Mary Scranton made plans to accompany her son to Korea. At this time, the WFMS asked her to consider going to Korea as its first representative.[14] Initially she was hesitant to accept because she was fifty-two, much older than the typical woman missionary. However, ultimately she did accept the appointment, and ironically her age proved to be an advantage in gaining the trust of Koreans because of the great respect for seniority within Korean culture.[15] As Wade Crawford Barclay notes, a "young unmarried woman could not have accomplished with Korean women what Mrs. Scranton did—middle-aged, widowed, the mother of a grown son."[16]

In October 1885 Mary Scranton purchased some property in Seoul, consisting of nineteen straw huts and a strip of unoccupied land, for the WFMS.[17] She also conveyed her intention to start a girls' school to the Korean government and got general approval from the King, who conferred the name *Ewha* on the school. In a contribution to the *Heathen Woman's Friend*, she told American readers how all this happened:

> [I] got the promise of the President [Kim Yun-sik] of the Foreign Office to do something for me which would show the people that I had the confidence of the Government . . . A few days after he sent the school name, . . . and there followed a *kenison*. The *kenisons* are soldiers who are attached to certain officials, always acting as escort whenever they go out. They carry letters, and do similar errands. They cannot be employed by any one except by special favor of the king; . . . I have to pay the man, of course; but I am glad to have the opportunity, for it will, I think, be an advantage to us and our work in many ways . . . The school name is in no degree wonderful; it is only the royal setting which gives it importance . . . The Koreans call women (when they wish to be specially sweet and poetic) *pear-flowers;* so our school is the Pear-Flower School. I am told that at first they gave it a name which would have suited me exactly; namely "Entire Trust School." Probably this meant less to Korean officials than it would have done to me. At any rate, they appear to think they have done a better thing by changing it to the one which now hangs over the big gate.[18]

In the Korean tradition, the King bestowed names only to special private academies as a sign of national distinction.[19] Thus the royal origin of the name *Ewha* gave the school an imprimatur of prestige that provided

Scranton with both power and authority to move forward with her project of educating Korean women.[20]

Given its symbolic significance, one can view the naming of the school as an example of negotiation.[21] Although grateful for the recognition, Scranton was not completely happy with the name. She thought the other option, Entire Trust, would have been more appropriate because it would better reflect Christian piety and uprightness. However, she was so eager to get approval from the royal court that she went along with the less satisfying name. The royal court's primary interest in modern education was not entirely matched with the missionaries' foremost desire to convert Korean women to Christianity. However, the parties needed each other to move toward modern civilization, sharing certain beliefs but highlighting different priorities—modernization versus Christianization.

The auspicious beginning of the school was somewhat undercut when Scranton was informed in the same message in which the King bestowed the name on the school that she would have to forego her plan to recruit girls from the upper classes because of the tradition of seclusion.[22] It was a great disappointment to her because she thought that daughters of the upper class would have greater influence on the future of Korean women. Facing this reality, Scranton turned her attention to orphans and poor children. However, even that was not easy at the beginning. Koreans' utter lack of familiarity with foreigners created situations where the missionaries' presence "on the street in too close proximity to the women's apartments was often times the signal for the rapid closing of doors and speedy retreat behind screens, while children ran screaming with as much lung power as they could bring to bear on the occasion."[23]

After some initial difficulties, Scranton began to receive students. Her very first student was known as Mrs. Kim, a concubine of a local official. Kim came to the school in the hope of learning English and becoming an interpreter for the Queen; however, she did not stay long due to illness. Scranton's first permanent student was from a very poor family. The primary motivation for sending her to the school was to make sure that she was fed.[24] At that time, there were rumors that foreigners would use food and clothing to lure children and kidnap them to the United States or, worse, would fatten them in order to suck their blood.[25] The mother of Scranton's first permanent student was so frightened by the rumors that she wanted to bring her daughter back home. In her efforts to keep the student, Scranton had to write a letter to the mother, assuring her that the child would never be taken out of the country.[26] The second permanent pupil was picked up with her sick mother near the city wall by William

Scranton. Eventually her entire family ended up working at the school for Mary Scranton.[27] Kim Chŏm-dong (a.k.a. Esther Pak), who was among the first permanent students and later became the first female physician trained in the United States, came to the school through her father's connection with a missionary. Her father worked for the Methodist missionary Henry Appenzeller and gave his daughter to Ewha Girls' School to alleviate some of the burden of feeding his family.[28] By and large, the first class comprised children from impoverished families, daughters of widows, or the children of Koreans who worked for American missionaries. Only occasionally did Ewha receive daughters of the upper class who had Enlightenment-oriented fathers, such as Pak Yŏng-hyo.[29]

Mary Scranton later recalled that in the midst of Koreans' suspicion about mission schools, those who sent their daughters to Ewha "appeared as if they were conferring a favor" on the school.[30] However, as missionaries had hoped, Koreans gradually began to trust the school after they saw that the students were happy and well treated.[31] They even acknowledged the benefit that their daughters received. Growing confidence in the school over the years led to a steady increase in the number of students. By 1895 Ewha had become dangerously overcrowded and, due to its limited facilities, could not accommodate all those who wanted to attend. Eventually, the original Korean-style building had to be demolished and a Western-style, two-story brick building called Main Hall was erected in its place in 1900.[32] Some students were so eager to attend the school that they were willing to pay their own lodging fee as long as they were admitted.[33] According to Lulu Frey and Jessie Marker, both teachers at Ewha, from 1904 "no girls have been received who do not clothe themselves, furnish their own bedding, rice bowl, and many other things formerly supplied by the school."[34] Thus, in a relatively short period of time, the school had evolved from being something seen as a support resource for desperate families to an educational institution for families with at least some means to support their daughters.

This gradual but significant change in attitude among Koreans ran parallel with Korea's ongoing effort to modernize the country and a series of political upheavals. After Korea signed the 1905 Protectorate Treaty with Japan, Koreans enraged by the treaty believed that their semicolonized nation could be salvaged only through education and a self-sufficient economy. Upon returning to Korea from furlough in December 1905, Josephine Paine, a teacher at Ewha, instantly noticed that "the great longing of the people now is for an education,"[35] and the "Koreans have suddenly awakened to the fact that they must have education and now is the time when

Christian education can be pushed as never before. I never had more faith in our work and in what can be done for a country like this through Christian education than I have at present."[36] By 1910, enrollment had reached 177.[37] With the growth in enrollments, Ewha was able to shift its practice from offering free education toward paid education. An entrance fee of one *yen* became obligatory beginning with the 1907–8 academic year, and tuition began to be charged the year after that. As a result, by 1910 the majority of students were paying either all or part of their tuition and dormitory expenses.[38] Leaping from the solid foundation it had gained, Ewha took a significant step in 1910 by beginning to offer college-level education and graduated its first college-level class in 1914 (shown in figure 9). Within a quarter-century, Ewha transformed itself from something akin to an orphanage, providing food, clothing and lodging for poor or abandoned children, to Korea's most prominent institution for women's education, literal and symbolic center of new womanhood in the country.

THE NATIONALIST ZEAL FOR EDUCATION

Prior the 1905 Protectorate Treaty, girls' education was offered predominantly through mission schools. There were about seventeen girls' schools established between 1886 and 1905, all but two of which were mission schools. The Korean government devoted its attention exclusively to modern education for boys and men despite all of its rhetoric about the importance of modern education. The newspaper *Tongnip sinmun* pointedly criticized this lack of attention to girls' education. It stated, "although the government established several schools for children, there is none for girls. How can the government claim to educate the children of the people when it discriminates against girls? Aren't girls children of Korea as well? While brothers have a right to study at school, their unfortunate sisters are confined to the inner quarters and are indoctrinated to obey men like servants. We feel outrage and have great sympathy for girls."[39] Kim Hwak-sil, a twelve-year-old girl from Anju who attended a mission school, lamented the lack of Korean schools for girls and praised the role of mission schools in filling this gap. She wrote:

> The rise and fall of the nation depends on women's education . . . the more education women receive, the more advanced the country is, as exemplified by western countries . . . Of the twenty million people in our country, half are men and the other half are women . . . but women have been treated like slaves and received no education. That's why we have come to this [miserable] situation. I have heard that people

have started to establish boys' schools but I regret that I haven't heard anything about girls' schools. My church already realized the importance of education for girls and established one. My parents sent me to the school and let me study. First, I thank the blessings of God, second, I thank the enthusiasm of the church, and third, I thank my parents for their benevolence.[40]

Concerned about the future of the nation and grateful for having the opportunity to receive an education at a mission school, Kim captured the reality that mission schools satisfied Koreans' growing interest in women's education in the absence of Korean schools. Perhaps the most dramatic example of this yearning for education in the nation can be captured in the story of Ha Nan-sa, one of the most prominent graduates of Ewha. Ha was born in P'yŏngyang in 1875 in a Kim family and later became a secondary wife of the government official Ha Sang-gi in Chemulp'o.[41] Following the suggestion of George Heber Jones, a missionary in Chemulp'o, Ha Nan-sa sought to enroll at Ewha to study but was not admitted because she was married and there was no more space available.[42] Not discouraged a bit, she went to see Lulu Frey, a teacher at Ewha, at night. In the middle of their meeting, she blew the light out in the lantern and said to Frey, "Our country is in the dark like this. We mothers should learn something and teach our children, and [if you do not admit me,] what should I do?"[43] Impressed by Ha's seriousness and determination, the missionary teachers decided to admit her in 1896 under the condition that she would pay tuition and the other expenses for her education.[44] In 1900, eager to continue her education beyond what Ewha was able to offer at the time, she went to Japan and studied there for a year, and then she went to the United States in 1902 for a college education. Many missionary women who came to Korea had graduated from Ohio Wesleyan University, including Lulu Frey, Mary Hillman, and Jessie Marker, and they had encouraged Ha Nan-sa to attend their alma mater. She received her BA from Ohio Wesleyan University in 1906, becoming the first Korean woman to obtain a BA from an American university and beginning a long tradition in which Ewha graduates attend Ohio Wesleyan. Returning to Korea, Ha divided her time between Ewha and Sangdong Church, making herself invaluable to missionaries.[45] She worked closely with Mary Scranton at Sangdong Church, teaching English and the Bible to attendees, who were largely widows, concubines, entertainers, and a few palace women. Teaching women from a background similar to hers, Ha made a significant impact on the future generation of influential Korean Methodist women.[46] While maintaining close ties with missionaries, Ha was also engaged in Korea's independence movement. According to Sin Hŭng-u, a prominent Christian intellectual, she had close ties with the second son of King Kojong while she was studying in the United States, and they appear to have worked together to reveal the illegitimacy of Japanese colonialism.[47] She was later sent to the Paris Peace Conference of 1919 via Peking, China, but she died there and the cause of her death remains uncertain.[48]

As indicated earlier, the lack of schools for girls came into sharp focus with the crisis of Korea's loss of diplomatic sovereignty in 1905, and Korean schools mushroomed. As one woman contributor wrote in *Taehan maeil sinbo* in 1907, the idea that "learning is the foundation of civilization and national independence" prevailed, and women's education was accordingly emphasized.[49] Between 1905 and 1910, twenty private schools and one public school for girls were established by Koreans, while thirteen mission schools were newly established.[50] The erupting passion for female education among Koreans after 1905 stemmed from their urgent desire to strengthen the nation in the face of Japanese colonization.

Despite Koreans' passion for the idea of educating their young women, they often encountered difficulties due to lack of experience. The Koreans often turned to missionary teachers for advice because of their greater experience in establishing and administering schools. Missionaries gladly extended their help, offering lessons or sending their graduates as teachers to those newly established Korean schools. For example, when Lady Ŏm established Chinmyŏng Girls School in 1906, Mary Scranton, who had a cordial relationship with the royal court from the beginning of her mission, spared some time to teach at Chinmyŏng and was proud of the fact that Ewha graduates began to play a significant role in women's education as the first class of teachers in Korea. She wrote in 1906:

> I have recently become actively interested in the school in the Northern part of the city established by Lady Om. In the past we have not looked to her for help along educational lines. She now says of herself, "During the past twelve years I have had much power, I have done many things without ever wishing to do anything for schools. But God has changed my heart, and now, this is a work I greatly desire to do." . . . Our Mrs. Mary Whang, one of Ewa's first pupils, has been placed in charge of the school and thus far appears to be giving entire satisfaction. I give to this school two mornings in the week, but am hoping that some one younger, who has had more recent training along the required lines, will soon take my place. Mrs. Miller also is helping the new enterprise by giving instruction in music . . . I hope we shall be able to live up to our profession.[51]

The symbiotic relation between missionaries and the Koreans in the promotion of education for girls played out in various forms. The Mary Helm School and the Chŏngsin Girls' School are noteworthy examples for understanding the ways in which the two parties helped each other to advance their own primary agendas—for the missionaries, the evangelization of Korea, and for Koreans, the building of a modern, independent state. The Mary Helm School (a.k.a. Songgye haktang) was initiated by Korean women of the upper class who were widows, and they were largely inspired by the idea that women should be as educated as men are. They also saw opportunities to transform their own lives through education, which they believed would help them contribute to the new nation.[52] However, they did not know how to start. Rosella Cram, a Southern Methodist missionary who was brought in to help implement the Mary Helm School, recounted the beginning of the school:

> In the spring of 1907 there was a great stir in the city of Seoul about the education of the neglected women of Korea. The contagion spread to Songdo, and a few high-class young women met together and were being taught by the brother of one of the young women; but it did not prove satisfactory, so the young man came to Mr. Yun [Yun Ch'i-ho], the President of the Anglo-Korean College, Songdo, and laid the matter before him, saying that these young women would like for some lady of the mission to instruct them. Mr. Yun came to me and asked me what I could do, saying that he thought it an opportunity that ought not to be neglected. After thinking the matter over, I decided to begin work immediately. These were high-class young women, who did not want to appear on the streets in the daytime, so a night class was organized . . . From the beginning the school was opened with Scripture-reading, singing, and prayer. At first none of the girls attended church, nor were they urged to do so; but by and by they began attending the night services . . . Almost all of the girls who attended the school were high-class young widows. They had been married between the ages of ten and thirteen, and their husbands had died while they were yet young.[53]

The complementary aspects of the missionary and Korean motives and their different goals for education come together in Cram's description. The Korean students valued the learning Cram could offer, such as reading skills, although they were not necessarily interested in the religious subjects she offered. Cram reported that none of the girls attended church in the beginning, and she never urged them to attend. However, by using Scripture as the text for teaching the students how to read, she cultivated the ground for the spread of Christianity. Ultimately these students began to attend church services, and thus the missionary goal of introducing the Gospel was met.

While enrollments in mission schools kept growing, financial constraints often led to serious problems such as inadequate facilities and teacher shortages.[54] Given that education remained second to evangelism in missionary priorities, the mission board preferred closing those schools and concentrating on its main goal of evangelism. When financial hardship threatened the existence of the Chŏngsin Girls' School, the flagship girls' school of the Presbyterian church, Koreans were willing to help to rescue it from its demise because of their belief that women's education was a key to national reconstruction. In 1920, O. R. Avison, chairman of the Seoul Station Education Committee, wrote a letter to Arthur Brown, secretary of the Board of Foreign Missions of the Presbyterian Church, reporting that "I have long watched it [Chŏngsin Girls School, a.k.a Seoul Girls' School, or Woman's Academy in Seoul] with deep anxiety as it has struggled against difficulties just to maintain its existence without thinking of advance at all; and now its circumstances are such that I can no longer refrain from writing you and trying to put you in touch with its really pitiful condition."[55] Alarmed by the prospect that the school might have to close, prominent Koreans in New York, including P'il-lye Kim Ch'oe, who had worked as teacher at Chŏngsin from 1916 to 1919, met with Arthur Brown and pledged to raise funds to save the school.[56] John Soo Ahrn, chairman of the Korean Church Building Committee in New York, informed Brown that the Korean community in New York and their countrymen would probably be able to contribute a yearly amount of $1,500 to $2,000. In the same letter, Ahrn made a persuasive plea why Chŏngsin should continue to exist:

> Mrs. Pillye Choi has informed us that your board has decided to discontinue the work of Chungsin [Chŏngsin] School of Seoul, Korea with all its educational activities because of the lack of fund to carry it on. It is really sad news to us all, especially to those who have been closely connected with this institution and watched with keenest interest its growth and achievement. In our opinion this Chungsin School has produced more woman leaders of highest type than any other girl schools in Korea that we know of. Among them we have Mrs. Pillye Choi one time principal of the school, at present a student in Columbia, Miss Maria Kim one of the educational leaders, at present a student in Chicago University and many others who are prominent in the religious and educational circles. Today, in Korea we need woman leaders more than men leaders to guide our modern young girls who are just released from their involuntary seclusion and have no moral standard to follow.[57]

A much more substantial donation came in 1933 from "Lady X," a wealthy Korean Christian woman who wanted to donate her rice fields to "create an endowment fund for the Chungsin [Chŏngsin] Girls' School." She wished "to put part of her money into a work that will accomplish something rather than see it go to a grandson who she thinks will waste it." J. G. Holdcroft, chairman of the Executive Committee of the Korea Mission of the Presbyterian Church, made a note that Lady X's rice fields would "bring in each year in the neighbourhood of 2800 bags of rice" and "the property is said to be worth about ¥200,000.00."[58] In these substantial contributions from overseas as well as domestic Koreans, one notices a nationalistic mandate to educate women for the country's future. As Ahrn noted above, with a strong hint of moral obligation to guide "modern young girls" who "have no moral standard to follow," Korean Christian intellectuals saw greater promise for the better future of Korea in women's education and Christian teachings than any other activity. Here, Koreans' nationalistic desire went hand in hand with Christian education at mission schools.

IN PURSUIT OF CHRISTIAN DOMESTICITY AND MODERN WOMANLY VIRTUE

Speaking of the general educational policy of the Presbyterian Church, William Baird argued in 1897 that the "main purpose of a mission school should be to develop the native church and its leaders for aggressive Christian work among their own people. Schools of other kinds and with other purposes have their place and utility but let us not burden ourselves with them while the great commission is still unobeyed. Benevolence, philanthropy, and education are all good servants, but they must be second to evangelism or they cease to become missionary."[59] He acknowledged that "the primary idea of a school is to educate in the various branches of useful knowledge, and thus fit the pupils for the various duties and responsibilities of active life." However, he made a clear distinction between mission schools and secular schools, insisting on the primacy of evangelical goals in mission schools. Lulu Frey, a teacher at Ewha, echoed this central goal of mission education, reporting that "we teach English, arithmetic, general history and the native language, but most important of all are the Bible studies. The textbooks, in which they learn to read the Korean character, are the catechisms, Old Testament stories, and translations of other Christian books."[60] Naturally, the study of the Bible and other subjects related to Christianity composed the core element of the curriculum.[61] Even when religious instruction was prohibited by the Korean government in the early history of the Korea mission, the Bible remained the main text for reading at mission schools. At Ewha Girls' School, for example, students studied the Bible and learned to pray on the first day of the week, and the Bible was the only text used until 1890, when several new subjects were introduced into the curriculum.[62] Even when teaching other subjects, missionaries actively related them to Christianity. Lillian Nicholas, who was the principal of Holston Girls' School in Songdo, noted that "[t]he part played by Physics and Chemistry may be toward a better understanding of the reliability of God. If the student can see God back of all natural law, all cause and effect, she may be led to see more of His resourcefulness, His almighty power, and His dependability." Similarly, the subjects of "Physiology and Zoology may be so taught as to arouse a feeling of wonder and awe at the mystery and sublimity of life that may bring the student to a new dependence upon and appreciation of the Father of all life. A conception of the human body as the temple of the living God will serve to create a greater interest in keeping fit mentally, physically, and spiritually."[63] In this way, ostensibly nonreligious subjects could provide opportunities for Christian teaching because mission schools ultimately aimed for "the full Christianization of the country."[64]

In realizing the goal of evangelization, missionary teachers had to face certain resistance from Koreans toward the new religion. Furthermore, Koreans were concerned that girls at mission schools would ignore Korean traditions and imitate a Western lifestyle.[65] In the face of this public suspicion and unwillingness to send their daughters, missionaries strategically emphasized that their educational goal was not "Westernization" but making students "better Koreans" with "home-grown Christian characters."[66] Mary Scranton made this point very clear when she described her aim for the education at Ewha Girls' School:

> I emphasize the fact that they [Korean students] are not being made over again after our foreign ways of living, dress, and surroundings, because it occasionally appears from home and even in the field that we are thought to make a change in all ways. This is not so. We take pleasure in making Koreans better Koreans only. We want Korea to be proud of Korean things, and more, that it is a perfect Korea through Christ and His teachings. In the short time we have been at work here we see that we are slowly doing what is in our hearts to do and are allowing Korea Korean possibilities.[67]

Scranton's emphasis on Korean ways was shared and emphasized by other missionaries. Lillias Underwood argued that "it is a great mistake to unfit these girls by a foreign education for the home they are to fill, and we only seek to make Christian Koreans of them, not American ladies."[68] George Gilmore further argued that girls' schools should train Korean girls to become "model housewives under the conditions in which they must pass their lives, and to make them missionaries of the Cross among their relatives and associates."[69] Missionaries were keenly aware of the detrimental effect it would have on the mission if their girls were perceived by the Korean community as "unfit" and "Westernized." Trying to dissipate public suspicion and to gain local acceptance, missionaries strategically emphasized that they trained girls not to become Westernized ladies but rather to become better Koreans and model housewives.

At the core of respecting Korean ways and avoiding conflict with the local culture lay the conviction that a woman's ideal sphere should be in the domestic arena. Louise Rothweiler, who taught at Ewha Girls' School from 1887, acknowledged the vast possibilities for female education and yet urged her fellow missionaries to focus on domesticity as a strategy to appeal to the Korean community:

> We must lay the foundation broad and deep, not so narrow and shallow that there is no chance to build further on it neither must we give them an education that, while it may fit them ever so well for one purpose shall in any way unfit them for other duties or for their station and mode of life. Whatever may be the private opinion of any one concerning woman's sphere and proper occupation we must, for the present, at least act under the supposition that in Korea domestic life is her sphere and destiny. Whatever else we may want our girls to do or be, it must be all secondary to this first calling . . . They must learn to prepare food, cut, make and repair their clothing, keep themselves and their rooms neat and this all in purely Korean style except where we can improve on that without weaning them from their people, making them discontented with their surroundings or creating demands in them that cannot be supplied when they leave us.[70]

Rothweiler implied that there were differing opinions among the missionaries about what was the appropriate domain of women. Like many women missionaries of her generation, she herself was a college graduate who had teaching experience in public schools in the United States before she came to Korea as a missionary in 1887.[71] One might anticipate someone in her position might hold an opinion in which the sphere for women would extend beyond home and family. After all, a life of professional commitment in an international arena was clearly manifested in her own involvement in the foreign missionary enterprise. Yet she observed that Korean girls lived in a different environment and thus their education should fit their own local condition. For this, the teaching of domestic skills should be second only to religious training.

One may think that this emphasis on domesticity was a strategic choice in the initial stage of mission education to gain the confidence of Koreans. However, this focus remained largely unchanged through the history of the mission schools for girls. For example, even after Ewha started to offer "college" courses in 1910, the school kept emphasizing that "woman's most important place will always be the home."[72] The inclusion of *Naehun* (Instructions for Women), as well as sewing, cooking, and child-rearing classes, as part of the core curriculum at Ewha is indicative of its emphasis on domesticity.[73] Ewha boasted what was popularly known as "Ewha style" or "Ewha etiquette," which created trends in clothing, home decoration, and cooking and "raised the tone of general culture."[74] This does not mean that Ewha taught only courses related to home economics. It played a pioneering role in offering more diverse and advanced subjects, including chemistry, physics, English literature, world geography, geometry, algebra, psychology, music, and physical education, while its counterparts, such as the government-run Hansŏng Girls' School, offered only a rudimentary curriculum.[75] Ewha, as the first girls' school to offer a more advanced curriculum, produced many prominent writers and other professionals who became active in the 1920s and after.[76] Nonetheless, Ewha never failed to center its education on women's "most proper place"—the home and the family. Velma Snook, a Presbyterian missionary and principal of the Women's Academy in P'yŏngyang (a.k.a. Sungŭi Girls' School) beginning in 1904, noted that "Korean customs are rapidly changing and there is much danger to young women, in that for generations they have known no freedom and they do not yet know how to use the freedom which is coming to them, so *we encourage them to observe all the good Korean customs and to be quiet and willing to stay in the home-ground*" [emphasis added].[77] Continuing Snook's educational philosophy, it became the staple tradition of the Women's Academy in P'yŏngyang that it provided "new scholarship" but avoided any radical changes and emphasized the virtuous conduct of wife and mother.[78] Holding the rapid changes in check became almost a point of pride. Missionary teachers at Chŏngsin Girls' School took pride in their calculated pace in keeping their educational directives "a little ahead of the prevailing customs of the people" but standing against "the over-rapid departure from Korean ideals of propriety which is dangerous to the transition stage between repression and freedom."[79] At this juncture, Alice Appenzeller, a teacher at Ewha, expressed both her deploration of the sheer speed of the changes and her strong desire to help guide Korean girls and women "so that this new freedom may not be abused." She suggested, "Now is Korea's great day of need for the strongest leaders, men and women of vision and power who shall inspire this old East with the best that the West can give."[80]

Missionaries, in keeping with Victorian ideals, envisioned that "the best that the West can give" to the old East would be a true Christian home.[81] Believing that women were innately endowed with the properties of caring, giving, and self-sacrifice, missionary teachers felt that those qualities should be used to help weak, ignorant, sinful people, and they aimed to prepare students for their moral, spiritual, and social roles in creating Christian families. Here there is an interesting intersection between Victorian ideals of womanhood and Confucian-prescribed womanhood. In Catharine Beecher's discourse on Christian domesticity in Victorian America, she referred not simply to domestic chores, such as cooking, sewing and cleaning, but also to women's moral, spiritual, and social responsibilities. According to Beecher, the Christian family was characterized by "self-sacrificing labor of the stronger and wiser members to raise the weaker and more ignorant to equal advantages . . . The family state then, is the aptest earthly illustration of the heavenly kingdom, and in it woman is its chief minister. Her great mission is self-denial, in training its members to self-sacrificing labors for the ignorant and weak; if not her own children, then the neglected children of her Father in heaven."[82] The Christian home, in which woman is "its chief minister," is the essential site to cultivate the body and mind not only of private families but of the broader society. Similarly, as discussed in chapter 2, Confucian gender norms did not merely stress women's sphere in the domestic arena, in which women should be responsible for household work and raising children, but greatly valued the moral influence of mothers and wives. In this context, the missionary goal in female education was dual: to "educate the girls and lift them out of the ignorance and superstition" through the instruction of the Christian faith and ethics, and to teach them to be good wives and wise mothers.[83]

The missionaries' emphasis on Korean ways and domesticity was well matched with the outlook of many conservative Korean intellectuals, who envisioned the role of an educated woman as a "wise mother and good wife" with Korean sensibility. The central focus on "wise mother, good wife" in women's education was manifested as early as 1906, when a Korean-initiated girls' school, Yanggyu ŭisuk, opened its doors with twenty students.[84] Two years later, in 1908, the first government-run girls' school,

Hansŏng Girls' School, also declared that its primary goal was to educate women so that they would fulfill their duties as *hyŏnbae chamo* (wise companion, benevolent mother).[85]

The modernized form of "wise mother, good wife" emphasizing "scientific" home management and child-rearing was actively promoted by elite men and women. Yun Ch'i-ho summarily pointed out the central importance of domestic science in female education:

> Let us first remember that the Korean girls who are being educated in mission schools are to live and work in Korean homes, many of them in poor homes. So to educate them as to make them unsuitable to a Korean home would be a great mistake. For instance, to prepare food and to make dresses have been the exclusive province of the Korean woman. The inability or unwillingness of a newly educated girl to take up these duties does more than any one thing to prejudice the Koreans against female education. It is my firm belief that it is more useful for a Korean girl to learn to cook and sew well than to play on a piano, for the simple reason that she will have far more occasions to cook and sew than to play on a piano in a Korean home. By all means emphasize domestic science in the curriculum more than any other kind of science. Teach abacus more thoroughly than algebra. Cultivate the taste (passion!) for flowers and pictures, rather than waste time in dabbling in astronomy and botany.[86]

Echoing Yun's argument, Chu Yo-sŏp lamented the wastefulness of teaching algebra, geometry, physics, chemistry, or musical instruments to girls, who he assumed would become housewives after graduation. He argued that women's education should not aim at inculcating "knowledge" or teaching physical exercise but rather should prepare students to be useful in real life. To him, all those academic subjects hardly bear any relevance to Korean homes. What was needed, in his view, was practical, common-sense knowledge. For instance, he proposed that in home economics class, teachers should eliminate Western-style cooking in favor of Korean-style cooking classes. Deploring a monotonous and unchanging dinner menu of pollack stew with steamed tofu for ten consecutive days prepared by an "educated" housewife with a diploma from a girls' high school, Chu urged educators to teach girls how to prepare dinner more creatively with a diverse combination of ingredients.[87]

In the curricula of girls' schools, the importance of the domestic sciences to train young Korean women to set a splendid dinner table and manage a household efficiently ultimately stressed the role of women as mothers.[88] In the discourse of new womanhood, educated mothers were envisioned as the most important element in the foundation of a strong nation. Yi Kwang-su, a prominent male writer, specifically called for female education centering on motherhood:

> The central duty in women's life is to become someone's mother. Half of women's life is spent in raising children. The character of children is formed at the bosom of their mothers. . . . Becoming a good mother and raising good children is the only duty women have to humankind, to the nation and to the society. This duty can be fulfilled by none other than women. To produce good citizens we need to produce good mothers. Especially in our special situation where national reformation is urgent, we want good mothers more than anything else . . . Today, unless we offer motherhood-centered education to Chosŏn women, education will be meaningless.[89]

In her analysis of Korean women who went to Japan for advanced study during the colonial era, Pak Sŏn-mi argues that the glorification of domestic science and educated motherhood was actively promoted by conservative male and female intellectuals.[90] For example, Hŏ Yŏng-suk, who was trained as a medical doctor in Japan, put forward the idea of woman as "the mother of the nation," who would cultivate, reform, and revitalize the Korean people and the nation. In line with what her husband, Yi Kwang-su, advocated in his famous essay "Minjok kaejoron" (On National Reconstruction) published in 1922, she saw women as the most immediate and powerful agency in the reconstruction of national character in their role as mother, and thus early, proper education for girls became essential in instilling this true calling for women.[91] Hŏ thus distanced herself from the Western model of liberal feminism, represented in the figure of Nora in Ibsen's play *A Doll's House*.[92] This strategy of active distinction between Western and Korean modern womanhood stemmed from the conservative elite's frustration and disappointment with the outcome of women's education, which was often branded as too Westernized and out of touch with indigenous family life. As the population of female students grew and a greater variety of courses was introduced, the print media and the literary world (dominated by male intellectuals) started to put out sensational alerts about the "problem of the girl student" who wore luxurious clothes, loved foreign products, belittled her less-educated elders, and refused housework.[93] This "problem" had already emerged when women's education had just begun to take hold in Korea.[94] In his novel *Kŭmsu hoeŭirok* (Record of the Animals' Assembly), An Kuk-sŏn sarcastically portrayed educated women as having a little bit of knowledge but thinking they were above all others and ignoring traditional womanly virtues such as gentleness, obedience, and respect for seniors.[95] The public had doubts about "educated women," whom they perceived as trying to undermine traditional ways of life in the name of "new knowledge."

Missionaries were clearly aware of this widespread perception and thus adopted educational policies that were to "stay within the Korean tradition" as much as they could. They explicitly expressed their distaste for any attempt on the part of Koreans to imitate foreign styles in pursuit of "so-called progress." They chided such attempts as "appalling" and delusional, saying they were based on "radical misconceptions" of Anglo-Saxon women and believing that those unwarranted imitations would "trample down the most firmly established customs and the conservatism of centuries."[96] In this way, missionary teachers' ideal was largely in harmony with conservative Korean intellectuals' vision of an educational model for women that centered on domesticity and cherished Koreanness.

However, this unwavering emphasis on traditional propriety and domesticity eventually backfired and generated severe criticism of mission education from the Korean public in the 1920s and later. The cultural critic Kim Chin-song notes that 1920s Korean society went beyond the trite pursuit of "enlightenment." Instead, an influx of new ideas generated complex, fluid, and conflicting identities based on class, gender, nation, and ideologies. The powerful discourse of "civilization and enlightenment" led by elite intellectuals and missionaries began to lose its attraction by the 1920s. The modern, experimental, and rebellious pursuit of self-identity in everyday life started to take root in colonial Korea.[97] In the midst of a whirl of new ideas and images, the visibility of girl students and the discourse about them reflect both desire for and anxiety about the modern.[98] In her examination of new women in China during the May Fourth Era, Jin Feng argues that "the figure of the girl student proves to be not only the 'earliest' type, but also the 'archetype' of all new women."[99] Similarly, the image of new women in Korea was embodied in "girl students," whose thoughts, attitudes, fashion, and private lives became almost a public obsession. It is no wonder that many leading journals of the 1920s and 1930s, including *Sin yŏsŏng* (New Women), devoted much of their space to a close examination of girl students.

While Korean society was undergoing rapid cultural changes, mission schools tended to remain unchanged, leading to public criticism for "anachronistic" educational policy. The main charge against mission schools was lack of freedom and the excessively stringent regulation of school life. For example, a pseudonymous writer criticized the Holston Girls' School in Kaesŏng (a.k.a. Songdo) for its oppressive educational policy, which the author believed was inappropriate to the changing reality of Korea: "You came from a country with advanced civilization. You are Protestant missionaries. Therefore, we should assume that your educational policy is relatively liberal. However, isn't it true that you still use the exact same policy that you adopted when you first came to Korea decades ago?"[100] The author specifically pointed out the rigid practices in dormitory life, where students were so strictly supervised that they could not meet even their own parents alone during their visitation, and incoming letters were opened by missionary teachers to examine the contents. At the end of the article, the author urged the mission schools to offer education appropriate to the current times.

In a more critical assessment of mission schools, another contributor, Cho Sang-hang, first acknowledged the great benefit mission education brought to Korean society. He did not question the legitimacy of the primary goal of mission education in evangelism. However, he wondered if they were sincerely concerned about a better future for Koreans or more interested in their own honor and ambition. He observed that missionary teachers' "attitude and policy is too anachronistic, unpractical, oppressive, and even anti-Christian." He reasoned that the frequent strikes by students at mission schools had to do with inappropriate educational policy. For example, students at Sungŭi Girls' School went on strike on October 15, 1923, demanding reforms, including major changes in dormitory regulations. They specifically demanded that Ra Chin-gyŏng, the head of the dormitory, resign. When it was apparent that no resolution between the school authority and the students would come, several influential community members, especially Christian leaders, tried to intervene to solve the problem. Nonetheless, the school's advisory board, composed of missionary teachers, stood in support of Ra and took stringent action against the students, which prompted an uproar among the Korean public.[101] Cho was disturbed to hear that missionaries' response to the strikes was: "if you don't want our education, go home. We don't care if we have to close the school," which prompted him to question the sincerity of missionaries as teachers. He further noted that the Woman's Academy in P'yŏngyang (Sungŭi) had been known (admittedly with hyperbole) as the city's second "prison."[102] Worse yet, the absence of freedom, he sternly asserted, was indicative of the missionaries' arrogance and their sense of superiority to Koreans.[103]

Students who graduated from mission girls' schools also joined in the public criticism, commenting on negative experiences during their study.[104] Their comments were largely in line with those above, but as insiders they could offer a more concrete view. A graduate of Ewha pointed out that while it was the first girls' school and thus garnered a widespread public perception that it offered a high quality education, she felt otherwise. The reason, she wrote, had nothing to do with facilities or curriculum. Rather, the methods and philosophy of teaching at Ewha were inadequate and behind the times.[105] Similarly, a student at Chŏngsin Girls' School complained that dormitory life resembled prison life, with no privacy and very stringent regulations.[106] A graduate of Paehwa Girls' School had hoped to learn subjects other than the Bible and prayers when she entered the school, but to her disappointment the school required students to spend much of their time in prayer.[107] An anonymous student who attended a mission school urged the school administrators to separate education from religion and to stop forcing students to become Christians.[108] A student from Lucy Girls' School imagined that her school would be a showpiece if there were an exhibition of schools. However, "the school's excellent facilities were solely prepared for its own promotion." Furthermore, even though it was a Christian school, she could not find Jesus' love in the place; instead, it was filled with resentment and oppression. She wrote, "The school seems to exist not for education but for evangelism. Teachers are not concerned for students. Rather they are busy in gaining trust from the mission board. Of course, I know this is an inevitable phenomenon in the capitalist system. But I am writing this because the whole situation reached the level of ridicule . . . I plead to you [missionary teachers] that you do not center on evangelism too much. Please respect students' individual character and try to offer student-centered education."[109]

From the perspective of missionaries, the parts of students' lives that were spent away from the supervision of their teachers were an area of grave concern. Margo Lewis, the principal of Chŏngsin Girls' School, urged Korean families to supervise their daughters more carefully. She specifically noted a trend in which young female students frequented theaters showing romantic plays or films to which unmarried young ladies in the West would have been denied access.[110] A teacher from Ewha Girls' School expressed a particular concern about students who came from other provinces and stayed at private lodges outside the campus. These students, he argued, were free to move their lodging from one place to another and to do anything they pleased without any supervision from parents or teachers.[111] As the mistress of a private rooming house observed, girl students in her lodge tended to lead a more luxurious lifestyle and to date more frequently.[112] The Korean male intellectual Chu Yo-sŏp went so far as to suggest that girls' schools admit only that number of students who could be accommodated in the school dormitories and forbid residence in private lodging.[113]

To missionary teachers, Christian religiosity was the panacea for the miserable conditions that Korean women lived in, "without mental culture or a knowledge of the outside world."[114] They also cherished domestic virtue, a component of their own gender ideology that conformed to local values. While these twin goals of Christianity and domesticity worked in the beginning, missionary teachers increasingly had to cope with the demands from students who wished to learn about more secular subjects and to have greater freedom and independence. Missionaries considered the changes in Korean society to be either too fast or too dangerous. In the 1928 Jerusalem Meeting of the International Missionary Council, W. Arthur Noble discussed "the opposition of secular civilization to Christianity" and the urgency to address "concrete statements [that] should be directed largely to youth, who are the greatest sufferers in this civilization."[115] As the tensions between Christian religiosity and secular civilization loomed large, missionaries were willing to go "a little ahead of the prevailing customs of the people," but they thought "over-rapid departure from Korean ideals of propriety" would be dangerous.[116] Thus, over time divergent paths emerged in the Korean students' desire for modern secular knowledge and the missionaries' adherence to religiosity and domesticity.

THE GENDERED POLITICS OF LITERACY

Upon arriving in Korea, early missionaries faced an immediate problem: none of the students knew how to read or write. As Mary Scranton reported, "When they [the students] first came, not one knew even a letter of their own language."[117] In order to teach the Bible and Christian literature, literacy training became the most urgent task at mission schools. In traditional Korean society, perceptions about women's inferiority in intellectual capacity prevailed, and traditional female roles often did not require literacy at all. Literacy was largely monopolized by men of the upper class, becoming a sign of privilege and social status. A prominent Confucian scholar of eighteenth century Korea, Yi Ik (1682–1764), remarked, "reading and learning are the domains of men. For a woman it is enough if she knows the Confucian virtues of diligence, frugality, and chastity."[118] To be sure, there were some exceptionally intelligent women, mostly from the upper class, whose literary, philosophical, or artistic accomplishments are recognized today, exemplified by Hŏ Nansŏlhŏn (1563–89), Sin Saimdang (1504–51), Im Yunjidang (1721–93), and Kang Chŏngildang (1772–1832).[119]

Some women of the upper class were able to receive formal training in Chinese classics along with their brothers; however, the majority of women, especially those of the lower classes, were left without any formal, institutionalized training in literacy.[120] Thus, introducing literacy to populations who had not had access to it for reasons of class and gender was a challenge in and of itself.

In addition, there was the question of what language to use for literacy training: Korean, Chinese, or English. Missionaries soon discovered that Koreans used "two forms of characters"—the "native Ernmun *[han'gŭl]* and the Chinese," with the former being the "low" language for women and men of the lower classes and the latter the "high" language for men of the upper class in Sino-centered traditional Korea.[121] Missionaries also needed to teach English to their students, especially in the beginning, in order to be able to communicate with them while the teachers themselves were tackling Korean. In fact, some Korean students sought to enter mission schools with the sole purpose of learning English as a source of upward mobility. In this context, the choices that the missionaries made in selecting the languages for literacy training significantly demonstrated the ways in which they negotiated with local cultural and political preferences. If we consider literacy as a key sign of the move toward modernity and the construction of nationalist consciousness, literacy training at mission schools is a fascinating window into both the affinity and the tensions felt by American missionaries and Korean intellectuals in their pursuit of their respective notions of modernity. The choice of language vividly mirrored the declining or ascending value of certain languages in the new era. At the same time, the new world available to women through literacy was also a cause of anxiety. In the following sections, I specifically demonstrate how the debate over language was an integral part of the transformation of womanhood.

Chinese as a Prestige Language

During the Chosŏn dynasty Chinese was the script of prestige and status, reserved for the exclusive use of upper-class men. If a young man had not received instruction in Chinese, it was considered tantamount to having no education at all. As a result, in mission schools for boys, Chinese instruction always constituted an essential part of the curriculum. As Henry Appenzeller described in the case of Paejae Boys' School, the first mission school for boys, offering Chinese was an efficient strategy to recruit students, and "the Chinese classics formed a prominent part" of the curriculum.[122] However, the offering of instruction in Chinese to girls varied.[123] Some missionaries regarded classical Chinese as useless for girls, while others argued for the value of Chinese instruction, which was seen as equivalent to Latin and Greek instruction in the West.[124] Louise Rothweiler at Ewha Girls' School advocated teaching Chinese as an important part of intellectual training:

> Since we can hope only in very exceptional cases to have girls make enough progress in Chinese during their few school years to enable them to read Chinese with much benefit it is denounced by some as utterly useless. But may it not be useful as a drill for mind and memory? Will it not help them to understand the numberless Chinese expressions met within all books and letters and even in conversation to know even by ear only the *Hanmoun* [Chinese script] and its corresponding *Enmoun* [Korean script] reading which will cling even though the character be forgotten?[125]

For the first two years, Ewha Girls' School offered courses in English and the Bible only.[126] However, on October 6, 1888, Scranton indicated that Ewha would begin to offer reading in Chinese, Korean, and English.[127] By 1892, Louise Rothweiler was proudly reporting that some of her students were making real progress in Chinese.[128]

However, Chinese instruction ended at Ewha in 1893 due to cultural and practical constraints, as well as the priority that the missionaries placed on teaching the Bible. Margaret Bengal noted the change of direction at Ewha, reporting that "we have endeavored to make our school Bible Training School and have therefore dropped the study of Chinese and a number of secular studies and have laid more stress upon the study of the Bible, Catechism etc."[129] Mary Scranton described the background that went into the decision:

> Early in the season we changed our plan of study. From the beginning of the school until this year we have devoted considerable time to the study of Chinese. Our older girls however dropped out of the Chinese classes more than a year ago, because according to the customs of the country it was no longer proper for them to receive instruction from a male teacher, and a Korean woman capable of taking his place was not to be found. Some of the girls had made commendable progress and yet they had not advanced far enough to be greatly benefited by the instruction they had received. Under such state of affairs we decided to give up the study altogether and turn their attention [to] other things.[130]

In her explanation of the change in the curriculum, Scranton implies a practical consideration in that there was a potential loss of students. Some older students at Ewha dropped out of the Chinese classes because of the impropriety of being taught by male teachers. For instruction in Chinese, it was almost impossible to find women teachers who could teach Chinese and work outside their homes. The missionaries had to hire local teachers because their own knowledge of Chinese was inadequate. As a result, the missionaries were forced to hire a man to teach Chinese. The man taught from behind a screen in the classroom, in accordance with the doctrine of the separation of the sexes.[131] In addition, the missionary teachers had concluded that only a few students tended to make progress in the language, none to the level of competent use.

What is most notable in this case is that Chinese instruction was restored in 1897 at the request of several students. Their request for Chinese can be interpreted as a "new spirit" in the students and a demand for learning equal to that received by male students.[132] Those female students came forward to express what they wanted to learn and successfully convinced the faculty to restore Chinese to the curriculum, which was an indication of their active commitment to education. Alice Hammond reported in 1902 that "we have added Chinese to the course for the more advanced. This is intended for an incentive to diligent study in the lower classes."[133] In other words, the opportunity to study Chinese was attractive enough that the missionaries were able to use it to encourage more rigorous study among the girl students who had demonstrated significant progress and would be likely to succeed in a more challenging subject. Furthermore, the fact that girls were educated in Chinese was an important step toward equality of content in education and a manifestation that girls had an intellectual capacity equal to that of boys. Mary Knowles, a teacher at Ewha, described how much the girls' ability to read Chinese impressed the general public. She wrote, "during the public exams visitors seemed delighted with the progress the children made. The men opened their eyes wide with astonishment at the way the girls recited Chinese . . . It was a revelation to many that Korean girls had minds capable of learning along with the boys if only taught."[134]

By 1905, instruction of Chinese was firmly established in mission schools for girls. Mary Scranton noted at the 1906 annual meeting that teachers at Ewha "have no thought of permitting the neglect of Enmoun [Korean vernacular] or Chinese," suggesting that Chinese instruction was no longer subject to elimination as had been the case in the past. Similarly, according to the 1905 Report of the Committee on Curriculum for Girls' Schools in Korea prepared by Margaret Best and Mary Barrett, both of whom served in the Presbyterian Church, the reading and writing of Chinese was included from the first year in elementary school.[135] In 1908, Lulu Frey and Jessie Marker, teachers at Ewha, reported that there were already two male teachers of Chinese at their school, and some students brought significant knowledge of Chinese upon entering Ewha. For instance, they reported that one "ambitious girl who came to us from Hai Ju last fall had studied in the boys' school for several years, and knew so much Chinese that we had to examine her in a number of books before we could find one she could not readily read."[136]

Although they had begun with mixed opinions about the value of Chinese instruction either as an intellectual device for learning or spurious waste of time, missionaries eventually accommodated Korean girls' strong desire to learn Chinese because they continued to consider it the prestige language of the country. No longer monopolized by boys and men of the upper class, Chinese instruction became a central subject of learning for girls and henceforth began to break the longstanding prejudice against intellectual capacity of women.

Korean as the National Language

Teaching Korean as a core subject was the least controversial and the most beneficial choice for missionary teachers, as it satisfied both Korean reformers and missionary goals. It had great appeal for Korean reformers, who had just begun to appreciate the value of the Korean script in creating a better educated populace for a strong nation. It also proved to be the most efficient tool in spreading the gospel as fast as one could imagine. Invented in 1443 by King Sejong and his associate scholars, the Korean vernacular writing system, *han'gŭl*, was created to facilitate the literacy of women and men of the lower classes. Since Chinese was considered a language of prestige and true scholarship, men of the upper class looked down upon *han'gŭl* as an easy, vulgar, and "female system of letters."[137] Although *han'gŭl* had a far-reaching impact on the Korean cultural and literary tradition, especially on women's literature, Sinocentric cultural and literary preferences overshadowed its value and utility. It was only in the late nineteenth century that the significance of *han'gŭl* came to be recognized by foreign residents, including missionaries, and reform-oriented Korea intellectuals. Isabella Bird Bishop, who traveled in Korea from 1894 through 1897, observed the inferior status of the Korean writing system: "*En-mun*,[138] the Korean script, is utterly despised by the educated, whose sole education is in the Chinese classics. Korean has the distinction of being the only language of Eastern Asia which possesses an alphabet. Only women, children, and the uneducated used the *En-mun*."[139]

Against this background, American missionaries passionately advocated the use of the Korean script. As Homer Hulbert declared, the Korean vernacular writing system "has not its superior in the world" in terms of its "simplicity of construction and phonetic power."[140] Its simplicity was to lead Koreans to universal literacy, which would only help to spread the Gospel. Horace Underwood noted that *han'gŭl* "is claimed by scholars to be the second-best alphabet in the world" in terms of its ingenious system.[141] Given this linguistic distinction, Lillias Underwood found it ironic for Koreans to adore "absurd" foreign things while degrading their "wonderful" native heritage:

> It is a great pity that it is human nature, to go forever adopting some absurd, ungainly, inconvenient, inefficient custom of foreigners and neglect or despise its own, simpler and far more useful . . . these foolish Koreans who have a wonderful alphabet of twenty-six letters which has not its peer in the East, hardly in the world, an alphabet which is the wonder of savants and which with the constitutional monarchy sets her far above her haughty neighbours, China and Japan, yet despises her chief glory, considers the Ernmun as it is called unfit for scholars and gentlemen, relegates it to the common and vulgar and writes its official documents, its gentlemanly calling cards, and its scholarly books all in indefinite, difficult, sight-ruining Chinese. A Korean gentleman would scorn to read a book, or write a letter in any character but Chinese, but since missionaries have come they have printed the New Testament and the hymns that the people love in the Ernmun and are trying to teach them what a jewel they have hidden away there in the dust.[142]

Underwood implied above that missionaries rescued *han'gŭl*, a "jewel" and Korea's "chief glory," and tried to propagate the exceptional value of the Korean vernacular writing system. George Heber Jones stated that the Korean writing system "had been a practically abandoned literary factor in Korean life until the coming of the Christian missionaries. They immediately *discovered* its value and proceeded to put it into use. The translation of the Bible is published in this alphabetic script and so is practically all the Christian literature of the present day. This mission of carrying the contents of the Christian Bible out into Korean thought life has resulted in the redemption of the native script from the contempt in which the educated native once held it and is regarded as one of the three notable contributions of Christianity to Korean advancement."[143] Similarly, James Gale recalled that "The native character, the contemptible script, as its name *unmun* reads, had been left to slumber in the waste-paper basket for four hundred years, and now came forth anew in hymn, and song and sacred story."[144] In this way, missionaries immediately recognized the unrivaled value of the Korean script not only as an expedient tool for teaching Christian texts and Western knowledge but also a true marker of Korean uniqueness and cultural heritage that Koreans should be proud of. For this, Korean linguists have commended the role of missionaries in the "revival, reform and propagation of *han'gŭl*."[145]

Newly converted Korean Christians fully shared the viewpoints of missionaries in their advocacy of the Korean script. In his analysis of the contribution of Western missionaries to the modernization of Korean, Ross King suggests that Western scholars and missionaries "initiated a wide-ranging discussion of Korean writing which soon spilled over into the Korean Christian community. This discussion ran parallel with, and seems likely to have helped instigate, similar discussion in Korean among Korean reformers and intellectuals."[146] Especially given the close association of missionaries with some of the most prominent Korean Enlightenment-oriented intellectuals, such as Sŏ Chae-p'il, Yun Ch'i-ho, and Chu Si-gyŏng, the advocacy of *han'gŭl* must have been one of the strongest rallying points to share.[147] Proud of the unrivaled distinction of the Korean writing system, which demands a "place in the front rank of written languages," Yang Chu-sam, a leading Christian man, believed that "the first and foremost duty of every wellwisher of the cause of education in Korea" was to make full use of the impeccable Korean script.[148]

Missionaries' exceptional emphasis on the Korean vernacular writing system ran parallel with the emerging social movement in the late 1890s, led by Korean Enlightenment-oriented intellectuals, for the use of Korean script over and above other scripts. These intellectuals strongly supported the use of Korean over Chinese as a medium of public communication and dissemination of modern knowledge to the wider population. The shift to Korean would not only help Korea's modernization but redefine Korean national identity as unique.[149] In addition, the use of Korean was expected to eliminate centuries-old gender and class inequality marked by the knowledge of Chinese. *Tongnip sinmun, Cheguk sinmun,* and *Taehan maeil sinbo* made *han'gŭl* their main medium of communication precisely to reach out to women and the general populace who were not literate in Chinese. Sin So-dang, the principal of Kwangdong School and a reader of *Taehan maeil sinbo,* highly praised its policy of using *han'gŭl.* She commended that "your paper decided to use *kungmun* [lit., "national script"] for women and commoners, and we are very grateful. From now on, we all can breathe the air of civilization regardless of gender and age."[150]

What runs through Koreans' advocacy for *han'gŭl* is a strong sense of linguistic nationalism. Korea's unique writing system emerged as a marker of national identity that was to unify the people regardless of their class and gender and to enable all of them to contribute to the nation to their utmost ability, equipped with modern knowledge acquired through the Korean language. Perhaps the most forceful advocate of the Korean writing system was the leading newspaper, *Tongnip sinmun*. The fact that for the first time in Korean history it adopted the policy of using pure Korean script without any Chinese characters is indicative of its full commitment to the promotion of Korean. An editorial from the newspaper offers a rationale for the use of the Korean writing system in its effort to enlighten the people regardless of social class or gender and to invigorate Korea's potential to become a modern nation.

> The purpose of using Korean script instead of Chinese is to enable everybody to read regardless his/her class . . . It should be a rule that Koreans learn Korean first and only after they are well versed with it, they can further study foreign languages. However, Koreans do not learn han'gŭl; instead they study Chinese. As a result, very few Koreans know enough about the Korean script. If Korean is being compared with Chinese, the former has many advantages—first, Korean is easy to learn and second, Korean is the language for Koreans, so when we report things in Korean instead of Chinese, everyone can read and understand regardless of social class. Since Chinese has been much more frequently used than Korean, Koreans have a more difficult time in understanding Korean on the page. This is a deplorable situation . . . One should not think of anyone who does not know Chinese as an ignorant person. In fact, those who know Korean and have much knowledge and current information are more intelligent and superior to those who know Chinese but do not know any other information. Chosŏn women of all classes, who know Korean well and have good knowledge of current issues and thus broaden perspectives, are superior to aristocratic men who know Chinese well but do not know anything else.[151]

In line with the language policy of *Tongnip sinmun*, Chu Si-gyŏng, a leading linguist at the time, urged the Korean populace to learn Korean instead of Chinese. He said, "If the people of our country continue to study only the Chinese classics and neglect new subjects, our nation will remain ignorant and weak . . . Let no one waste precious time learning yet another Chinese graph. The Korean letters that were developed by our great scholars for our use are easy to learn and write, and they should be used in recording everything. Everyone in his youth should take the time to study for practical employment and, by doing his work, should become the foundation, and the pillar, for our national independence."[152]

The sociopolitical and cultural context of late-nineteenth-century Korea provided both Koreans and American missionaries a perfect stage for claiming the legitimate and even superior status of the Korean script. From a Korean's point of view, previously disrespected *han'gŭl* became the consummate symbol of Korean national identity and patriotism, representing one of the most valued cultural artifacts in the country's history.[153] Furthermore, the Korean language was perceived as an expedient medium for cultivating the mind of the larger population. Especially for women, who had been deprived of literacy, becoming literate in Korean and through it gaining access to new knowledge and information constituted an important prelude to new womanhood. Millie Albertson, a Methodist missionary, observed that the greatest disadvantage Korean women had was "the fact that they have been denied the privilege of study in childhood," but "the Korean alphabet is so simple that the woman of average intelligence may learn to read very quickly, therefore, she can, to a certain extent, retrieve her lost opportunities."[154] Largely interested in the wider distribution of the gospel, missionaries saw the greatest potential in *han'gŭl* in terms of its economy and effectiveness in reaching out to the largest segment of the population. Especially when missionaries presented the goal of mission education to the Korean public by emphasizing "Korean style" Christian education, the provision of the Korean language course as a central part of the curriculum further demonstrated their commitment to Korean ways.[155]

English as a Language of Modernity

The English language became associated with privilege and prestige in Korea beginning in the late nineteenth century. Due to its increased contact with other countries, Korea needed personnel capable of interacting with the outside world, and knowledge of English became an important resource for the nation. Individuals with this knowledge could assure themselves upward mobility and social status.[156] In 1886 the Korean government opened its first public school, *Yugyŏng kongwŏn*, "to fit men, by the study of the English language and customs and by study of the useful branches of knowledge, to serve the Government as foreign ministers and diplomats."[157] For this purpose the government hired three American teachers, Homer Hulbert, Dalzell A. Bunker, and George W. Gilmore.[158] However, there was no counterpart in girls' education. Mission schools filled the void by including English lessons in the curriculum. As mentioned earlier, the first student at Ewha was a concubine of a government official who came to the school hoping to become an interpreter for the Queen. Such instances indicate the rising demand for English among the elite.[159] Commoners also recognized the market value in the knowledge of English.[160] The value of English was so widespread that Korean-run schools for girls enthusiastically included English as part of their core curriculum. For instance, Yŏja pohagwŏn, established in 1907 by Yŏja kyoyukhoe (the Association of Women's Education), offered English along with Chinese, Korean, and other subjects.[161] In the case of Chinmyŏng Girls' School, founded in 1906 by Lady Ŏm, all instruction was done in English. Ch'oe Hak-ju, who entered Chinmyŏng in 1907 and was one of the members of the first graduating class, vividly remembered the way she learned arithmetic, reciting in English "two times two is four."[162]

Lacking proficiency in Korean, missionaries initially offered English lessons out of the simple need to communicate with their students and teach the Bible. At Ewha, "the rudiments of the English language"[163] were taught from the very beginning, and students learned how to pray in English as well.[164] Mary Scranton's recollection of one of her first students' usage of English in her prayers gives us a glimpse into the ways in which students spoke English. The student said, "I love Jesus; I pray every day Korean; I pray every day English." When asked what she prayed for, she replied: "God many things give, thank you; rice give, all food give, thank you; clothes give, wood give, thank you."[165] The student had constructed English sentences using Korean word order. In spite of the grammatical errors, she was able to communicate with Scranton. In addition, her prayers were quite telling in that they expressed a "secular" interest in gaining resources for survival rather than focusing on religious devotion. Only when she was told that she must ask God to help her be a good girl, she replied that "O Yes . . . make all good inside—take all bad away."

Missionaries were wary of students who came to learn English rather than Christianity. Just as the provision of food, clothing, and lodging was a huge inducement for Koreans to attend mission schools, so was the English instruction. Male students in particular were eager to learn English as a means to making a living in the newly emerging arenas of trade and industry. Missionaries began to realize that teaching English would not help them spread the Gospel because students would leave after acquiring basic skills in English rather than become workers for Christianity. The missionaries were divided in their viewpoints on the provision of English instruction at mission schools.[166] Generally speaking, the majority of Presbyterian missionaries were against teaching English because it was seen as a pitfall in their evangelical work, while Methodist missionaries tended to be more lenient and willing to argue for the intellectual and religious benefits of English instruction.

Most Presbyterians firmly believed that English instruction should not be a central focus of their teaching activities. Frederick S. Miller, who was in charge of a Presbyterian boys' school in Seoul, gave specific reasons for not teaching English. He wrote, "We did not teach English as we found out that when they learned a little English they would go off to the ports or the mines and become interpreters, and those were bad places for the young folks in those days. For another reason we found we could learn Korean better if they knew no English! I used to put pictures up on the wall and ask them 'What is this?' so I learned."[167] William Blair noted that "[w]e began our work in Korea with the definite determination not to give the people anything as an inducement to believe but the Gospel; neither rice, nor money, *nor an English education,* nor any sort of an education; but to go directly to the people with the Gospel message" [emphasis added].[168] Speaking of the girl students at Presbyterian schools, Lillias Underwood reported in 1890 that they *"are taught no English,* but to read Chinese, and their own native 'Erumun' language, and above all, are taught the Gospel and Gospel living" [emphasis added].[169] In their annual meeting in 1895, Presbyterian missionaries declared that the "evangelistic bent of the Missions is unmistakable and all controlling," and from that vantage, the "Mission does not believe in Schools for the teaching of English—at least for themselves."[170] Thus, the Presbyterians, with only a few exceptions, decided not to offer instruction in or about English. Instead they adhered to the exclusive use of the Korean language to teach Christian ideals.[171]

In comparison, Methodist missionaries saw both evangelical and intellectual opportunities in offering English lessons. Henry Appenzeller, the first Methodist missionary in Korea, realized the teaching of English provided "the most fertile field" for gathering converts to Christianity.[172] Louise Rothweiler of Ewha Girls' School argued that English served not only to impart Christian ideas but also to mold students' minds by exposing them to Western civilization. Rothweiler believed that knowledge of other societies through the medium of English would enhance the students' ability to think and learn:

> A knowledge of English, the reading of English books, pursuing studies that would and could not be taught in *Enmoun* as yet, will give just that broadening of mind, thought and aspiration which we want our girls to have and which they need if they are to be successful helpers and which the *Enmoun* alone still fails to provide. Through English they will gain general knowledge and learn to know and appreciate the differences between Eastern and Western nations as in no other way.[173]

In Rothweiler's view, the benefit of learning English would go beyond religious purposes. Literacy in English would serve as a bridge between the East and the West, for mutual understanding and the reconciling of differences. The positive effect of teaching English was further argued by William Scranton:

> Every school should at this time put their greatest stress on the teaching of English, and this study should be fostered and even forced in order to bring the Korean people the more rapidly out from darkness into light, out from ignorance to keep abreast with the rest of the world, and out from every form of bondage into freedom and equality with the rest of humanity, where they can stand side by side with all men. . . . I class the English language the best agency for enabling the Korean people in the pursuit of learning, and I covet it for them that they may have it for their possession to enable them to do nobly, to strive bravely, and to succeed in these their trying days of new birth and responsibility in the family of Nations.[174]

To Scranton, the English language represented Western democracy and civilization. Korea, as a state in "new birth," had to catch up with the West, and English was perceived as the best agent for that purpose. George Heber Jones even considered the English language to be a marker of true civilization.[175] Josiah Strong stated that "the English language, saturated with Christian ideas, gathering up into itself the best thought of all ages is the great agent of Christian civilization throughout the world; at this moment affecting the destinies and molding the character of half the human race."[176] Thus, one of the fastest and most effective ways to disseminate Christianity to the world was to offer English instruction, which could serve as a vehicle for learning Christian civilization. However, in facing the same dilemma that the Presbyterians had, those missionaries who advocated English instruction were cautious about Korean students who were primarily interested in English for its secular value.[177]

The greater challenge for missionaries was to resolve the clash between the benefit of learning English and perceptions among the Korean community that learning English was part of a process that would Westernize young women. As discussed earlier, missionaries were aware that Koreans were hostile to "Westernized" girls who had been educated at mission schools. In an effort to soothe the Koreans' concerns, missionaries emphasized "Korean style" Christian character and ardently denied the charge that they trained Korean girls to become Western ladies. However, the English lessons continued to be perceived by Koreans as a symbol of Westernization. Speaking English or, worse yet, being proud of speaking English was equal to a "life of translation," as opposed to a true life based on Koreanness.[178] The hostility toward teaching English to girls was so great that many missionaries grew to fear that literacy in English "would be prejudicial to the highest good and influence of the girls when they return to their homes"[179] and might alienate these students from the local community.[180] Indeed, leading Korean intellectuals confirmed the worst fears of the missionaries. O Ch'ŏn-sŏk, an influential male educator, wrote, "if I summarize the accomplishment of Westerners in women's education in Korea in a stroke, it is that they take Korean women as raw materials and turn them into immature Western women."[181] Strongly echoing O's viewpoint, Chu Yo-sŏp proposed that English language instruction should be removed from the curriculum and instead the instruction of Korean should be strengthened. His main argument was that the majority of girls would never benefit from learning English because they were destined to remain in Korean homes as mothers and wives.[182]

Regardless of what missionaries or Korean male intellectuals thought, knowledge of English as a skill and medium for new ideas became a form of cultural capital. Thus, the curriculum evolved to include English as a staple.[183] By the 1920s, many English terms had been incorporated into Korean, such as *ppŏssŭ kkŏl* (bus girl), *p'aen* (fan), *nŏn sensŭ* (nonsense), and *p'aesŭp'ot'ŭ* (passport). They were widely used in newspapers and magazines, which reflected the cultural value and popularity that English had come to have in Korea. Advanced knowledge of English also prepared some students for study overseas and helped them find jobs, mostly in teaching positions, whereby they gained economic independence through their capacity to earn.[184] The learning of English by women, therefore, constituted an important element of modern womanhood in the sense that it helped them have access to the new realms of life and work beyond the traditional gender boundaries. At the same time, from a missionary point of view, English served as an important vehicle for disseminating Christian civilization. However, it also demanded a careful negotiation with the local expectations of "educated" women who would cherish things Korean more than foreign things.[185]

For both missionaries and Korean intellectuals, education was a crucial platform for pursuing their parallel primary goals of Christianization and national sovereignty. Sharing the belief in the power of education, they cooperated and complemented each other. However, the difference in their ultimate goals demanded constant negotiation and flexibility in representing and administering school work. While never compromising a core curriculum that prioritized Christian ideas, missionary teachers represented their educational work as an effort to help create "a perfect Korea" through "home-grown" Christian spirituality with emphasis on domestic virtues for girls. Missionaries' strategic emphasis on Korean ways and domesticity lessened some of the Korean anxiety about "educated women" who might be headstrong and unwilling to engage in domestic duties. However, from the 1920s, the relatively harmonious relationship between missionaries and Koreans began to be undermined by a growing number of educated women who were more interested in and intrigued by the secular modern or socialist gender reforms in their pursuit of modern subjectivities. In particular, the incisive critique by a group of socialist women fundamentally questioned the place of religion in modern education because they saw "religion as an opium" that paralyzed class consciousness.[186]

Nevertheless, to many students, mission schools were like a haven where they felt they were "protected from the tragedy of a childhood betrothal and early marriage, trained in mind and soul." Some missionary teachers positively responded to Korean students' passion for education and strove to offer the best education they could. When Lulu Frey, a teacher at Ewha, advocated college education for women, a majority of missionaries opposed that idea because they feared that college-educated Korean women "would be spoiled for service to their own people" and thus would be rejected by Korean communities.[187] In an essay written in 1932, Alice Appenzeller, president of Ewha College (1922–39), wrote that Koreans were not necessarily opposed to elementary or middle school education for girls, but they feared that higher education would produce "arrogant" women with no skills in household work and only a desire for luxury.[188] This negative perception drove a number of prospective students away from college education. Despite the sheer lack of support from Koreans and missionaries, Frey put forward her vision of college education out of her conviction that missionaries "should plan to give Korean women nothing less than the best."[189] Reminded of the history of Mount Holyoke College, founded by Mary Lyon, Annie Baird marveled at the beginning of college education in Korea: "in an incredibly short space of time the women of Korea have begun to rouse up from a state of utter mental inertness, and are looking about hungrily for something wherewith to train and occupy their growing powers . . . it is plainly up to the missionaries to satisfy the desire which the Gospel they preach has operated to create."[190] The gradual development of Ewha as a women's college was, in Marion Conrow's words, a "history of the dreaming of dreams."[191] Here the differing dreams of Koreans and missionaries in their passion for education converged, allowing them to negotiate and reshape their pursuit of their distinct ideals.

5. Imagining the Other

Discursive Portraits in Missionary Fiction

There has been significant research that argues that colonial expansion was not merely a phenomenon "out there." It was instrumental in constructing national identity, intellectual discourse, and the life of imagination in the metropole.[1] In a similar fashion, foreign missions were not just a phenomenon out there. Rather, they captured the American public's fascination with stories of the exotic, "heathen" world, and served as an important cultural ground to feed the imagination of Americans and their identity as superior to the Other. In particular, as Patricia Hill points out, the romanticized image of foreign missions was "the focus of ambition and the stuff of dreams for young women," some of whom later joined the foreign mission to save heathen sisters.[2] While foreign missions were imagined and romanticized by American writers at home, American missionaries themselves also actively engaged in producing "missionary fiction" in which they employed literary devices to represent foreign missions and dramatize their role in saving souls from the "ages of mental and moral degradation."[3] By *missionary fiction* I mean narratives in English and authored by missionaries with elaborate plots and detailed character development. In the Korea mission field, missionaries used the term as one of the categories on their required reading list.[4] In his analysis of missionary novels from China, Patrick Hanan defines them as "narratives (in the form of novels) that were written in Chinese by Christian missionaries and their assistants."[5] The different linguistic medium of the narratives is a critical factor in understanding their target audience and their motivation. While missionary novels written in Chinese were circulated among current and potential Christian converts as "the main proselytizing instrument" in the nineteenth century, missionary fiction in English primarily targeted American readers at home as a way to maintain and promote interest in foreign missions. Mostly published by Christian presses, such as the Fleming H. Revell Company, missionary fiction in English was a vital vehicle for distributing information on foreign missions to constituents at home.

Missionary fiction was significantly different from popular fiction in the United States at the time.[6] While popular fiction was often written by American writers who had never been to any foreign mission field, missionary fiction based its plot and character development on missionaries' intimate knowledge of and close interaction with the local subjects of conversion. Missionary authors often claimed that their stories were based on "facts and incidents" they observed, but in order to make the stories more interesting, they added "fictional" elements. Missionary fiction should also be distinguished from other official missionary records, such as mission journals, annual reports, and correspondence, which focused heavily on institutional mission policies and activities in the field. In general, missionary fiction dramatized the local, private, and intimate lives of people whom missionaries encountered. While missionary zeal to convert the Other was never compromised in the stories, missionary fiction offers a unique window into missionaries' more subtle and complex desires and experiences. The authors' intimate gaze at the Other produced rich ethnographic details. More important, in the novels their gaze was sometimes returned by the Other in a humorous and sometimes self-depreciating fashion. Missionary desire and outlook centering on the superiority of Christianity was interwoven with local people's resistance to the new religion and pride in their own tradition and civilization. In this way, missionary fiction is an interesting discursive arena that defies typical binarisms, affording the reader an opportunity to look into a dynamic site of transcultural interactions and representations.

This chapter analyzes three examples of missionary fiction from Korea that shed light on the complexity and diversity of missionary discourse. I focus particularly on the portrayal of new ideals for women. Each fiction presents a distinct image of the new woman, which reflects both historical changes in Korea and missionaries' response to those changes from their own subject positions. Annie Baird's *Daybreak in Korea: A Tale of Transformation in the Far East* closely follows the turbulent life of a Korean girl, Pobai, in a small rural village.[7] Pobai, represented as "the wretched and depraved product of oppressive patriarchy,"[8] goes through an unspeakable ordeal and is rescued by Christianity, which finally gives her eternal comfort. W. Arthur Noble's *Ewa: A Tale of Korea* depicts two young men and a woman who are drawn into the political turbulence that followed the Sino-Japanese War (1894–95) and gradually experience spiritual and political awakening in the face of encroaching Japanese colonial forces.[9] Unusually political in tone and content vis-à-vis other missionary fiction, Noble strategically takes a Korean perspective as the main vehicle of narration. In doing so, he attempts to represent the emerging nationalist identity of Koreans and portray Ewa, the female title character, as a symbol of dedication and sacrifice for the new nation. Ellasue Wagner's unpublished manuscript entitled *The Concubine* is a fascinating story of a modern American woman, Eva, who unwittingly becomes the concubine of a U.S.-educated Korean man from a prominent *yangban* (upper class) family.[10] Juxtaposing the American Eva, who is daring, frivolous, and anti-Christian, with the Korean Pobai, who is compliant, devoted, and a pious Christian, Wagner offers a cautionary tale of the danger of modern womanhood. Regardless of the author's express intentions in writing these works, the literary representations of new womanhood in the stories open up fluid and complex interpretations of the nature of missionary discourse involving what constituted new womanhood for a new Korea.

FROM DARKNESS TO DAYBREAK IN KOREA

Annie Baird (figure 10) was a Presbyterian missionary, arriving in the Korea mission field in 1891 with her husband, William Baird. She died of cancer in 1916. During her twenty-five years of service, she engaged actively in evangelical, educational, and literary work mainly in the P'yŏngyang station. As her fellow missionary, Harry Rhodes noted, she was one of the most prolific missionaries in producing Christian literature.[11] She frequently contributed articles to mission journals, touching on a variety of topics especially concerning Korean women and the role of women missionaries in the field. She published three books—*Fifty Helps for the Beginner in the Use of the Korean Language* (1897), *Daybreak in Korea: A Tale of Transformation in the Far East* (1909), and *Inside Views of Missionary Life* (1913). All three were considered important works of Christian literature and were widely circulated among missionaries and readers at home. James Gale recalled the pervasive influence of her book, *Fifty Helps*, noting that she "would easily rank as first teacher of the foreign community."[12] Furthermore, being well versed in Korean language and culture, Baird also wrote two short stories in Korean: "Ko Yŏng-gyu chŏn" (A Story of Ko Yŏng-gyu) and "Pubu ŭi mobon" (Examples of Husband and Wife). Published in 1911, these two stories were aimed at Korean readers as a means to promote Christian faith and ways of life.[13] Both her publications and her involvement in evangelical work make it amply clear that she was one of the most influential women missionaries to serve in Korea.

Baird wrote *Daybreak in Korea* almost two decades after she first arrived in the country. The book, which comprises nine chapters and a preface, demonstrates her intimate and in-depth knowledge of Korean people and customs, detailing the motives and circumstances under which Koreans were converted to Christianity. Unlike male missionaries, whose discourse tends to focus on a wide range of social, political, and economic issues, Baird engages in a highly individualized, intimate, and almost ethnographic observation of Korean customs and people. The protagonist of her story is Pobai, a twelve-year-old Korean girl living in a small village.[14] Her choice of a girl instead of an adult seems to reinforce not only the "maternal" nature of women's missionary work but also the more influential or necessary early intervention of Christianity in cultivating and transforming Korean womanhood.[15] Right after Baird arrived in Korea in 1891, she wrote a letter to a friend in which she gave a very detailed picture of a Korean girls' school run by a woman missionary. In that letter, she described how the work of the mission had brought about much change, transforming Korean girls from "miserable little bundle[s] of rags and dirt" to "sweet and helpful" people.[16] The story of Pobai in *Daybreak* is a full-blown dramatic tale of transformation from a degraded life in a Christless world to the dawn of a new life "under the transforming power of the Gospel."[17] The title evokes the power of natural law: as night inevitably gives way to daybreak, so is Korea destined to ascend to Enlightenment through Christian spirituality.

In insinuating the role of missionaries in this transformation, Baird uses two interesting narrative strategies. One is to adopt the plot of "transformed melodrama," which Judith Walkowitz defines as a story line "complete with stereotyped characters, extreme states of being and danger, rapid action, and the vindication of virtue over vice."[18] This plot form, designed to "reinforce and valorize a Protestant-based morality," was quite popular among Christian women in the United States at the turn of the twentieth century.[19] Baird vividly portrays the wretched lives of Korean women and the vicious customs that cause them violence, humiliation, and death. Filled with pagan characters whose lives are in turmoil, this melodramatic story ends when heathen vices subside under the light of Christian virtue.

Baird's second strategy is a highly individualized and personal approach to the representation of Koreans and their culture, one that is almost psychoanalytic in nature. In the course of her work Baird was able to gather intimate details that were not available to male missionaries. Due to the "inside-outside rule" discussed in chapter 3, only women missionaries were allowed to visit women's inner chambers, which became a main stage for evangelical efforts. It was in the women's quarters that women missionaries learned about Korean women's lives. More important, such privileged contact often enabled women missionaries to develop close bonds with native women, which allowed them a degree of access that enabled them to portray those women with authority.

Zooming in from a distance and gradually approaching the house of Pobai on a summer afternoon, Baird begins her narration with a description of Pobai,

> nearly twelve years old, with round cheeks that glowed red under the olive skin, and a heavy braid of glossy black hair hanging down her back. Only perfect cleanliness was lacking to make her a very wholesome little girl to look upon, but Pobai was almost always rather dirty. She would have liked to be clean, but so much of her time and strength went into helping her mother keep the men of the family immaculately clad, that she hardly ever had time to think of herself.[20]

Baird compares Pobai's life with "the happy lot" of girls the same age in the United States.[21] The drudgery Korean girls and women must perform daily—cooking, cleaning, and ironing for the family, especially the men—defines women's standard routine. Worse yet, young girls like Pobai are expected to get married early. The fearful Pobai is instructed by her grandfather that getting married is one of the three major phases in life—birth, marriage, and death—and if she does not marry, she "would be no better than a *pyung-sin* [handicapped person] or a *tol-gye-jip* [lit., "stone woman," an infertile woman]."[22] As discussed in chapter 3, the extremely early age for marriage in Korea shocked incoming missionaries, and opposition to early marriage became one of their most important agendas for social reform.[23] At the 1908 Annual Meeting of the Korea Woman's Conference of the Methodist Episcopal Church, Lulu Frey specifically asked her fellow missionaries "to use your influence against early marriages."[24] Pobai's situation illustrates for the American reader the kind of customs practiced in pagan society. Although the centuries-long custom had recently begun to be questioned, Pobai is represented as a typical Korean girl who is destined to be a victim of premature marriage.

The shock the reader feels at the custom of early marriage only grows with Baird's more detailed descriptions of married life in Korea, with its harsh physical labor and virtually no love between wife and husband:

> Pobai's married life began, only one of many faltering little barks that set sail on unknown seas in lands where tender mercies are cruel . . .

All day long and from year's end to year's end she wrought, through the bright years of her girlhood, and got in return something to wear, a scanty two meals of food a day, and a place to sleep at night . . . she had never cared much for her husband, or he for her, and he paid her very little attention except to complain when his clothes were not washed and ironed properly, or his food not prepared to his liking.[25]

A woman's life after marriage is portrayed as being no better than slavery. And yet an even more bitter experience awaits Pobai at age eighteen, when she gives birth to a daughter. Understanding the traditional Korean preference for sons, Baird describes how anxiously her parents-in-law wait for a grandson, and how "Pobai was more anxious than any one else. What little happiness she knew, and any earthly honour that she could hope to attain, depended upon her becoming the mother of a son."[26] Sadly, Pobai fails to satisfy her mandate and must face life as a sonless woman. Son preference in Korea is the epitome of the Confucian patriarchal system that reigned during the Chosŏn dynasty.[27] One of the essential reasons for son preference has to do with highly structured patrilineages in which only sons inherited the family line and had legal connections with the family. For purposes of perpetuating genealogy, sons were (and have continued to be) preferred over daughters.

Things get worse when Pobai's husband suddenly dies, and she is beset by numerous calamities. Her parents-in-law are about to sell her to "whomever would give the money," and her baby daughter catches the "dreadful guest" (a colloquial reference to smallpox). Desperate, Pobai seeks help from a shaman to save her daughter. To pay the shaman she attempts unsuccessfully to steal some stacks of straw from her parents-in-law. The very next day she is sold to a drunken man named Mansik and is dragged to his home with a rope tied around her waist as if she were an animal. This horrifying episode reaches a climax when her only child dies soon after she arrives at Mansik's home. Baird wonders:

[W]hy Pobai did not put an end to her wretched life in the days and weeks and months and years that followed, I do not know, except it was because the good God had something better in store for her. Often, as she sat at the riverside with her heap of washing, and watched the dark current flowing swiftly by, the thought of how sweet it would be to sink beneath those waves and never come back to a world so bereft of hope, welled up in her mind and almost overpowered her.[28]

This worsening series of incidents—a forced and loveless marriage, the abuse she suffers as a sonless woman, the backbreaking workload, the lack of protections for her as a widow, and the loss of her only child—all serve as lucid examples of the harsh life of Korean women under pagan customs. Baird raises the level of intimacy by giving expression to Pobai's inner thoughts. This glimpse into Korean life might have provoked disgust and, at the same time, sympathy among a Western audience. Baird speaks for Pobai, the innocent, powerless victim of pagan custom who imagines death to be better than this cruel life, "a world so bereft of hope." At this climatic moment, Baird quietly ponders why Pobai does not end her life, concluding that "the good God had something better in store for her." The missionary zeal to rescue this misery-stricken Korean woman is apparent, and indeed the deus ex machina arrives in the story in the form of the "transforming power of the Gospel."

In the chapter "An Absorption of New Ideas," Baird begins to describe the "daybreak" that is transforming life among Koreans. When Yung Kyoo, who is working for some missionaries, is asked by village people about the new doctrine, he says, "It's about somebody that they call Jesus. They say he 'saves' them, and they seem to get a lot of comfort out of it." When Pobai hears this, her ears perk up:

> "Comfort out of it!" Oh, how sweetly those words fell upon Pobai's listening ear, and what desperate strength of longing awoke in her to know more of anything that promised comfort! She took her spindle and went into the house, and with beating heart sat down to think it over.[29]

Pobai's encounter with Christianity transforms her life in just one day, and she finally recovers her sense of worth. In *Inside Views of Mission Life*, Baird claims that "until the introduction of Christianity the one reason in Korean minds for the existence of women was the exercise of the maternal function. To be a mother was their one claim to consideration."[30] Baird implies that Christianity values women as human souls rather than simply for their maternal function. While only motherhood made women's lives worthwhile in traditional Korea, in the Christian tradition women had genuine worth as human beings. And thus Christianity is imagined to play a role in transforming the Korean view of women from mothers only to individuals genuinely equal to men.[31] Of course, as I discussed in chapter 2, Western Christian women were not equal to men, either in the church or in society in general. Yet conversion to Christianity is presented as a great liberator with the suggestion that women are granted dignity and honor beyond their maternal role. Ignoring gendered inequalities in power and authority, Baird idealizes the "equal" realm of gender within Christian

ethics. This selective recognition of gender equality under the Christian
God is the dominant picture of new womanhood in missionary discourse.

Pobai's conversion to Christianity clearly symbolizes the end of hardship and the heathen life. However, her inner transformation is not sufficient to give her life new meaning because it is still in the hands of her
husband. Discovering that Pobai has gone to church "to do the Jesus doctrine," Mansik "threw her to the ground and bound her with rope."[32] In
the face of threats of more beatings, Pobai responds: "You may beat me to
death if you will, or saw me asunder, but I cannot give up my Lord." Pobai
becomes a true Christian when she "did not feel much pain [from Mansik's
beatings], but instead her spirit was possessed by a sense of high privilege
in sharing Christ's suffering."[33] Here Baird contrasts the saintlike Pobai,
who sustains herself despite cruel violence done to her, with Mansik, the
incarnation of vice and, implicitly, paganism. Pobai's endurance of her suffering under the relentless terror at home maximizes her sanctification
under Christianity. The true transformation is yet to come.

At this point, Baird turns attention to Mansik, portraying him as a deeply
frustrated man with strong opposition to anything foreign. Baird writes
that he violently objects to Pobai's going to church because he "resented
the idea of obtaining it [anything that could be of advantage] through
the medium of foreigners." He shouts, "Upstart barbarians, every one of
them . . . They [foreigners] only come here to steal our land and put foolish
notions into the heads of our women. What doctrines have they that are any
better than those we have? Our Confucius, has there ever been a sage like
him?"[34] Through Mansik, Baird expresses Koreans' hostile attitude toward
foreigners and indirectly contextualizes the political background against
which the story takes place. Mansik is by no means a representative of all
Koreans. Yet his harsh view of foreigners clearly reflects Korean anxiety
and suffering at the turn of the twentieth century, when foreign powers,
especially Japan, Russia, and China, contested for hegemonic power over
Korea.[35] In this political turmoil, the general policy of mission organizations was "an entirely non-committal and neutral policy in reference to the
national problems."[36] Missionaries were strongly advised to steer clear from
any political engagement or statement, and thus it is not too surprising to
notice that Baird does not explicitly refer to any larger political context in
her novel. It is only through the angry voice of Mansik that Baird illustrates
a broader antiforeign sentiment.

Mansik, of course, is ultimately transformed into a loving man and
husband, forming a happy Christian family with Pobai. His radical transformation follows a great humiliation in which he attempts, unsuccess-

fully, to buy into a higher social class by forging a *chokpo* (genealogy). This bitter experience provides the critical momentum through which he realizes that his low status is fixed. He might have felt betrayed by the Confucian ideology that he had upheld as the backbone of Korean morality. In the midst of this deep sense of humiliation and betrayal, one day he is drawn to a gathering in the street and finds himself "in the presence of one of the hated foreigners."[37] Although Mansik is scornful of the foreigner's preaching, he thinks about the missionary's message all night and the next day repents his wrongdoing. In the morning he confesses to Pobai, telling her that he has "found your Saviour, and he has shown me what a brute I have been. I have been worse than any beast" to her, and he seeks her forgiveness by promising that he will "never lay hand on you again except in love."[38] Mansik's redemption from cruel, uncivilized pagan to caring Christian completes the true transformation that Baird projects in the story. The misery and hardship caused by "pagan" customs and cruel patriarchy finally ends with the vindication of virtue over vice and Christianity over paganism. In the ending of the story, Baird writes, "And so out of the wreck and wastage of their former lives these two people began together to build the fair edifice of a happy home, that rich ornament which seldom precedes a Christian civilization, but follows it everywhere in its march throughout the world."[39] Clearly, the daybreak of the title symbolizes hope and a new beginning that enables Koreans to join in the march toward universal Christian civilization. Ironically, this upbeat tone takes place at the historical point when Koreans were undergoing Japanese colonization, the ultimate humiliation for the Korean nation and the total loss of national autonomy, which can be characterized as a "dark" period in its history.

Privileging personal, inner, and spiritual salvation while downplaying national political crisis, the storyline effectively serves as a classic example of missionary discourse in which stereotypical pagan characters, who display extreme states of cruelty, violence, and manipulation, are rescued by Christianity. Within this transformation plot Baird put forward a model of new womanhood whose virtue lies in patience, endurance, devotion, and (most important) Christian faith. In a significant way, Baird portrays Pobai and her life as typical of "heathens" of the commoner classes. The only way out of the "wreck and wastage of their former lives" is to accept the Gospel, signified by daybreak. Just as daybreak is the law of nature, so conversion to Christianity is the law of humanity. The transformation of Korean women in the new era is thus characterized by Christian spirituality and inner peace and separate from national political tumult.

GENDERED MARTYRDOM FOR THE NEW NATION

If Annie Baird's *Daybreak in Korea* is discreet about Korea's political crisis, W. Arthur Noble's *Ewa: A Tale of Korea* (1906) is an explicitly political story with an intimate portrayal of Korean customs and new gender relations with a hint of modern romance defined by noble forms of masculinity. Arthur Noble and his wife, Mattie Noble, were sent to Korea in 1892 by the Methodist Church in the U.S. Like the Bairds, the Nobles worked largely in P'yŏngyang during their forty-two-year tenure in Korea. Arthur Noble was one of the most respected missionaries in Korea, by both Koreans and his fellow missionaries. A Korean preacher noted in 1920 that Noble "was not large, nor especially attractive looking, nothing in his appearance to draw forth such unbounded praise as I had always heard, and I more deeply wondered 'What is the secret?' . . . His fine sympathy with all & quick righteous judgment and non sparing of self I found at last was the secret, & I became one of his admirers & staunch friends."[40] Noble's sympathy with Koreans reached its height when, right after Korea was colonized by Japan in 1910, he publicly criticized Bishop Harris for his pro-Japanese activities.[41] In a significant way, Noble's *Ewa* captures his great empathy with Koreans and their unfortunate path toward colonization.

Published in 1906, *Ewa* is composed of twenty-seven chapters. In his preface, Noble states his goal in writing the book is to "represent Korean affairs from the standpoint of the Korean." More specifically, Noble intends "to show the great struggle of new Korea for a better life; to illustrate the type of manhood that is leading the people toward reform; [and] awaken sympathy for a people who have become the victims of an unjust exploitation by a foreign power" [Japan]. Given the general mission policy of strict political neutrality, Noble opts for a *literary* representation of Korea in the first-person narrative of a Korean man, Sung-yo. Through this narrative strategy, he endeavors to represent a Korean perspective, especially the concerns of Enlightenment-oriented intellectuals in the face of Japanese colonization. More interesting, he interweaves emerging nationalist sentiment with a modern form of romance. In doing so, he challenges traditional Korean gender relations and envisions a new womanhood as well as a new manhood. In the end, he invokes the image of a virtually martyred female protagonist, Ewa, whose sacrifice gives birth to a generation of new men who are bound to the duty of regaining Korea's sovereignty.

In the story, there are three main characters. Sung-yo, the narrator, is the son of a concubine in the "great Kim clan of the North."[42] Groomed as a member of the *yangban* (upper class), he has been "discouraged from taking robust physical exercise" and has "developed the physical effeminacy which is supposed to be the mark of a gentleman."[43] Tong-sik, a senior friend of Sung-yo, is not from "a family of rank" but represents a character of Enlightenment who has studied in Japan.[44] His interest in nation-building with new moral standards, including Christianity, significantly influences Sung-yo. Sung-yo's parents have arranged a marriage for him, but he finds out his bride-to-be is a "hunchback, short and ugly" without a "trace of intelligence." He eventually falls in love with Ewa, the title character. Ewa is the daughter of a respectable family, but she has lost her parents because of political corruption. She is sold as a slave to Mr. Yi, who later turns out to have been a conspirator who was responsible for destroying Ewa's father and her family.[45] Ewa has to go through an unspeakable ordeal, but her discovery of Christianity and her encounter with Sung-yo empower her. In a significant way, the story is a melodramatic romance with a tragic ending in which Ewa faces death in order to protect Sung-yo, her husband, and hold onto her Christian faith.

When Noble's book was reviewed by the journal *Korea Mission Field*, the review criticized "the love story [between Ewa and Sung-yo] as too highly drawn and as not true to the usual tenor of social life."[46] Indeed, there are plenty of words and descriptions that might allow a reader to mistake the missionary novel for a typical Western romance, as in this passage, right after Ewa and Sung-yo have found each other after a long period of searching:

> Ewa: "I am yours forever and ever. I am happy, happy," and tears
> stood out on her long lashes. A delirium of ecstasy swept through me
> [Sung-yo], and somewhere down in the elemental regions of the soul,
> arose feelings that caressed with the voice where words were dumb;
> and all my years of struggle and pain were as if they had never been.
> The moonlight swept back the shadows of the mountain and I found
> her large dark eyes gazing into mine, and I said many things and
> she replied in words that I have long since hid away in the sanctuary
> of my memory. Nor will I do violence by entering there. In lonely
> hours I walk around its closed walls with gentle tread and dumbly
> feel its surface, and when I press my lips against the wall it glows
> and palpitates with dear words and looks that will never die.[47]

In this imagined Korean modern romance projected from the vantage point of Western sensibilities, Noble's narrative serves to promote both nationalist and Christian ideals, two essential components in new womanhood. As discussed in chapter 2, Enlightenment-oriented intellectuals in Korea criticized traditional gender practices as one of the reasons for

Korea's lagging behind advanced countries. Their critique was ultimately to bring women to the project of nation-building. Sharing the view whole-heartedly with Koreans, Noble portrays how transcultural encounters between Koreans and Westerners had an impact on the changing views of Koreans on the status of women. He goes even further, challenging male-dominant nationalist discourse and making a space for women to exercise their power as agents in shaping history and a new society. In the voice of Tong-sik, Noble discusses Korean womanhood:

> . . . would you believe it . . . their [Westerners'] women meet all visi-tors, talk with them, and they are treated more politely by the men than the men treat each other. It shocked me first, and I thought there must be something terribly wrong with such a people, but here is a point that puzzles me. Confucius has done much for us, but he never made us equal, nor womanhood respected. Perhaps the foreigner is right, and they should be respected and put on a plane of equality with men . . . [48]

> I need not remind you . . . of the status of our women. Do we ever think enough of a girl to give her a name? A woman in our country has no more personality than a horse or an ox . . . The land is full of men that need to be bolstered up by women . . . there are many men who have little vigor than an oyster, and the vision of a strong woman would put them to flight.[49]

Critiquing the low status of women in traditional Korea, Noble intends to reveal the unjust oppression of women by men. Clearly aware of the traditional rule of the separation of genders, he presents a new model of gender interactions. Significantly, this new model is practiced by Christian converts. When Ewa and Sung-yo go to a church to marry, Sung-yo is surprised to see men and women mingling together without screens to separate them. Responding to Sung-yo's shock, a Korean pastor tells him that "Christian communities live differently. We speak to the women, and they are not afraid of being greeted. We are all on a plane of equality . . . she is not beneath us in point of respect or privileges."[50]

The idea of equality between women and men is dramatized when Ewa takes the initiative in her relationship with Sung-yo. Although he is the one who pursues her doggedly despite all the upheavals, it is ultimately Ewa who moves their relationship forward at critical moments. Two important events show her defining role in their relationship. One is when she shows her "cross" tattoo to him and puts the same symbol on his wrist as a sign of a "marriage contract."[51] The other is when Sung-yo, excited about the possibility that he and Ewa can "flee" to the north (meaning his hometown P'yŏngyang), paints "in glowing colors the future," Ewa calmly suggests that they first marry at a church.[52] She says, "I am yours for your own dear sake, and if that will make your arm strong and your heart brave to dare I shall be content; but listen—fifty *li* from here is a Christian chapel where, sometimes, is performed the marriage rite. I am a Christian. I was not born a slave. I am by right a free woman, and if I will, I may accompany you there."[53] Suggesting that their relationship must be formally recognized by the church, she wants to make the record clear before they "flee."

The importance of the Christian marriage ritual is worth noting. Men of the upper class in old Korea used to take women of their liking as *ch'ŏp* (secondary wives) without formal rituals. There was a formal ceremony only for marriage to the primary wife.[54] Given this tradition, Ewa's calmly reasoned attitude in this matter signals the enhanced power of women as agents in shaping their lives with their own will. Her rational, self-composed, measured action is an interesting contrast to Sung-yo's naïve, emotional, and passionate attitude. Rationality constitutes one of the core elements of modernity and is often associated with maleness, but Ewa's rational thinking and attitude contradicts a stereotypical gender-bound personality trait in which women are expected to be the more emotional, irrational, and unstable.[55] Thus, it is ultimately Ewa who defines and shapes their relationship.

Another dramatic change represented in the plot is that Sung-yo, a son of the upper class, marries a slave woman. Although Ewa is originally from the upper class, the fact that she has had her status reduced to that of a slave is what matters most in the eyes of others. Theoretically and practically their marriage would not have been possible according to the customs of the late Chosŏn dynasty. However, Sung-yo is ready to give up his status as *yangban* in order to be united with Ewa. He says, "I gave up a life of ease to follow you. To serve as a slave at your side, though despised of men, would have been all I asked. Do not think I am not proud, but you were more than rank, wealth and parents to me."[56] Noble's storyline, which emphasizes individual will over ascribed status, makes their union possible. Sung-yo's falling in love with Ewa signals an emergence of selfhood. One may think of this emphasis on individuality as a Western view, and Tong-sik articulates this view:

> I never heard of a young man falling in love with a woman who was a stranger, much less a slave, and follow her about, as a dog his master. They say in the western world, where they boast of their civilization, that such things are common.[57]

Emphasizing individuals' own feelings and desires, Tong-sik suggests a new practice of marriage, removed from the family-centered, status-oriented system. Noble consistently suggests that the daring claims of the individual will constitute one of the core ideas necessary for a modern Korea. Sung-yo's decision to reject his parents' bride choice already unheard of. What adds a more dramatic turn is that he, as a son of the upper class, takes a slave woman as his *primary* wife. This entirely unconventional and scandalous development culminates in a Western-style Christian wedding without family members, which is in itself unconventional by the late-nineteenth-century Korean standards.

The romance reaches its height when Ewa sacrifices herself for Sung-yo and her new religion. Sacrifice is a keyword here. Noble consistently proffers that the essence of nationalism is self-sacrifice on behalf of the nation. Emphasis on sacrifice is not new to nationalist discourse. Indeed, self-sacrifice, or repression of personal desire, constitutes a core value of nationalism.[58] As the historian Thomas Dubois points out, reformers in Asia in the late nineteenth century admired "the sense of individual responsibility and sacrifice" they saw in the West, and deplored "the lack of such virtues among their own people."[59] Noble echoes this archetypical nationalist discourse. Further, he finds the origin of "self-sacrifice" in the West as the prime force for advancement, and thus he suggests that Koreans should learn this spirit in order to regain their sovereignty.[60]

Ewa, who epitomizes the spirit of self-sacrifice, becomes a virtual martyr for her religious and national causes.[61] When she rejoins her beloved Sung-yo and marries him after a series of turbulent events, she could remain happy for the rest of her life. However, "for conscience' sake" she intentionally returns to the house of her slave master, Mr. Yi. She does this because she is afraid that Yi might think Christians to be deceptive if she were to run away for her own personal interest. She does not want to give Christianity a bad reputation but wants to demonstrate Christian faith and honesty by sacrificing her personal happiness.[62] Upon arriving at Yi's house, Ewa and Sung-yo face the outraged Yi, who has Ewa beaten nearly to death for fleeing and marrying Sung-yo. Shocked by the horrible beating, Sung-yo tries to take Ewa away from Yi's house. However, Ewa insists that he should leave alone. She argues that since she is a slave, marrying her makes Sung-yo a slave as well "in the eyes of our law," and thus she will only be a burden and curse on his life.[63] In addition, she urges Sung-yo to devote his life to a greater cause—national liberation. In her effort to persuade Sung-yo to follow her suggestion, she implores, "I have thought it all out. You must return to your people and fight the battles for our country with your friend."[64]

To Ewa, ultimate happiness lies not in secular time and space but in the spiritual world. She tells Sung-yo that "I am your wife. Cruel death may find me sometime, but it will be as your virgin wife."[65] Their spiritual bonding is best captured by Noble's symbolic use of the cross. On the one hand, it represents a feudal past. Ewa's owner tattoos a cross on her wrist as a sign of her enslaved status, symbolizing the oppressive, inhumane, and unequal society of old Korea. On the other hand, the cross is the central symbol of Christianity, alluding to Jesus' sacrifice and representing a future of salvation. Thus, the cross engraved in the bodies of Ewa and Sung-yo signals "the hope of Korea, and not her misery and ruin."[66] In this mixing of the old and the new, the East and the West, the crisis and the reform, one witnesses the unmaking and remaking of Korea. Ewa plays a key role in this process with her Christian piety and womanly devotion and sacrifice. Sung-yo observes that Ewa has given her life for him.[67] In return, he is obliged to carry out "a great work" for Korea, which "shall be made free."[68] The last words Ewa speaks before her death is, "The cr—oss, S—Sung-yo."[69] Metaphorically and literally, the cross and Sung-yo represent the hope and future of Korea, The cross, representing Christianity, becomes a marker of a better future. Sung-yo as the future of Korea gains a new life through Ewa's Jesus-like sacrifice of her own life.[70]

Although Noble's novel is named after its female protagonist, the book makes clear that male protagonists will play the central role in nation-building. The heroic Ewa helps her husband recapture his role in shaping the modern nation-state through her endurance and ultimate sacrifice. Metaphorically, she helps to beget the nation through Sung-yo, but she herself has no public role in the new Korea—indeed, she is beaten to death by her owner, the symbol of all that is backward and cruel in the "old" Korea. One can see a contrast in the way in which Sung-yo is informed by Tong-sik—an archetype for the new man of intelligence, rationality, and cutting-edge.[71] Tong-sik signifies the new man, one who takes center stage in building the nation by awakening men and women to their new roles. In comparison, Ewa takes a peripheral, private, and ultimately invisible role in the nation-building project. Thus, both the new nation and new womanhood informed by Korean Enlightenment and Christianity in missionary fiction unwittingly continues to center on a patriarchal order—women's roles, although broadened, are still subordinated.

A CAUTIONARY TALE OF MODERN WOMAN

Ellasue Canter Wagner (in Korea 1904–40), sent by the U.S. Southern Methodist Church, was one of the most active and prolific missionaries in Korea (see figure 11). She pioneered and developed a girls' school, the Holston Institute in Songdo (presently Kaesŏng in North Korea), served as the superintendent of the Social Evangelical Center in Seoul, and also worked as the editor of *The Korea Mission Field*.[72] Wagner had a long list of publications that informed American audiences about the history and cultural characteristics of Korea. The majority of her publications shared the views expressed in other missionary writings in that they describe the terror of paganism, the oppressed lives of women, and their eventual transformation after conversion to Christianity. In particular, the plot of Wagner's short story "The Dawn of Tomorrow" is remarkably similar to Annie Baird's *Daybreak in Korea* in tracing the cruel path of women's lives.[73]

Wagner's novel *The Concubine* differs from her other writings on two accounts. One is that the story was never published. The 272-page, double-spaced typescript comprises nineteen chapters with a dedication page, a three-page long "Sketch of Story," and two pictures of Korea. It is very clear from the dedication page and the tone of her introductory "Sketch of Story" that Wagner wanted to publish it for an American audience. Wagner was already an experienced writer, having published several books as well as numerous articles that appeared in mission journals. Even after she returned to the United States in 1940, she continued to make efforts to publish books about Korea.[74] Amid all her productivity and enthusiasm for publication, we are left with the question: Why was this novel, seemingly complete, written by an established author, never published? Archival data do not give any clear indication why. Nor is it clear when the novel was completed. Judging from the reference to certain historical events in the story, such as the nationwide Independence Movement of 1919, activities of communist groups, and the appearance of the "New Woman" in Korea, the manuscript was certainly completed sometime after the late 1920s. Interestingly, a letter of Wagner's dated May 24, 1948, suggests that she might have completed the manuscript in the 1940s, inspired by an actual event in Korea—an American woman who had fallen in love with a Korean man. In the letter, she wrote, "I've forgotten, but of course you remember Allyeu [Wagner's sister]. I still laugh when I remember how shocked Allyeu was in Seoul at Ann Wallace and her Korean sweetheart. By the way, did you see Ann while you were in Seoul? She evidently has had a pretty tough time, but what could she expect?" (see figure 12).[75] If she wrote the story in the 1940s, it is also possible that she read Pearl Buck's well-known novel *East Wind, West Wind*, published in 1930, which has a subplot in which a Chinese man marries an American woman while studying in the United

States. Although the stories differ, both authors were clearly engaged in the literary representation of intercultural and interracial formation.

The other distinctive feature of the novel is that *The Concubine* explicitly and primarily deals with "modern girls." To be sure, the novel shares some of the traditional themes of other missionary literatures—saving souls and pious Christian womanhood. However, it also offers an intriguing tableau for uncovering the tensions between tradition and modernity, between religiosity and secularity, between the East and the West, and between the races. Unlike the novels by Annie Baird and W. Arthur Noble, which were published on the eve of colonization, *The Concubine* takes place against the background of Japanese colonial rule and the dynamic cultural change that swept through Korea in the 1920s and 1930s.[76] One of the cultural elements that had entered public consciousness at the time in Korea was the phenomenon of New Women and Modern Girl. In this same period in the United States, the sensualized image of "the flapper" attracted a great deal of public attention and became a target of criticism by fundamentalist Christians.[77] Wagner herself portrayed "the flapper of the West" as an outcome of the "extreme belief in the romantic code" and blamed the cinema and "yellow journals and penny novels [which] teem with the vilest and most shameless stories of sex life" for the grossly "distorted and false pictures of Western life" that had a bad influence on young men and women in Korea.[78]

When we read Wagner's novel in the contexts of both the United States and Korea in the 1920s and 1930s, it is highly suggestive of what constitutes true "modern" womanhood in missionary discourse and how the missionary vision for modern womanhood was in tension with the phenomenon of the *secular* New Women and the early women's movement. In a significant way, the novel illustrates both the anxiety and ambivalence felt by missionaries in the face of growing challenges to the "cult of true womanhood."[79] By choosing to focus on the concubine system as a plot device, Wagner affords herself the chance to critique the "pagan" and "premodern" nature of Korean traditions, but more important, she challenges audacious, secular modernity, invoking a conservative gender ideology of "wise mother, good wife" accompanied by Christian spirituality as the core value of true modernity.[80]

The center of the story is Eva Bowers, a white American woman. In the story, Eva is described as a "thoughtless and self-centered girl from a godless home." She loves to wear fashionable, revealing dresses and enjoys worldly pleasures such as dancing and going to theaters, invoking the popular U.S. image of the 1920s flapper.[81] Her middle-class upbringing in a well-educated family teaches her to despise religion and adore science. Eva is presumably under the influence of her father, a professor of mathematics and a man of science. Her outlook illustrates the contrast between modernity governed by science and rationality and the premodern past ruled by religion. More important, Wagner's depiction of Eva echoes the typical rhetoric of early-twentieth-century Christian literature, which lamented the rapid change in gender relations away from the Victorian ideal of true womanhood.[82] In this vein, the choice of the protagonist's name as Eva might have been strategic.[83] As Ann Ardis points out in her analysis of the New Woman novels, some (male) writers characterized the New Woman as *Eve* "in her bid for emancipation from the Victorian cult of true womanhood" and she was "accused of instigating the second fall of man."[84] With this Biblical connotation attached to the name, Eva also represents the "corruption of Western godliness" in the words of Rev. George Pentecost, who diagnosed that the "ungodliness of the American and European communities that have invaded the East for the sake of trade and empire" was one of the "darkest spots in the missionary outlook."[85] Ungodly and unwieldy, Eva embodies the new modern subjectivity which disturbed the missionary sensibility and inspired a desire to constrain or discipline it.

Eva falls in love with Tai Jin Pak, a native of Korea from a prominent *yangban* family while he is studying in the United States. Despite the opposition of her parents, Eva decides to marry Tai Jin and leave her country to be with him. She even gives up her American citizenship before sailing to Korea.[86] In Korea, Tai Jin's parents disapprove of the marriage because Tai Jin has been pledged to be the bridegroom of a Korean woman, Pobai, from the time they were children. In fact, Pobai is already living in Tai Jin's parents' house. To Tai Jin's parents, Pobai is the legitimate bride and Eva merely a concubine. But no one, including Tai Jin, informs Eva of this reality. While living in a chamber at Tai Jin's house, Eva continues to shock family members with her "immodest dress, discourteous manners, and her bad temper."[87] In the end, Eva discovers her actual position in Tai Jin's family. Deeply hurt and ashamed, Eva decides to leave Korea. The bold, sensual, defiant, and godless modern woman fails to gain happiness, while Pobai, the pious Christian who respects tradition and authority, ultimately wins Tai Jin's heart and lives happily ever after.

Wagner's motive is obvious—constructing an ideal womanhood whose Christian piety acts as an antidote to the maelstrom of secular modernity. Wagner makes it very explicit that her story is meant to show how the godless and rebellious Eva unwittingly falls into the heathen, premodern custom of concubinage. Eva and Pobai are vividly contrasted. While the free-spirited, fashionable, and secular Eva "hates religion and despises the missionaries as hypocrites and parasites," Pobai possesses great integrity, dignity, and morality. She is a Christian girl educated at a mission school, where she learns various modern subjects, most importantly home economics, which provides her with useful skills for her role at home. She is particularly well prepared to cook "Western food" such as crisp biscuits, broiled steak, and coffee, Tai Jin's favorite meal.[88] However, she also conforms to the expectations of Korean tradition. Her respect for tradition and her willingness to conform to parental authority is shown in her acceptance of the arranged marriage with Tai Jin, putting her into stark contrast with Eva, who chooses her own husband against her parents' wishes. At the story's climax, when Eva learns that she has been trapped in concubinage, she repents her own vanity and lack of substance. In this hyperbolic melodrama, the secular modern girl from the United States is punished by her experience in Korea, which ultimately disciplines her to become more respectful of tradition and piety.

A unique aspect of Wagner's story is the racial discourse that is intricately woven into Wagner's discourse on modern womanhood. In addition, the ways in which race and gender intersect in her novel differ significantly from what previous feminist studies often argue—that is, that Western women felt "superior in race, inferior in gender" in the colony or mission field.[89] Wagner does not always privilege the white race; indeed, she uses the guiding principle of Christian piety to subject white Westerners to harsh criticism. The novel thus employs race as a strategic tool to maximize its cautionary effect on secular modern womanhood. Wagner, a veteran missionary woman who worked in Korea for decades and gained a great deal of cultural knowledge about Korea and Asia, deploys this knowledge to ridicule, pity, and punish the transgressive white American woman, while the Korean characters are either redeemed or beyond reproach. Race is thus not the essential marker of enlightenment, civilization, or modernity—the true marker is Christianity. Wagner distinguishes Christian Americans from non-Christian Americans (Eva's family is secular), privileging the Christian faith as the essential criterion. In an interesting reversal, non-Christian Americans, embodied in Eva, become "the Other," or "these people from the West."[90]

The plot involving Eva's and Tai Jin's interracial marriage dramatizes the audaciousness of modern, "free American ways." According to Martha Banta, the influx of immigration made some members of the American public fearful about the degeneration of the pure Anglo-Saxon race by "the lost races," such as Native Americans, Jews, blacks, and Asians.[91] Out of general racism and a sense of threat to WASP heritage, the popular press and prominent authors made an effort to define an "all American girl," the "Gibson Girl" being a prime example of this public fervor about racial definition in early twentieth-century America. Against this socio-cultural background, the free-spirited Eva falls in love with Tai Jin, "the man for whom she had defied the whole world." In return, Tai Jin comes to love "this fair, young thing who had trusted him so implicitly, who had been willing to brave the wrath of friends and relatives and to face the unknown world, a strange land and a strange people, for his sake."[92] Tai Jin "was fascinated, infatuated by the blond beauty and vivacity of this girl." When Eva urges him to propose marriage (another act of boldness), Tai Jin cannot resist "this fantastic, irresistible, devastating little being."[93] To Eva, Tai Jin is a "slender young Oriental with his lacquered hair as black as a blueblack of the black bird's wing, in his gentle eyes so brown and kindly, all the romance of the ages."[94] In these fantasized images of other-ness, Eva's willingness to cross racial boundaries defines her as a modern woman who defies tradition.

Obviously, Wagner includes this interracial twist to demonstrate how far a modern woman could go against her parents' wishes and the status quo. It is important to recall in this context the pervasiveness of miscegenation laws in the United States, especially the Racial Integrity Act of 1924, which felonized marriage between white and nonwhite people.[95] Yet the same plot could be interpreted as an indirect, subversive attempt to criticize the racial prejudice prevalent in the United States. On the one hand, Wagner exudes superiority as a Christian missionary who conveys the Gospel to Koreans whose lives are filled with "superstition, ignorance, and misery."[96] On the other hand, the novel shows a great deal of cultural understanding, which Wagner gained through her career in the Korea mission. In displaying her knowledge of Korean culture, she stands in contrast to those who lack knowledge about the Other, including highly educated Americans such as Eva and her parents. Wagner adds that while the "Oriental" people are despised in the United States, they have the "pride of race and country" that comes from a four-thousand-year history.[97] Representing the Koreans' point of view, Wagner scolds those prideful Americans for their "white barbarian" and "indelicate and vulgar" behaviors toward the Orient.[98]

Wagner's sympathetic tone toward Koreans and harsh critique of non-Christian Americans do not necessarily reflect a liberal viewpoint on race, of course. Throughout the novel, Wagner sends a subtle but obvious mes-sage that the prospect for interracial union is doomed. This message meets its climax when Tai Jin's father talks about a "Eurasian" grandchild as totally unacceptable for continuing the family genealogy. Senior Pak says to Tai Jin:

> "Not only do I think of the childless wife, but about the grandson that should be here to cheer the old days of your father? Do you want a Eurasian son?" "Eurasian?" there was a slight sneer in Tai Jin's voice. "Well hardly, the very word is hateful. Poor things, they are neither one nor the other; they are as birds that fly in the sea or fish that swim in the sky, where ever they are foreign, and owned by neither the sea or the sky. I am, in truth thankful that Eva has no child; she does not care for children."[99]

Eva's European heritage ultimately disqualifies her to continue the Pak family line. In a sense, her body is deemed inappropriate for either biological or cultural reproduction. A Eurasian grandchild, in the senior Pak's mind, only symbolizes a "lost race," belonging nowhere. The disruption in family genealogy is the most important concern to the senior Pak, who symbolizes patriarchal power.[100] The modernity signaled in Tai Jin and Eva's unshackled, free-spirited, and individualistic lifestyle is shattered in the face of centuries-long tradition. Wagner does not present an alternative argument in favor of disregarding racial boundaries. Indeed, the only other option considered is that Eva remain childless. In the end, Senior Pak's point of view prevails. This triumph of parental authority and tradition over Western modernity means a reversal of fortune for Eva, who used to be a privileged "modern" woman but is now relegated to the status of concubine.

Eva's degraded status interestingly echoes the volatile experience of many Korean New Women at the time. In the first half of the twentieth century, many young Korean men from the upper class went overseas, mostly to Japan, to study but already had wives because of the custom of early marriage. While studying overseas, they often fell in love with young, attractive, and intelligent Korean women who were also studying overseas. When they returned to Korea, these highly educated Korean New Women would find that their fiancés or husbands already had a "primary legal" wife at home and thus ended up as a concubine or a secondary wife.[101] Wagner was keenly aware of this reality of the "small wife," referring to concubines,[102] and twisted the situation in her novel so that the educated young woman was not Korean but American. Eva thus could represent a new modern woman not only of the West but also of Korea. When Eva is plunged into concubinage without her knowledge, Wagner has trapped her between tradition and modernity as a dislocated woman and plotted the story in a way that eventually requires that Eva repent her wrongdoings, vanity, and audaciousness. Concubinage is a despicable lifestyle for a New Woman of either the West or Korea, and it is effectively employed here as discipline and punishment.

In this cautionary tale, Wagner tends to put women missionaries to the sideline. Yet the occasional appearance of women missionaries is used in two strategic ways. One is to challenge stereotypical images of missionary women at the time; the other is to contrast the secular modern woman with the pious modern women. The American public often ridiculed missionary women with clichéd images of spinsters wearing unstylish dress and wire-rimmed glasses, or as long-suffering wives.[103] By using the unsympathetic Eva, who echoes these stereotyped perceptions, Wagner attempts to rehabilitate the image of missionary women. She even subtly hints at the superiority of the women missionaries to the New Woman by subverting the typical understanding of the woman missionary and the modern new woman. That is, Eva, a fashionable and privileged new woman in the United States, becomes an oddity and a concubine in Korea, while the women missionaries are career women with sophisticated cultural knowledge of Korea who lead very "normal" happy lives in which they even maintain a fashionable style in their clothes and residences.[104] Wagner thus shatters the stereotypical image of the missionary woman and critiques secular modern womanhood.

Between Eva and Pobai is Tai Jin, the embodiment of tormented male subjectivity during the colonial era who is located at the intersection of competing binaries: between tradition and modernity, East and West, filial duty and pursuit of individuality, and collective nationalist aspiration and private, bourgeois sensibility. While Eva and Pobai are contrasting prototypes of the secular modern woman and the pious true woman, respectively, Tai Jin's character also offers an interesting observation about the role of highly educated male intellectuals in bringing new ideas and practices to colonial Korea. Tai Jin clearly represents a privileged class, studying overseas and inheriting significant wealth from his father. Yet upon returning to colonial Korea he began to feel powerless to advance his nation and society. One day he visits a "club" organized by "radical youngsters," supposedly a communist group, with an intention to participate in the independence movement. But soon Tai Jin hears the news that one of the "club" members has been arrested on the charge of murder, and the accused was "long sought for by the police believed to be under the direction of Russia."[105] Realizing he has barely escaped a similar charge, Tai Jin feels that "anything seemed possible. Not a hunted criminal; not a potential or actual murderer! O, thank

God for that! What joy to be free again! O, yes, he was ready for business now." Wagner describes Tai Jin's relief and a renewed sense of life as a "resurrection" and a "miracle": "Drawing a deep breath of unutterable relief he relaxed and felt the warm blood again tingle through his cold limbs. He smiled to himself at his fancy, but it seemed that this was a sort of resurrection; his old self had died, this was a new life; his life had been restored to him by a sort of miracle. If the Communist had not been arrested he very well knew that he would have paid, and paid dearly, for his rashness of the night before."[106] Saved from the harsh watch of the colonial authority, Tai Jin is more than willing to follow his father's wish to continue the family business, which he never previously had been interested in. Tai Jin is ready to accept his assumed role as the eldest son, which in turn signifies the beginning of conformity. At the personal level he also fails to persuade his parents to accept his love marriage with Eva, and gradually begins to appreciate the womanly virtue of Pobai. In the end, he chooses Pobai as his wife and becomes Christian, ending the trouble-ridden life he had led since he came back home and heralding a new Christian life with the pious and virtuous Pobai.

Wagner envisions new womanhood in the era of modernity, centering on Christian piety as its essential and universal element. The ideal new woman almost has tunnel vision for the light of Christianity, excluding and trivializing rapidly emerging secular lifestyles and the self-conscious development of modern subjectivities. However, Wagner's own position as a veteran missionary woman in Korea seems to play a significant role in creating a complex narrative in which she supports and subverts the cross-cultural and interracial issues of her time. One can argue that Wagner herself was located at the intersection of tradition and modernity, religion and secularism, East and West. In that sense, *The Concubine* is not only the manifestation of Wagner's unflinching commitment to Christian piety as the universal element for virtually everything but also a realization of emerging tensions and cleavages in traditional gender relations.

Unlike official records and promotion-oriented documents, missionary fiction afforded writers the chance to present detailed melodramatic stories that served not only to recapitulate the prevailing discourse of Christian modernity but also reflected the varied experiences and desires of missionaries. Depending on their own subject positions and the specific historical circumstances they faced, missionaries envisioned a new, transformed Korea differently. What runs through their stories is that the degraded life of women, manifested in such customs as early marriage, slavery, and the concubine system, was a sign of Korea's backwardness, and that conversion to Christianity signaled a new beginning, a "daybreak." However, while the three novels use gender as a leitmotif for the transformation of Korea, they represent newly transformed womanhood with varied emphasis on Christian religiosity, Korean nationalist sentiment, and the lure of modernity.

6. Doing It for Her Self

Sin yŏsŏng *(New Women) in Korea*

The phenomenon of New Women [*sin yŏsŏng*] in the 1920s and 1930s marks a significant milestone showing Korea's progress toward modernity that began in the late nineteenth century. The discourse on modern womanhood that had been dominated by male intellectuals began to be transformed by the first generation of educated women in the print media and urban space. It also started to reveal growing tensions between competing narratives put forward by Korean men and women intellectuals as they had more exposure to Western and Japanese modernity. In a significant way, the New Women were both the culmination of and a challenge to the Christian and nationalist drive for "civilization and enlightenment." As Theodore Jun Yoo aptly points out, the newly emerging class of educated women was a product of efforts by Enlightenment-oriented male intellectuals who regarded newly educated women "as symbols of modernity, civilization and nationalism." At the same time, these New Women began to pose unexpected threats to "the stability of the family, compromising sexual morality and denigrating national character."[1] It was this negotiation of feminist agendas that the vanguard of educated New Women struggled to cope with in their work and everyday life.

The emergence of New Women in Korea was significantly aligned with a global trend. The term *New Woman* was first introduced by Sarah Grand in the *North American Review* in 1894 and was effectively employed by English and American women who struggled "against the constraints of Victorian norms of femininity" in their pursuit of an alternative life.[2] Refusing to have their proper place defined by men, the newly emerging group of women began to agitate against centuries-old gender norms and engage in new cultural production and political activities. In this vein, Rita Felski argues that the New Woman became a "powerful symbol of modernity, change, and the future."[3] Commonly identified "with the modern and the disruptive, that is with challenges to existing structures of gendered identity,"[4] New Women were intimately linked with capitalist consumer economy and a changing political climate, generating dynamic gender politics in a wide range of issues including citizenship, education, work, fashion, leisure, the body, and sexuality.[5] By the 1910s, the concept of the New Woman had been translated into various Asian languages (*sin yŏsŏng* in Korean, *xin nüxing* in Chinese, *atarashii onna* in Japanese) and had sparked a new women's movement in East Asia by addressing the unique female constraints imposed by Confucian gender norms.

While it was a global phenomenon, the New Woman was also inexorably tied to the specific historical and cultural elements of each distinct society it emerged in. In particular, the ways in which the forces of (semi)colonialism, nationalism, and modernity framed and appropriated the woman question shed light on local variations of the experience of the New Women that went beyond the mere importation of Western-originated ideas of New Women.[6] The New Women's movement in Korea was inevitably shaped by its unique historical circumstances of Japanese colonial rule, anticolonial movements, and a growing desire for the new and the modern. Within this broader political and cultural context, various factors contributed to the emergence and development of New Women in Korea, including the increased population of educated women,[7] the shift of the Japanese colonial policy toward "Cultural Rule" after the 1919 March First Independence Movement, the gradual industrialization and urbanization of the Korean economy, the explosion in the number of social and cultural organizations, and the proliferation of vernacular presses and publications.[8] More notably, the intellectual influence of Western and Japanese women's movements on Korean women was an indispensable factor in the emergence of the New Women in Korea. In the 1920s and 1930s, translations of a number of foreign writers who put forward new feminine ideals became available, including Harriet Beecher Stowe, Henrik Ibsen, Ellen Key, Alexandra Kollontai, Guy de Maupassant, and Leo Tolstoy.[9] Nora, the protagonist in Henrik Ibsen's *A Doll's House* became an especially potent symbol for New Women in East Asia.[10]

There are a variety of definitions of New Women in Korean scholarship.[11] However, the popularized image of New Women in 1920s and 1930s print media was often associated with the image of "girl students" and a small group of elite women in urban spaces.[12] They attracted the admiration of the public, especially those who studied overseas and had accomplished something unprecedented in the fields of art, literature, education, or journalism. Simultaneously, they also drew relentless criticism for challenging Confucian gender norms, advocating gender equality, rejecting the sacred nature of motherhood, engaging in scandalous love affairs, and indulging themselves in the worldly pleasures of shopping, reading romance stories, watching "motion pictures of crude Americanism,"[13] and wearing Western-style clothing, high heels, and bobbed hairstyles. A growing number of readers and writers propelled the ever-more sensationalized image of the New Woman. A few prominent examples of the New Women became minor celebrities, famous for simply being themselves.[14] They were often in the spotlight, and their private lives were constantly scrutinized, particularly in the event of divorce or love affairs. A mix of praise and harsh moral judgment filled the pages of the print media. As Barbara Sato points out in her analysis of a similar social situation in interwar Japan, the popularized and sensationalized image of the New Women was not based on the actual life of "real women" but the "possibilities for what all women could become."[15] In this sense, the image of the New Women reveals "the temper of an age symbolized by changing women's identities" in the making.[16] The New Women in Korea shared this symbolic power, offering exhilarating hopes and possibilities for the new era. At the same time, they also invited deep anxiety and uncertainty about the new order of gender relations, especially among male intellectuals.[17]

What is unique about Korean New Women vis-à-vis those in other cultures is that they had a significant connection with Protestant Christianity. As the New Woman Hwang Sin-dŏk observed in 1931, the sheer majority of New Women had exposure to Christianity through mission schools and churches.[18] Many of them came from Christian families and were baptized as children. Christian spirituality was one of the bonding solidarities among students studying overseas.[19] Some married in Christian-style weddings and were professionally involved in national and international Christian organizations, most prominently represented by the Korean Young Women's Christian Association (YWCA), founded in 1922.[20] Just as the early Enlightenment-oriented male intellectuals were deeply influenced by Christian civilization, so was the first-generation of New Women in Korea. To these women, Christianity was more than a new religion. It offered them a wide range of novel experiences through church attendance, rituals, music, sports, and group activities, which served as a platform for understanding the world beyond domestic routines and developing their identities as individuals.

However, the responses of New Women to Christianity were by no means uniform. Quite the contrary, the ways in which these women incorporated Christian religion into their public and private lives demonstate the variety of their religious encounters with Christianity. Ranging from a lifetime commitment to Christian spirituality to outright rejection, the choice of New Women for or against Christianity reveals their individual strategies in carving out their public and private spaces. The tensions they felt between their religious and secular interests and between collective (read: nationalistic) and individual desires resulted in remarkably diverse life paths. In this chapter, I focus on some examples of New Women whose public discourse and private lives shed light on the complex relationships they had with Christianity, Japanese colonialism, Korean nationalism, and secular modernity. Analyzing several key debates on modern womanhood, I pay special attention to the points of connection and disconnection between missionary and nationalist mandates and Korean women's own understanding of the modern.

CHRISTIAN MODERN AND NEW WOMEN

A number of mission publications regularly cited examples of the new ideal for "Oriental" women who had been transformed by Christianity. In particular, those who were sponsored by missionary teachers to study overseas drew a great deal of attention because they would potentially become leaders in the woman's world upon returning to Korea.[21] For example, Esther Pak, who became the first woman doctor trained in Western medicine in the United States, was proudly presented by her mentor, Rosetta Sherwood Hall, as an example of "one new life in the Orient."[22] Pak's transformed life and her devotion to healing the bodies and minds of Korean women exemplified the ideal outcome of women's missionary work. Kim Maria and Kim P'il-lye, both of whom studied in Japan and the United States, were hailed as ideal Christian women who represented the future of Korean womanhood.[23] Just as converting women to Christianity was crucial for the proliferation of Christian communities because "no nation can become Christian without Christian mothers," so fostering Christian women to become future leaders was imperative to ensure that present and future Christian women were under good guidance. The Korea mission produced a good number of Christian women leaders who left a significant footprint through their work at mission schools and a variety of small and large scale Christian institutions. Most of these organizations primarily aimed at the spiritual growth of their members and the instruction of a Christian lifestyle. However, they were also deeply engaged in social "enlightenment" activities, largely through offering literacy training to children and women in rural communities.[24] These diverse Christian groups and organizations were an important platform for New Women to learn leadership skills, strengthen solidarity, and reach out to other women in all walks of life.

"Grace Sufficient": Kim Hwal-lan

If Ewha Girls' School signaled the beginning of new womanhood in the late nineteenth century, the establishment of the Korean YWCA in 1922 manifested a certain maturity in Chrsitian womanhood that provided women with greater opportunities to get involved in educational, social, and economic issues. Kim Hwal-lan (1899–1970), who represented both Ewha and the YWCA through her leadership of both of these institutions, symbolized ideal Christian womanhood and exemplified the most desired outcome of Christian education in Korea. Kim is no doubt one of the most influential women leaders in twentieth-century Korea, especially in the area of women's education, but she is arguably the most controversial woman intellectual because of her collaboration with the Japanese colonial power during the Second World War.

Born in Inch'ŏn in 1899, Kim attended a primary school, Yŏnghwa, which had been founded by a Methodist missionary, Margaret Bengal Jones, in 1892.[25] When her family moved to Seoul in 1907, she entered Ewha, where her two older sisters were already in attendance. She was admitted on scholarship by Lulu Frey, the school's principal. After she finished high school in 1913, she wanted to pursue college education, but her father objected strongly, mainly because she was already "of marriageable age and going to school for five more years was unthinkable" to him.[26] However, with a "determination to prepare my self through education to serve my people and my nation" and with the support of her mother and missionary teachers such as Jeannette Walter and Alice Appenzeller, she pursued a college education at Ewha and went on to study overseas. She received a BA in1924 from Ohio Wesleyan University, an MA in 1925 from Boston University, and the PhD in 1931 from Columbia University.[27] In 1939, she became the first Korean president of Ewha (see figure 13). Given this background, it is impossible to separate the history of Ewha from that of Kim Hwal-lan. She was fostered by American missionaries throughout her education and career, culminating in her position at Ewha. Furthermore, since Ewha was one of the two institutions that offered college education to women until Korea's independence in 1945, Ewha and Kim together symbolized modern education for women.[28]

Kim Hwal-lan also left a significant mark on the Korean YWCA, the first Christian women's organization with nationwide networks crisscrossing different denominations and that engaged not only in religious activities but also in secular social and political movements, such as the women's movement, the rural community movement, and the nationalist movement. Kim was one of the founding members of the Korean YWCA, along with Kim P'il-lye and Yu Kak-kyŏng.[29] In 1922, Alice Appenzeller introduced her to Kim P'il-lye, who had been interested in organizing a Korean branch of the YWCA since she had first been exposed to the organization during her study in Japan in 1908.[30] Kim Hwal-lan accompanied Kim P'il-lye to Peking (Beijing) to attend the Student Christian Federation Conference to explore the establishment of a Korean affiliate of the World YWCA.[31] Korea's status as a Japanese colony complicated such an affiliation, but they were able to get support from their Japanese counterpart, which agreed to allow Korea to stand as an independent member.[32] Kim followed up on this preliminary success at Peking when she attended the World Committee Meeting of the YWCA in Washington, D.C., to request formal affiliation. She described the difficulties in convincing the YWCA to hear and accept her arguments for the establishment of a Korean branch of the YWCA, because "through all YWCA history, in no other country had the women of the land taken the entire initiative and responsibility for the beginning of their organization." Despite the lack of any precedent, she was able to gain a "pioneer membership" awarded to the Korean YWCA,[33] and its pioneer membership changed to the regular full membership in 1930.[34] Kim Hwal-lan served as the president of the Korean YWCA intermittently from the mid-1920s to the late 1930s.[35] As Ch'ŏn Hwa-suk rightly points out in her study of the Korean YWCA, the establishment and development of that organization cannot be reduced to the role of a few prominent leaders. Rather, it represents the growing modern consciousness among Christian women and the ever-expanding grassroots organizations centering on mission schools and local churches. Nonetheless, as Ch'ŏn also notes, its leadership was dominated by a few women, including Kim Hwal-lan, Kim P'il-lye, and Yu Kak-kyŏng, and these leaders came from either Ewha or Chŏngsin—the flagship girls' schools run by the Methodist and Presbyterian churches, respectively.[36] In this vein, Kim Hwal-lan's long-term leadership in the YWCA marks a key linkage between mission education and other Christian activities, between the local and the national, and between Korea and the world Christian community of women. Kim was exceptionally prepared to play this leadership role through her education at Ewha and her exposure to the world as a student at American institutions of higher education and participant in missionary meetings worldwide. In her autobiography, *Grace Sufficient*, Kim Hwal-lan remembered the powerful inspiration she drew from fellow

Christians she met at international mission conferences. She detailed the experience when she first attended the Executive Committee Meeting of the Woman's Foreign Missionary Society of the Methodist Episcopal Church in 1923. She recalled how inspirational it was to see "hundreds of church-women come together to pray and work for their common objectives and responsibilities concerning missions in all parts of the world." The poised leadership of the president of the committee strongly impressed young Kim, and she took the president as a constant source of inspiration.[37]

Throughout her career, Christian spirituality was the backbone that provided her with support. When American missionaries were forced to leave Korea by the Japanese in 1940, Kim recalled that she felt overwhelmed with a "sense of loneliness and helplessness." She had to face not only financial problems without the subsidies from the missions but also increasing Japanese oppression. However, she said, she was "fully aware of the presence of Almighty God everywhere, ready to help, comfort, sustain, and continue to bless Ewha and all these who remained with her . . . During those difficult days courage and fortitude, wisdom and guidance were needed daily and hourly from above. We had all these blessings commensurable to our needs."[38] Under increasing pressure to collaborate with Japan during the Second World War, Kim Hwal-lan offered her services to the colonial power in the form of public speeches to mobilize men and women for the war effort and actively engaged in pro-Japanese organizations.[39] Along with other prominent women, such as Pahk Induk [Pak In-dŏk], Mo Yun-suk, and Ko Hwang-gyŏng, Kim Hwal-lan propagated the slogan *naesŏn ilch'e* (Japan and Korea are One Entity), a Japanese propaganda effort designed to eradicate Korean national identity.[40] When her critics accused her of collaboration with the Japanese colonial power in the 1930s and 1940s, she justified her action as being necessary in order to keep Ewha open under the harsh colonial policies. Her collaboration with the Japanese was in keeping with the Methodist Church's general policy of minimizing conflict with the colonial authorities. The Methodist mission had gone so far as to conform to the policy of *sinsa ch'ambae* (Homage to Shinto Shrines), taking it not as a religious act but a ritual imposed by the state.[41] She further argued that even her public speeches supporting the Pacific War and the colonial government carried "unspoken words" that were understood by her students,[42] and her sole purpose in collaborating with the colonial power was to protect Ewha.[43] Whether her actions were an exigency to keep the school open or were the result of her own personal ambition, her collaboration stood out prominently due to her stature as a pioneer in women's education, the first PhD holder, the first Korean president of Ewha, and a leader of the Korean YWCA.

As one of the officially designated "Japanese collaborators," Kim Hwal-lan is arguably the most controversial woman intellectual in twentieth-century Korea. Opinions about her legacy differ vastly depending on the political standpoints of the commentators. A huge controversy arose in 1998 when Ewha Womans University announced its plan to mark the 100th anniversary of Kim Hwal-lan's birth by establishing the "Uwŏl Kim Hwal-lan Award,"[44] to be given to an exemplary woman or women's organization.[45] Public sentiment was overwhelmingly negative. Even Ewha students protested the award, criticizing Kim's pro-Japanese speeches and activities that urged Korean men and women to volunteer to join the Pacific War to become true *hwangguk sinmin* (imperial subjects of Japan). However, the Korean feminist Kwŏn In-suk has argued that one needs to keep in mind the complex politics of memory and historiography when it comes to the place of women in national history. Kwŏn observes that there has been "disproportionate public attention" to Kim Hwal-lan and a few other women "collaborators" (6 in total) in comparison with male collaborators (708 in total), suggesting that such an imbalance in the treatment reveals "the gendered patriarchal character of current Korean nationalist discourse" and leaves "the simplified impression that renowned women intellectuals in the decades ranging from the 1920s through the 1940s were collaborators."[46] To be sure, the rare presence of women intellectuals in the colonial era makes them easy, fast, and frequent targets of criticism. But by the same token there have also been a few women intellectuals, such as Kim Maria, who have emerged as heroic figures for their anti-Japanese activities. This binary framework in which individuals are either collaborators or freedom fighters completely ignores the inherent complexity in the lives of individual historical subjects. The lives of women, especially prominent ones, have been conveniently deployed either to praise their sacrifice for the nation or to demonize their self-ambition. The prevailing evaluation of Kim Hwal-lan reflects this dichotomous approach and reminds us of the ongoing tensions between nationalist and feminist agendas.

While the debate over Kim Hwal-lan's legacy needs to be further developed, there is a clue that Kim's collaboration might stem from her persistent interest in the advancement of women's issues. When she attended the 1928 meeting of the International Missionary Council in Jerusalem as a Korean delegate, she gave a speech that reconfirmed the critical role of Christainity in helping Korean women to find their intrinsic value regardless of gender, class, or age. She further saw the discovery of the self endowed with equality by God as a platform for critiquing the male-dominant church organizations:

When Christ taught the way of life to the Samaritan woman at the well, He withheld no privileges and made no conditions as to her right to bear witness to Him. The same was true of His attitude to men and women of all classes. But His life and teachings seemed to have been misrepresented since, perhaps unconsciously and in some cases with good intentions, and we find today certain conditions even in churches under Christ's name that make the vision of Christ a little blurred to the less discerning eyes of youth. For example, while Christ has never forbidden any to bear witness for Him, in some churches of to-day women are not allowed to preach in pulpits, not because they are lacking in ability or in zeal, but just because they are women. I think Christ would pity us women, if we still are timid and hesitate about bearing witness to Him in all the walks of life, not only in domestic life, but also in the industrial, commercial, political and international life of humanity. I think He would say to us, "Women, have not I freed you? Why are you still so timid? Go forth courageously with my message into all the phrases of human life. They need you there, and there you have a distinct contribution to make at this stage of human society."[47]

Here Kim expressed a vision for Korean women that went beyond the private and embraced a public arena. Her expanded view of women's ideal sphere was further crystallized by the impact of the Pacific War on Korean women. Like many intellectuals at the time, Kim publicly described the war as a "sacred war" led by "righteous Japan" in order to "rescue the Asian people from the invasion of the Anglo-Saxon race." Focusing on new opportunities, she urged women to devote themselves fully to the war effort, which she believed would bestow upon them the "privilege and glory of imperial subjects."[48] Although the situations differed greatly, there was an important parallel between Kim's public justification of the war and the participation in the war effort by Japanese women's groups. That is, collaborating with the (colonial) state was understood as a way to broaden the scope of women's work and influence. Sheldon Garon argues that many Japanese women activists used the war "as an opportunity to elevate the position of Japanese women within the state" and the state recognized "their value in promoting economic development, social stability, and wartime mobilization." Furthermore, Japanese women's groups that "embraced the modern state's ideology of separate spheres for men and women (the 'good wife and wise mother')" were more successful in advancing their agendas than those feminist women who challenged the state and demanded political rights.[49] In this vein, while Kim's advocacy is typically understood as the work of a colonial puppet, it can also be understood as a historical intervention, one that privileged the expansion of women's spheres of influence while downplaying Korean national identity. Better yet, her speeches and actions in support of Japan could be understood as falling in the interstices between outright collaboration and feminist advocacy. Kim Hwal-lan's life and work reflect the volatile public history of Korean women in the face of continuing patriarchal gender norms, an increasingly oppressive Japanese colonial authority, and demands for allegiance to the Korean nation. The prevailing interpretation of her life has been highly nationalistic in its orientation. However, a more nuanced approach is needed that pays attention to the full complexity and ambiguity embedded in her political, cultural, and individual choices.

The case of Kim Hwal-lan adds one more dimension to this ongoing debate: the role of religion, specifically Christianity. Kim was perhaps the best-known protégé of American missionary teachers at Ewha, who had groomed her to become a leading woman educator. She received advanced degrees from American universities with missionary sponsorship, pioneered in founding Christian women's organizations, and represented Korean womanhood on the world Christian stage. In a significant way, she acquired intimate knowledge of the inner workings of the big organizations through a close working relationship with missionaries and national leaders. She learned a great deal from her Methodist missionary colleagues about how to deal with the precarious relationship between religion and politics. To protect churches and evangelical work, missionaries took pains to comply with the policy of worship at Japanese Shinto shrines. In a similar fashion, in order to protect Ewha she bowed to pressure from the Japanese colonial authorities to mobilize Korean men and women for the war. To her, protecting Ewha might have meant more than simply preserving a women's college. Ewha was a critical platform for the expansion of the scope of women's lives and work, and Christianity was a major enabling agent in it. As Kwok Pui-Lan argues in the case of Chinese women, "Christianity offered women new symbolic resources with which to look at the world and themselves, helping them to affirm their sense of worth and dignity."[50] Similarly, Kim understood that Christianity inspired women to find their own intrinsic value and individual dignity that had been ignored. Thus, her primary mandate was to proliferate Christian education for women as a way to ensure the advancement of women's status and rights. One may argue that Kim Hwal-lan's complete devotion to and trust in God was part of her strategy for both coping with the turbulent political situation and bringing a new womanhood to realization within that context. Given the historical and symbolic statue of Ewha and the impact of Christianity in the history of women, Kim's vision and her critical choices for Christian

education for women in these most trying times reveal the profound tensions between the expected role of women in nationhood and the presumed
role of nationhood in the advancement of womanhood.

"Korea's Joan of Arc": Kim Maria

In ways different from Kim Hwal-lan, the life of Kim Maria (1892–1944),
another prominent Christian woman leader, sheds light on how Christianity, nationalism, and feminism intersected. Although Christianity was
central to both women's lives, they differed significantly in their visions
for Korean women and for the nation. Whereas Kim Hwal-lan has been
singled out as an imperialist collaborator, Kim Maria has been hailed as a
patriotic independence fighter. While Kim Hwal-lan gave highest priority
to women's education and spiritual devotion, Kim Maria regarded Korean
national independence as the ultimate goal. In her article on women's
education published in the magazine *Yŏjagye*, Kim Maria wrote that the
"characteristic of modern civilization is said to be 'liberation.' Political liberation, occupational liberation, abolition of slavery, academic freedom and
liberation of women; these are the spirit of the civilization today. Human
beings are not human beings just because they are born as human beings.
They become human beings only after they develop the full capacity of
their body and mind. We need to teach Korean women so that they are
appropriate and useful to Korean society and can devote themselves to
Korea."[51] The "liberation" she emphasized was both national and individual, and her life illustrates her attempt to weave the two together. For her
devotion to national liberation, she was called "Korea's Joan of Arc" among
Korean students studying in the United States,[52] and a popular magazine,
Samch'ŏlli, referred to her as an "immortal sovereign of the stars."[53]

Kim Maria was born in Sorae. Her family included pioneering Christian
leaders. One of her aunts was Kim P'il-lye, mentioned earlier as one of
the founders of the Korean YWCA, and some other relatives were actively
engaged in independence movements. Her family also had close ties with
Canadian and American missionaries such as William McKenzie, Horace
Underwood, and Oliver Avison, as well as Christian Korean leaders such
as An Ch'ang-ho and Kim Kyu-sik. Like her aunt and sister, she attended
Chŏngsin Girls' School (Presbyterian) and later taught there. While teaching at Chŏngsin, Kim was encouraged by the principal of Chŏngsin, Margo
Lewis, to continue her education in Japan. Lewis, who came to Korea in
1910 and served the Presbyterian mission until 1940, became a strong
advocate for Kim Maria financially and morally throughout her life. Both
remained unmarried for life, devoting themselves completely to their

respective passions: the mission for Margo Lewis, and national independence and Christian education for Kim Maria. Despite their close relationship and mutual respect, they sometimes experienced tension especially around political matters. For example, when a rumor spread in early 1919 that King Kojong was poisoned by the Japanese, students at Chŏngsin put black ribbons in their hair as an expression of anger and despair. The missionary teachers were afraid of retaliation from the Japanese authorities and tried to ban the black ribbons. Those students who defied the school policy were ordered on probation. Outraged students went on strike—the first strike in the history of Chŏngsin. Lewis sought help from Kim, who was in Japan studying at Tokyo Women's College at the time. At Lewis's urging, Kim returned to Korea. But Kim disagreed with Lewis on the school policy, and upon her return she threw herself into organizing anti-Japanese women's organizations together with Na Hye-sŏk, Pahk Induk, Hwang Esther, and others. These leaders were arrested for their role in organizing the anti-Japanese demonstrations around the March First Movement in 1919. Kim Maria was released from prison in July 1919, and when she returned to Chŏngsin, the vice principal, Lillian Dean, invited her to stay at her house. Soon the house became a key site for the independence movement.[54] Kim was arrested again in November for independence-related activities, along with other key members of the Taehanminguk aeguk puinhoe (Korean Association of Patriotic Women). Kim was severely tortured, her body and mind devastated.[55] In May 1920 she was released from prison in order to receive medical treatment. While undergoing treatment she began to contemplate exile for good. She eventually managed to escape, going to Shanghai in disguise in June 1921. However, she soon discovered the factional strife within the Korean Provisional Government located in Shanghai.[56] Disappointed, she went to the United States in 1923 and enrolled at Park University in 1924 with a recommendation from George Shannon McCune, who wrote that she was the most ideal Christian among her fellow Koreans and that no one was better known.[57] After graduating from Park, Kim went to the University of Chicago and Teachers College, Columbia University, for advanced degrees. There were only a small number of Korean women studying in the United States at the time, and in 1928 Kim founded another women's group, Kŭnhwahoe (Association of Sharon Rose), to promote patriotism and solidarity among Korean students.[58]

When Kim finally returned to Korea in 1932, the Korean media welcomed her with high praise for her patriotism, courage, and determination. Yi Kwang-su, a prominent writer and intellectual, wrote a poem in her honor in which he encouraged her to devote her youth, love, and life to the future of Korea.[59] Kim was still under intensive surveillance by the Japanese police, so her public activities were greatly constrained. She was appointed as a professor at Marta Wilson Women's Theological Seminary, founded by a Canadian woman missionary, Louise H. McCully. She devoted her time to training future women leaders in Chrsitian communities as well as engaging in the revitalization of rural communities. She also became vocal about gender discrimination within the Christian community, citing and reinterpreting the Bible.[60] And she remained uncompromising around the policy of Homage to Shinto Shrines. Her resistance ultimately affected Martha Wilson Theological Seminary, which was forced to close in 1943. After its closure, Kim Maria had a stroke from which she never recovered. She died in 1944, one year before Korea's liberation from Japan.

"Korea's Nora Has Left a Doll's House": Pahk Induk

The life of Pahk Induk (1896–1980) succinctly captures the turbulent transition from old to new womanhood in Korea, and the tensions between Christian ethics and secular modern desires. Born in Chinnamp'o and educated at mission schools through college, Pahk was one of the most prized students among missionary teachers. She had an exceptional reputation during her days at Ewha, known for being "well-spoken, fluent in English, talented in music, and exceptionally beautiful."[61] She was particularly good at public speaking, which eventually led to contracts for numerous speaking engagements in Christian missions overseas. Her academic excellence, exceptional speaking skills, and religious devotion prompted Alice Appenzeller, the principal of Ewha (1922–39), to consider sending Pahk to the General Conference of Methodist Churches in America as a representative for the Methodist mission in Korea. It was eventually decided that Pahk was too young to be a delegate, but Appenzeller thought that Pahk should go to the United States as a student. A month later, Appenzeller informed Pahk that she had been granted a full scholarship to Ohio Wesleyan University. This exceptional opportunity arose while Pahk was being pursued by a wealthy Korean man, Kim Un-ho. Pahk wrote that her "emotions were stirred" for the first time in her life. Throughout her school life, she had looked up to her missionary teachers as her models. Her teachers had been, for the most part, unmarried professional women who had given full dedication to their mission, so she had rarely given much thought to marriage. Indeed, "the right of a girl to remain unmarried" was being gradually recognized at the time, and the Christian educator Ch'oe P'il-lye even called it "the greatest freedom of all."[62] Further, Pahk "loathed the Confucian scheme of using girls primarily as instruments for continuing the family." However, the attraction she felt for Kim Un-ho was "beyond her analytical thinking," and she found herself hopelessly drawn to him. The problem was that he was a divorced man. She recalled, "although it was legally right to marry this man whom I loved, the Church was greatly opposed to marriage to a divorced person and almost if not completely ostracized members who so married."[63] Torn between her feelings for Kim and her loyalty to the Church, she ultimately chose to accept his marriage proposal and turned down the scholarship. Her decision greatly disappointed many people. Alice Appenzeller, in particular, "was heartbroken with disappointment" at her decision and said to her, "Induk, you are very unwise; you don't know what you are doing. This emotion will pass. Go to America and study for a couple of years and then if you still want to marry this man on your return, how beautiful your marriage will be."[64] Despite all the opposition from her loved ones, Pahk married Kim. She recalled that her "quiet wedding," which took place with only a few close friends present, "seemed more like a funeral."[65]

A rude awakening hit her shortly after her marriage, which came to be filled with betrayal, deception, and poverty as her husband squandered his wealth. While working as a teacher at Paehwa Girls' School, she confided with Mrs. Anna Chaffin, principal of the Women's Bible School, that she wanted to pursue further study in the United States and asked Chaffin if she could help her find a scholarship. To her great disappointment, Chaffin discouraged her plan, reminding her that her two children would be a great handicap. However, Pahk's missionary colleague Rubie Lee at Paehwa volunteered to look for possible scholarships for her and eventually secured one for her to study at Wesleyan College in Macon, Georgia. Pahk saw this new chance to study in the United States as "a springboard upon which I would catapult into new life."[66] Indeed, it turned out to be exactly that. She began her study in the United States as a junior in 1926, taking courses in the Bible, philosophy, psychology, English literature, sociology, music, and physical education. She further developed her talent for public speaking through increasingly frequent invitations to give talks. One of the most important speaking opportunities came when she attended the Quadrennial Convention of the Student Volunteer Movement for Foreign Missions in Detroit from December 28, 1927, to January 1, 1928. She was invited by the organization's general secretary to speak for fifteen minutes on the topic, "What Jesus Christ Has Meant to Me." In the speech, she told the audience that "[a]ccording to my thinking, of all the discoveries made in the latter part of the nineteenth century, the discovery of womanhood in Korea, as representative of all Asia, was the greatest of all. This discovery was due to Christianity by means of which my mother had been privileged to embark on a new way of life and through her I in turn benefited."[67]

The enthusiastic reception for her speech resulted in innumerable requests that Pahk be given the opportunity to travel and speak to college students. The Student Volunteer Movement Organization subsequently appointed her as a traveling secretary for the organization during the year 1928–29. She became "the only secretary of foreign birth at that time and also the first Oriental secretary."[68] She traveled widely, speaking at more than three hundred colleges. In 1929, she was also invited to speak at the sixtieth anniversary convention of the Women's Foreign Missionary Society of the Methodist Church in Columbus, Ohio. Most of her American teachers at Ewha belonged to the WFMS, and she had fully understood the significance of that organization in the work of women missionaries. She had come full circle, from a child educated by American women missionaries to a traveling secretary speaking to the members of WFMS. She expressed her gratitude to her missionary teachers, saying "Had it not been for these women, where would I be today?"[69] By the time she completed her appointment as traveling secretary, she also acquired an MA from Columbia University. On her way back to Korea, she decided to travel in Europe, where she was given opportunities to speak to students. Starting out in London, she eventually traveled to Belgium, Denmark, Germany, Austria, Italy, Turkey, Soviet Union, Beirut, Jerusalem, Egypt, India, Singapore, Hong Kong, and China. Pahk originally intended to stay in the United States only for two years to pursue her BA, but various opportunities made her postpone her return to Korea. In the end, the almost six years that she spent studying and traveling provided her with unique and unusual opportunities to see the world and people from all walks of life. She felt that "probably I was the first Korean woman in history to have a chance to know intellectual America as widely and intimately as had been my opportunity, and surely few Korean women had ever had an opportunity to encompass the globe with so many thoughtful friends in every country to interpret contemporary life. What could I now do with my understanding?"

Pahk was elated by the dream of contributing to women's development in Korea. When she returned to Korea, in an interview with *Sin yŏsŏng* she told the reporter that "above all, my plan is to become a friend to ten million women." Described as cheerful, kind, and fashionable like an "American lady," she also expressed her views on the status of women in other countries. She noted that she was most deeply impressed by Indian women, who were "gentle, contemplative, and good at organization," by German women who were "the strongest," and by American and English women who excelled in their social roles. Most of all, she was convinced that "If we want to work, we should establish good relationships with American women because that's the way we can accomplish things quickly . . . I think American women are the most progressive and advanced. The next group is Chinese women, who are intelligent and cautious."[70] With her overseas degrees, multiple talents, and prominent social profile, Pahk was positioned and expected to make a significant impact on the women's world as well as the Christian community.

While energized by the dream to contribute to society, she was agonized by the precarious state of her marriage. Her husband was irresponsible and was rumored to have taken a concubine while she was studying in the United States. Ultimately, she decided to end the turbulent marriage. She recalled that she knew very well that the Christian teachers and fellows would not approve of her divorce and she "would have no influence in educated circles; no prestige; indeed, probably no entrée. I would even seem to reflect discredit upon America."[71] Nonetheless, she saw contradictions between what she called "the Christian way of life" and her husband's life of infidelity, irresponsibility, and abuse of power. She said, "unless ills were cured they would go on hurting. I would rather have an arm amputated and live than to die because it was diseased . . . Being bound by age-old concepts and traditions was the worst burden of all. I had learned that the most precious thing in the world is freedom to do what one believes is right and now I must choose between the Korean custom of remaining with my husband 'no matter what,' or starting out on an independent way of life."[72] In the end, she asked for the divorce, "becoming the first woman to divorce her husband for infidelity under new laws introduced by the colonial authorities."[73]

As she expected, harsh criticism followed, both in private and in public. The divorce became a public scandal and even might have triggered public concern about the ever-increasing divorce rate. According to a report in 1931, Seoul recorded the highest number of divorces compared to cities such as Tokyo, Osaka, P'yŏngyang, and Taegu.[74] Pahk's case provided her critics with the opportunity to challenge the women's movement and in so doing to reinforce certain patriarchal gender roles. One article published in *Sin yŏsŏng* began by acknowledging Pahk's influential role in Korean society in order then to chide her for her divorce, which the author viewed as selfish and a reflection of her misunderstanding of feminism. To this author, Pahk should not have gone against Korean custom; should not leave simply because a husband is sick, poor, or jobless; should have considered her most sacred maternal duty to her two daughters; and should have been willing to support her family if she truly were a pioneer in the women's rights movement. The article further scolded Pahk for vanity and hypocrisy in claiming that the divorce was a form of sacrifice for the younger generation of women by setting a model for the future.[75]

Another article, which appeared two years after her divorce, offers a more sympathetic view. The title of the article was "Pahk Induk, Korea's Nora, Has Left a Doll's House."[76] Noting the worldwide impact of the iconic figure of Nora in Henrik Ibsen's play *A Doll's House*, the article lays out competing views on Nora's choice to leave her family in order to find herself as a human being. Although there are people who accuse Nora of "heartlessness" in giving up her children for the sake of her own freedom and independence, the article looks for a deeper, more sympathetic understanding of her choice. Pahk, as a Korean Nora, is portrayed as the New Woman who had to "escape the oppression of her husband in order to become a human being before she could really fill her role as wife and mother."[77] The impact of Ibsen's Nora was immeasurable on the newly emerging class of women in East Asia. The story was translated, widely distributed, and performed in theaters.[78] Leading feminists admired Nora's awakening from patriarchal bondage and her courage to lead an independent life as her own individual. Nora was indeed "an ideal of new power and a symbol of revolution" to Korean new women.[79] Pahk's divorce thus could embody Nora's search for new selfhood in the face of the centuries-old notions of *namjon yŏbi* (men honored, women despised) and *yŏp'il chongbu* (women ought to follow men). However, she also had to face numerous accusations that her decision was egoistic, callous, and even immoral.

The largely callous response of both the media and her close associates, including family members, led Pahk to withdraw from public view for a while. She landed a few small jobs related to church work and expanded her work to focus on education for women and children in rural communities through a peripatetic school. Her interest in rural education began when she visited Denmark on her way back to Korea in 1931 and was impressed by the power of rural development. And by the early 1930s, the revitalization of rural communities had become a central project in the educated classes as part of their efforts in social, economic, and cultural reform.[80] Students from mission schools often opened Bible classes in their own communities,[81] and night schools for the rural population became common. In an article in *The Korea Mission Field*, Pahk described her motivation for starting such a school:

> Having grown up in the country I know somewhat the life of a farmer's wife. She exists within the four walls of poverty, ignorance,

disease and superstition. Above these is the roof of oppression by her husband. She toils under these circumstances all through her life from birth to death. It seems that it is her destiny, for there is no way of getting out of it. Many of our grandmothers went through such a life, and many women of to-day are going through practically the same routine . . . Because of my own experience in a country village in childhood I have been thinking very seriously how I could help our women to a better way than what they have, and ever since I had the knowledge of Jesus I was more anxious to teach them the way, the truth, and the life of Jesus.[82]

Echoing her American missionary teachers in their deploration of the misery and oppression of Korean women, Pahk pitied rural women and showed her intention to carry out what her missionary teachers had initiated years ago. She laid out the goals of her peripatetic school: (1) to inculcate the living spirit of Jesus, (2) to advance culture, (3) to disseminate knowledge, (4) to encourage the formation of cooperative societies, and (5) to give guidance in cottage industries. To that end, she offered instruction on Christianity and other subjects, including "hygiene and sanitation, baby care, emergency needs, raising chickens, pigs, cows, rabbits, and silkworms, budgeting, dyeing, sewing etc. We teach them to read and write. Only ten out of every hundred women can read in these villages. Not only are these subjects eagerly studied but the women love to learn to sing and to play games."[83]

In 1935 Pahk was invited to speak at the Quadrennial Convention of the Student Volunteer Movement in Indianapolis and also at the Chain of Missionary Assemblies in Florida. These invitations meant a welcome opportunity to renew herself away from her now "miserable, lonely and disappointing" life after her divorce.[84] In addition, unlike her earlier trip to the U.S. as a student, this time she felt she was "a kind of missionary to America," sharing the stories of Korea and asking for the "brotherhood of mankind." From December 1935 to September 1937 she made 642 speeches and covered 80,000 miles.[85] She was very successful in raising funds for her rural development projects, especially for the purchase of livestock to help farmers. Those cows purchased were often named after donors. For example, "Betsy Moo" was named after Betsy (Mrs. Dwight L.) Moody with funds raised in Northfield, Massachusetts, and "Ox-Ford" was named to recognize the contributions by the Kappa Phi women of Miami University in Oxford, Ohio. Other donations eventually were used to start the Training Center for Rural Leaders in Korea.[86]

When she came back to Korea in September 1937, the Sino-Japanese

War had already broken out and Japan's war efforts were on a rapid rise. Pahk established the Tŏkhwa yŏsuk (Tŏkhwa Institute) in 1941, which was designed to offer female graduates from high schools a year-long intensive course in homemaking. It quickly gained a reputation for producing graduates who were "particularly good wives and daughters-in-law."[87] While her school seemed apolitical and with a decided focus on women's domestic education, Pahk's pro-Japanese activities began more explicitly in her capacity as Tŏkhwa's principal. Her school for future wives and mothers became a site for the fervent mobilization of women as Japan got deeper into the Pacific War. Pahk was in full support of the military training for female students because she believed that such training would promote cooperative spirit, orderly life, and sound body.[88] Just as imperial Japan mobilized its own women in the metropolis, so it did the women of its colonies, with considerable collaboration from leaders among the colonized.[89] Joining Kim Hwal-lan of Ewha and Yi Suk-jong of Sŏngsin Girls' School, Pahk actively promoted Japan's war efforts and became one of the passionate supporters of its "Greater East Asia Co-Prosperity Sphere." She articulated the role of women in bringing war victory to home, emphasizing efficient and economic household management, scientific child-rearing, and active participation in agricultural work. If necessary, she further argued, "women should be ready to devote their energy and work in factories that produce weapons and mines that excavate iron and coal. Further, even when explosives are raining down and swordfights are everywhere, women should be brave in delivering arms to our soldiers. In the last instance, women should carry guns and fight at the battlefront. For this, women should prepare themselves to be both psychologically and physically fit. In other words, women should be prepared to shed blood, and when the time comes, they must shed blood."[90] In this way, Pahk seamlessly extrapolated the "national" role and duty of Korean women as imperial subjects in order to contribute to a Japanese victory.

Her high regard for the United States could not but be deeply compromised by her pro-Japanese speeches and activities. One of her editorials, contributed to *Tae tonga* (Greater East Asia) in 1942, succinctly captures her strategic conversion. Praising the imperial navy's attack on Pearl Harbor in 1941 and other Japanese victories against the British military, she wrote, "the shadow of the influence from the US and Britain will helplessly disappear, and the new aura of the new East Asia finally shines through like morning sunlight."[91] Here she publicly demonstrated full allegiance to Japanese imperial expansion, deploying the discourse of Asian liberation from the West.[92] However, she effectively discarded or abandoned her strategic allegiance with Japan once Japan was defeated by the Allied Forces in 1945. In her commercially successful autobiography, *September Monkey*, published in 1954 by Harper & Brothers, Pahk appealed to American readers by describing the liberating power of Christianity brought by American missionaries in transforming the lives of her mother and herself. In the foreword, she wrote that her book had two goals. One was to "witness what can happen in a life when the power of God grips a heart, mind and soul. My mother was a village woman born in the days when the weighty traditions and conventions accumulated throughout the centuries had become especially burdensome. Christianity acted as a lever and fulcrum to dislodge her from the stony soil of the past and to lift her above tragedy, fear and superstition. It also brought the living water which made the soil fertile again. And in this new soil I was rooted and nourished." The other goal was to "express my gratitude to my friends who have contributed so much that is endearing and broadening and inspirational to my life on two continents. In my heart Koreans and Americans are all one family."[93] In her praise for the positive impact of Christianity and Americans on her life, Pahk entirely omitted her collaborationist and anti-Western activities during the Pacific War; instead, she not merely distanced herself but made herself a victim of Japanese oppression: "[T]he suffering we were enduring was like birth pangs and the Allied Forces were like the midwives who would deliver us . . . God always opened other and greater doors when one was shut against us."[94] In a significant way, her connections with both the Japanese colonial power and American missionary teachers served as important catalysts for her to explore and expand opportunities in life. As she taught her students at Tŏkhwa, she knew "how to conform to the old customs and yet to be resilient, resourceful."[95] Once her loyalty to the Japanese colonial power began to lose currency as it became clear that Japan was doomed to defeat, she wasted no time in reinventing herself as one of the beneficiaries of the American missionary enterprise in Korea. Her autobiography, written in English, captured the imagination of the American readers. *The Christian Science Monitor* interviewed her after her autobiography became a commercial success. It described her as a woman who "discussed world problems with a comprehension born of experience, embracing not only the worlds of the East and West, but also, century-old traditions and the new ideas to which they are giving place. She has bridged during her lifetime, the gulf between the age-old customs which threatened to restrict her girlhood, and the modern status of Korean women."[96]

Christian women leaders such as Kim Hwal-lan, Kim Maria, and Pahk Induk were expected to play a central role in creating both a Christian

Korea and a Christian new womanhood. This anticipation led to mission-ary-sponsored opportunities to study in the United States. As an author in the missionary journal *Woman's Work* put it, "it would be difficult to over emphasize the opportunities and responsibilities of leadership which await the American-educated Oriental woman on her return to her country."[97] To a significant extent, they satisfied the expectation of their mission-ary teachers as many of them did largely devote their lives to Christian spirituality and its promotion. However, as the Kim Maria's life shows, some tensions existed especially when it came to the matter of political engagement under Japanese colonial rule. Pahk Induk's decisions to marry and divorce also caused significant strain on the otherwise ideal relation-ship between the missionary teachers and their protégé. What these three women had in common is that they firmly held onto their Christian belief as a spiritual guide as they advocated women's advancement in society. Yet they significantly differed in their choices and strategies in coping with the colonial reality in their own pursuit of new womanhood.

SECULAR MODERN IN PURSUIT OF SELFHOOD

Of the leading New Women with a Christian background, Kim Wŏn-ju and Na Hye-sŏk stand out because they rarely identified themselves as Christian and almost exclusively focused on secular feminist agendas through their public writings and private lives. In a significant way, no one is a better fit than Kim and Na for the most popularized image of New Women in the 1920s print media. They were the symbol of educated, talented women. At the same time, they posed a serious threat to the sta-bility of gender morality and the family. They challenged the oppressive nature of Confucian gender ideology and the double-standard that had been applied to women and men. Their scandalous love affairs funda-mentally defied the ideal of chastity. They even questioned the sanctity of motherhood that had been the centerpiece of patriarchal social arrange-ments. Kim and Na led distinct lives, but their paths crossed at significant junctures, and they forged an alliance in their lonesome struggle as public women intellectuals.

Sin yŏja *(New Women): Kim Wŏn-ju (a.k.a. Kim Ir-yŏp)*

Kim Wŏn-ju (1896–1971) was born into a Christian family in South P'yŏngan. Her father was a pastor, so she grew up with Christian teachings. In an autobiographical essay she recalled that when she was eight years old, she was frightened to learn that those who did not believe in Christ would go to hell. Out of her desire to rescue those nonbelievers, she had already made plans to become a Bible woman and work in a distant island where she imagined cannibals lived.[98] However, despite the strong influence of her Christian father and missionary teachers, Kim grew to doubt her faith. She wondered, for example, "if Christians called Buddha an idol, wouldn't the sacred pictures of the Christian deity be idols as well? Would God, Jesus and the Holy Ghost—the Trinity—be just an empty surface?" Her pastor father could not help her reconcile her growing doubts about Christianity, and she ended up rejecting all the claims about heaven and hell she had accepted as a young girl.[99] Her faith grew even weaker as she experienced a series of tragic events, including the deaths of several family members and the traumatic end to an engagement with a wealthy man. Her growing skepticism might have been one of the reasons why she almost never mentioned her missionary teachers at Ewha in her writing. Nonetheless, one can still detect the influence of Christianity in her intellectual and personal life. Her writings, such as the short story "Kyesi" (Revelation) and an essay, "Tongsaeng ŭi chugŭm" ("My Sister's Death"), prominently incorporate Christian rituals and devotions.[100] Kim also expressed uneasy feelings about her disillusionment with Christianity given her close bond with her father, who she believed embodied the ideal of Christianity. In a memorial essay written after her father's death, Kim expressed guilt that what she came to believe in as a feminist drew harsh criticism from society and, she worried, might have defamed her father's name. By this time (the mid-1920s), Kim was already a well-known, outspoken feminist who advocated freedom, independence, and free love, and criticized the absurdity of the ideology of chastity, which had been imposed only on women. Kim Wŏn-ju pursued love as the purpose of her life not just in rhetoric but in practice, and she had loving relationships with several men. Despite public criticism, she was determined to adhere to what she truly believed.

Kim Wŏn-ju literally and symbolically started the New Women's movement when she founded the magazine *Sin yŏja* (New Women) in 1920. Its publication marks a historical turning point: prior to the 1920s, American missionaries and Korean male intellectuals dominated the public discourse on the woman question and institutional reforms for women. Missionary journals such as *Korea Mission Field*, *Korean Repository*, *Gospel for All Lands*, and *Woman's Missionary Friend* were a crucial venue for presenting women missionaries' leadership in shaping a Korean new womanhood centered on religious piety and domesticity. Korean male intellectuals had taken the initiative in publishing earlier magazines, including *Kajŏng chapchi* (Home Journal, 1906), *Yŏja chinam* (Guide for Women, 1908–9),

Hak chi kwang (Light of Learning, 1914–30) and *Yŏjagye* (Women's World, 1917–21), which served as an important platform for them to convey new gender norms. To be sure, a few Korean women were able to publish important writings in those journals that helped them begin to cultivate new ground for future feminist discourse. Most representatively, Na Hye-sŏk's "Isang chŏk puin" (Ideal Woman), published at *Hak chi kwang* in 1914, presented a new woman's voice that looked out to the world for its inspiration of an ideal new womanhood, while looking at the hypocrisy and tyranny of traditional gender relations.[101] However, despite their connection to several prominent women, these print media were primarily led by male intellectuals and often regarded the "woman question" as subsidiary to nationalist and modernist projects. Thus, Korean women's magazines published before 1920 are largely in line with the spirit of the Patriotic Enlightenment movements.[102]

Sin yŏja publicly opened the door for the discursive construction of a new gender ideology by women and for women in Korea.[103] It was created through women's own work, from its inception to its execution. Its articles focused on women's inner voices and desires, as well as their concerns about social issues. Kim Wŏn-ju cultivated a network of women by forming Ch'ŏngt'aphoe (the Bluestocking Society) with her colleagues, including Kim Hwal-lan, Pahk Induk, and Na Hye-sŏk, all of whom were contributors to *Sin yŏja*.[104] They held weekly meetings to discuss new ideas and literature and set the goals and directions of the magazine.[105] In its first issue, Kim Wŏn-ju emphasized that she had made a conscious effort to "work with women's hands only" and that "the entire staff is composed of women only."[106] Its publisher and financier was Mrs. Billings, the wife of a Methodist missionary, Bliss Billings, who was the vice president of Yŏnhŭi College (now Yonsei University).[107] Kim further emphasized that the magazine was for all women of Korea and would "welcome any pieces written by women," regardless of their social standing.[108] This "de-masculinized" endeavor, in Yu Chin-wŏl's words, and the inclusive policy of inviting contributions from any and all women opened up new possibilities for women to voice publicly their inner desires and daily experiences in the face of oppressive family life, harsh treatment by men and in-laws, and the general denial of basic human rights for women.[109] The major journal *Korea Mission Field* enthusiastically reported the founding of *Sin yŏja* and even translated one of the editorials into English. Its report mentioned that two American writers "who have had a chance to know something of the magazine, have been delighted to find such a high toned and progressive paper being carried on by women." Further, it noted the magazine's impressive sales—up to 2,000 copies per issue—assessing the new magazine as "the best gotten-up and most worth while of the three woman's magazines which have appeared in Korea."[110]

In the preface to the first issue, Kim Wǒn-ju historicizes the emergence of the New Women as an inevitable global trend:

> Reform! This is the outcry of humankind after moaning with pain in the midst of terrifying gunshots for five years [referring to the First World War]. Liberation! This is the outcry of women ourselves who were traditionally confined to the deep inside of the house for long. Excessive ambition and egoism broke the peace and brought mountains of death and oceans of blood. If this war was against the will of heaven and the right way of humankind, it is also against the humanity to force women, who are as capable as men are, to stay in the inner chambers, and to regard women as a weaker kind than men and treat women as if they were slaves . . . We have to reform our society. In order to reform the society we must first reform the family, which is the most basic and fundamental unit of society. In order to reform the family we have to liberate women, who are the masters of the house. We must liberate women first if we are interested in catching up and winning over others and transforming our entire social structure. We are not interested in seeking empty notions of equality or respect for women. Our magazine is only interested in contributing to the betterment of society.[111]

Kim begins by referring to the aftermath of the First World War and its subsequent impact on women globally. Her subsequent writings often mention "the influence of the world war," "the trend of the world," "rapid changes of the world destiny," or "transitional period," intending to place her agenda for New Women into the broader context of the times.[112] Keenly aware of the global changes that began to transform gender discourse and practices most represented by New Women,[113] Kim establishes a new discourse with an urgency for gender reform as the inevitable path to a better society and a better world.

There are some hints that *Sin yǒja* might have taken its earliest ideas from its Japanese counterpart, *Seitō* (Bluestocking). Not only did Kim Wǒn-ju form an organization of the same name (Ch'ǒngt'aphoe in Korean), but the intellectual connection is evident in the two magazines' goals. For example, both intended to be instrumental in identifying and introducing "female geniuses." When Hiratsuka Raichō and Yasumochi Yoshiko drafted main goals for the Bluestocking Society of Japan, they wrote, "we hereby launch our society's magazine, *Seitō*, which will be open to unknown women who share literary interests with us or who are willing to work for the same cause with us. We hope and also trust that *Seitō* will produce eminent *joryū ten-*

sai (female geniuses) some time in the future."[114] Some of the better-known literary feminists, such as Yosano Akiko and Okamoto Kanoko, emerged in the pages of *Seitō*, where they addressed the plight of women bound by the Japanese patriarchal marriage system.[115] Similarly, in the second issue of *Sin yŏja*, Kim Wŏn-ju explicitly stated that "the magazine is to introduce some of the eminent works by the members of Ch'ŏngt'aphoe and simultaneously to discover hidden geniuses."[116] And indeed, through *Sin yŏja* Kim Wŏn-ju and contemporaries such as Na Hye-sŏk and Kim Myŏng-sun began to be recognized as leading writers and feminists. Although short lived, closing down after only a year due to financial problems,[117] *Sin yŏja* literally and figuratively initiated the phenomenon of the New Woman, and its core members and writers were instrumental in setting a new standard for the roles, duties, and rights of women.[118]

After the closure of *Sin yŏja*, Kim continued to be active in her writing career, contributing key pieces on new womanhood. However, in 1928 she made a dramatic turn when she became interested in Buddhism. She began to socialize with the staff of the magazine *Pulgyo* (Buddhism). As she recalled, she was never interested in Buddhism and considered it a superstition. But her frequent contact with the Buddhists in this group changed her views, and she eventually married a former monk.[119] She recalled that "when I first heard the teachings of Buddhism, I was so delighted that I even thought of becoming a nun. However, I also thought that unless I could overcome my sexual desire, it would be better to marry a man who is a sincere Buddhist and pursue a Buddhist way together. Once I reached this conclusion, I was able to marry a [former] monk."[120] In the end, however, she did become a Buddhist nun in 1933 in order to pursue "unchanging truth." Her departure from the secular world and embrace of celibacy drew public attention in view of her numerous love relationships and daring feminist statements.[121] When a reporter asked for her thoughts about the women's movement in 1934, she answered that the women's movement "is nothing other than a temporary solution to an emergency. It cannot be a permanent truth."[122] Even so, she continued to submit essays to magazines, but her later writings largely focused on Buddhist philosophy.

"Chastity Is a Taste": Na Hye-sŏk

Born in Suwŏn, Na Hye-sŏk (1896–1948; see figure 14) came from an affluent family that had a great interest in "Enlightenment" and women's education. She attended Samil Girls' School for elementary education, which was founded by Mary Scranton, and Chinmyŏng Girls' High School, where she received the highest honor in her graduating class.[123] She continued her education in Japan, studying Western painting. It was during her stay in Japan that she received her first significant exposure to Japanese and Western feminist movements and came to engage in a progressive women's movement that departed from Enlightenment-oriented gender discourse. At the core of that departure was the increasing emphasis on the self, a prime characteristic of modern identity. The discovery of selfhood entailed a number of changes in perspective. Na began to scrutinize the patriarchal constraints on women that had suppressed selfhood and glorified women's role in the family as wife and mother. In both her writings and her life, she began to resist the prevailing notion of "wise mother, good wife" rooted in Confucian gender ethics *[pudŏk]*, Japan's Meiji gender ideology *[ryōsai kenbo]*,[124] and American missionaries' Victorian notions of domesticity. In so doing, she undermined the presumed "naturalness" of the selfless woman as a devoted wife and mother, laying new ground for modern womanhood.

In her first essay, "Isang chŏk puin" (Ideal Woman), Na first questions what would constitute an "ideal woman." She uses exemplary female figures—both real and literary—from Western and Japanese societies, including Ibsen's Nora, the Japanese feminists Hiratsuka Raichō and Akiko Yosano, and the American author Harriet Beecher Stowe, to challenge the existing gender ideology of the "good wife, wise mother." She points out that while women are instructed to become good wives and wise mothers, there is no similar education for men to become "good husbands and wise fathers" *[yangbu hyŏnbu]*.[125] She interprets this disparity as a reflection of the patriarchal scheme to reduce women to the status of de facto slaves and to demand women's conformity and meekness.[126] Na's critique of "wise mother, good wife" ideology points not only to uneven, gender-specific social expectations but also to women's absence of individuality *[kaesŏng]* and selfhood. Na's colleague Kim Wŏn-ju echoed her critique and emphatically argued in *Sin yŏja* that new women want to achieve "a complete self-realization," declaring that "we, as new women, intend to break away from all customary habits, and create new rational morality that does not limit women on the basis of gender and offers freedom of equality, freedom of rights, freedom of duties, freedom of work and freedom of pleasure so that women can pursue self development and realize the best life of their own."[127]

Na Hye-sŏk's exceptional artistic ambition was challenged when she became pregnant.[128] In her essay "Mo toen kamsanggi" (Reflections on Becoming a Mother),[129] she reflects upon the devastation she felt upon becoming pregnant, fearing the end of her artistic and literary career. Referring to Western and Japanese women including Akiko Yosano, who had many children and continued to be productive in her career as a writer, Na reports that she resisted the common idea that once a woman becomes a mother, her life is basically over.[130] Nonetheless, her despair was acute, for she felt she was just beginning to understand "what art is, what life is, what Koreans should do, and what Korean women should do." She "had a lot of work to do"[131] to achieve her life's mission, and she worried that motherhood would derail her. She even contemplated suicide or abortion.[132] Her essay vividly portrays the inordinate pain and suffering she experienced while giving birth. To her, "the child is a devil that takes away the flesh of its mother." The sleep deprivation that accompanies motherhood is a "cruel curse worse than God's punishment of Eve for her taking of the forbidden fruit from the tree of knowledge."[133] Questioning the essentialization of maternal instinct, she writes that "people often say that motherly love is already innate in the mother's mind. But I do not think so."[134] To her, motherly love is learned, not a natural gift given to all women.[135]

Her firm denial of "natural" and "sacred" motherly love drew scathing criticism from a male intellectual, pen-named Paekkyŏl. He argues that "women should know that pregnancy is a sacred task endowed to them, their value lies in their capacity to get pregnant, and pregnancy [and producing children] is one of the most important duties of women toward humankind."[136] To him, Na's denial of this sacred duty and unique capacity is a clear indication of how wrongly the so-called New Woman understands her place in the world. He acknowledges that it is important to overcome bad customs. Yet once that has been done, a woman needs to have good values to put in the place of those old values. In his view, New Women, represented by Na Hye-sŏk, have abandoned the old but offer no new values that would guide them to a better life.

In her response to Paekkyŏl, Na makes the piercing point that while his essay pretends to criticize her personally, it actually targets Korean women in general, and Korean New Women in particular. She detects a tone of "curse, criticism and cynicism" when he describes "pioneering New Women in Korea," "those who consider themselves as New Women," or "New Women calling for liberation." Na suggests that her writing about her private emotional experience has triggered an evolving resentment, especially among male intellectuals, against New Women, who call for liberation, selfhood, and independence. When Na admits her forbidden feelings, denies the sacredness of motherhood, and instead longs for her own sacred site of selfhood, she directly challenges all notions of traditional womanhood. Children were conceived to be the only source of pride and satisfaction for many women in traditional society, but Na wants to find such pride and happiness through her creative work.

Na's fundamental transgression is her discovery of the self, in particular, her ability and courage to put the self at the core of her own life. Her novella, *Kyŏnghŭi* (1918), brilliantly captures the birth of selfhood inspired by a feminist vision that questions the patriarchal order that determines the "proper" space for women in the domestic sphere.[137] Na frankly scrutinizes the bodily constraints caused by pregnancy and motherhood and recognizes that they could hinder women's pursuit of self and creative work. Therefore, those keenly interested in self-realization might not be interested in marrying or getting pregnant. To male intellectuals, however, this desire to prioritize her own dreams is selfish, decadent, and even dangerous to society. If motherhood is the foundation of the nation, then eschewing it in favor of individual ambition is a profound threat. When Na talks about the suffering and the inconvenience of motherhood, male intellectuals envision far-reaching, detrimental effects of such a viewpoint on the nation. The purpose of their criticism, as Na well understood, is to tame and discipline all independent and daring women through public humiliation and ridicule.

Na endured the criticism—after all, she was a mother. In addition, her status as the wife of a prominent political figure, Kim U-yŏng, who was a vice consul in Manchuria at the time, worked as a safety net to protect her from potential ostracism.[138] The degree to which her marriage shielded her can be taken from the aftermath of her divorce.

Na divorced in 1930. Three years earlier, she had had an extramarital affair with Ch'oe Rin, a leader of Ch'ŏndogyo (Religion of the Heavenly Way) during a brief stay in Paris.[139] In 1934, she published an article entitled "Ihon kobaekchang" (Confession about Divorce), addressed to her former husband.[140] Filled with feelings of incredulity and devastation, her confession describes in detail how she and her husband ended up divorcing and how sincerely she had pleaded with him to reconsider and try to begin a new life. She had begged him to forgive her in order to protect their four children. She had suggested that if they lacked capacity to renew their trust, they should remember how Jesus sacrificed his life to save millions of people.[141] In order to save her marriage, she had even promised to become a *hyŏnch'ŏ yangmo* (wise wife, good mother), the very ideal she had criticized earlier.[142] In the end, all her pleas were in vain.

While admitting that she had made a mistake in having the affair, Na nonetheless portrayed herself as a pioneer who dared to challenge the contradictions and hypocrisy, especially in the idea of chastity, that were embedded in patriarchal oppression. She writes, "the mind of the Korean man is strange. They do not embrace the idea of chastity for men. But they demand chastity of their wives and all other women. Worse, they try to violate other women's bodies. In the case of people in the West or in Tokyo, if they do not cherish the idea of chastity, they understand and respect the view of others who do not hold the idea of faithfulness." To Na, such discriminatory sexual morality is itself an act of immorality and a sign unenlightenment. Contemplating the "level" of modernity among the intelligentsia, she writes:

> I feel pity for the men of the educated class in Korea. They were prevented from participating in the political arena, men's foremost stage of work. Their knowledge has no use. There is no critical mass who can understand various theories these educated men talk about. They try to find an outlet in love, but they are constrained by the [old] family system and unintelligent wives. Therefore, they feel bitter and sour. They go to bars, drinking heavily and playing with entertainers . . .

> I also feel pity for the women of the educated class, the so-called new women. They still spend their childhood and marriage within the feudal family system so that their lives are incredibly complex and chaotic. Half-baked knowledge does not help them strike the necessary balance between the old and the new, and it only provokes a depressing temper. They learn a philosophy of life in college and have the opportunity to observe family life in the West or Tokyo, don't they? They have ideals and will as high as the sky, but their bodies and work are on earth, aren't they? They marry based on sweet love, but husband and wife follow their own separate ways so that they do not find any meaning in life. The wife only worries about what to prepare for dinner from morning to evening. They envy single women to the point where they have a nervous breakdown or completely reject marriage as an institution. People often call women weak, but women are strong. Women may be small, but it is women who are truly powerful. Happiness depends on the ability to control everything. Women! Control your family, your husband, your children and the society. Then the ultimate victory will lie in women.[143]

Na's narrative succinctly captures the feelings of powerlessness among colonized intellectuals. Frustrated and hampered by their lack of political influence and the failure of the masses to understand their high ideals, these new women and men were caught between the old and the new. Under these circumstances, Na emphasized that women needed to keep hope so they could create a truly ideal womanhood. Her writing, especially in the passage above, reveals a strong belief that women's strength will enable them to overcome numerous social challenges and constraints. She uses her "mistake" and its devastating impact on her personal life not to discourage other women but to encourage them to continue to pursue their ideals. Na suggests that unlike European and American societies, Korean society is not prepared to embrace women as geniuses; indeed, budding genius is crushed. Na implies that her life was crushed by a harsh public and her own family. Nonetheless, she seems to believe that her "mistake" can be an important signpost for other women, and thus she feels her mission has been fulfilled. This sense that she was leaving a legacy for the women of the next generation through mistakes was eerily expressed in the earlier piece "Chapgam" (Miscellaneous Thoughts), published in *Hak chi kwang* in 1917. Using the analogy of a person in deep snow, she implies that pioneering women might make mistakes in their efforts to find a path to their goal, but that even those mistakes—"getting lost, stepping on ice or falling into a hole"—guide others not to repeat the same mistakes.[144]

Five years after her divorce, she wrote a new essay, "Sin saeghwal e tŭlmyŏnsŏ" (Beginning a New Life),[145] in which she described her dream of going to the West, specifically Paris, to study. Na tells a friend, "I don't like Chosŏn, which knows my past, present and future. I don't like Chosŏn people." In the face of unsympathetic treatment from family members and society in general, she longs for a different cultural environment that might give her another chance to revive herself. Paris, where she explored new artistic genres and had the affair that led to her divorce, represents the possibility for rebirth: "[I]t was Paris that killed me. It was also Paris that made me a woman."[146] Touching on the temptation of Eve and Adam, Na portrays her brief romance with Ch'oe in Paris as a fatal incident in which she was tempted by "forbidden fruit." Yet she believed that it was an inevitable process for her growth, one that helped her become a "woman" who had truly experienced emotional freedom and fantastic moments of intimacy. Her experience was like "a rose in the midst of a desolate road" when she stepped away from the safety of conventionality: "[T]he deeper the temptation is, the more profound and complex reality she can understand. More hardship might make her seem agonized in her outer appearance, but she is able to live with unfathomable emotional depth in her inner life."[147] The price of her audacity was her comfort zone—family and social acceptance—but that same audacity also transformed her existential self.

Reflecting on love and chastity, she writes:

> Chastity is neither morality nor law. It is only a taste. Just as we eat rice when we want to eat rice, and we eat rice cake when we want to eat rice cake, chastity depends on our will and usage. We should

not be constrained . . . In order to keep chastity, we often suppress
our natural desire, our irresistible passion and our point of view.
How ironic is it? Therefore, our liberation begins with our liberation
from chastity. I believe that we have to look to a reality where sexual
anarchy makes some people want to keep chastity. In Paris, where
sexual anarchy prevails, there are men and women who keep chastity.
They do so after they have already experienced everything and return
to the old fashioned ways. Like Parisians, we also need to experience
everything and then choose whichever. That is a less dangerous and
more proper way.[148]

Clearly influenced by Ellen Key's writings on love and marriage,[149] Na
offers a radical view of sexual desire as natural and expansive; to her it
is chastity that is unnatural. She goes so far as to say that chastity is "a
taste," a minor, transitory preoccupation. Such a perspective radically
challenges the core of Chosŏn-dynasty gender ideology, which instructed
women to remain chaste even at the cost of their own lives. Na exposes the
"virtuous woman" trope as a manmade construct to suppress and inhibit
women's natural desire, thus shattering centuries' old norms.

  After Na's highly publicized divorce, she felt shunned in Korea. She
could neither sell her paintings nor find a job. Her financial situation was
utterly unstable. In the end, she never recovered from the social isolation,
public ridicule, and the subsequent poverty. She died alone and essentially
homeless in Seoul in 1948.

The women included in this chapter do not necessarily represent all of
Korea's New Women in their full diversity. However, they were undoubtedly central figures in the print media and societal or religious organizations in envisioning an ideal new womanhood. They were also actively
engaged in the formation of gender discourse through their work in the
burgeoning print media and in autobiographical writing. Further, their
dramatically different life paths fundamentally challenge the homogenized
image of New Women, shedding light on the diversity and complexity of the
women who created a novel space for women on one hand while constantly
negotiating the old customs and gender practices on the other. As many
scholars argue, the New Women's emphasis on "self" was discursively denigrated by androcentric and nationalistic discourses that privileged nation,
family, and men. The autonomous voices of women were mounting head-
on challenges to a male-centered social order and the cultural practices that
resulted from it, and for this they were denigrated throughout the 1920s as
frivolous, selfish, and sexually promiscuous by male intellectuals and con-

servative women alike.[150] According to Sally Ledger, even this stereotypical image of the New Women could have allowed feminists a space in which they could discuss their radical views about women's rights.[151] In other words, while the male-dominant discourse meant to crush women's voices, it may have unexpectedly helped women create a "reverse discourse" to promote feminist agendas. Na Hye-sŏk's alleged mistake and the criticism it brought did offer her with the opportunity to assert her true ideal of modern womanhood. The heated debate in popular magazines and newspapers clearly reflects this dynamic discursive space for a new womanhood in the making. Such public arguments and counter-arguments, with women intellectuals actively participating, paved the way for the shifting notions of what it means to be a woman, a significant move away from collective identity in pursuit of an individual self.

7. Conclusion

New Women, Old Ways

A few years ago I organized a bilingual reading by writers from Korea at my university. At that time, one of the invitees, a poet known for her feminist work, met our dean, an American woman professor. The poet told the dean that American women did not have any problem, while Korean women still had huge barriers to overcome. This rather casual exchange pointedly illustrates the enduring image of Western or American women as modern, liberated, and progressive—an image that is deeply engrained in the minds of Koreans. In comparison to the situation in Korea, there may be some truth to this image. However, much research on the history of Western women amply demonstrates that such a simplified and overgeneralized conclusion distorts a complex history. The above anecdote ended with the American dean saying that she felt American women still had many problems to struggle against. I have argued in this book that the gap between the reality of Western women and their imagined status in the minds of Koreans is a key for understanding the formation of modern womanhood in Korea, because such a gap is not accidental. Instead, it reveals the politics of knowledge and power relations between genders, nations, and various ideological groups who have different historical mandates in their imagining and experiencing of the modern.[1]

I have specifically focused on American women missionaries and their relationship with Koreans as a starting point for the genealogies of modern womanhood in Korea mainly because the missionaries were the first group of Western women to introduce "modern" knowledge and culture to Korean women through education and various other activities, and also because they have been represented as pioneers of modern Korean womanhood. I have argued that the close association of American women missionaries with modern womanhood in Korea was derived from the perception of the West as modern and advanced—an image that originated in the late nineteenth century within the context of Korea's pursuit of a modern nation-state. Further, this derivative image was an integral part of the Korean nationalist discourse in which the advancement of women was understood as a prerequisite to building a modern nation-state. The role and status of Western women was represented in the print media as advanced, liberated, and progressive—the model for Korean women to copy for the modern nation of Korea.

However, as the preceding chapters have shown, women missionaries' devotion to "women's work for women" centering on domesticity and religious piety was a natural match with a traditional Confucian gender norm that assigned women's primary sphere to the domestic. Ellasue Wagner, a veteran missionary from the Southern Methodist Church, succinctly captures the kind of ideal womanhood that missionaries projected. In her celebratory remarks for the thirty-six anniversary of Holston Girls' School in 1940, she reminisced about the progress in the status of Korean women, who are finally considered "as persons, and more and more they are having their word and rights considered." Then, Wagner reaffirms that "the ideal woman of Korea to-day is, as it should be, the ideal wife and mother. We believe that there is no higher destiny than this. We remember the old saying that 'the hand that rocks the cradle rules the world.' In Korea to-day, however, there is a new realization of the fact that the woman who wields this influence needs the best of education and training. We have heard it said over and over lately that the best families now demand an educated daughter-in-law."[2] The ideal of "educated" daughter, wife, and mother was considered crucial for the creation and proliferation of the Christian family who would adhere to religious devotion while applying "scientific" knowledge to homemaking. Indeed, it cannot be gainsaid that the modern construction of "wise mother, good wife" in Korea significantly absorbed elements from Victorian true womanhood introduced by women missionaries. More important, this modern ideology was strategically employed by Korean reformers—both male and female—in order to strengthen the family as the basis of the modern nation.[3] Women's novel roles in society were rehashed according to this juxtaposition of the family with the nation. As chapters 2 and 3 have shown, gender equality was invoked as a new moral order and women's participation in the public realm was encouraged. Yet a close examination of such rhetoric and gender practices make it clear that the place of women was firmly located in "women's work for women" and the domestic domain, in which women were expected to utilize their "feminine virtues" such as love, caring, and sacrifice for the family and (by extension) the nation.

The ideal of American missionary women based on Christian modernity ultimately came to be challenged as an anachronism by Koreans looking for greater opportunities that went beyond religiosity and domesticity. The growing gap between what missionaries strove for and what Korean women desired to achieve was most sharply felt in the area of the secular modern, especially from the 1920s when an emerging group of educated women known as New Women began to challenge the privileged status of domesticity and take the initiative in transforming the "woman question." With the increased exposure to Japanese and Western modernity through the print media and their experiences studying overseas, a small but influential group of New Women fundamentally challenged the assumptions embedded in centuries-old gender philosophy and practices. In their pursuit of selfhood, romance, and independence, they laid bare the treatment of women as secondary members of society, the hypocritical approach to sexuality, and the absence of individuality in the hyperbolic, sacred image of motherhood as the backbone of the nation.

It is noteworthy that some of the most prominent New Women who had passionately confronted the oppressive nature of patriarchal gender relations did not have a lasting relationship with their missionary teachers or, indeed, with Christianity. As chapter 6 has shown, both Kim Wŏn-ju and Na Hye-sŏk had significant backgrounds in Christianity, and yet Chrsitianity did not figure prominently in their discourse on new womanhood, especially after they became leading public feminists.[4] Perhaps what is most interesting is when and why these women chose to invoke Christian ideals. In the case of Kim Wŏn-ju, she mentions her Christianity when she expresses guilt for not living up to the expectations of her father, a Christian pastor, to be a "proper" woman. Na Hye-sŏk invoked Christian compassion to persuade her husband to remain in their union after her extramarital affair, promising to become a good wife and wise mother—a compromise very different from the independent position she had advocated not long before. Despite their long histories of taking generally secular stands on issues related to the "woman question," these exemplars of new womanhood returned to their Christian background in the context of their own families, representing Christianity as a way to become a filial daughter and conform to the traditional role of woman as a good wife and wise mother.

The centrality of domesticity and womanly virtue embedded in Christian modernity still paved the way for greater opportunities for Korean women as well as American women missionaries.[5] For the Fiftieth Anniversary Celebration of the Korea Mission of the Presbyterian Church in the U.S.A., Margaret Best succinctly captured what missionary women perceived to be their contribution to Christian modern womanhood in Korea and what benefits Korean women drew from their interactions with women missionaries:

> If you ask Korean Christians, what the Gospel has done for Christian women, they will say first of all that it has brought them salvation from the guilt and power of sin. Then will come a long list of blessings, social, moral, educational and religious, sometimes quaintly expressed in English like the following: "It broke the door that kept them in houses." It gave them liberty to believe in Jesus Christ. It gave them rights to become members of their own families and not merely necessary and useful appendages. It gave them names. It gave them liberty of soul and action. It gave them an education based on Christianity. It gave them work for homes, churches and their own people. It gave the bride-to-be a voice in the choice of the bridegroom and the bridegroom a voice in choice of his bride. It brought about a more personal, and responsible relation between young husband and wife in the home than existed under old conditions, and a deeper feeling of their own responsibility for the training and nurture of their children. It has given many a Christian wife the real love and admiration of her husband and given them both a home where little children are trained in the nurture and admonition of the Lord, and where God is honored in other ways and acknowledged as head, of the home.[6]

In Best's appraisal, Korean women have been empowered by the "rights," the "liberty," the "choice," and the "voice" that Christianity had afforded them. Significantly, these keywords representing the modern transformation are predicated on spiritual devotion and domestic virtues, echoing the central motto of the women missionaries, "Christianizing the Home."[7] However, despite the emphasis on the domestic, women missionaries also stressed how important it would be to have "the very finest, most highly educated Korean young women in the leadership of the Church." To produce and support such women leaders was considered "one of the great opportunities open to our American missionary women."[8] Here, the primary place of women in the domestic sphere is seamlessly linked with women's engagement in the public and even global sphere. The "women's work for women" in the foreign mission field backed by the Victorian gender ideology of "separate spheres" provided women missionaries with fertile ground for making a lifetime commitment to their calling, to exercise power and authority in various mission organizations, and to expand the horizon of intellectual and cultural life. In doing so, they were able to make invaluable contributions to the foreign mission, albeit within the constraints of church organizations that were highly patriarchal.

In the same fashion, Korean women's involvement in church activities began to alter the scope and quality of their lives, offering them opportunities to learn not only religious teachings but also cultural and social skills in the public sphere. After all, in the late nineteenth century in Korea, attending church was radical in the sense that it literally and symbolically "broke the door" of the inner chambers, which Confucian gender norms had constructed as women's proper space. As chapters 2 and 3 have shown, Korean Christian women's testimonials amply attest to how they felt liberated in the physical and cultural space of spiritual devotion joined by their fellow women. In addition, other facets of Christian practice gave women new standing in Korean society, both symbolically and practically. As a woman did not have a name of her own, getting a baptismal name meant gaining a sense of human dignity as an individual.[9] Learning how to read and write at Bible sessions or mission schools was a crucial step for women to prepare themselves for new roles and self-identity in the family and society. Within a generation of the first group of American missionary women arriving in Korea, Korean women themselves were already serving as missionaries themselves in foreign missions. This fact demonstrates a particularly dramatic transformation of women's lives that went far beyond the domestic and the local spheres.

Gender and mission encounters in Korea were extraordinarily complex. Rather than following a singular progression from old to new womanhood, or from premodern to modern womanhood, women's transcultural encounters induced dynamic interactions between American and Korean notions about gender and national ideologies through which concerned parties formed alliances and also experienced tensions. In a significant way, it was in the mission field that largely conservative American women missionaries came to be regarded as "modern" women by Koreans and by women missionaries themselves, who felt they held relatively greater freedom and independence than Korean women. It was also their deeply cherished values of domesticity and womanly virtue that ultimately enabled women missionaries to expand the scope of their lives and work beyond the domestic. Korean women's responses to the new religion of Christianity and to its educational and cultural opportunities were divergent. Mission schools and church organizations offered Korean women novel opportunities to explore multiple meanings of the modern within the constraints of the patriarchal gender ideology and practices embedded in church organizations. However, there was a group of Korean women who thought idealized Christian womanhood to be too limited to satisfy their desire for the new. It is this latter group of women who fundamentally destabilized the old gender system by disputing the patriarchal oppression of the family, embracing the value of selfhood and setting a new standard for being a modern woman.

The pursuit of "modern" womanhood in Korea since the late nineteenth century has been deeply intertwined with the reified image of the Christian West, male-centered Korean nationalism, the patriarchal nature of the various social systems, and the growing desire for selfhood. I have argued that American missionaries' and Korean male intellectuals' discourses on modern womanhood often de-oriented gender in order to put forward either Christian or nationalist goals. The rhetoric of gender equality as a new moral order remained abstract without substantial changes in gender practices. Indeed, such empty rhetoric was actively deployed to further justify the priority of Christian or nationalist modernity. Nonetheless, women's actual experiences reveal that, equipped with the new rhetoric, they found novel opportunities even under the old patriarchal system. Bound by continued patriarchal constraints, women made full use of their limited opportunities to explore and expand the scope of their life and work. The ideal of new womanhood was often practiced in old ways just so that the limited goals of the mission or the nationalist movement could be accomplished. However, the tenuous coexistence of these new ideals with old practices became a source of dissatisfaction for some, especially New Women, whose radical practices, in concert with their new ideals, stirred up both fascination and abomination from the public.

The wide range of gender questions raised in the late nineteenth and early twentieth centuries are still relevant to Korean society in the twenty-first century. To be sure, there has been remarkable progress in the status of women in Korea. Just to mention a few examples, in 2001 the South Korean government instituted the Ministry of Gender Equality in order to enhance the status of women through legal and administrative policies to protect rights and provide equal opportunities. Women's representation in the National Assembly has grown from 1.3 percent in 1958 to 13 percent in 2004,[10] and the first female prime minister was appointed in 2006. The abolition of *hojuje* (Household Head System) in 2005 is a clear sign that the social, political, and economic system may be shifting away from its traditional patriarchal structure. However, a profound contradiction continues between the promise of modernity and the gender talk and practice of everyday life.[11] Hong Se-hwa, a public intellectual and columnist for the Korean daily newspaper *Han'gyŏre,* reflecting on a prominent case of sexual harassment in Korea in 2000,[12] deplored that "the Korean society is an exceedingly macho society." At the core of the "exceedingly macho" social arrangements is a male-centered, nationalistic way of thinking that has trivialized other social issues especially around gender. It is only in recent years that the almost sacrosanct metanarrative of nationalism has come under critical scrutiny. In addition, as the opening paragraph of this chapter indicated, there is still a rather uncritical assumption about the West as the origin of the modernity that helped women become liberated. Such an assumption is arguably the reflection of a colonized mind that continues to endorse the hierarchical status of the West as superior and the Other as inferior. As Rey Chow notes, "We live in an era in which to critique of the West has become not only possible but mandatory."[13] Given the strong presence of American women missionaries in the early history of modern womanhood in Korea, it is essential to question what constituted the modern in the minds of women missionaries. More importantly, it is crucial to investigate how Korean women and men responded to or appropriated the notion of Christian modern womanhood.[14] What I have intended in this book is a historically specific, textured analysis of the genealogies of American missionary knowledge and Korean intellectuals' ideas about the modern, while paying attention to concrete lives of women. Its goal is ultimately to rescue the complex and dynamic life experience of women from male-centered historiography and to bring to the fore a fuller picture of modern womanhood—a picture that can provide the historical insights that help us better understand contemporary women's issues.

Abbreviations

The following abbreviations are used throughout the notes and in the bibliography:

AMMEC   Minutes of the Annual Meeting of the Korea Mission of the Methodist Episcopal Church. General Commission on Archives and History, The United Methodist Church, Drew University, Madison, New Jersey

AMPC   Minutes and Reports of the Annual Meeting of the Korea Mission of the Presbyterian Church in the U.S.A.

ARPCUSA   Annual Report of the Board of Foreign Missions of the Presbyterian Church in the U.S.A.. Presbyterian Historical Society, Philadelphia, Pennsylvania

ARWFMS   Annual Reports of the Woman's Foreign Missionary Society of the Methodist Episcopal Church. General Commission on Archives and History, The United Methodist Church, Drew University, Madison, New Jersey

GCAH   General Commission on Archives and History, The United Methodist Church, Drew University, Madison, New Jersey

GAL   *Gospel in All Lands*

HWF   *Heathen Woman's Friend*

KMF   *The Korea Mission Field*

KR   *The Korean Repository*

KWCMEC   Annual Reports of the Korea Woman's Conference of the Methodist Episcopal Church. General Commission on Archives and History, The United Methodist Church, Drew University, Madison, New Jersey

PHS	Presbyterian Historical Society, Philadelphia, Pennsylvania
RG	Record Group, Presbyterian Historical Society, Philadelphia, Pennsylvania*
WFMS	Woman's Foreign Missionary Society
WMA	*Woman's Missionary Advocate*
WMF	*Woman's Missionary Friend*
WW	*Woman's Work*
WWW	*Woman's Work for Woman*

*There are two major Record Groups that are particularly relevant to the Korea Mission. One is Record Group 140, which includes documents of the Presbyterian Church in the United States' Korea Mission, 1903–72. The other is Record Group 360, the Foreign Missionary Personnel File. In the text, numbers following the RG numbers refer to box and folder numbers (e.g, "RG 140-10-51").

Notes

For abbreviations used throughout these notes and in the bibliography, see p. 185.

PREFACE

1. Martina Deuchler, "Propagating Female Virtues in Chosŏn Korea," in *Women and Confucian Cultures in Premodern China, Korea, and Japan,* ed. Dorothy Ko, JaHyun Kim Haboush, and Joan R. Piggott (Berkeley and Los Angeles: University of California Press, 2003), 142.

CHAPTER 1

1. J. S. Ryang [Yang Chu-sam], foreword to *Fifty Years of Light,* prepared by the Missionaries of the Woman's Foreign Missionary Society of the Methodist Episcopal Church in Commemoration of the Completion of Fifty Years of Work in Korea (Seoul, 1938).

2. Among the diversity of foreign missionary denominations in Korea between 1884 and 1910, close to eighty percent of the entire missionary force was sent by the U.S. Methodist Episcopal Church and the Presbyterian Church. Therefore, this book largely focuses on the two denominations. For a detailed denominational breakdown of foreign missionaries in Korea, see Sung-Deuk Oak, "The Indigenization of Christianity in Korea: North American Missionaries' Attitudes towards Korean Religions, 1884–1910" (Th.D. dissertation, Boston University, 2002), 480.

3. Louise Rothweiler, "What Shall We Teach in Our Girls' Schools?" *KR* (March 1892): 89–93 (from 89).

4. Annie Baird, "Higher Education of Women in Korea," *KMF* 7 (1912): 113–16 (from 13).

5. Annie Baird, *Daybreak in Korea: A Tale of Transformation in the Far East* (New York: Fleming H. Revell Company, 1909), 5.

6. Anna Bergman, a Presbyterian missionary, wrote: "I did hear our sew-

ing woman, just this last week tell of the difference Christianity had made in the lives of women in Korea. She heard our girls laughing and cheering at a basketball game down on the court and said, 'That happy sound surely cheers my heart.' Then she turned to me and told about the way girls were treated when she was little. They were never allowed outside their own courtyard. The boys had all the best food and clothes and little girls got what was left if there was anything. They were never allowed to run and play but were put to work as soon as they were around five years old." Anna Bergman to Dear Friends, June 21, 1931, Personnel File, RG 360, PHS.

7. Jeannette C. Hulbert, "Ewha College: 1910–1938," in *Fifty Years of Light*, 21–22.

8. Pierce R. Beaver, *American Protestant Women in World Mission: A History of the First Feminist Movement in North America* (Grand Rapids, Mich.: William B. Eerdmans, 1980).

9. Yi Pae-yong in cooperation with Son Sŭng-hŭi, Mun Suk-chae, and Cho Kyŏng-wŏn, "Han'guk kidokkyo yŏsong kyoyuk ŭi sŏnggwa wa chŏnmang—Ewha yŏja taehakkyo rŭl chungsim ŭro" (Accomplishment and Prospect of Korean Christian Education for Women—With Focus on Ewha Womans University), *Ewha sahak yŏn'gu* 27 (2000): 9–36.

10. For a brief overview of the premises and problems embedded in the notion of gender equality in Christianity, see Hyaeweol Choi, "A New Moral Order: Gender Equality in Korean Christianity," in *Religions of Korea in Practice*, ed. Robert Buswell (Princeton, N.J.: Princeton University Press, 2006), 409–20. Yun-Sung Kim argues that the discourse on gender equality was intrinsically hampered by premises rooted in Christian theology and Confucian ethics. Also, he continues, the discourse on the eradication of superstition led by missionaries and Korean Christians resulted in despair over rather than hope in women's religious life, as it linked women and superstition to premodernity and inferiority. Focusing on the gender hierarchy and gendered division of labor within the church structures, Yang Hyŏn-hye demonstrates how women were systematically excluded from opportunities to become pastors and to participate in decision-making processes. See Yun-Sung Kim, "The Predicament of Modern Discourses on Gender and Religion in Korean Society," *Korea Journal* 41, no. 1 (spring 2001): 114–36; and Yang Hyŏn-hye, "Han'guk kaesin'gyo ŭi sŏng ch'abyŏl kujo wa yŏsŏng undong" (The Structure of Sex Discrimination in Korean Protestant Christianity and the Women's Movement), in *Han'guk yŏsŏng kwa kyohoeron*, ed. Ewha yŏja taehakkyo yŏsŏng sinhak yŏn'guso (Seoul: Taehan kidokkyosŏhoe, 1998), 200–248. See also Nam-Soon Kang, "Creating 'Dangerous Memory': Challenges for Asian and Korean Feminist Theology," *The Ecumenical Review* 47, no. 1 (1995): 21–31; Lee Hyo-Chae, "Protestant Missionary Work and Enlightenment of Korean Women," *Korea Journal* 17, no. 11 (November 1977): 33–50; Sŏ Kwang-sŏn, "Han'guk yŏsŏng kwa chonggyo" (Korean Women and Religion), in *Han'guk yŏsŏngsa* 2 (History of Korean Women), ed. Han'guk yŏsŏngsa p'yŏnch'an wiwŏnhoe (Seoul: Ewha yŏja taehakkyo ch'ulp'anbu, 1972), 492–531; and Yu Tong-sik,

Han'guk chonggyo wa kidokkyo (Korean Religions and Christianity) (Seoul: Taehan kidokkyosŏhoe, 1965), 37–39.

11. Pak Yong-ok, *Kim Maria: Na nŭn Taehan ŭi tongnip kwa kyŏlhon hayŏtta* (Kim Maria: I Married Korea's Independence) (Seoul: Hongsŏngsa, 2003), 419–20; and Helen Kim, "Women and the Missionary Enterprise: Discussion," in *The Christian Life and Message in Relation to Non-Christian Systems: Report of the Jerusalem Meeting of the International Missionary Council* (London: Oxford University Press, 1928), 370.

12. There is much research that focuses on the gender hierarchy embedded in the foreign mission structure. To mention just a few, Jane Hunter, *The Gospel of Gentility: American Women Missionaries in Turn-of-the-Century China* (New Haven: Yale University Press, 1984); Patricia R. Hill, *The World Their Household: The American Woman's Foreign Mission Movement and Cultural Transformation, 1870–1920* (Ann Arbor: The University of Michigan Press, 1985); Leslie A. Flemming, ed., *Women's Work for Women: Missionaries and Social Change in Asia* (Boulder: Westview Press, 1989); and Dana Robert, *American Women in Mission: A Social History of Their Thought and Practice* (Macon, Ga.: Mercer University Press, 1996).

13. In this book, "Victorian" refers to American Victorian culture and society. See Thomas Schlereth, *Victorian America: Transformations in Everyday Life, 1876–1915* (New York: HarperCollins, 1991); and Susan Curtis, *A Consuming Faith: The Social Gospel and Modern American Culture* (Baltimore: Johns Hopkins University Press, 1991).

14. Alice Chai, "Integrative Feminist Politics in the Republic of Korea," in *Feminist Nationalism*, ed. Lois West (New York: Routledge, 1997), 177; Yi, "Han'guk kidokkyo yŏsong kyoyuk"; and Insook Kwon, "'The New Women's Movement' in 1920s Korea: Rethinking the Relationship between Imperialism and Women," *Gender and History* 10, no. 3 (November 1998): 381–405.

15. Nancy Fraser, *Unruly Practices: Power, Discourse, and Gender in Contemporary Social Theory* (Minneapolis: University of Minnesota Press, 1989), 113–43; Michael W. Apple, ed., *Cultural and Economic Reproduction in Education* (London: Routledge Kegan Paul, 1982); and Gael Graham, *Gender, Culture, and Christianity: American Protestant Mission Schools in China 1880–1930* (New York: Peter Lang, 1995), 3.

16. Charles Taylor, *Modern Social Imaginaries* (Durham: Duke University Press, 2004); Lydia Liu, *Translingual Practice: Literature, National Culture, and Translated Modernity* (Stanford, Calif.: Stanford University Press, 1995); Dilip Parameshwar Gaonkar, ed., *Alternative Modernities* (Durham: Duke University Press, 2001); and Rita Felski, *The Gender of Modernity* (Cambridge, Mass.: Harvard University Press, 1995).

17. The term "modern" itself has close ties with Christianity, as it derives from the fifth-century Latin term *modernus*, which distinguished a "Christian present" from a "pagan past." But in the nineteenth century, Western modernity was defined by much more complex philosophical, sociopolitical, and aesthetic terms that were not always compatible with each other and were

in fact competing categories. See Barry Smart, "Modernity, Postmodernity and the Present," in *Theories of Modernity and Postmodernity*, ed. Bryan S. Turner (London: Sage, 1990), 14–30.

18. Talal Asad, *Formations of the Secular: Christianity, Islam, Modernity* (Stanford, Calif.: Stanford University Press, 2003); Peter van der Veer, *Imperial Encounters: Religion and Modernity in India and Britain* (Princeton, N.J.: Princeton University Press, 2001); Joris Geldhof, "'Cogitor Ergo Sum': On the Meaning and Relevance of Baader's Theological Critique of Descartes," *Modern Theology* 21, no. 2 (April 2005): 237–51; Hyaeweol Choi, "Christian Modernity in Missionary Discourse from Korea, 1905–1910," *East Asian History* 29 (June 2005): 39–68; and Ussama Makdisi, "Reclaiming the Land of the Bible: Missionaries, Secularism, and Evangelical Modernity," *American Historical Review* 102, no. 3 (June 1997): 680–713.

19. Felski, *The Gender of Modernity*, 212.

20. There is a growing list of research on the New Woman. Works range from biographical accounts of New Women to theoretical attempts to revise male-centered historiography, literary criticism, and social theories. To mention just a few, Theodore Jun Yoo, *The Politics of Gender in Colonial Korea: Education, Labor, and Health, 1910–1945* (Berkeley and Los Angeles: University of California Press, 2008); Kim Su-jin, "1920–30-yŏndae sin yŏsŏng tamnon kwa sangjing ŭi kusŏng" (Excess of the Modern: Three Archetypes of the New Woman and Colonial Identity in Korea, 1920s to 1930s) (PhD dissertation, Seoul National University, 2005); Jennifer Jung-Kim, "Gender and Modernity in Colonial Korea" (PhD dissertation, UCLA, 2005); Kelly Jeong, "Multiple Beginnings: Crisis of Gender, Masculinity, Nationhood, and Many Arrivals of Modernity in Modern Korean Literature and Cinema (PhD dissertation, UCLA, 2003); Kim Kyŏng-il, *Yŏsŏng ŭi kŭndae, kŭndae ŭi yŏsŏng* (Modernity of Women, Women of Modernity) (Seoul: P'urŭn yŏksa, 2004); Mun Ok-p'yo, ed., *Sin yŏsŏng* (New Women) (Seoul: Ch'ŏngnyŏnsa, 2003); Yi Sang-gyŏng, *In'gan ŭro salgo sipta* (I Want to Live as a Human Being) (Seoul: Han'gilsa, 2000); Ch'oe Hye-sil, *Sin yŏsŏngdŭl ŭn muŏt ŭl kkum kkuŏnnŭn'ga* (What Did New Women Dream?) (Seoul: Saenggak ŭi namu, 2000); Yung-Hee Kim, "Creating New Paradigms of Womanhood in Modern Korean Literature: Na Hye-sŏk's 'Kyŏng-hŭi,'" *Korean Studies* 26, no. 1 (2002): 1–60; and Yung-Hee Kim, "From Subservience to Autonomy: Kim Wŏn-ju's 'Awakening,'" *Korean Studies* 21 (1997): 1–21; *Yŏsŏng kwa sahoe* (Women and Society) 11 (2000).

21. Kumari Jayawardena, *Feminism and Nationalism in the Third World* (London: Zed Books Ltd, 1986).

22. Kim Yŏng-ok, ed., *"Kŭndae," yŏsŏng i kaji anŭn kil* ("Modernity," A Path Not Open to Women) (Seoul: Tto hana ŭi munhwa, 2001). Although the title's literal translation would be "Modernity: A Path Women Have Not Gone To," this gloss better captures the book's contents.

23. In her attempt to establish a new methodology in feminist research based in psychoanalytic methods, Kim Su-jin argues that the New Woman is a social and cultural site that reflects male intellectuals' unconscious anxi-

ety about the colonized nation and modernity. In this reinterpretation of the New Woman, it is interesting to see a parallel in the Chinese case. Ching-kiu Stephen Chan argues that the May-Fourth male writers in early 20th century China appropriated gender issues as a way to express their frustration with the Chinese patriarchal family and the experience of having their subaltern subjectivities undermined by the "superior" West. In their unconscious or conscious desires and identity crises, their writings on New Women and their advocacy for women's rights were an attempt to reaffirm their own superiority to Chinese women. See Kim Su-jin, "'Sin yŏsŏng,' yŏlyŏ innŭn kwagŏ, mŏjŏ innŭn hyŏnjae rosŏ ŭi yŏksa ssŭgi" ("'New Woman,' Writing History as the Open Past and Stagnant Present"), *Yŏsŏng kwa sahoe* 11 (2000): 6–28; and Ching-kiu Stephen Chan, "The Language of Despair: Ideological Representations of the 'New Women' by May Fourth Writers," *Modern Chinese Literature* 4. no. 1–2 (1988): 19–38. See also Wang Zheng, *Women in the Chinese Enlightenment: Oral and Textual Histories* (Berkeley and Los Angeles: University of California Press, 1999), especially chapter 1, "Creating a Feminist Discourse," 35–66.

24. Michel Foucault, "Nietzsche, Genealogy, History," in *The Foucault Reader*, ed. Paul Rabinow (New York: Pantheon Books, 1984), 76–100; and Foucault, *The Archaeology of Knowledge and the Discourse on Language* (New York: Pantheon Books, 1972).

25. To mention just a few representative studies, Chung-shin Park, *Protestantism and Politics in Korea* (Seattle: University of Washington Press, 2003); Wi-Jo Kang, *Christ and Caesar in Modern Korea: A History of Christianity and Politics* (Albany: SUNY Press, 1997); Chai-shin Yu, ed., *Korea and Christianity* (Seoul, Berkeley: Korean Scholar Press, 1996); No Ch'i-jun, *Ilcheha Han'guk kidokkyo minjok undong yŏn'gu* (A Study of the Korean Christian Nationalist Movement under Japanese Rule) (Seoul: Han'guk kidokkyo yŏksa yŏn'guso, 1993); Yi Man-yŏl, *Han'guk kidokkyo wa minjok ŭisik* (Korean Christianity and National Consciousness) (Seoul: Chisik sanŏpsa, 1991); Kenneth Wells, *New God, New Nation: Protestants and Self-Reconstruction Nationalism in Korea, 1896–1937* (Honolulu: University of Hawai'i Press, 1990); Donald Clark, *Christianity in Modern Korea* (Lanham, Md.: University Press of America, 1986); James Grayson, *Early Buddhism and Christianity in Korea: A Study in the Emplantation of Religion* (Leiden: E.J. Brill, 1985); David Chung, *Syncretism: The Religious Context of Christian Beginnings in Korea*, ed. Kang-nam Oh (Albany: SUNY Press, 2001); Timothy Lee, "Born-Again in Korea: The Rise and Character of Revivalism in (South) Korea, 1885–1988" (PhD dissertation, University of Chicago, 1996); and Oak, "The Indigenization of Christianity in Korea."

26. There were a few earlier studies that provided biographical profiles of early Korean Christian women as part of the history of Christianity in Korea. Examples include Chang Byung-wook, *Han'guk kamnigyo yŏsŏngsa* (The History of Methodist Women in Korea) (Seoul: Sung Kwang Publishing Co., 1979); and Yi Tŏk-chu, *Han'guk kyohoe ch'ŏŭm yŏsŏngdŭl* (Early Christian

Women in Korea: Life Stories of 28 Women Who Loved Christ and Their Nation) (Seoul: Kidokkyomunsa, 1990). For more recent research studies, see Ruth Compton Brouwer, *Modern Women Modernizing Men: The Changing Missions of Three Professional Women in Asia and Africa, 1902–69* (Vancouver: University of British Columbia Press, 2002); Donald N. Clark, *Living Dangerously in Korea: The Western Experience 1900–1950* (Norwalk, Conn.: EastBridge, 2003); Elizabeth Underwood, *Challenged Identities: North American Missionaries in Korea, 1884–1934* (Seoul: Royal Asiatic Society—Korea Branch, 2004); Robert Buswell and Timothy Lee, eds., *Christianity in Korea* (Honolulu: University of Hawai'i Press, 2006); Ryu Tae-yŏng, *Ch'ogi Miguk sŏn'gyosa yŏn'gu: 1884–1910* (Early American Missionaries in Korea: 1884–1910) (Seoul: Han'guk kidokkyo yŏksa yŏn'guso, 2001); and Kang Sŏn-mi, "Chosŏn p'agyŏn yŏ sŏn'gyosa wa (kidok) yŏsŏng ŭi yŏsŏngjuŭi ŭisik hyŏngsŏng" (Women Missionaries Sent to Korea and the Formation of Feminist Consciousness among Christian Women) (PhD dissertation, Ewha Womans University, 2003).

27. Nicole Beger defines "feminist historiography" as "a historical methodology that has emerged in the process of attempting to write histories that look at women not as outsiders, different from the male norm or at best subsumed in it, but as autonomous shapers and creators of their history. Feminist historiography highlights the historical construction and changeability of gender, criticizes the marginalization of women in dominant forms of writing history, sees sexual difference and other forms of difference as relational, and fosters changes in the power imbalances between men and women in today's social settings." Beger, *Present Theories, Past Realities: Feminist Historiography Meets "Poststructuralisms"* (Frankfurt: Viademica-Verlag, 1997), 1.

28. Numerous studies pay special attention to gender as an analytical category in the context of Western imperialism and the foreign missionary enterprise. To mention just a few examples, Nupur Chaudhuri and Margaret Strobel, eds., *Western Women and Imperialism: Complicity and Resistance* (Bloomington: Indiana University Press, 1992); Susan Thorne, *Congregational Missions and the Making of an Imperial Culture in Nineteenth-Century England* (Stanford, Calif.: Stanford University Press, 1999); Mary Taylor Huber and Nancy Lutkehaus, eds., *Gendered Missions: Women and Men in Missionary Discourse and Practice* (Ann Arbor: University of Michigan Press, 1999); and Reina Lewis, *Gendering Orientalism* (London: Routledge, 1996).

29. Books representing the history of Western women missionaries include Hunter, *The Gospel of Gentility*; Hill, *The World Their Household*; Brouwer, *Modern Women Modernizing Men*; Flemming, *Women's Work for Women*; Robert, *American Women in Mission*; Daniel Bays, ed., *Christianity in China: From the Eighteenth Century to the Present* (Stanford, Calif.: Stanford University Press, 1996); Graham, *Gender, Culture, and Christianity*; Kathleen Lodwick, *Educating the Women of Hainan: The Career of Margaret Moninger in China 1915–1942* (Lexington: University Press of Kentucky, 1995); Huber and Lutkehaus, *Gendered Missions*; Thorne, *Congregational Missions*

and the Making of an Imperial Culture; and Chaudhuri and Strobel, *Western Women and Imperialism.*

30. For works emphasizing the significance of and difficulty in gathering the direct narratives of local converts, see Kwok Pui-lan, *Chinese Women and Christianity 1860–1927* (Atlanta: Scholars Press, 1992); and Margo S. Gewurtz, "'Their Names May Not Shine': Narrating Chinese Christian Converts," in *Canadian Missionaries, Indigenous People,* ed. Alvyn Austin and Jamie S. Scott (Toronto: University of Toronto Press, 2005), 134–51.

31. Lila Abu-Lughod, ed., *Remaking Women: Feminism and Modernity in the Middle East* (Princeton, N.J.: Princeton University Press, 1998).

32. Donald Baker, "Christianity 'Koreanized,'" in *Nationalism and the Construction of Korean Identity,* ed. Hyung Il Pai and Timothy R. Tangherlini (Institute of East Asian Studies, University of California, Berkeley, 1998), 108–25.

33. V. Ravindiran, "Discourses of Empowerment: Missionary Orientalism in the Development of Dravidian Nationalism," in *Nation Work: Asian Elites and National Identities,* ed. Timothy Brook and Andre Schmid (Ann Arbor: University of Michigan Press, 2000), 51–81. Ravindiran critiques the simplistic approach of Saidian orientalism, arguing that "Far from being a hegemonic 'colonialist imposition' upon a passive 'Orient,' European orientalism was dependent upon and responsive to the discourse of locally dominant groups and reflected many of their visions and interests. Similarly, far from being passive victims of orientalism, dominant groups in the colonies actively participated in the construction, maintenance, and propagation of orientalist knowledge." (52).

34. Charles Taylor, "Two Theories of Modernity," in *Alternative Modernities,* ed. Dilip Parameshwar Gaonkar (Durham: Duke University Press, 2001), 172–96; See also Felski, *The Gender of Modernity,* 12–13; Laurel Kendall, ed., *Under Construction: The Gendering of Modernity, Class, and Consumption in the Republic of Korea* (Honolulu: University of Hawai'i Press, 2002), 2.

35. Antoinette Burton, "Thinking beyond the Boundaries: Empire, Feminism and the Domains of History," *Social History* 26, no. 1 (January 2001): 60–71 (from 69).

36. James Hevia presents a classic example that shows the power of discourse in shaping certain reality in the context of conflicts between Western missionaries and "the Other." See "Leaving a Brand on China: Missionary Discourse in the Wake of the Boxer Movement," *Modern China* 18, no. 3 (July 1992): 304–32. See also Stuart Hall, ed., *Representation: Cultural Representations and Signifying Practices* (London: Sage, 1997); Bernard S. Cohn, *Colonialism and Its Forms of Knowledge* (Princeton, N.J.: Princeton University Press, 1996); Burton, "Thinking beyond the Boundaries"; and Beger, *Present Theories, Past Realities.*

37. Hunter, *The Gospel of Gentility,* 229–55; Kwok, *Chinese Women and Christianity;* Hua R. Lan and Vanessa L. Fong, eds., *Women in Republican China: A Sourcebook* (Armonk: M. E. Sharpe, 1999); Gail Hershatter, *Women*

in China's Long Twentieth Century (Berkeley and Los Angeles: Global, Area, and International Archive/University of California Press, 2007), 79–88; Heidi A. Ross, "'Cradle of Female Talent': The McTyeire Home and School for Girls, 1892–1937," in *Christianity in China: From the Eighteenth Century to the Present*, ed. Daniel Bays (Stanford, Calif.: Stanford University Press, 1996), 209–27; Judith Liu and Donald P. Kelly, "'An Oasis in a Heathen Land': St. Hilda's School for Girls, Wuchang, 1928–1937," in Bays, *Christianity in China*, 228–42; Helen Hopper, *A New Woman of Japan: A Political Biography of Katô Shidzue* (Boulder: Westview Press, 1996); Barbara Rose, *Tsuda Umeko and Women's Education in Japan* (New Haven, Conn.: Yale University Press, 1992); and Sharon L. Sievers, *Flowers in Salt: The Beginnings of Feminist Consciousness in Modern Japan* (Stanford, Calif.: Stanford University Press, 1983).

38. Kwok, *Chinese Women and Christianity*, 187–93; and Jan Bardsley, *The Bluestockings of Japan: New Woman Essays and Fiction from Seitō, 1911–16* (Ann Arbor: Center for Japanese Studies, The University of Michigan, 2007), 51–52, 128–31.

39. Hwang Sin-dŏk, "Chosŏn puin undong ŭn ŏttŏk'e chinaewanna" (How Has the Women's Movement Developed in Korea?), *Sin kajŏng* (April 1933): 22–23. Cited from Kim Kyŏng-il, *Yŏsŏng ŭi kŭndae, kŭndae ŭi yŏsŏng*, 74.

40. Yi Man-gyu, "Chosŏn samdae chonggyo konggwaron: Kidokkyohoe ŭi kong kwa kwa" (Discussion of the Contribution and Shortcomings of Three Major Religions in Korea: The Contribution and Shortcomings of Christianity), *Kaebyŏk* 1 (November 1934): 27–31, 42.

41. Timothy Lee, "A Political Factor in the Rise of Protestantism in Korea: Protestantism and the 1919 March First Movement," *Church History* 69, no.1 (March 2000): 116–42 (especially, 120–22); and Clark, *Christianity in Modern Korea*, 6–8.

42. Hevia, "Leaving a Brand on China"; Lee, "A Political Factor," 122; Ka-che Yip, "The Anti-Christian Movement in China, 1922–1927, with Special Reference to the Experience of the Protestant Missions" (PhD dissertation, Columbia University, 1970).

43. Lee, "A Political Factor," 125. I am not arguing that Christianity was easily and eagerly accepted by Koreans. I merely suggest that American missionaries in Korea had a unique platform that often proved advantageous for them. For example, Edward McFarland reported that Japanese harassment of Korean Christians created antagonism against the Japanese but a sense of alliance with American missionaries. W. Arthur Noble described a "massacre by the Japanese soldiers" and the "widespread tragic suffering" of Korean Christians after the March First Independence movement in 1919. See "Annual Personal Report of Edward F. McFarland, Taiku, Korea, 1907–1908," RG 140-8-1; and J. Tremayne Copplestone, *History of Methodist Missions*, vol. 4, *Twentieth-Century Perspectives* (The Methodist Episcopal Church, 1896–1939) (New York: The Board of Global Ministries, The United Methodist Church, 1973), 1177.

44. In their analysis of Chinese elite women in late nineteenth and early

twentieth centuries, Ellen Widmer and Joan Judge demonstrate that the Japanese gender ideology of "good wives and wise mothers" was explicitly promoted together with a Chinese nationalist goal and a racialized pan-Asianism. The influence of a leading Japanese educator, Shimoda Utako, and her school, Practical Women's School (Jissen Jogakkō) on the early generation of Chinese women intellectuals was especially profound, although tensions between Shimoda's goals and Chinese students' aspirations emerged later. In contrast, while a similar gender ideology of "good wives and wise mothers" was implemented at girls' schools in Korea, the outbreak of the Russo-Japanese War and the subsequent outcome, in which Korea became a protectorate of Japan, ignited strong anti-Japanese sentiments among Koreans that continued after Korea was officially colonized by Japan in 1910. As a consequence, it is no wonder why it is hard to trace any explicit influence of Japanese teachers in the public discourse of Korean women intellectuals, even though they had studied in Japan and were influenced by the Japanese model of "good wives, wise mothers." See Ellen Widmer, "Foreign Travel through a Woman's Eyes: Shan Shili's *Guimao lüxing ji* in Local and Global Perspective," *Journal of Asian Studies* 65, no. 4 (November 2006): 763–91; and Joan Judge, "Talent, Virtue, and the Nation: Chinese Nationalisms and Female Subjectivities in the Early Twentieth Century," *American Historical Review* 106, no. 3 (June 2001): 765–803. See also Pak Sŏn-mi, *Kŭndae yŏsŏng cheguk ŭl kŏch'ŏ Chosŏn ŭro hoeyu hada* (Modern Women Return to Korea via Empire) (Seoul: Ch'angbi, 2007), 183–229; and Hŏ Yŏng-suk, "Puin munje ŭi ilmyŏn" (An Aspect of Women's Issue), *Tonga ilbo*, January 1–4, 1926.

45. Dorothy Ko, *Teachers of the Inner Chambers: Women and Culture in Seventeenth-Century China* (Stanford, Calif.: Stanford University Press, 1994); Susan Mann, *Precious Records: Women in China's Long Eighteenth Century* (Stanford, Calif.: Stanford University Press, 1997); Ellen Widmer, "The Rhetoric of Retrospection: May Fourth Literary History and the Ming-Qing Woman Writer," in *The Appropriation of Cultural Capital China's May Fourth Project*, ed. Milena Doleželová-Velingerová and Oldřich Král (Cambridge, Mass.: Harvard University Press, 2001), 193–225; and Martha Tocco, "Made in Japan: Meiji Women's Education," in *Gendering Modern Japanese History*, ed. Barbara Molony and Kathleen Uno (Cambridge, Mass.: Harvard University Press, 2005), 39–60.

46. Yi Pae-yong et al., *Uri nara yŏsŏngdŭl ŭn ŏttŏk'e sarassŭlkka 1* (How Korean Women Lived) (Seoul: Ch'ŏngnyŏnsa, 1999); Chŏn Sin-yong, ed., *Han'guk ŭi kyubang munhwa* (The Domestic Culture of Korea) (Seoul: Pagijŏng, 2005).

47. Kim, *Yŏsŏng ŭi kŭndae, kŭndae ŭi yŏsŏng*, 270–305; Mun Ok-p'yo, "Chosŏn kwa Ilbon ŭi sin yŏsŏng" (New Women of Korea and Japan), in *Sin yŏsŏng*, ed. Mun Ok-p'yo, 245–82; Kim, "1920–30-yŏndae sin yŏsŏng"; Bardsley, *The Bluestockings of Japan*; Wang, *Women in the Chinese Enlightenment*.

48. Peter Lee, ed., *Sourcebook of Korean Civilization*, vol. 2, *From the Seventeenth Century to the Modern Period* (New York: Columbia University

Press, 1996), 337–60. Enlightenment-oriented Korean intellectuals at the time were significantly influenced by Westerners, especially Protestant American missionaries in understanding what modernity is about and in what ways Korean society should be transformed. Some of these intellectuals got sponsorship from missionaries and had the opportunity to study in the United States. See Yi Kwang-nin, *Han'guk kaehwasa yŏn'gu* (Study of the History of Korean Enlightenment) (Seoul: Ilchogak, 1981), 31; and Wells, *New God, New Nation.*

49. Peter Duus, "The Takeoff Point of Japanese Imperialism," in *Japan Examined: Perspectives on Modern Japanese History*, ed. Harry Wray and Hilary Conroy (Honolulu: University of Hawai'i Press, 1983), 154.

50. James Huntley Grayson, "A Quarter-Millennium of Christianity in Korea," in *Christianity in Korea*, ed. Buswell and Lee, 7–25.

51. Henry Appenzeller, August 1885, Missionary Correspondence, 1840–1912, GCAH.

52. See note 24. For an analysis of the tensions between the mission board and individual missionaries in their response to Japanese colonial policies between 1905 and 1910, see Choi, "Christian Modernity," 39–68.

53. Joseph M. Henning, *Outposts of Civilization: Race, Religion, and the Formative Years of American-Japanese Relations* (New York: New York University Press, 2000), 146, 163.

54. Christianity includes a vast range of religious traditions, including Roman Catholicism, Eastern Orthodoxy, Oriental Orthodoxy, and Protestantism. In Korean history, Catholicism was introduced a century earlier than was Protestantism. However, Protestant Christianity has been the dominant form in Korea, and the notion of Christianity *[kidokkyo]* among Koreans typically refers to Protestant Christianity. In this vein, when I use the term "Christian modernity," it specifically refers to Protestant Christianity, which was first introduced to Korea in the late nineteenth century. I thank Timothy Lee and Pang Wŏn-il for drawing my attention to this distinction.

55. Prasenjit Duara, "The Discourse of Civilization and Pan-Asianism," *Journal of World History* 12, no. 1 (2001): 99–130.

56. The notion of "Christian modernity" builds on and expands similar notions that have already been introduced. Most representatively, William Hutchison's idea of "moral equivalent for imperialism" or Ussama Makdisi's concept of "evangelical modernity" capture the dynamic and complex relationship between missionary endeavors and secularity and politics. However, the particular situations found in the Korea mission field tend to complicate and expand these concepts. To be more specific, Hutchison characterizes the American evangelical movement as a "moral equivalent for imperialism" with its "civilizing" emphasis largely in the "circumstance of non-colonialism." Unlike European imperial powers, the United States' "traditional abstention from formal or political imperialism" contributed to the positive image of American missionaries as they engaged in building modern institutions, such as schools and hospitals. However, despite his discussion on liberal theology

that enhanced cultural relativism and social gospel, a "moral equivalent for imperialism" tends to downplay the power and importance of the local population who accepted, rejected or appropriated the newly introduced religion for their own particular interest. As much research in postcolonial studies demonstrates, imperialism or colonialism was "a process of mutual interaction, of point and counterpoint that inscribed itself on the dominant partner as well as the dominated ones." Furthermore, Hutchison's notion is based on the premise that "Americans were inordinately proud of themselves for avoiding colonial entanglement," but as I will demonstrate, American missionaries in Korea had to cope with unique challenges posed by Japanese colonial power. Ussama Makdisi uses the term, "evangelical modernity," elaborating on certain themes of American missionary involvement in the Levant in the mid-nineteenth century. Borrowing Johannes Fabian's terms "religious time" and "secularized time," Makdisi explains "evangelical modernity" as a "struggle between two overlapping notions of religious and secular time" and demonstrates how the intercommunal war in 1860 Syria made missionaries reconfigure evangelical modernity toward a "more overtly secular and worldly, hierarchical and discriminatory modernity that William Hutchison has described as 'a moral equivalent for imperialism.'" Makdisi's approach to evangelical modernity as a fragile "process" of preserving and abandoning certain cultural claims in response to the local particularities provides us with valuable insights into the dynamic interactions between the missionaries and the missionized. However, the drastically different local situation in the Levant makes evangelical modernity as defined by Makdisi insufficient for explaining the ways in which Christianity and modernity were articulated by American missionaries in Korea in their response to the particular local politics and culture. See William R. Hutchison, "A Moral Equivalent for Imperialism: Americans and the Promotion of 'Christian Civilization,' 1880–1910," in *Missionary Ideologies in the Imperial Era: 1880–1920*, ed. Torben Christensen and William R. Hutchison (Aarhus: Forlaget Aros, 1982), 167–77; Ussama Makdisi, "Reclaiming the Land of the Bible: Missionaries, Secularism, and Evangelical Modernity," *American Historical Review* 102, no. 3 (June 1997): 680–713. See also Dane Kennedy, "Imperial History and Post-Colonial Theory," *The Journal of Imperial and Commonwealth History* 24, no. 3 (September 1996): 345–63; Andrew Porter, "'Cultural Imperialism' and Protestant Missionary Enterprise, 1780–1914," *The Journal of Imperial and Commonwealth History* 25, no. 3 (September 1997): 367–91; Mary Louise Pratt, *Imperial Eyes: Travel Writing and Transculturation* (London: Routledge, 1992); Robert Young, *White Mythologies: Writing History and the West* (London: Routledge, 1990); and Robert Young, *Colonial Desire: Hybridity in Theory, Culture and Race* (London: Routledge, 1995).

57. Gaonkar, ed., *Alternative Modernities*, 1–8.

58. Arthur Brown, *New Forces in Old China: An Unwelcome but Inevitable Awakening* (New York: Fleming H. Revell Company, 1904), 127.

59. Ibid., 318.

60. Talal Asad, *Formations of the Secular: Christianity, Islam, Modernity* (Stanford, Calif.: Stanford University Press, 2003), 1.

61. José Casanova, "Rethinking Religion, Secularization and Secularism," paper presented at the conference "Conflicts at the Border of Religions and the Secular: Alternative Modernities," Arizona State University, April 23, 2004 (from 23–26). See also Janet Jakobsen with Ann Pellegrini, "World Secularisms at the Millennium," *Social Text* 64, no. 3 (fall 2000): 1–27.

62. The overall conservative nature of missionaries in the Korea mission field is succinctly summarized by the Rev. Charles A. Clark: "From the beginning, nearly all members of the Mission have held notably conservative views on theology. The missionaries in their teaching have always laid strong emphasis upon the sinfulness of men, and the paramount need of getting rid of sin, and upon salvation through the blood of Christ alone. They have accepted the supernatural as presented in the Scriptures, and believe in the Bible as a book of authority. They have believed and still believe that the message of the Gospel is unique in the world, and that Christianity is not one among several coordinate religions 'searching after God,' but the one and final religion which, through revelation, has found Him." See "Fifty Years of Mission Organization Principles and Practice," in *The Fiftieth Anniversary Celebration of the Korea Mission of the Presbyterian Church in the U.S.A.*, June 30–July 3, 1934 (Seoul: Han'guk kidokkyo yŏksa yŏn'guso, 2000, rpt.), 56–66.

63. Hunter, *The Gospel of Gentility*, xv.

64. Kwok Pui-lan, "Chinese Women and Protestant Christianity at the Turn of the Twentieth Century," in *Christianity in China*, ed. Daniel Bays, 204.

65. For American missionary women in China who were critical of Chinese women's attempts to get the right to vote, see Graham, *Gender, Culture, and Christianity*, 100–101.

66. Barbara Welter, "The Cult of True Womanhood: 1820–1860," *American Quarterly* 18, no. 2 (summer 1966), 151–74. For a critical reflection on Welter's notion of "true womanhood," see Tracy Fessenden, "Gendering Religion," *Journal of Women's History* 14, no. 1 (2002): 163–69; and Mary Kelly, "Beyond the Boundaries," *Journal of the Early Republic* 21, no. 1 (2001): 73–78.

67. Chilla Bulbeck explores "why and how the stereotypes of 'other' women are so integral to white western women's constructions of themselves." See her *Re-Orienting Western Feminisms: Women's Diversity in a Postcolonial World* (Cambridge: Cambridge University Press, 1998), 1–2.

68. Jayawardena, *Feminism and Nationalism*; Aparna Basu, "Feminism and Nationalism in India, 1917–1947," *Journal of Women's History* 7, no. 4 (winter 1995): 95–107; Noriyo Hayakawa, "Feminism and Nationalism in Japan, 1868–1945," *Journal of Women's History* 7, no. 4 (winter 1995): 108–19; and the special issue on gender and nationalisms and national identities of *Gender and History* 5, no. 2 (summer 1993).

69. Andre Schmid, *Korea between Empires, 1895–1919* (New York: Columbia University Press, 2002), 55–100.

70. Ibid., 57–60.

71. Yi Pae-yong, "19-segi kaehwa sasang e nat'anan yŏsŏnggwan" (Viewpoints on Women Represented in the Enlightenment Thought of the Nineteenth Century), *Han'guk sasang sahak* 20 (2003): 127–34; See also Lee, ed., *Sourcebook of Korean Civilization*, 354–60.

72. Lee, ed., *Sourcebook of Korean Civilization*, 382–84.

73. Yu Kil-chun, *Sŏyu kyŏnmun* (Observations from My Travels in the West), trans. Hŏ Kyŏng-jin (Seoul: Hanyang ch'ulp'an, 1995), 350.

74. Craig Calhoun, *Nationalism* (Minneapolis: University of Minnesota Press, 1997), 11.

75. Ibid.

76. Kim Tong-ch'un, *Kŭndae ŭi kŭnŭl* (Shadow of Modernity) (Seoul: Tangdae, 2000), 375–91.

77. Yun Hae-dong, *Singminji ŭi hoesaek chidae: Han'guk ŭi kŭndaesŏng kwa singminjuŭi pip'an* (The Gray Zone of a Colony: Korean Modernity and a Critique on Colonialism) (Seoul: Yŏksa pip'yŏngsa, 2003); Im Chi-hyŏn, *Minjokchuŭi nŭn panyŏk ida* (Nationalism Is Treason) (Seoul: Sonamu, 1999); and Gi-Wook Shin and Michael Robinson, eds., *Colonial Modernity in Korea* (Cambridge, Mass.: Harvard University Press, 1999). In *Colonial Modernity in Korea*, see especially Shin and Robinson, "Introduction: Rethinking Colonial Korea"; Carter J. Eckert, "Epilogue: Exorcising Hegel's Ghosts: Toward a Postnationalist Historiography of Korea"; Kenneth M. Wells, "The Price of Legitimacy: Women and the Kŭnuhoe Movement, 1927–1931"; and Kyeong-Hee Choi, "Neither Colonial nor National: The Making of the 'New Woman' in Pak Wansŏ's 'Mother's Stake 1.'"

78. Yun T'aeng-nim, "Minjokchuŭi tamnon kwa yŏsŏng: Yŏsŏngjuŭi yŏksahak e taehan siron" (Women and the Discourse of Nationalism: A Thought on Feminist Historiography), *Han'guk yŏsŏnghak* 10 (1994): 86–119; Kim Ŭn-sil, "Minjokchuŭi tamnon kwa yŏsŏng: Munhwa, kwŏllyŏk, chuch'e e kwanhan pip'anjŏk ilkki rŭl wihayŏ" (Women and the Discourse of Nationalism: Toward a Critical Reading of Culture, Power, and Subjectivity), *Han'guk yŏsŏnghak* 10 (1994): 18–52.

79. Wells, "The Price of Legitimacy," 191–220.

80. Chŏng Chin-sŏng, "Minjok mit minjokchuŭi e kwanhan Han'guk yŏsŏnghak ŭi nonŭi: Ilbon kun wianbu munje rŭl chungsim ŭro" (A Debate on Nation and Nationalism in Korean Feminism: The Issue of Comfort Women during the Japanese Colonial Era), *Han'guk yŏsŏnghak* 15, no. 2 (1999): 29–53; Chŏng Hyŏn-baek, "Chendŏ, minjok, kukka: Minjokchuŭi wa p'eminijŭm" (Gender, Nation, and the State: Nationalism and Feminism), *P'eminijŭm yŏn'gu* 1 (2001): 9–52. The viewpoints of Chŏng Chin-sŏng and Chŏng Hyŏn-baek are largely in line with the main argument of Kumari Jayawardena, who emphasizes the constitutive, not separate, nature of the feminist movement in the nationalist movement. See Jayawardena, *Feminism and Nationalism*. With specific focus on India, Aparna Basu offers a balanced point of view, touching on both gains and losses from women's participation in independence movements. She concludes, "Fighting for the country's freedom brought women out

of their homes and made them politically conscious but it did not emancipate or improve the position or status of the vast majority." Aparna Basu, "Feminism and Nationalism in India, 1917–1947," *Journal of Women's History* 7, no. 4 (winter 1995): 95–107 (from 105).

81. Rita Felski, *Doing Time: Feminist Theory and Postmodern Culture* (New York: New York University Press, 2000), 1–32.

82. In his analysis of the "last phase of the East Asian world order" in late nineteenth century, Key-Hiuk Kim describes the ways in which Korea's entry into the international system in 1882 with the United States, Britain, and Germany was brought about by the Qing empire, which helped Korea negotiate with western powers in response to the growing influence and potential threat from Japan and Russia. See Kim, *The Last Phase of the East Asian World Order: Korea, Japan, and the Chinese Empire, 1860–1882* (Berkeley and Los Angeles: University of California Press, 1980). For discussion of "civilization and enlightenment" in global and regional contexts, see Gerrit W. Gong, *The Standard of 'Civilization' in International Society* (Oxford: Clarendon Press, 1984); Schmid, *Korea between Empires;* Henning, *Outposts of Civilization;* and Kai-wing Chow, Kevin M. Doak, and Poshek Fu, eds., *Constructing Nationhood in Modern East Asia* (Ann Arbor: University of Michigan Press, 2001).

83. Although the most significant impact of the United States on the Korean political economy and culture began after the end of the Second World War, when U.S. military forces occupied the southern part of the Korean peninsula, the largely positive image of the United States had set in by the late nineteenth century. It was only in 1980s that such an image was significantly challenged.

84. Timothy Mitchell, ed., *Questions of Modernity* (Minneapolis: University of Minnesota Press, 2000), 2.

85. Ibid., 1.

86. Dipesh Chakrabarty, *Provincializing Europe: Postcolonial Thought and Historical Difference* (Princeton, N.J.: Princeton University Press, 2000), 2. See also Gyan Prakash, "Subaltern Studies as Postcolonial Criticism," *The American Historical Review* 99, no. 5 (December 1994): 1475–90.

87. Mary Louise Pratt, *Imperial Eyes: Travel Writing and Transculturation* (London: Routledge, 1992), 6. See also Steven Kaplan, ed., *Indigenous Responses to Western Christianity* (New York: New York University Press, 1995).

88. Choi, "Christian Modernity"; Jang Sukman, "Protestantism in the Name of Modern Civilization," *Korea Journal* 39, no. 4 (winter 1999): 187–204.

89. Hunter, *The Gospel of Gentility,* 26.

90. Kwok, "Chinese Women and Protestant Christianity," 194–208.

91. Brouwer, *Modern Women Modernizing Men.*

CHAPTER 2

1. Josiah Strong, *Our Country,* 17th ed. (Cambridge, Mass.: The Belknap Press of Harvard University Press, 1963; New York: The American Home Missionary Society, 1885), 200–202. Citations are to the Belknap edition.

2. Ibid., 16–17.

3. Mrs. J. F. Willing, "Under Bonds to Help Heathen Women," *HWF* 1 (August 1869): 20. See also Hill, *The World Their Household*, 36.

4. Duara, "The Discourse of Civilization," 100; Michael H. Hunt, *Ideology and U.S. Foreign Policy* (New Haven, Conn.: Yale University Press, 1987), 126–27; Frank Ninkovich, "Theodore Roosevelt: Civilization as Ideology," *Diplomatic History* 10 (summer 1986): 238; Hunter, *The Gospel of Gentility*, 8–9.

5. Korean intellectuals fostered close relationships with American missionaries because the latter were perceived as important sources of Western knowledge and technology. Newspapers often reported the activities of missionaries in the fields of education, social work, medicine, and religion, which conveyed a strong level of trust and expectation. See *Tongnip sinmun*, March 30, 1897; August 26, 1897; August 31, 1897; June 4, 1898; May 24, 1899. See also Ryu Tae-yŏng, *Kaehwagi Chosŏn kwa Miguk sŏn'gyosa* (Chosŏn of the Enlightenment Era and American Missionaries) (Seoul: Han'guk kidokkyo yŏksa yŏn'guso, 2004).

6. *Tongnip sinmun*, September 29, 1896; May 31, 1899.

7. Ibid., May 31, 1899.

8. *Taehan maeil sinbo*, July 2, 1907. For the role of *sin sosŏl* in the formation of new modern subjectivities, see Susie Jie Young Kim, "The Ambivalence of 'Modernity': Articulation of New Subjectivities in Turn of the Century Korea" (PhD dissertation, UCLA, 2002).

9. In his analysis of the development of modern Korean identity, Chung Yong-Hwa argues that the nineteenth-century representation of the West as superior negatively affected Koreans' sense of modern self and caused an inferiority complex with respect to Western culture. See "The Modern Transformation of Korean Identity: Enlightenment and Orientalism," *Korea Journal* 46, no. 1 (spring 2006): 109–38.

10. Homer Hulbert, *The Passing of Korea* (New York: Doubleday, Page and Company, 1906), 6. See also Ernest W. Clement's article arguing that Christianity is contributing to the "elevation of Japanese women": "The New Woman in Japan," *American Journal of Sociology* 8, no. 5 (March 1903): 693–98.

11. Strong, *Our Country*, 16–17.

12. James Gale, *Korea in Transition* (New York: Educational Department, The Board of Foreign Missions of the Presbyterian Church in the U.S.A., 1909), 95–106 (from 106).

13. Mrs. E. W. Rice, "A Woman of Korea," *HWF* 17, no. 8 (February 1886): 182–83.

14. Ellsue Wagner, "Girls and Women in Korea," *KMF* 4, no. 6 (June 1908): 82.

15. Ellasue Wagner, *Children of Korea* (London: Oliphants Ltd., 1911), trans. Sin Pongryong as *Han'guk ŭi adong saenghwal* (Seoul: Chipmundang, 1999), 31–34. Rosella Hogan Cram, a Methodist missionary, expressed similar sentiment when she wrote, "No more perplexing problem and no more difficult work

confronts the missionary than that of uplifting the degraded and neglected womanhood and establishing a right place for her in the church and home." R.H. Cram, "Song Do Girls' School," *The Korea Methodist* 1 (1905): 163–64.

16. In his analysis of the crisis of Korea facing the Japanese colonial conquest in the early 1900s, Homer Hulbert explicitly blamed the bad influence of China, stating that "Chinese law, religion, dress, art, literature, science and ethics became the fashion, and I am convinced that from that day began the deterioration of the Korean people, which has culminated in her present helpless condition." Hulbert, *The Passing of Korea*, 50, 76–77.

17. The Five Moral Imperatives include, in addition to *pyŏl*, righteousness [*ŭi*] between sovereign and subject, proper rapport [*ch'in*] between father and son, proper recognition of sequence of birth [*sŏ*] between elder and younger brothers, and faithfulness [*sin*] between friends. See Martina Deuchler, *The Confucian Transformation of Korea* (Cambridge, Mass.: Harvard University Press, 1992), 110. The third-year course of study included Confucian texts. See AMMEC (1899), 48–49.

18. George Heber Jones, "The Status of Woman in Korea," *GAL* (October 1896): 458–62 (from 459).

19. George Heber Jones, "Open Korea and its Methodist Mission," *GAL* (September 1893): 391–96.

20. *Samjong* already appeared in *Samguk sagi*, long before Confucianism was thoroughly institutionalized in the mid-Chosŏn dynasty. See Kim Chin-myŏng, "Kabujang tamnon kwa yŏsŏng ŏgap: Naehunsŏ mit Ŭiryesŏ ŭi punsŏk ŭl chungsim ŭro" (Patriarchal Discourse and the Oppression of Women), *Asea yŏsŏng yŏn'gu* 33 (1994): 63. See also Deuchler, *The Confucian Transformation of Korea*, 231–81.

21. The Committee for the Compilation of the History of Korean Women, *Women of Korea: A History from Ancient Times to 1945*, ed. and trans. Yung-Chung Kim (Seoul: Ewha Womans University Press, 1979), 52–53.

22. Mattie Noble, ed., *Victorious Lives of Early Christians in Korea: The First Book of Biographies and Autobiographies of Early Christians in the Protestant Church in Korea [Sŭngni ŭi saenghwal]* (Seoul: The Christian Literature Society, 1927). The book, written in Korean, bears the Korean title *Sŭngni ŭi saenghwal*. It gives an unusual window into the lives of early Christian women, given the fact that in late nineteenth and early twentieth centuries, women's literacy was so low that it was rare to find any writings by women. There are plenty of missionary reports about Korean converts, but those are still different from Korean women's own writings. In this sense, *Victorious Lives* provides examples of the vivid voices of Korean Christian women.

23. Kim Se-dŭi, "Na ŭi kwagŏ saenghwal" (My Past Life), in *Victorious Lives*, ed. Noble, 34–48.

24. Kim Syŏ-k'ŏ-sŭ, "Ŭnhye manŭn na ŭi saenghwal" (My Life Filled with Blessings), in *Victorious Lives*, ed. Noble, 71–76.

25. Yi Kyŏng-suk, "Yesu nŭn nae saenghwal ŭi pohyesa" (Jesus as the Protector and Benefactor of My Life), in *Victorious Lives*, ed. Noble, 54.

26. Mrs. T. J. Gracey, "Something about the Koreans," *HWF* 23, no. 12 (June 1892): 282–83.

27. Kim, "Ŭnhye manŭn na ŭi saenghwal," 71–76.

28. Yang, "Han'guk kaesin'gyo ŭi sŏng ch'abyŏl kujo," 215.

29. The phrase "equality of purpose" comes from Ann White's article, "Counting the Cost of Faith: America's Early Female Missionaries," *Church History* 57, no. 1 (March 1988): 29.

30. Elizabeth Cady Stanton and the Revising Committee, *The Woman's Bible* (New York: European Publishing Company, 1895; rpt., New York: Arno Press, 1974), 8; See also Rita Gross, *Feminism and Religion* (Boston: Beacon Press, 1996), 37–38.

31. Stanton, *The Woman's Bible*, 9.

32. Ellen Carol DuBois, *Feminism and Suffrage: The Emergence of an Independent Women's Movement in America 1848–1869* (Ithaca: Cornell University Press, 1978), 46.

33. Clark, *Living Dangerously in Korea*, 169.

34. After her husband, William Hall, passed away, Rosetta Sherwood Hall, a medical missionary, applied for appointment to Korea through the Board of the Methodist Episcopal Church. However, she was advised to apply to the WFMS because the Board "does not send out lady physicians." Minutes of the Committee on Japan and Korea, 1886–1896 (Oct. 31, 1895), Administrative Files, GCAH, 377. Not all single women missionaries were sent by the WFMS. Five single women missionaries were sent by the General Board. One of them was Maud Keister Jensen, and she recalls her experience as follows: "I did not go out (I will have to admit) as a missionary under the women's board, the Woman's Foreign Missionary Society. I never wanted to work under women . . . I usually felt that many of the women were not people who made it pleasant to serve under them. The Board of Foreign Missions was the main mission board of the church, and that's what I wanted to work with. . . . The Board of Foreign Missions usually took married couples and men, single men, but they did (although most people didn't seem to know it) occasionally take single women when there was a place for them. Usually single women went out under the women's board, but I went out under the General Board that they called 'the men's board' in those days mostly, when people referred to it." See *United Methodist Women's Oral History Project: Maud Keister Jensen*, six interviews (1984), 17–18, GCAH; and "Chronological List of Missionaries to Korea: Methodist Episcopal Church," Charles A. Sauer Collection, United Methodist Church Archives, GCAH.

35. Arthur Brown, *One Hundred Years: A History of the Foreign Missionary Work of the Presbyterian Church in the USA* (New York: Fleming H. Revell Company, 1936), 141–42.

36. The main goal of such a separate conference was "to unite the members of the Woman's Foreign Missionary Society, the women of the General Missionary Society, and such Korean women as may be admitted, for the purpose of discussing methods of work, hearing reports of missionaries in charge of

work, and planning for the work of bringing the Gospel of Christ to the women and children of Korea." It had a slate of officers, consisting of a president, two vice-presidents, a recording secretary, a corresponding secretary, a statistical secretary, and a treasurer, with an array of committees, such as the executive committee, the standing and special committees, the committee on estimates for appropriations and on appointments of workers. KWCMEC (1899), 7–8.

37. Ibid., 7.

38. Married women accompanied their husbands, so they were not officially appointed by the WFMS. Mattie Noble, who married W. Arthur Noble, wrote in her diaries some of the procedures she and her husband went through before their departure for Korea. She said that she "did not need to pass an examination" and a church official in New York asked her only about her health. Mattie Noble, Diaries, July 2, 1892. GCAH.

39. While the Woman's Conference was largely run by women missionaries, the president of the woman's conference was the bishop, who presided over the meetings.

40. Brown, *One Hundred Years*, 141.

41. Lillias Underwood, "Shall Married Women Have a Vote on Mission Matters," *KMF* 8 (1912): 345–46 (from 345).

42. AMPC (1904), 87.

43. Underwood, "Shall Married Women Have a Vote on Mission Matters," 345.

44. Ibid., 346.

45. For example, Mrs. E. W. Koons describes the situation: "with a small foreign community in an isolated country town, the question of getting something to eat and getting it cooked looms up in serious fashion." See "House-Keeping Problems of a Small Station," *KMF* 3, no. 2 (1907): 30–32.

46. Jane Hunter's analysis of American missionary women in China indicates a situation that is very similar to the one found in Korea in terms of the lower expectations for married women in comparison to single women and the former group's struggle between "their original mission ambition and their limited possibilities." Hunter, *The Gospel of Gentility*, 90–127.

47. Annie Baird, "Votes or Not for Married Women in Station and Mission," *KMF* 9, no. 2 (1913): 35–37.

48. AMPC (1913), 77–78.

49. Rules and By-Laws of the Korea Mission of the Presbyterian Church in the United States of America (1916), Section 54 on voting privileges. PHS.

50. Those who applied to the foreign mission board as single women almost always answered negatively to the question, "Do you contemplate marriage?" Some married to male missionaries they met in the same mission field, but others remained single and devoted all of their time to the mission work until they retired. See RG 360; and Lura McLane Smith to Miss Hughes, July 1, 1915, RG 208-1-2.

51. *WWW* 9, no. 8 (August 1894): 214.

52. *WMA* (April 1900): 308.

53. Victoria Arbuckle, May 18, 1893, Missions Correspondence and Reports Microfilm series, Presbyterian Church in the USA Board of Foreign Missions, vol. 4, 90, PHS.

54. "What do we wear and how do we act to be perfectly proper out in Chosen? The Koreans themselves ask Miss Margo Lee Lewis of Seoul, Chosen," Margo Lee Lewis' file, RG 360.

55. Ann White, "Counting the Cost of Faith: America's Early Female Missionaries," *Church History* 57, no. 1 (March 1988): 26; Martha Huntley, "Presbyterian Women's Work and Rights in the Korea Mission," *American Presbyterians* 65, no. 1 (1987): 37–48.

56. The salary gap was even worse for Korean women Christians, who were at the bottom of the church hierarchy. According to a report in 1921, the salary for American missionaries was about 179 *won* (Korean currency), for Korean male pastors 48 *won*, for his male assistant 30 *won*, and for Korean Bible women 18 *won*. The sharp discrepancy in salary eventually led some Bible women to submit a plea to raise their salary in 1922. In the case of married women missionaries, they did not receive any salary at all until the 1960s, regardless of the hours or years they spent in work outside and inside the home. See AMPC (1902), 34–35; 50–54; Yang, "Han'guk kaesin'gyo ŭi sŏng ch'abyŏl kujo," 224; and Huntley, "Presbyterian Women's Work and Rights," 37–48.

57. Hunter, *The Gospel of Gentility*, 89.

58. White, "Counting the Cost of Faith," 29.

59. One of the exceptional cases can be found in Abby M. Colby, a missionary in Japan who spoke up for women's rights. At a time when women missionaries were regarded as inferior, earned a lower salary, and were largely restricted to women's work, Colby protested unequal pay for single men and women and expressed a belief in the moral superiority of women. She believed women should vote in order to purify the government. See Sandra Taylor, "Abby M. Colby: The Christian Response to a Sexist Society," *New England Quarterly* 52, no. 1 (March 1979): 68–79; and also Sheila Rothman, *Woman's Proper Place: A History of Changing Ideals and Practices, 1870 to the Present* (New York: Basic Books, 1978), 127–32.

60. Hill, *The World Their Household*, 35.

61. Jane Haggis argues that "Rather than an emancipatory struggle to break through the bounds of convention, it was precisely convention which enabled the making of the female missionary. . . . The outcome, however, is remarkably similar to that produced in the more overtly feminist story of struggle." See "'A Heart That Has Felt the Love of God and Longs for Others to Know It': Conventions of Gender, Tensions of Self, and Constructions of Difference in Offering to Be a Lady Missionary," *Women's History Review* 7, no. 2 (1998): 171–92 (from 172).

62. Schmid, *Korea between Empires*, 55–100.

63. Deuchler, *The Confucian Transformation of Korea*, 22.

64. Yi Sug-in, "Kaehwagi (1894–1910) yuhakchadŭl ŭi hwaltong kwa sidae insik" (Activities and Perspectives of Confucian Scholars during the Enlight-

enment Era, 1894–1910), *Tongyang ch'ŏlhak yŏn'gu* 37 (2004): 8–42. Yi traces the complex lineage of Confucian scholars whose intellectual background and praxis differed in terms of their responses to the political and sociocultural changes.

65. An Pyŏng-ju, "Yugyo ŭi iron powan: P'eminijŭm ŭi suyong kwa kwallyŏn hayŏ" (Complementing Confucian Theories: In Relation to the Accommodation of Feminism), *Yugyo sasang yŏn'gu* 12 (1999): 7–19. Here An specifically introduces a Chinese intellectual, Kang Youwei, and his critique of the precedents of Confucian practices and advocacy of gender equality through a thorough transformation of Confucianism.

66. Schmid, *Korea between Empires*, 80–82.

67. Kyung Moon Hwang, "Country or State? Reconceptualizing *Kukka* in the Korean Enlightenment Period, 1896–1910," *Korean Studies* 24 (2000): 1–24.

68. Yi Kwang-nin, *Han'guk kaehwasa yŏn'gu* (A Study of the History of Korean Enlightenment) (Seoul: Ilchogak, 1981), 47–56.

69. My analysis of Pak Yŏng-hyo's "Memorial on Domestic and Political Reforms" is based on the full translation in Korean, "Pak Yŏng-hyo ŭi kŏnbaeksŏ," by Kim Kap-ch'ŏn, published in *Han'guk chŏngch'i yŏn'gu* 2 (1990): 245–92. I also refer to a partial translation of the Memorial in English in Peter Lee, ed., *Sourcebook of Korean Civilization*, vol. 2 (New York: Columbia University Press, 1996), 354–60. For the intellectual connection between Pak and Fukuzawa Yukichi, see Yi Pae-yong, "19-segi kaehwa sasang e nat'anan yŏsŏnggwan" (Views on Gender in Nineteenth Century Enlightenment Thought), *Han'guk sasang sahak* 20 (2003): 127–34.

70. Pak, "Memorial," 254–55.

71. Lee, *Sourcebook of Korean Civilization*, 358.

72. Charles Taylor, "Modern Social Imaginaries," *Public Culture* 14, no. 1 (2002): 91–124 (from 98).

73. Pak, "Memorial," 271, 283, 290, 292.

74. Ibid.; Yi, "19-segi kaehwa sasang," 127–34.

75. Yi, "19-segi kaehwa sasang," 127.

76. *KR* (January 1896): 4.

77. *HWF* 17, no. 8 (February 1886): 190–91.

78. *HWF* 17, no. 1 (July 1885): 10–11.

79. "Mrs. M. F. Scranton Writes to Dr. Reid from Tokio, Japan, May 25th," *GAL* 11 (1885): 329.

80. "Chaemi itnŭn mundap" (Interesting Questions and Answers), *Tongnip sinmun*, April 15, 1899.

81. Yi T'aek-hwi et al., *Sŏ Chae-p'il* (Seoul: Minŭmsa, 1993), 17. According to *The Korean Repository*, Sŏ Chae-p'il received his medical degree from Johns Hopkins University. See "The Independence Club," *KR* (August 1898): 282.

82. *Yun Ch'i-ho ilgi* (The Diaries of Yun Ch'i-ho), February 12, 1895. Yun's diaries are available online at the site of Kuksa p'yŏnch'an wiwŏnhoe (http://db.history.go.kr/).

83. When Sŏ returned to Korea in 1895, he was greatly interested in starting a Korean-English newspaper as a medium for enlightening the public. Sŏ sought collaboration from Yun Ch'i-ho, who had himself been interested in starting a newspaper, especially one published in English. For the beginning and ending of *Tongnip sinmun*, see Yi Kwang-nin, "Sŏ Chae-p'il ŭi 'Tongnip sinmun' kanhaeng e taehayŏ" (About the Founding of "Tongnip Sinmun" by Sŏ Chae-p'il), *Chindan Hakpo* 39 (1975): 71–104.

84. *Tongnip sinmun*, April 7, 1896.

85. *Tongnip sinmun*, April 21, 1896; September 5, 1896.

86. Kim Suk-ja, "Tongnip sinmun e nat'anan yŏsŏng kaehwa ŭi ŭiji" (The Goals for Enlightening Women Reflected in Tongnip Sinmun), *Han'guksa yŏn'gu* 54 (1986): 59–74.

87. Editor, "The Independence Club," *KR* (August 1898): 281–87 (from 286). The official organ of the Independence Club was the *Bulletin of the Independence Club of Great Chosŏn*. Ki-baik Lee, *A New History of Korea* (Seoul: Ilchogak, 1984), 303.

88. Yi U-jin, "Sŏ Chae-p'il ŭi chaeMi hwaltong" (Sŏ Chaep'il's Activities in the United States), in *Sŏ Chae-p'il*, ed. Yi, 262–63.

89. "A Korean's Confession," *GAL* (June 1887): 274–75. In his examination of Yun Ch'i-ho's study in Japan, Yi Kwang-nin argues that the initial influence of Christianity on Yun began when he first studied in Japan between 1881 and 1882 through Japanese teachers and possibly Korean Christians, including Yi Su-jŏng. However, in Yun's "Confession," he states, " I had not heard of God before I came to Shanghai . . . " See Yi Kwang-nin, *Kaehwap'a wa kaehwa sasang yŏn'gu* (Study of the Enlightenment Group and Its Thoughts) (Seoul: Ilchogak, 1989), 43–62.

90. *Yun Ch'i-ho ilgi*, February 19, 1893.

91. "Editorial," *The Independent*, November 14, 1896.

92. Yung-Hee Kim, "Under the Mandate of Nationalism: Development of Feminist Enterprises in Modern Korea, 1860–1910," *Journal of Women's History* 7, no. 4 (1995): 120–36.

93. *Tongnip sinmun*, January 4, 1898.

94. Ibid. A public debate was held at Chŏngdong Church on December 31, 1897. The topic for debate was whether men and women should have access to equal education and equal rights. Note that this event was designed to teach student members of the Chŏngdong Church how to conduct a debate. Sŏ Chaep'il and Yun Ch'i-ho intentionally took opposite positions to provoke thought and points of argument, and to encourage students to engage in the debate.

95. *Tongnip sinmun*, September 29, 1896. See also May 31, 1899.

96. Kim Kyŏng-ae, "Tonghak ŭi yŏsŏnggwan e taehan chae goch'al" (A Reexamination of the Views on Women in Tonghak), *Han'guk sasang sahak* 20 (2003): 90–95.

97. The letter from Yun Ch'i-ho to Young J. Allen can be found in Hyung-chan Kim, *Letters in Exile: The Life and Times of Yun Ch'i-ho* (Covington, Ga.: Rhoades Printing Company, 1980).

98. Regarding the influence of *Wanguo gongbao*, see Yi Kwang-nin, *Han'guk kaehwasa yŏn'gu* (A Study of the History of Korean Enlightenment) (Seoul: Ilchogak, 1981), 45–46.

99. Cited from Hu Ying, *Tales of Translation: Composing the New Woman in China, 1899–1918* (Stanford, Calif.: Stanford University Press, 2000), 2.

100. Kim, *Letters in Exile*, 65.

101. *Yun Ch'i-ho ilgi*, December 12, 1893.

102. Ken Wells, "Expanding their Realm: Women and Public Agency in Colonial Korea," in *Women's Suffrage in Asia: Gender, Nationalism and Democracy*, ed. Louise Edwards and Mina Roces (London: RoutledgeCurzon, 2004), 152–69 (from 153).

103. Kim, *Letters in Exile*, 65.

104. T. H. Yun, "The Sort of Education Korean Girls Need," *The Missionary Voice* (April 1918): 114–15.

105. The circulation of the newspapers remained rather tiny. For example, the largest circulation of *Tongnip sinmun* reached about 3,000 by July 1898. Yi, "Sŏ Chae-p'il ŭi 'Tongnip Sinmun,'" 88–89.

106. The decision to use Korean script in the cases of *Tongnip sinmun* and *Cheguk sinmun* was particularly important because it made the new information in newspaper accessible to women. Chang Myŏng-hak, "Tongnip sinmun sasŏl e nat'anan kŭndaehwa kihoek" (The Project of Modernity Reflected in the Editorials of *Tongnip Sinmun*) *Yŏksa wa sahoe* 3, no. 30 (2003): 1–15.

107. The *T'ongmun* is often cited as *Yŏkwŏn t'ongmun*, but the element of the name, "Yŏkwŏn" (women's rights) is not in the original text. See the original text in *Tongnip sinmun*, September 9, 1898.

108. Ibid.; *Hwangsŏng sinmun*, September 9, 1898. It was proclaimed by Yi Sosa and Kim Sosa on September 1, 1898. The title *sosa* is a general title for women. It is inferred that Yi Sosa and Kim Sosa might be the two leaders Yangsŏngdang Yi ssi and Yanghyŏndang Kim ssi, respectively, who played a central role in founding Ch'anyanghoe in order to promote women's education. See Han'guk yŏsŏngsa p'yŏnch'an wiwŏnhoe, *Han'guk yŏsŏngsa* 2, 62.

109. Ando Shoeki (1703–1762), a Japanese philosopher, pointed to the problem of the binary distinction between heaven/yang/male and earth/yin/female as the natural order. See Tetsuo Najita, "Presidential Address: Reflections on Modernity and Modernization," *Journal of Asian Studies* 52, no. 4 (November 1993): 845–53 (from 846).

110. Sohye Wanghu Han ssi, *Ŏje naehun* (rpt., Seoul: Hongmungak, 1990), 178–89.

111. Ibid., 167

112. Ibid., 45–48.

113. The translation is from John Duncan, "The *Naehun* and the Politics of Gender," in *Creative Women of Korea: The Fifteenth through the Twentieth Centuries*, ed. Young-Key Kim-Renaud (Armonk: M. E. Sharpe, 2004), 26–57 (from 31).

114. Charles Taylor argues that one of the most prominent differences be-

tween premodern and modern social imaginaries is "the idealizations of natural law theory." In premodern social imaginaries, modes of hierarchical complementarity prevail in shaping human relationships, while in modern social imaginaries the hierarchical nature is challenged. See Taylor, *Modern Social Imaginaries*, 11.

115. Duncan, "The *Naehun* and the Politics of Gender," 26–57.

116. Martina Deuchler, "Propagating Female Virtues in Chosŏn Korea," in *Women and Confucian Cultures in Premodern China, Korea and Japan*, ed. Dorothy Ko, JaHyun Kim Haboush and Joan Piggott (Berkeley and Los Angeles: University of California Press, 2003), 142–69 (from 148).

117. Exploring the connection between Confucianism and feminism is part of the emerging effort of scholars who acknowledge the undemocratic elements embedded in Confucianism and yet try to reinterpret it not as an anachronistic philosophy but as an alternative to Western capitalism and democracy. See Ch'oe Yŏng-jin, "Yugyo wa p'eminijŭm, kŭ chŏpchŏm ŭi mosaek" (Confucianism and Feminism: Exploring Their Intersections), *Yugyo sasang yŏn'gu* 14 (2000): 115–31.

118. Yi Sug-in, "Yugyo ŭi kwan'gye yulli e taehan yŏsŏngjuŭi chŏk haesŏk" (Feminist Interpretations of Relational Ethics in Confucianism), *Han'guk yŏsŏnghak* 15, no. 1 (1999): 39–69.

119. In explaining the transition from the feudal society to the modern, Charles Taylor elucidates new Western political theories emerging from the seventeenth century that advocate equality of people who "stand outside all relations of superiority and inferiority." Taylor, *Modern Social Imaginaries*, 3–22.

120. Ch'anyanghoe was alternately referred to as Yangsŏngwŏn.

121. *Tongnip sinmun*, September 15, 1898.

122. *Tongnip sinmun*, October 7, 1898, reports that a Western woman gave a speech at a meeting of Ch'anyanghoe, and Yun Ch'i-ho translated her speech into Korean. See also Pak Yong-ok, "1896–1910 punyŏ tanch'e ŭi yŏn'gu" (A Study of Women's Organizations 1896–1910), *Han'guksa yŏn'gu* 6 (1971): 106–12.

123. *Tongnip sinmun*, October 12, 1898.

124. Pak, "1896–1910 punyŏ tanch'e ŭi yŏn'gu," 111.

125. There was a criticism that Ch'anyanghoe was largely for women of the upper class and ignored poor women. The majority of women in leadership positions were likely from the upper class in Seoul, which also explains the close ties between them and the male intellectuals of the Independence Club. See *Tongnip sinmun*, December 10, 1898.

126. *Taehan maeil sinbo*, August 1, 1908.

127. The "inside-outside rule" refers to both physical and symbolic differences between women and men. Physically, women are expected to stay inside the house, attending to domestic matters, while men are in charge of external and public affairs.

128. *Taehan maeil sinbo*, August 1, 1908. At the end of the article, a male newspaper reporter, observed that when women depend on men, women cannot have rights, that when people depend on the government, their rights are limited, and that when one country depends on another, its rights are weakened. He adds his hope that the submitted article would stimulate new ideas among women and result in their being less dependent on others.

129. Yi Kang-ja, "Yŏja ŭi chayu" (Women's Freedom), *Yŏja chinam* 1, no. 1 (1908): 28–29. (Rpt., Ewha yŏja taehakkyo Han'guk yŏsŏng yŏn'guso, ed., *Han'guk yŏsŏng kwan'gye charyojip* [Sourcebook of Korean Women] [Seoul: Ewha yŏja taehakkyo ch'ulp'anbu, 1981], 48–49).

130. Pak Ch'an-sŭng, *Han'guk kŭndae chŏngch'i sasangsa yŏn'gu* (A Study of the History of Modern Political Thought in Korea) (Seoul: Yŏksa pip'yŏngsa, 1993), 29–107.

131. Yun Chŏng-wŏn, "Ponguk chehyŏng chemae ege" (To Brothers and Sisters at Home), *T'aegŭk hakpo* (September 1906).

132. Fred Dallmayr, "Confucianism and the Public Sphere: Five Relationships Plus One?" in *The Politics of Affective Relations*, ed. Hahm Chaihark and Daniel A. Bell (Lanham, Md.: Lexington Books, 2004), 41–60.

133. "Yŏja wa nodong sahoe ŭi chisik ŭl pogŭpk'e hal tori" (Mission to Distribute Knowledge to Women and Laborers), *Taehan maeil sinbo*, December 29, 1908.

134. There is a significant parallel between Korea and China in terms of the nature of women's citizenship in early twentieth century. See Joan Judge, "Citizens or Mothers of Citizens? Gender and Meaning of Modern Chinese Citizenship," in *Changing Meanings of Citizenship in Modern China*, ed. Merle Goldman and Elizabeth J. Perry (Cambridge, Mass.: Harvard University Press, 2002), 23–43.

135. "Chosŏn yŏja ŭi sahoe chŏk chiwi" (The Social Status of Korean Women), *Sin yŏsŏng* 3, no. 10 (1925): 4.

CHAPTER 3

1. Huldah A. Haenig, "From West Gate to East Gate," *WMF* 43, no. 1 (January 1911): 9–11.

2. Mrs. Ella D. Appenzeller, "Korean Girls," *HWF* 20, no. 2 (August 1888): 47–48; W. B. Scranton, "Report of Pastor, Baldwin Chapel and Ewa Hak Tang—1893," *AMMEC* (1893), 44–46; George W. Gilmore, "Social Phases in Korea," *HWF* 22, no. 1 (July 1890): 3–5 (from 3); Augustus R. Buckland, *Women in the Mission Field: Pioneers and Martyrs* (New York: Thomas Whittaker, 1895), 16–18.

3. *Cheguk sinmun*, January 11, 1898; December 12, 1899; and January 11, 1900. Cited from Kim In-uk, "Hanmal yŏsŏng kyemong undong e taehan il yŏn'gu: 'Cheguk sinmun' ŭi yŏkhal ŭl chungsim ŭro" (A Study of the Enlightenment Movement for Women in Late Chosŏn Dynasty with a Special Focus on Cheguk Sinmun), (MA thesis, Hanyang University, 1985), 32–35.

4. Seyla Benhabib, *Situating the Self: Gender, Community, and Postmodernism in Contemporary Ethics* (New York: Routledge, 1992), 89–120.

5. Amanda Vickery, "Golden Age to Separate Spheres? A Review of the Categories and Chronology of English Women's History," *The Historical Journal* 36, no. 2 (1993): 383–414; and Joan B. Landes, "Further Thoughts on the Public/Private Distinction," *Journal of Women's History* 15, no. 2 (summer 2003): 28–39. For a more recent and thorough discussion on the analytical categories of the public and private in women's history, see the special issue of the *Journal of Women's History* 15, no. 1 (spring 2003). Included in the issue are solid case studies of British, Brazilian, and Middle Eastern women.

6. Deuchler, "Propagating Female Virtues in Chosŏn Korea," 142–69; and Duncan, "The *Naehun* and the Politics of Gender," 26–57.

7. JaHyun Kim Haboush, "Versions and Subversions: Patriarchy and Polygamy in Korean Narratives," in *Women and Confucian Cultures in Premodern China, Korea and Japan*, ed. Dorothy Ko, JaHyun Kim Haboush and Joan Piggott (Berkeley and Los Angeles: University of California Press, 2003), 279–303.

8. Leonore Davidoff and Catherine Hall, *Family Fortunes: Men and Women of the English Middle Class, 1780–1850* (Chicago: University of Chicago Press, 1987).

9. Leslie Peirce, *The Imperial Harem: Women and Sovereignty in the Ottoman Empire* (Oxford: Oxford University Press, 1993).

10. Paula Baker, *The Moral Frameworks of Public Life: Gender, Politics, and the State in Rural New York, 1870–1930* (New York: Oxford University Press, 1991).

11. Leonore Davidoff, "Gender and the 'Great Divide': Public and Private in British Gender History," *Journal of Women's History* 15, no. 1 (spring 2003): 22.

12. Mary Ryan, "The Public and the Private Good: Across the Great Divide in Women's History," *Journal of Women's History* 15, no. 2 (summer 2003): 10–27; Elizabeth Thompson, "Public and Private in Middle Eastern Women's History," *Journal of Women's History* 15, no. 1 (spring 2003): 52–69 (from 53).

13. Martha Vicinus, ed., *A Widening Sphere: Changing Roles of Victorian Women* (Bloomington: Indiana University Press, 1977).

14. Hattie Heron, "Behind Sealed Doors in Korea," *WWW* 1, no. 3 (March 1886): 82–83.

15. Gilmore, "Social Phases in Korea," 3.

16. Kim Yong-suk, *Han'guk yŏsoksa* (The History of Women's Customs in Korea) (Seoul: Minŭmsa, 1990), 63.

17. Deuchler, *The Confucian Transformation of Korea*.

18. Martina Deuchler, preface to *Korean Women: View from the Inner Rooms*, ed. Laurel Kendall and Mark Peterson (New Haven, Conn.: East Rock Press, Inc., 1983), 1–3.

19. The historian Chŏng Chi-yŏng argues that while Confucianization put new and greater restrictions on the scope of life for women, it is important to pay attention to the ways in which women conformed to, resisted, or ignored such regulations. See "Chosŏn sidae punyŏ ŭi noch'ul kwa oech'ul: Kyuje wa

t'ŭmsae" (Escaping the Inner Room: Women between Regulation and Resistance in the Chosŏn Dynasty), *Yŏsŏng kwa yŏksa* 2 (June 2005): 149–81.

20. Mrs. Horace Underwood, "Woman's Work for Women in Korea," *WMA* (February 1906): 286–90.

21. Ellen Strong, "Woman's Work in Korea," *WWW* (August 1893): 213–14.

22. A. M. Nisbet, "Seclusion of Korean Women," *KMF* 4, no. 6 (June 1908): 90.

23. Harriet G. Gale, "Hosanna, A Korean Woman," *WWW* (August 1894): 205; Emily G. Kemp, *The Face of Manchuria, Korea and Russian Turkestan* (London, Chatto & Windus, 1910), 76. In a situation where a male visitor came to a house but the man of the house was absent, his wife was not supposed to talk to the visitor directly. What typically happened in this situation is that the visitor said loudly "Come here," which implies that a servant came to the visitor and let the owner know of his visit. The wife hid herself in the kitchen or a room and said "Tell him the man of the house is not at home right now," as if she ordered her servant to tell the visitor as such. The commoners did not own servants, but the wife and the male visitor communicated in this way using an indirect speech style in order to avoid any direct contact. See Yi Nŭng-hwa, *Chosŏn yŏsokko* (Investigation of Women's Customs in Korea), trans. Kim Sang-ŏk (Seoul: Tongmunsŏn, 1990), 347.

24. Gilmore, "Social Phases in Korea," 3.

25. Heron, "Behind Sealed Doors in Korea," 82–83.

26. Baird, *Daybreak in Korea*, 58–59.

27. Isabella Bird Bishop, *Korea and Her Neighbors: A Narrative of Travel, with an Account of the Recent Vicissitudes and Present Position of the Country* (New York: Fleming H. Revell Company, 1897), 342.

28. Lillias H. Underwood, *With Tommy Tompkins in Korea* (New York: Fleming H. Revell Company, 1905), 228–29.

29. Sherwood Hall, *With Stethoscope in Asia: Korea* (McLean, Va.: MCL Associate, 1978), 27–28.

30. "Customs in Korea," *GAL* (August 1888): 366–67.

31. Kim Mi-jŏng, "Chosŏn sidae saramdŭl ŭi p'aesyŏn kamgak" (The Fashion Sense of Chosŏn People), in *Chosŏn sidae saramdŭl ŭn ŏttŏk'e sarassŭlkka* 2, ed. Han'guk yŏksa yŏn'guhoe (Seoul: Ch'ŏngnyŏnsa, 1996), 199–211.

32. "From Mrs. Wilson, in Korea," *WMA* (December 1900): 168–69.

33. Annie Baird, *Inside Views of Mission Life* (Philadelphia: Westminster Press, 1913), 18–19.

34. Barbara Burman and Carole Turbin, "Material Strategies Engendered," *Gender and History* 14, no. 3 (November 2002): 371–81.

35. Davidoff, "Gender and the 'Great Divide,'" 11–27. See also Norbert Elias, *The Civilizing Process: The History of Manners*, trans. Edmund Jephcott (New York: Urizen Books, 1978). In the section "Changes in Attitude toward Relations between the Sexes" (pp. 169–91), Elias demonstrates how standards of shame or propriety in manners in sexual relations have changed over time. He notes, "In the civilizing process, sexuality too is increasingly removed behind the scenes of social life and enclosed in a particular enclave, the nuclear

family. Likewise, the relations between the sexes are isolated, placed behind walls in consciousness." (180)

36. Nandini Bhattacharya argues that "due to noncommunication or mutual linguistic incomprehension . . . the Western observers intensified visual symbolism and metaphorized Indian women's bodies. These observers' intense focus on the body led to the construction of the colonial female body as a metonym of Indian culture." See Nandini Bhattacharya, *Reading the Splendid Body: Gender and Consumerism in Eighteenth-Century British Writing on India* (Newark: University of Delaware Press, 1998), 15.

37. Baird, *Inside Views of Mission Life*, 18–19.

38. Yun Ka-hyŏn, "Sŏng kwa sŏng ŭisik ŭi pyŏnhwa" ("Sexuality and the Change in Sexual Consciousness") in *Chŏnt'ong kwa sŏgu ŭi ch'ungdol* (Clash between Tradition and the West), ed. Yŏksa munje yŏn'guso (Seoul: Yŏksa pip'yŏngsa, 2001), 53–72. Yun notes that in certain regions of Korea, women customarily exposed their breasts as a sign of pride after they gave birth to a son. He further argues that it is only from the 1980s or so that Korean women began to avoid breastfeeding in public space, as their breasts were rapidly becoming associated more with sexuality than with motherhood. Song Yŏn-ok argues that women's breasts began to signify sexuality rather than motherhood as early as the 1920s, and that this change was symptomatic of gendered modern experience. See Son Yŏn-ok, "Chosŏn 'sin yŏsŏng' ŭi nae-syŏnŏllijŭm kwa chendŏ" (Nationalism and Gender in Chosŏn New Women), in *Sin yŏsŏng*, ed. Mun Ok-p'yo, 83–117.

39. Baird, *Inside Views of Mission Life*, 18–19.

40. Yu Su-gyŏng, *Han'guk yŏsŏng yangjang pyŏnch'ŏnsa* (A History of the Adoption of Western Dress among Korean Women), (Seoul: Ilchisa, 1990), 143.

41. *Paehwa 60-yŏnsa* (The Sixtieth History of Paehwa) (Seoul: Paehwa chunggodŭng hakkyo, 1958), 110.

42. *Kijŏn 70-yŏnsa* (The Seventieth History of Kijŏn) (Chŏnju: Kijŏn 70-yŏnsa p'yŏnch'an wiwŏnhoe, 1974), 47–48. Another reason given in the book for the strike was that Principal Colton had severely abused two Korean girls she had adopted.

43. The incident at Kijŏn Girls School also signaled a growing distance between the younger Korean generation and American missionaries in their respective vision for new womanhood. This gap became much more evident in the 1920s and later, when mission schools were criticized by the Korean public for their "anachronistic" and "oppressive" regulations for dormitory life and other disciplinary rules imposed on students. There were regional differences, however, especially between urban and rural areas. While mission schools in Seoul were able to adopt more "liberal" gender practices, their counterparts in provincial cities like Chŏnju, Taegu, or P'yŏngyang continued to adhere to the old custom of covering the face and body in public up to the 1910s. See "Kaesŏng Hosŭdon yŏgo kyojang ege," *Sin yŏsŏng* 2, no. 10 (November 1924): 68–70.

44. Margaret Best, "Fifty Years of Women's Work," in *The Fiftieth Anniversary Celebration of the Korea Mission of the Presbyterian Church in the U.S.A, June 30–July 3, 1934* (Rpt., Han'guk kidokkyo yŏksa yŏn'guso, 2000), 83.

45. Welter, "The Cult of a True Womanhood, 1820–60," 151–74.

46. Mary Swale Wilkinson, "The Place of the Missionary Training School," *WMF* 35, no. 11 (November 1903): 384–85.

47. Susan Thorne, "Missionary-Imperial Feminism," in *Gendered Missions: Women and Men in Missionary Discourse and Practice*, ed. Mary Taylor Huber and Nancy Lutkehaus (Ann Arbor: University of Michigan Press, 1999), 39–65 (from 50).

48. In her analysis of women missionaries, Carol Marie DeSmither emphasizes the "career" aspect of missionary work over "calling." She makes an argument that "these women were less evangelists pursuing a life of sacrifices and dedication to religious ideals to secure a 'converted' Christian world than they were early professional women in America—a social type so new as to be unrecognized in this milieu—and that they were, in fact, pursuing professional careers through one of the few fully institutionalized opportunities open to educated women at this point in the 20th century." However, it is clear that many women missionaries were eager to engage in specifically "evangelical work," rather than educational or medical work. See DeSmither, "From Calling to Career: Work and Professional Identity among American Women Missionaries to China, 1900–1950," (PhD dissertation, University of Oregon, 1987), 2.

49. Robert, *American Women in Mission*, 36–38.

50. Henry G. Appenzeller, "Protestant Progress in Korea," *GAL* (June 1888): 263–64.

51. Chang Byung Wook, *The History of Methodist Women in Korea* (1885–1945) (Seoul: Sung Kwang Publishing Co., 1979), 147.

52. *HWF* (April 1886): 249.

53. Gilmore, "Social Phases in Korea," 3–5.

54. Hunter, *The Gospel of Gentility*, 27–51.

55. Clifton J. Phillips, "The Student Volunteer Movement and Its Role in China Missions, 1886–1920," in *The Missionary Enterprise in China and America*, ed. John K. Fairbank (Cambridge, Mass.: Harvard University Press, 1974), 91–109 (from 102–3).

56. Hunter, *The Gospel of Gentility*, 46–47.

57. Oak, "The Indigenization of Christianity in Korea," 488; Wade Crawford Barclay, *The Methodist Episcopal Church 1845–1939*, vol. 3, *Widening Horizons 1845–95* (New York: The Board of Missions of the Methodist Church, 1957), 754.

58. "Marjorie Lucy Hanson," RG 360.

59. Lulu Frey, Mission Biographical Reference Files, GCAH.

60. *WMF* 38, no. 3 (March 1906): 94.

61. Rosetta Sherwood Hall, "Woman's Medical Mission Work, Seoul, Korea," *GAL* (July 1893): 334–35 (from 335).

62. Ann White, "Counting the Cost of Faith: America's Early Female Missionaries," *Church History* 57, no. 1 (March 1988): 19–30; Robert, *American Women in Mission*, 93.

63. Marie E. Church and Mrs. R. L. Thomas, "Lulu E. Frey Who Went to Korea," *The One Who Went and the One She Found* (Woman's Foreign Missionary Society, 1929), 150–57; Annie Baird, "Higher Education of Women in Korea," *KMF* 8, no. 4 (1912): 113–16; "Ewa Hakdang Commencement," *KMF* 8, no. 5 (February 1912): 143.

64. Annie Ellers Bunker, "Personal Recollections of Early Days," Korea Methodist News Service Jubilee Address Reprints. (Rpt. from "Fiftieth Anniversary Addresses" delivered at First Church, Seoul, Korea. 1934), 1–2.

65. Esther Shields to the Board of Foreign Missions of the Presbyterian Church, November 13, 1896, RG 360.

66. Nell B. Johnson Null to Mrs. Pratt, August 12, 1901, RG 360.

67. Lillias Underwood, RG 360. It is unclear whether the term "Indians" refers to Native Americans or South Asian Indians.

68. Esther Shields, "Memorial Minutes," RG 360.

69. Margo Lee Lewis to Dr. Stanley White, February 8, 1910, RG 360.

70. Edith Blair to Dear Friends, February 1, 1929, RG 360.

71. Maude Cook, "Some Glimpses of Mrs. Welling Thomas Cook," RG 360.

72. Ellasue Wagner, "Songdo Woman's Work," *WMA* (January 1906): 248–50.

73. E. M. Cable, "Women's Work on the West District," *The Korea Methodist* 1 (1905): 139–40.

74. W. B. Scranton, "Report of Pastor, Baldwin Chapel and Ewa Hak Tang—1893," AMMEC (1893), 44–46.

75. Wm. Scranton, "Woman's Foreign Missionary Society," AMMEC (1895), 38–40.

76. Margaret Best, "Memorial Minutes Adopted by the Presbyterian Board of Foreign Missions, April 20, 1942," RG 360.

77. Alice Butts to Dear Friends, August 8, 1934, RG 360.

78. Rose M. Baird, "Dr. Margaret Best is Honored," *Pyengyang News* (August 1936). From Margaret Best's Personnel File, RG 360.

79. Hunter, *The Gospel of Gentility*, xiii. The larger proportion of women has to do with the fact that men tended to go to the mission field as married men accompanied by their wives, and the number of single women missionaries far surpassed the number of single male missionaries.

80. Barbara Welter, "She Hath Done What She Could: Protestant Women's Missionary Careers in Nineteenth-Century America," *American Quarterly* 30 (winter 1978): 624–38 (from 624 and 638).

81. Oak, "The Indigenization of Christianity in Korea," 480–84.

82. In her analysis of American women's involvement in the missionary movement, Shirley Garrett points to the prevailing phenomenon of the "feminine constituency," which had grown to become such a large proportion of the mission personnel that "in 1944 a male speaker at the Foreign Missions

Conference reported that women rather than men were familiar with the missionary movement." See Shirley S. Garrett, "Sisters All. Feminism and the American Women's Missionary Movement," in *Missionary Ideologies in the Imperialist Era: 1880–1920*, ed. Torben Christensen and William Hutchison (Aarhus: Forlaget Aros, 1982), 222–23.

83. "Are There Too Many Women in the Church?" *KMF* 33, no. 10 (October 1937): 199.

84. Helen McCune to Dear Friends, February 8, 1929, RG 401-82-22.

85. "Partial List of Books Translated or Prepared by Mrs. Annie A. Baird," RG 172-1-4.

86. Annie Baird, "The Relation of the Wives of Missionaries to Mission Work," *KR* (November 1895): 416–20 (from 417).

87. "Back to Korea: Mrs. Annie Adams Baird Writes Letter to Topeka Friends," RG 172-1-5.

88. Richard Baird, *William Baird of Korea* (Oakland, Calif.: Baird, 1968), 86.

89. James Gale, "An Appreciation: Mrs. Baird," *KMF* 12 (1916): 190–91.

90. KWCMEC (1899), 18–19.

91. "Weakness Made Strong," *WW* 29, no. 2 (February 1914): 33.

92. Ibid., 34.

93. Ibid.

94. Henrietta P. Robbins, "Report of Evangelistic Work on Pyeng-An and Whang-hae Do District," KWCMEC (1906), 51.

95. KWCMEC (1899), 18–19.

96. *The Korea Methodist* 1, no. 5 (1905): 50.

97. "Weakness Made Strong," 34.

98. Estelle Freedman, "Separatism as Strategy: Female Institution Building and American Feminism, 1870–1930," *Feminist Studies* 5, no. 3 (fall 1979): 512–29.

99. Rosemary Skinner Keller, "Creating a Sphere for Women," in *Women in New Worlds: Historical Perspectives on the Wesleyan Tradition*, ed. Hilah F. Thomas and Rosemary Skinner Keller (Nashville: Abingdon, 1981), 247.

100. Welter, "She Hath Done What She Could," 637; Adrian A. Bennett, "Doing More Than They Intended," in *Women in New Worlds*, vol. 2, ed. Rosemary Skinner Keller, Louise L. Queen, and Hilah F. Thomas (Nashville: Abingdon, 1981), 249–67.

101. Margaret L. Bendroth, "Women and Missions: Conflict and Changing Roles in the Presbyterian Church in the United States of America, 1870–1935," *American Presbyterians* 65, no. 1 (spring 1987): 51.

102. W. B. Scranton, "Report of Pastor, Baldwin Chapel and Ewa Hak Tang—1893," AMKMMEC (1893), 44–46.

103. Kim Tŏk-sŏn, "Midŭm ŭro igin nae ilsaeng" (My Life Won with Faith), in *Victorious Lives*, ed. Noble, 112–13.

104. Chang, *The History of Methodist Women in Korea*, 137.

105. ARWFMS (1888), 47, GCAH. See also Lillie Reed Smith, *Korea Aflame for Christ* (Abilene, Tx., privately published, n.d.), 112.

106. ARWFMS (1890), 52.

107. Barclay, *The Methodist Episcopal Church*, 752. In 1920, after several decades in mission work, Helen Henderson reported that she and her husband would still "separate at the door and sit on opposite sides of the room according to Korean custom." Helen Henderson to Dear Friends, December 14, 1920, RG 140-10-51. See also Sung-Deuk Oak, "Ch'ogi Han'guk kaesin'gyo yebaedang ŭi palchŏn kwajŏng kwa t'ŭksŏng: Kidokkyo kŭndaesŏng kwa t'och'akhwa ŭi munje, 1895–1912" (Spatial Characteristics of the Early Protestant Churches in Korea: Christian Modernity and Indigenization, 1895–1912), *Tongbang hakchi* 141 (March 2008): 267–321.

108. Best, "Fifty Years of Women's Work," 90.

109. Gilmore, "Social Phases in Korea," 4. "No reluctance to meeting [Western] gentlemen" came only after Korean women became acquainted with those foreigners. The 1892 annual report describes what the typical initial encounter looked like: "now and then a woman after having gotten a look at a foreign man's face takes fright and runs away," ARWFMS (1892–93), 80.

110. *Taehan maeil sinbo*, August 17, 1909.

111. Daniel Gifford, *Every-Day Life in Korea: A Collection of Studies and Stories*, trans. Sim Hyŏn-nyŏ (Seoul: The Institute for Korean Christian History, 1995), 41–44.

112. Margaret Best, "Memorial Minutes Adopted by the Presbyterian Board of Foreign Missions, April 20, 1942," RG 360.

113. Kim Mirisa, "Ch'unp'ung ch'uu 50-yŏngan e tarudahan han na ŭi yŏksa" (My Life History over the Past Fifty Years of Tears and Agony), *Pyŏlgŏn'gon* 11 (February 1928): 54–58.

114. Pil Ley Choi, "The Development of Korean Women during the Past Ten Years," *KMF* 18, no. 4 (1923): 222–23.

115. KWCMEC (1899), 18–19.

116. Margaret Best, "Country Bible Classes for Women," *KMF* 9 (1913): 102–4.

117. "Mrs. M. F. Scranton," *KMF* 6, no. 1 (January 1910): 12.

118. Lulu Frey, "The Bible Woman," *KMF* 3, no. 2 (February 1907): 42.

119. Sung-Deuk Oak, *Sources of Korean Christianity, 1832–1945* (Seoul: Han'guk kidokkyo yŏksa yŏn'guso, 2004), 188.

120. Mrs. Herbert Blair, "Women's Work in Kang Kai," *KMF* 7, no. 11 (1911): 314–17.

121. Kate Cooper, "The Bible Woman," *The Korea Magazine* (January 1917): 6–10 (from 7).

122. "Biblewomen," *The Korea Review* 6, no. 4 (April 1906): 140–47 (from 140).

123. Cooper, "The Bible Woman," 8.

124. Oak, *Sources of Korean Christianity*, 197.

125. For the social and cultural background of Bible women in early church history, see Yang Mi-gang, "Ch'ogi chŏndo puin ŭi sinang kwa hwaltong" (The Faith and Activities of Early Bible Women), *Han'guk kidokkyo wa yŏksa* 2

(1992): 91–109; Ha Hŭi-jŏng, "Ch'ogi chŏndo puin ŭi sinang kwa sinhak" (The Belief and Theology of Early Bible Women), *Han'guk kiddokkyo yŏn'guso sosik* 34 (1999): 11–24. See also Clark, *Living Dangerously in Korea*, 172–74.

126. Yang, "Ch'ogi chŏndo puin"; Noble, ed., *Victorious Lives*.

127. Mary Scranton, "Woman's Work in Korea," *KR* (January 1896): 9.

128. Yang, "Ch'ogi chŏndo puin," 96 and 105.

129. ARWMFS (1899), 91.

130. Rosetta Sherwood Hall, "Kwang Hya Nyo Won or 'Woman's Dispensary of Extended Grace,'" KWCMEC (1899), 14.

131. ARWFMS (1897–98), 90.

132. Margaret Best, "Country Bible Classes for Women," *KMF* 9, no. 4 (1913): 102–4.

133. The *li* (approximately 393 meters) is a traditional measurement of distance in Korea.

134. Olgar Shaffer, "Yeng Byen Women's Bible Class," *KMF* 9, no. 11 (1913): 284–86.

135. Miss Shields, "The Gospel in Syen Chun," *Assembly Herald* (November 1903): 519–20. Cited from Oak, *Sources of Korean Christianity*, 188. See also Shaffer, "Yeng Byen Women's Bible Class," 284.

136. Oak, *Sources of Korean Christianity*, 188.

137. Miss Butts, "Report of Workers Class of Bible Institute, Pyeng Yang," *KMF* 9, no. 1 (1913): 11; Margaret Best, "Courses of Study and Rules of Admission of the Pyeng Yang Presbyterian Women's Bible Institute," *KMF* 6, no. 6 (June 1910): 152–54; Yang, "Ch'ogi chŏndo puin," 101.

138. N. R. Scholes, "Developing Women Leaders" *KMF* 12, no. 7 (1916): 187–89.

139. Shaffer, "Yeng Byen Women's Bible Class," 284–86. See also "Some Pyeng Yang Paragraphs," RG 172-1-4.

140. Lura McLane Smith, "Korean Bible Women," *KMF* 33, no. 10 (1937): 213.

141. ARWFMS (1894–95), 72.

142. Ibid.

143. For descriptions of Bible women, see Mrs. O. R. Avison, "A Bible Woman's Work," *KMF* 2, no. 11 (1906): 212–13; and Mrs. G. S. McCune, "The Syen Chyun Women's Bible Study Class," *KMF* 8, no. 8 (1912): 249–50.

144. "Biblewomen," *The Korea Review* 6, no. 4 (1906): 140–47 (from 141).

145. Cited from Yang, "Ch'ogi chŏndo puin," 99.

146. KWCMEC (1903), 50–51.

147. Lulu Frey, "The Bible Woman," *KMF* 3, no. 2 (1907): 42. A similar story is also found in the mission field in China. According to Julia Bonafield, a missionary in China, "Bible-women or Bible-readers . . . many of them, knowing from a personal experience the depths of the ignorance and superstition of heathenism, have peculiar tact and wisdom in bringing others out." See Julia A. Bonafield, "The Work of a Bible-Woman in China," *WMF* 27, no. 9 (March 1896): 259.

148. ARWFMS (1912), 169.

149. Chŏn Sam-dŏk, "Nae saenghwal ŭi yangnyŏk" (History of My Life), in *Victorious Lives*, ed. Noble, 12.

150. ARWFMS (1899), 90.

151. ARWFMS (1892–93), 81.

152. Mary Scranton, "Woman's Work in Korea," *KR* (January 1896), 5.

153. Yi Tŏk-chu, *Ch'ogi Han'guk kidokkyosa yŏn'gu* (Study of the Early History of Christianity in Korea) (Seoul: Han'guk kidokkyo yŏksa yŏn'guso, 1995), 49–84.

154. Ibid., 68.

155. Lulu Frey, "Evangelistic Work First M.E. Church, Chong Dong, Seoul," KWCMEC (1901), 4–6.

156. ARWFMS (1913), 186.

157. Edith Blair, Extracts taken from article in *Pyengyang News* for November, 1934, RG 360.

158. "The Mission to China sent out by the Korean Church," RG 140-11-23.

159. Best, "Fifty Years of Women's Work," 83–92.

160. "The Church of Chosen Sends Out a Korean Woman as Missionary to China" (1931), RG 140-11-23; Best, "Fifty Years of Women's Work," 91.

161. Miss Shields, "The Gospel in Syen Chun," *Assembly Herald* (November 1903): 519–20. Cited from Oak, *Sources of Korean Christianity*, 189.

162. Margaret Best, "A Phase of Women's Work in Pyeng Yang," *KMF* 8, no. 1 (1912): 29.

163. Han'guk kidokkyo yŏksa yŏn'guso yŏsŏngsa yŏn'guhoe, *Han'guk kyohoe chŏndo puin charyojip* (A Sourcebook on Bible Women in the Korean Christian Church) (Seoul: Han'guk kidokkyo yŏksa yŏn'guso, 1999), 98–102.

164. "The Church of Chosen Sends Out a Korean Woman as Missionary to China" (1931), RG 140-11-23.

165. Han'guk kidokkyo yŏksa yŏn'guso yŏsŏngsa yŏn'guhoe, *Han'guk kyohoe chŏndo puin charyojip*, 169–70.

166. Best, "Fifty Years of Women's Work," 91.

167. C. T. Collyer, "The Work of a Women's Missionary Society," *KMF* 15, no. 10 (1919): 211–12.

168. Ibid., 211.

169. Ibid., 211–12.

170. Yi Tŏk-chu, *Han'guk kyohoe ch'ŏŭm yŏsŏngdŭl* (Early Christian Women in Korea: Life Stories of 28 Women Who Loved Christ and Their Nation) (Seoul: Kidokkyomunsa, 1990), 198–205; and Han'guk kidokkyo yŏksa yŏn'guso yŏsŏngsa yŏn'guhoe, *Han'guk kyohoe chŏndo puin charyojip*, 330.

171. Marie E. Church, "The Woman's Missionary Society of the Korean Methodist Church," in *Fifty Years of Light*, 111.

172. Anna Chaffin, "North District, Manchuria," in *Fifty Years of Light*, 114–15; Han'guk kidokkyo yŏksa yŏn'guso yŏsŏngsa yŏn'guhoe, *Han'guk kyohoe chŏndo puin charyojip*, 244–45. For studies on Koreans in Manchuria, see Hoon K. Lee, "Korean Migrants in Manchuria," *Geographical Review* 22, no. 2 (April 1932): 196–204; Hyun Ok Park, "Korean Manchuria: The Racial Poli-

tics of Territorial Osmosis," *The South Atlantic Quarterly* 99, no. 1 (winter 2000): 193–215.

173. Church, "The Woman's Missionary Society," 111.

174. Ibid., 113.

175. Ibid., 111.

176. Best, "A Phase of Women's Work," 28–30.

177. *Yun Ch'i-ho ilgi*, June 1, 1897. Some of the most prominent Korean Christian leaders also raised a similar issue about the condescending attitudes of American missionaries toward Koreans. See Oak, *Sources of Korean Christianity*, 446–47.

178. Best, "A Phase of Women's Work," 28–29.

179. Ibid., 30.

180. Edith Blair to Dear Friends, December 3, 1923, January 14, 1927, November 13, 1929, and January 1, 1931, RG 360.

181. Edith Blair to Dear Friends, January 12, 1932, RG 360.

182. Edith Blair, extracts taken from article in *Pyengyang News* for November 1934, RG 360.

183. Edith Blair, Abridged Personal Report of Edith A. Blair: 1936–37, RG 360.

184. The Committee for the Compilation of the History of Korean Women, *Women of Korea*, 129–44.

185. Church, "The Woman's Missionary Society," 112.

186. Kim, "Midŭm ŭro igin nae ilsaeng," 116.

187. KWCMEC (1910), 73–77.

188. Ch'ŏn Hwa-suk, *Han'guk yŏsŏng kidokkyo sahoe undongsa* (History of the Social Movement of Korean Christian Women) (Seoul: Hyean, 2000).

189. Yang, "Han'guk kaesin'gyo ŭi sŏng ch'abyŏl kujo," 224–25.

190. Garrett, "Sisters All," 221.

191. "Nae ka yŏja myŏn, nae ka yŏja myŏn!! Nae ka namja myŏn!!" (If I Were a Woman, if I Were a Woman!! If I Were a Man!!), *Samch'ŏlli* 10 (1927): 98–100.

192. Yang Mi-gang, "Ch'amyŏ wa paeje ŭi kwanchŏm esŏ pon chŏndo puin e kwanhan yŏn'gu: 1910-yŏn-1930-yŏndae rŭl chungsim ŭro" (A Study of Bible Women in Terms of Participation and Exclusion: From the 1910s to the 1930s), *Han'guk kidokkyo wa yŏksa* 6 (1997): 139–79.

193. Han'guk kidokkyo yŏksa yŏn'guso yŏsŏngsa yŏn'guhoe, *Han'guk kyohoe chŏndo puin charyojip*, 7–8.

194. Han'guk yŏsŏngsa p'yŏnch'an wiwŏnhoe, *Han'guk yŏsŏngsa 2*, 118.

195. ARWFMS (1891–92), 83.

196. ARWFMS (1890–91), 67.

197. J. O. Paine and L. E. Frey. "Report I—Ewa Haktang, Seoul," KWCMEC (1901), 1–2.

198. J. O. Paine and L. E. Frey. "Report I—Ewa Haktang, Seoul," KWCMEC (1903), 7–8.

199. J. O. Paine and L. E. Frey. "Report I—Ewa Haktang, Seoul," KWCMEC (1901), 1–2; Lulu Frey and Jessie Marker, "Ewa Haktang," KWCMEC (1908), 8.

200. J. O. Paine and L. E. Frey. "Report I—Ewa Haktang, Seoul," KWC-MEC (1901), 1–2.

201. Rosetta Sherwood Hall, "One New Life in the Orient," *WMF* 28, no. 12 (June 1897): 342–43.

202. AMKMMEC (1895), 38–40.

203. "The New Woman of the East," *KMF* 8, no. 1 (1912): 28.

204. William Baird, "Should Polygamists be Admitted to the Christian Church?" 15–16, Personnel File, RG 360, PHS.

205. Deuchler, *The Confucian Transformation of Korea*, 232.

206. The Committee for the Compilation of the History of Korean Women, *Women of Korea*, 96–97.

207. "The Annual Meeting of the Methodist Mission," *KR* 2 (September 1895): 356–57.

208. For detailed analysis of the missionary debate on polygamy, see Oak Sung-Deuk, "Ch'ogi Han'guk kyohoe ŭi ilbudach'ŏje nonjaeng" (Debates on Polygamy in the Early Korean Church), *Han'guk kidokkyo wa yŏksa* 16 (2002): 7–34.

209. Ibid., 21–24.

210. Ibid., 25–32.

211. Mattie Wilcox Noble, "The Missionary Home," *KMF* 27, no. 4 (1931): 75–77.

212. Mrs. A. M. Sharrocks, "Work among Korean Women," *KMF* 2, no. 2 (1905): 33–35.

213. Ryu, *Ch'ogi Miguk sŏn'gyosa yŏn'gu*, 56–73.

214. Sadie Welbon, "Foreign Woman's Evangelistic Work in City and Country," *KMF* 6, no. 10 (1910): 259–61.

215. Mattie Noble, Diaries, October 28, 1903; Ryu, *Ch'ogi Miguk sŏn'gyosa yŏn'gu*, 56–73.

216. Nellie Mary Cowan Holdcroft to Dear Friends, May 3, 1931, RG 360.

217. Susan Ross to Dear Friends, May 23, 1929, RG 360.

218. Nellie Mary Cowan Holdcroft to Dear Friends, May 3, 1931, RG 360.

219. Flemming, *Women's Work for Women*, 3.

220. Rothman, *Woman's Proper Place.*

221. Theodore Jun Yoo, "The 'New Woman' and the Politics of Love, Marriage and Divorce in Colonial Korea," *Gender and History* 17, no. 2 (August 2005): 295–324 (from 309–12).

222. Kim Mirisa, "Kyŏngje wa sigan munje" (Economy and the Time Problem), *Sin yŏsŏng* 2, no. 10 (1924): 26–27; Yi Kwi-yŏng, "Kajŏng saenghwal kaejo wa kŭ silche" (Reform and Reality of Family Life), *Sin yŏsŏng* 3, no. 1 (1925): 32–35; Hŏ Yŏng-suk, "Tonggyŏng e ŏtchae watdŭngo: Sanwŏn e taehan na ŭi kudo" (Why I Came to Tokyo: My Plans for the Maternity Ward), *Samch'ŏlli* 8, no. 4 (April 1936): 111–13.

223. Song Hwa-ja, "Anhae ege wŏlgŭp ŭl chura" (Pay Salary to Wives), *Sin yŏsŏng* 3, no. 1 (1925): 82–85.

224. Na Hye-sŏk, "Isang chŏk puin" (Ideal Woman), *Hak chi kwang* (1914). Cited from Yi Sang-gyŏng, ed. *Na Hye-sŏk chŏnjip* (Anthology of the Works of Na Hye-sŏk) (Seoul: T'aehaksa, 2000), 183–85; Pak Wŏn-hŭi, "Chosŏn yŏja kyoyuk ŭi hyŏnsang kwa kŭnbon chŏngsin" (The Reality and Main Philosophy of Women's Education in Korea), *Tonga ilbo* July 8, 1927; Kim Ŭn-hŭi, "Musan puin undongnon" (On the Movement of Proletarian Women) *Samch'ŏlli* 4, no. 2 (1932): 64–67.

CHAPTER 4

1. T. H. Yun [Yun Ch'i-ho], "The Sort of Education Korean Girls Need," *The Missionary Voice* (April 1918): 114–15.

2. "Commencement Month in Seoul" (1908), RG 360, 11–15; Ellasue Wagner, "Holston Institute Graduating Exercises," *KMF* 10, no. 5 (1914): 147–48; "A Girls' School Field Day," *KMF* 3, no. 6 (June 1907): 90–91.

3. From the missionary point of view, educational endeavors constituted one of three pillars of foreign missionary activities, along with evangelical and medical involvement. In this triangle, evangelization was the primary goal of any missionary work, and educational and medical activities were two strategic buttresses to promote evangelical goals. However, women missionaries had greater and more prominent success in educational work than in other activities. Robert, *American Women in Mission*, 81–124, 160–62.

4. Ibid., 160–62.

5. Kate E. Moss, "What We May Be To-Morrow," *WMF* 4, no. 4 (1908): 126–27 (from 126).

6. Emora T. Brannan, "A Partnership of Equality," in *Women in New Worlds*, vol. 2., ed. Rosemary Skinner Keller, Louise L. Queen, and Hilah F. Thomas (Nashville: Abindon, 1982), 132–47.

7. Beaver, *American Protestant Women in World Mission*, 41–42.

8. Brannan, "A Partnership of Equality," 137–47.

9. R. S. Maclay, "Commencement of the Korea Methodist Episcopal Mission," *GAL* (November 1896): 498; see also Allen D. Clark, *A History of the Church in Korea* (Seoul: The Christian Literature Society of Korea, 1971), 74.

10. Maclay, "Commencement of the Korea Methodist Episcopal Mission," 498–502; see also Clark, *A History of the Church in Korea*, 74.

11. Yi's letter of appeal is dated August 8, 1884. *HWF* 16, no. 7 (1885): 158–59.

12. Tsuda Sen was also the father of Tsuda Umeko, who was one of five Japanese girls sent to the United States in 1871 to be educated. She later founded one of the first schools to provide higher education for Japanese women. See Barbara Rose, *Tsuda Umeko and Women's Education in Japan* (New Haven, Conn.: Yale University Press, 1992), 13–16, 111–13.

13. Yi, *Kaehwap'a wa kaehwa sasang yŏn'gu*, 43–62.

14. *KMF* 6, no. 1 (1910): 12.

15. *HWF* 16, no. 8 (February 1885): 188–89; *KMF* 6, no. 1 (1910): 12.

16. Barclay, *The Methodist Episcopal Church*, 756.

17. Mary F. Scranton, "Woman's Work in Korea," *KR* 3, no. 1 (January 1896): 4.

18. *HWF* 19, no. 1 (July 1887): 11–12.

19. Ewha 100-yŏnsa p'yŏnch'an wiwŏnhoe, *Ewha 100-yŏnsa* (Seoul: Ewha yŏja taehakkyo ch'ulp'anbu, 1994), 53.

20. *HWF* 17, no. 10 (April 1886): 249.

21. There are differing interpretations of the origin of the school name, Ewha ("Pear Flower"). The official position of Ewha Womans University is that it originated from the characteristic of the location, Chŏngdong, where pear flowers were abundant. In addition, it was common at the time to name an institution for features of nature that surrounded it. Although unproven, another theory claims that Scranton bought the school property where a pavilion named Ihwajŏng (Pavilion of Pear Flower) already existed. See Ewha 100-yŏnsa p'yŏnch'an wiwŏnhoe, *Ewha 100-yŏnsa*, 55–56.

22. *HWF* 17, no. 10 (April 1886): 249.

23. *KR* (January 1896): 3; *HWF* 17, no. 10 (April 1886): 249.

24. *KR* (January 1896): 4.

25. Ewha 100-yŏnsa p'yŏnch'an wiwŏnhoe, *Ewha 100-yŏnsa*, 55.

26. *KR* (January 1896): 4.

27. *HWF* 19, no. 1 (July 1887): 11–12.

28. Ewha 100-yŏnsa p'yŏnch'an wiwŏnhoe, *Ewha 100-yŏnsa*, 52, 57.

29. Han'guk yŏsŏngsa p'yŏnch'an wiwŏnhoe, *Han'guk yŏsŏngsa* 2, 294.

30. L. George Paik, *The History of Protestant Missions in Korea 1832–1910*, 4th ed. (Seoul: Yonsei University Press, 1987), 134.

31. Louise Rothweiler, "Woman's Work in the Methodist Episcopal Mission in Korea," *GAL* (March 1893): 106; *KR* (January 1896): 5.

32. Ewha 100-yŏnsa p'yŏnch'an wiwŏnhoe, *Ewha 100-yŏnsa*, 61.

33. Ibid., 58–59.

34. KWCMEC (1908), 7–8.

35. KWCMEC (1906), 5.

36. *WMF* 38, no. 10 (October 1906): 365.

37. Data from mission journals, such as *HWF* and *GAL*, and annual reports by women missionaries in Korea.

38. Ewha 100-yŏnsa p'yŏnch'an wiwŏnhoe, *Ewha 100-yŏnsa*, 60–61.

39. *Tongnip sinmun*, May 12, 1896.

40. *Taehan maeil sinbo*, September 12, 1907.

41. Yi, *Han'guk kyohoe ch'ŏŭm yŏsŏngdŭl*, 61.

42. Most mission schools targeted young, unmarried students. In the case of Ewha, it had a specific policy not to accept married women as students with only a few exceptions—i.e. the very first student, Mrs. Kim, and Ha Nan-sa. However, partly due to the fever for education among Koreans and the imme-

diate need for teachers, Ewha did accept twenty-five married women in 1908. Ewha 100-yŏnsa p'yŏnch'an wiwŏnhoe, *Ewha 100-yŏnsa*, 60.

43. Ibid., 59.

44. ARWFMS (1899), 89.

45. KWCMEC (1908), 6.

46. Yi, *Han'guk kyohoe ch'ŏŭm yŏsŏngdŭl*, 63.

47. Chŏn T'aek-bu, *In'gan Sin Hŭng-u* (Seoul: Taehan kidokkyosŏhoe, 1971), 124.

48. Induk Pahk, *September Monkey* (New York: Harper & Brothers, 1954), 72.

49. *Taehan maeil sinbo*, May 23, 1907.

50. Han'guk yŏsŏngsa p'yŏnch'an wiwŏnhoe, *Han'guk yŏsŏngsa, purok* (History of Korean Women, Appendix) (Seoul: Ewha yŏja taehakkyo ch'ulp'anbu, 1972), 135–37.

51. M. F. Scranton, "Mead Memorial Church and Kyung-keui Do," KWCMEC (1906), 23–27.

52. Helen K. Kim, "Methodism and the Development of Korean Womanhood," in *Within the Gate*, ed. Charles A. Sauer (Seoul: The Korea Methodist News Service, 1934), 76–83; Yi, *Han'guk kyohoe ch'ŏŭm yŏsŏngdŭl*, 192.

53. Mrs. Rosella Cram, "Mary Helm School, Songdo, Korea," *WMA* (March 1910): 408–10.

54. Margo Lee Lewis, "Annual Report of Woman's Academy, Seoul," RG 140-7-31.

55. O. R. Avison to Arthur Brown, March 13, 1920, RG 140-13-8.

56. Arthur Brown to Mrs. Pilley Kim Choi, March 18, 1927, RG 140-13-8.

57. John Soo Ahrn to Arthur Brown, May 10, 1927, RG 140-13-8.

58. J. G. Holdcroft to C. B. McAfee, January 10, 1934; November 2, 1933; RG 140-13-8.

59. William Baird, "Read in the Mission in Seoul 1897. Our Educational Policy," RG 173-1-16.

60. Lulu Frey, "School Girls in Korea," *WMF* 27, no. 8 (February 1896): 227–28.

61. Martha Huntley, *Caring, Growing, Changing: A History of the Protestant Mission in Korea* (New York: Friendship Press, 1984), 87–96.

62. *HWF* 20, no. 7 (January 1889): 173–74; Ewha 100-yŏnsa p'yŏnch'an wiwŏnhoe, *Ewha 100-yŏnsa charyojip* (Seoul: Ewha yŏja taehakkyo ch'ulp'anbu, 1994), 340.

63. Lillian Nicholas, "The Religious Education Program at Holston Institute, Songdo, Korea," thesis draft, Scarritt College [n.d.], GCAH.

64. "Educational Policy of the Board," RG 140-7-31.

65. *KR* (March 1892): 90.

66. Annie Baird, "Higher Education of Women in Korea," *KMF* 8, no. 4 (1912): 113–16.

67. *GAL* (August 1888): 373.

68. Cited from Paik, *The History of Protestant Missions in Korea*, 132.

69. George Gilmore, *Korea from Its Capital* (Philadelphia: The Presbyterian Board of Publication, 1892), 300.

70. *KR* (March 1892): 90.

71. Louise Rothweiler, Mission Biographical Reference Files, GCAH.

72. Hulbert, "Ewha College: 1910–1938," in *Fifty Years of Light*, 21–22.

73. Ewha 100-yŏnsa p'yŏnch'an wiwŏnhoe, *Ewha 100-yŏnsa charyojip*, 341.

74. Hulbert, "Ewha College," 21–22.

75. Han'guk yŏsŏngsa p'yŏnch'an wiwŏnhoe, *Han'guk yŏsŏngsa* 2, 315.

76. Hulbert, "Ewha College," 22.

77. Velma Snook's letter does not bear a date, but it was filed in the Presbyterian Historical Society on June 26, 1913. RG 360.

78. Sungŭi yŏja chung kodŭng hakkyo, *Sungŭi 60-yŏnsa* (History of Sungŭi for the Past 60 Years) (1963), 81–82.

79. O. R. Avison to Arthur Brown, March 13, 1920, RG 140-13-8.

80. Alice Appenzeller, "The Need of Social Work among the Women of Seoul," *KMF* 14, no. 4 (1918): 77–79.

81. Colleen Mcdannell, *The Christian Home in Victorian America, 1840–1900* (Bloomington: Indiana University Press, 1986).

82. Barbara Cross, *The Educated Woman in America*: Selected Writings of Catharine Beecher, Margaret Fuller, and M. Carey Thomas (New York: Teachers College Press, 1965), 83–84; Mcdannell, *The Christian Home in Victorian America, 1840–1900*.

83. KWCMEC (1903), 7.

84. *Hwangsŏng sinmun*, June 12, 1906; Pak, *Kŭndae yŏsŏng*, 192.

85. Pak, *Kŭndae yŏsŏng*, 193.

86. Yun, "The Sort of Education Korean Girls Need," 114.

87. Chu Yo-sŏp, "Yŏja kyoyuk kaesinan" (Proposal for Reform of Women's Education), *Sin yŏsŏng* 5, no. 5 (1931): 8–12.

88. Yoo, "The 'New Woman' and the Politics of Love," 295–324.

89. Yi Kwang-su, "Mosŏng chungsim ŭi yŏja kyoyuk" (Women's Education Centering on Motherhood), *Sin yŏsŏng* 3, no. 1 (1925): 19–20.

90. Pak, *Kŭndae yŏsŏng*.

91. Hŏ Yŏng-suk, "Chosŏn yŏja ŭi ch'ŏnjik" (The Calling of Korean Women), *Tonga ilbo*, October 18, 1925.

92. Hŏ Yŏng-suk, "Puin munje ŭi ilmyŏn—namja hal il, yŏja hal il" (One Aspect of the Woman Question: Men's Work, Women's Work), *Tonga ilbo*, January 1, 1926, and January 4, 1926.

93. For example, a popular women's magazine, *Sin yŏsŏng*, frequently published special issues on schoolgirls. See the editions 2, no. 6 (1924); 2, no. 8 (1924); 3, no. 6 (1925); 4, no. 4 (1926); 7, no. 10 (1933). Some prominent educators, such as Kim Hwal-lan and Cho Tong-sik, complained about unreasonably exaggerated portrayals of girl students. See Kim Hwal-lan, "Yŏhakkyo kyoyuk munje" (Problems in Girls' Education), *Sin yŏsŏng* 7, no. 3 (1933): 10–13; Cho Tong-sik, "P'unggi wa Chosŏn yŏhaksaeng" (Moral Discipline and Korean Girl Students), *Sin yŏsŏng* 7, no. 10 (1933): 20–21.

94. *Taehan maeil sinbo*, March 13, 1909, and November 24, 1909.

95. An Kuk-sŏn, "*Kŭmsu hoeŭirok*" (Record of the Animals' Assembly), in *Han'guk sosŏl munhak taege* (A Series of Korean Novels), vol. 1, *Sin sosŏl* (New Fiction) (Seoul: Tusan donga, 1995), 448.

96. "Women's Rights in Korea," *The Korea Review* 6, no. 2 (February 1906): 51–59 (from 52).

97. Kim Chin-song, *Sŏul e ttansŭhol ŭl hŏhara* (Permit Dance Halls in Seoul) (Seoul: Hyŏnsil munhwa yŏn'gu, 1999), 20–50.

98. P'albong sanin, "Kŭmil ŭi yŏsŏng kwa hyŏndae ŭi kyoyuk: Mullanhan chung esŏ kŭdŭl ŭl sŏndo hagi wihayŏ yŏnae rŭl alge hara sŏng kyoyuk ŭl yŏhara" (Contemporary Women and Modern Education: Teach Romance and Sex Education in Order to Guide Them in the Midst of Moral Decay," *Sin yŏsŏng* 3, no. 6 (June 1926): 61–67; Yi Hŭi-gyŏng, "1920-yŏndae 'yŏhaksaeng' ŭi sahoe chŏk p'yŏsang" (Social Representation of "Schoolgirl" in the 1920s), *Han'gŭl kyoyuk yŏn'gu* 10, no. 1 (2004): 55–79.

99. Jin Feng, *The New Woman in Early-Twentieth-Century Chinese Fiction* (West Lafayette, Ind.: Purdue University Press, 2004), 18.

100. Songdo Mangin, "Hosŭdon yŏgo kyojang ege" (To the Principal of Holston Girls' School), *Sin yŏsŏng* 2, no. 10 (1924): 68–70.

101. "Sungŭi yŏgyosaeng tonghyu" (Students at Sungŭi Girls School on Strike), *Tonga ilbo*, October 18, 20, 27, 28, 29, 30, and November 4, 10, 14, 19, 24, and 25, 1923; see also *Kaebyŏk* 41 (November 1923): 113–14.

102. There was a widespread perception of school dormitories as "prisons" not only at mission schools but at Korean-run schools, as well. See Chu Yo-sŏp, "Yŏja kyoyuk kaesinan," 9.

103. Cho Sang-hang, "Sŏyang sŏn'gyosa tŭl ŭi hakkyo tanggukja ege" (To the Authorities of Western Missionary Schools), *Sin yŏsŏng* 2, no. 10 (1924): 81–82.

104. "Mogyo e taehan pulp'yŏng kwa hŭimang" (Complaints and Hopes about Alma Mater), *Sin yŏsŏng* 4, no. 4 (1926): 45–49.

105. Ibid., 46–47.

106. Ibid., 48.

107. Ibid., 47–48.

108. Chŏn Ŏn-hu, "Ilche sigi yŏhaksaeng ŭisik ŭi pyŏnhwa" (Change of Consciousness among Girl Students during the Japanese Colonial Era) (MA thesis, Ewha Womans University, 2000), 29.

109. "Mogyo e taehan pulp'yŏng kwa hŭimang," 48–49.

110. M. L. Lewis, "Chal kamdok hago chal ihae hara" (Supervise Well, Understand Well), *Sin yŏsŏng* 4, no. 4 (1926): 24.

111. An Ch'ung-jung, "Munje nŭn chibang haksaeng ŭi kamdok munje imnida" (The Problem is the Supervision of Students from Provinces), *Sin yŏsŏng* 4, no. 4 (1926): 23–24.

112. Kim Suk-ja, "Hasukok esŏ pon yŏhaksaeng" (Girl Students Seen from a Lodge), *Sin yŏsŏng* 4, no. 4 (1926): 42.

113. Chu Yo-sŏp, "Chosŏn yŏja kyoyuk kaesŏnan" (Proposal for the Improvement of Women's Education in Korea), *Sin yŏsŏng* 7, no. 10 (1933): 17.

114. *GAL* (September 1895): 456.

115. *Christian Life and Message in Relation to Non-Christian Systems: Report of the Jerusalem Meeting of the International Missionary Council,* vol. 1 (London: Oxford University Press, 1928), 410.

116. O. R. Avison to Arthur Brown, March 13, 1920, RG 140-13-8.

117. *GAL* (January 1889): 32–33.

118. The Committee for the Compilation of the History of Korean Women, *Women of Korea,* 154.

119. Yi Sŏng-mi, "Sin Saimdang: The Foremost Woman Painter of the Chosŏn Dynasty," in *Creative Women of Korea: The Fifteenth through the Twentieth Centuries,* ed. Young-Key Kim-Renaud (Armonk: M. E. Sharpe, 2004), 58–77; Kichung Kim, "Hŏ Nansŏrhŏn and 'Shakespeare's Sister,'" in *Creative Women of Korea,* ed. Kim-Renaud, 78–95; Yi Hye-sun and Chŏng Ha-yŏng, trans. and eds., *Han'guk kojŏn yŏsŏng munhak ŭi segye* (The World of Women's Classical Literature in Korea) (Seoul: Ewha yŏja taehakkyo ch'ulp'anbu, 2003).

120. The Committee for the Compilation of the History of Korean Women, *Women of Korea,* 154; Yong-Ok Pak, "A History of Korean Women," *Koreana* 4, no. 2 (1990): 34–45.

121. David J. Silva, "Western Attitudes toward the Korean Language: An Overview of Late-Nineteenth- and Early-Twentieth-Century Mission Literature," *Korean Studies* 26, no. 2 (2002): 272–75.

122. Henry Appenzeller, January 3, 1887, Missionary Correspondence, 1840–1912, GCAH; Barclay, *The Methodist Episcopal Church,* 755.

123. Paik, *The History of Protestant Missions in Korea,* 133.

124. Daniel Gifford, "Education in the Capital of Korea," *KR* (August 1896): 307.

125. *KR* (March 1892): 91–92.

126. *HWF* 20, no. 6 (December 1888): 150.

127. *HWF* 20, no. 7 (January 1889): 173–74.

128. "Woman's Work in the Methodist Episcopal Mission in Korea," *GAL* (March 1893): 106.

129. AMMEC (1893), 99–100.

130. Mary Scranton, "Korean Work: Woman's Foreign Missionary Society," AMMEC (1893), 79.

131. *HWF* 20, no. 9 (March 1889): 251–52.

132. Huntley, *Caring, Growing, Changing,* 85.

133. Alice Hammond, "Evangelistic Work—Mead Memorial Church and South Korea District," KWCMEC (1902), 13–14.

134. *The Korea Methodist* 1, no. 12 (1905): 165.

135. AMPC (1905), 33–35. The earliest record on the instruction of Chinese at Presbyterian mission schools for girls is found in the 1891 report by Susan Doty, who taught at Chŏngdong yŏhaktang. She indicated that her school taught

Chinese to the majority of students as it was "the literary language of the country." See ARPCUSA (1891), 136.

136. KWCMEC (1908), 6.

137. Mark Peterson, "The Sejong Sillok," in *King Sejong the Great*, ed. Young-Key Kim-Renaud (International Circle of Korean Linguistics, 1992), 15–18; Kim Dong-uk, "Women's Literary Achievements," *Korea Journal* 3, no. 11 (November 1963): 33.

138. *En-mun* refers to a modification of the *ŏnmun* (Korean script).

139. Bishop, *Korea and Her Neighbors*, 21.

140. Hulbert, *The Passing of Korea*, 92.

141. Horace H. Underwood, *The Call of Korea* (New York: Fleming H. Revell Company, 1908), 71.

142. Underwood, *With Tommy Tompkins in Korea*, 27.

143. George Heber Jones, *The Bible in Korea; or, The Transformation of a Nation* (New York: American Bible Society, 1916), 8–10.

144. *The Fiftieth Anniversary Celebration*, 11.

145. Ross King, "Western Protestant Missionaries and the Origins of Korean Language Modernization," *Journal of International and Area Studies* 11, no. 3 (2004): 7–38.

146. Ibid., 17.

147. Even before the first group of American Protestant missionaries arrived in Korea in 1885, Korean Christians, such as Yi Su-jŏng, were engaged in translating the Bible into Korean at the request of the American Bible Society. It was Yi's translation of the Bible that Henry Appenzeller and Horace Underwood brought with them to Korea when they first came in 1885. See Kim Pong-hŭi, *Han'guk kidokkyo munsŏ kanhaengsa yŏn'gu* (A Study of the History of Publications on Christian Tracts in Korea) (Seoul: Ewha yŏja taehakkyo ch'ulp'anbu, 1987), 22.

148. Annie Baird, "The Future of Unmoon," *KMF* 6, no. 8 (1910): 204–6. Baird quotes an essay written by Yang Choo Sam, who stated that "Men of truly enlightened nations declare of our Kookmoon alphabet that the fine discrimination of its principles, and its accuracy in indicating sound, are such as to constitute a cause for just pride, and to give it a place in the front rank of written languages. If, by the preparation of an unabridged dictionary, and by reducing the rules of grammar and composition to a system, the scope of the Kookmoon should be increased, then Chinese with its bare ideographs, Japanese with its imperfect alphabet, English with its inconsistencies of spelling, and others of like ilk, would be left to blush over their deficiencies."

149. Schmid, *Korea between Empires*, 64–72.

150. *Taehan maeil sinbo*, May 23, 1907.

151. *Tongnip sinmun*, April 7, 1896.

152. Chu Si-gyŏng, "Essay on the Korean Language," *Tongnip sinmun*, April 24, 1897. Translation in the *Sourcebook of Korean Civilization*, ed. Lee, 389–90.

153. *Taehan maeil sinbo*, December 30, 1908.

154. Millie Albertson, "Work for Women," *KMF* 10, no. 4 (1914): 111–13.
155. Ewha 100-yŏnsa p'yŏnch'an wiwŏnhoe, *Ewha 100-yŏnsa charyojip*, 340.
156. Paik, *The History of Protestant Missions in Korea*, 125–26.
157. *GAL* (February 1887): 95.
158. Clarence Norwood Weems, "Profile of Homer B. Hulbert," in *History of Korea*, Homer B. Hulbert, ed. Clarence Norwood Weems (New York: Hillary House Publishers Ltd., 1962), ED 23–62.
159. Mary F. Scranton, "Woman's Work in Korea," *KR* (January 1896): 2–9.
160. Henry Appenzeller, January 3, 1887, Henry G. Appenzeller, papers and correspondences, GCAH.
161. *Yŏja chinam* 1, no. 1 (1908): 47.
162. Han'guk yŏsŏngsa p'yŏnch'an wiwŏnhoe, *Han'guk yŏsŏngsa* 2, 316.
163. *HWF* 19, no. 9 (March 1888): 245–46.
164. Ibid.
165. *HWF* 20, no. 9 (March 1889): 239–40.
166. Hyaeweol Choi, "Women's Work for 'Heathen Sisters': American Women Missionaries and their Educational Work in Korea," *Acta Koreana* 2 (July 1999): 5–8. A similar debate took place in China, causing hostilities between proponents and opponents of English-language education. See Robert, *American Women in Mission*, 177–84.
167. Cited from Huntley, *Caring, Growing, Changing*, 89.
168. William Newton Blair, *Gold in Korea* (Topeka, Kans.: H.M. Ives & Sons, Inc., 1957), 83–85.
169. Cited from Paik, *The History of Protestant Missions in Korea*, 132.
170. *KR* (November 1895): 441–44.
171. Oak Sung-Deuk, "Ch'ogi Han'guk kyohoe ŭi ilbudach'ŏje nonjaeng" (Debates on Polygamy in Early Korean Church), *Han'guk kidokkyo wa yŏksa* 16 (2002): 18.
172. Paik, *The History of Protestant Missions in Korea*, 128.
173. *KR* (March 1892): 92.
174. AMMEC (1906): 31–32.
175. *GAL* (September 1893): 392.
176. Louis L. Snyder, ed., *The Imperialism Reader* (New York: D. Van Nostrand Company, Inc., 1962), 123.
177. Authorities of Paejae Boys' School, the Methodist school for boys, decided in 1904 that "all students who accept the benefits of instruction in English should pay a tuition fee of not less than fifty sen per month." This decision, missionaries felt, resulted in "purifying and strengthening influence on the school" because those students, who had a primary interest in the secular benefit of learning English but no desire to pay for it were automatically weaned out. However, the year after Paejae started charging tuition for English lessons, D.A. Bunker, a teacher at Paejae, reported that "[t]he pros and cons of teaching English were thoroughly discussed and an almost unanimous decisions arrived

at that for the present at least we should not teach English but instead use the native tongue." See "Pai Chai Haktang," AMMEC (1904): 54–55; D. A. Bunker, "Pai Chai High-school," AMMEC (1905): 75–78 (from 75).

178. "Modŏn yŏsŏng sipkyemyŏng" (Ten Commandments for Modern Woman), Sin yŏsŏng 5, no. 4 (1931): 71.

179. Robert, American Women in Mission, 180.

180. KR (May 1895): 197.

181. O Ch'ŏn-sŏk, "Sŏyangin ŭi Chosŏn yŏja kyoyuk pangch'im ŭl kŭnbonjŏk ŭro kaehyŏk hara" (Make a Fundamental Reform in the Direction of Women's Education Led by Westerners), Sŏul (June 1920). Cited from Kim, Sŏul e ttansŭhol ŭl hŏhara, 207–8.

182. Chu Yo-sŏp, "Yŏja kyoyuk kaesinan," 10.

183. "Report of the Posyung Girls' Middle School at Syen Chyun (Sensen), Korea," June 5, 1914, RG 140-7-31.

184. Pahk, September Monkey, 85–86.

185. "Modŏn yŏsŏng sipkyemyŏng."

186. Kim Ŭn-hŭi, "Musan puin undongnon" (On the Movement of Proletarian Women), Samch'ŏlli 4, no. 2 (1932): 64–67.

187. Marie E. Church and Mrs. R. L. Thomas, "Lulu E. Frey: Who Went to Korea," The One Who Went and the One She Found (Woman's Foreign Missionary Society, 1929), 150–57.

188. Alice Appenzeller, "Chosŏn yŏja kodŭng kyoyuk munje" (Problems of Higher Education for Women in Korea), Samch'ŏlli 4, no. 3 (March 1932): 45–47.

189. Church and Thomas, "Lulu E. Frey," 150–57.

190. Annie Baird, "Higher Education of Women in Korea," KMF 8, no. 4 (1912): 113–16 (from 113).

191. Marion Conrow, "The Future of the Women's College," KMF 26, no. 4 (April 1930): 76–77.

CHAPTER 5

1. Antoinette Burton, "Who Needs the Nation?: Interrogating 'British' History," in Cultures of Empire: Colonizers in Britain and the Empire in the Nineteenth and Twentieth Centuries: A Reader, ed. Catherine Hall (New York: Routledge, 2000), 137–53; Mitchell, Questions of Modernity; Thorne, Congregational Missions and the Making of an Imperial Culture.

2. Hill, The World Their Household, 8–22.

3. Mrs. E. W. Rice, "A Woman of Korea," HWF 17, no. 8 (February 1886): 182–83.

4. "Chosen Mission—Language School," extract from letter from Dr. C. A. Clark, Chosen, June 21, 1922, RG 140-1-15.

5. Patrick Hanan, "The Missionary Novels of Nineteenth-Century China," Harvard Journal of Asiatic Studies 60, no. 2 (December 2000): 413–43. (from 413).

6. Hill, *The World Their Household.*

7. Annie Baird, *Daybreak in Korea: A Tale of Transformation in the Far East* (New York: Fleming H. Revell Company, 1909).

8. Laurel Kendall and Mark Peterson, "Traditional Korean Women: A Reconsideration," in *Korean Women: View from the Inner Room,* ed. Laurel Kendall and Mark Peterson (New Haven, Conn.: East Rock Press, Inc., 1983), 6.

9. W. Arthur Noble, *Ewa: A Tale of Korea* (New York: Eaton & Mains, 1906).

10. The unpublished manuscript is located at GCAH.

11. Harry A. Rhodes, "Fifty Years of Christian Literature in the Korea Mission, Presbyterian Church, USA," in *The Fiftieth Anniversary Celebration,* 77.

12. James Gale, "An Appreciation: Mrs. Baird," *KMF* 12 (1916): 190–91.

13. So Chae-yŏng and Kim Kyŏng-wan, eds., *Kaehwagi sosŏl* (Novels from the Period of Enlightenment) (Seoul: Sungsil taehakkyo ch'ulp'ansa, 1999), 229–57.

14. For discussion on gender-bound discourse in colonial and missionary writings, see Sara Mills, *Discourses of Difference: An Analysis of Women's Travel Writing and Colonialism* (London: Routledge, 1991); Nupur Chaudhuri and Margaret Strobel, eds., *Western Women and Imperialism* (Bloomington: Indiana University Press, 1992); and Regina Lewis, *Gendering Orientalism* (London: Routledge, 1996). For samples of male missionary discourse from Korea, see Underwood, *The Call of Korea*; and Gale, *Korea in Transition.*

15. Barbara N. Ramusack, "Cultural Missionaries, Maternal Imperialists, Feminist Allies: British Women Activists in India, 1865–1945," in *Western Women and Imperialism,* ed. Chaudhuri and Strobel, 119–36.

16. Annie Baird to Gussie, March 6, 1891, RG 172-1-2.

17. Baird, *Daybreak in Korea,* 5.

18. Judith Walkowitz, *City of Dreadful Delight: Narratives of Sexual Danger in Late-Victorian London* (London: Virago Press, 1992), 91.

19. Alison M. Parker, "'Hearts Uplifted and Minds Refreshed': The Woman's Christian Temperance Union and the Production of Pure Culture in the United States, 1880–1930," *Journal of Women's History* 11, no. 2 (1999): 135–58.

20. Baird, *Daybreak in Korea,* 12.

21. Annie Baird to Gussie, March 6, 1891, RG 172-1-2.

22. Baird, *Daybreak in Korea,* 14–15.

23. Ella D. Appenzeller, "Korean Girls," *HWF* 20, no. 2 (August 1888): 47–48.

24. KWCMEC (1908), 8.

25. Baird, *Daybreak in Korea,* 24–27.

26. Ibid., 28–29.

27. Deuchler, *The Confucian Transformation of Korea,* 3–27; Mark Peterson, "Women without Sons: A Measure of Social Change in Yi Dynasty Korea," in *Korean Women,* ed. Kendall and Peterson, 33–44; Cha Jae-ho, Chung Bom-Mo, and Lee Sung-Jin, "Boy Preference Reflected in Korean Folk-

lore," in *Virtues in Conflict,* ed. Sandra Mattielli (Seoul: The Royal Asiatic Society Korea Branch 1977), 113–27.

28. Baird, *Daybreak in Korea,* 40.

29. Ibid., 71.

30. Baird, *Inside Views of Mission Life,* 18.

31. For discussion of gender equality in Christian discourse, see Kim, "The Predicament of Modern Discourses on Gender and Religion," 114–36.

32. Baird, *Daybreak in Korea,* 75.

33. Ibid., 76.

34. Ibid., 79–80.

35. Shin Yong-ha, *Formation and Development of Modern Korean Nationalism* (Seoul: Dae kwang munhwasa, 1989).

36. ARPCUSA (1908), 269.

37. Baird, *Daybreak in Korea,* 82.

38. Ibid., 84.

39. Ibid., 85.

40. Mattie Noble, Diaries, no. 5, "Tribute to Arthur," 13; "The Annual Meeting of the Methodist Mission," *KR* (September 1895): 355–58.

41. See the home page of the Korean Methodist Church at http://www.kmcweb.or.kr/index.html.

42. Noble, *Ewa,* 11.

43. Ibid., 19.

44. Ibid., 42.

45. There has been a series of debates about the history of the slavery system in Korea. For example, James Palais argues that "Korea was a bona fide slave society" as far back as the tenth century, while other scholars pay close attention to the differences between the Korean *nobi* system and slaves in America and Europe. For more details, see James Palais, *Confucian Statecraft and Korean Institutions: Yu Hyŏngwŏn and the Late Chosŏn Dynasty* (Seattle: University of Washington Press, 1996); and Yŏksa hakhoe, ed., *Nobi, nongno, noye: Yesokmin ŭi pigyosa* (Nobi, Serfs, and Slaves: Comparative History of Bonded Servitude) (Seoul: Ilchogak, 1998). Arthur Noble was aware of the fact that the 1894 reform in Korea abolished the slavery system. In Noble's story, Ewa's owner claims that Ewa is still his slave because she had been purchased before 1894. Noble further describes the transitional period when many slaves chose to stay on in their master's houses, although they had been given freedom under the law.

46. *KMF* 4, no. 1 (January 1908): 15–16.

47. Noble, *Ewa,* 294.

48. Ibid., 41.

49. Ibid., 197.

50. Ibid., 298–99.

51. Ibid., 170.

52. Ibid., 295.

53. Ibid., 296.

54. Deuchler, *The Confucian Transformation of Korea*, 267–73.

55. See Annie Baird, "Votes or Not for Married Women in Station and Mission," *KMF* 9, no. 2 (1913): 35–37.

56. Noble, *Ewa*, 189.

57. Ibid., 198.

58. Craig Calhoun, "Nationalism and Civil Society: Democracy, Diversity, and Self-Determination," in *Social Theory and the Politics of Identity*, ed. Craig Calhoun (Oxford: Blackwell, 1994), 314.

59. Thomas David Dubois, "Hegemony, Imperialism, and the Construction of Religion in East and Southeast Asia," *History and Theory* 44, no. 4 (December 2005): 113–31.

60. Noble, *Ewa*, 223.

61. In his discussion of nationalism, Calhoun points out that "nationalisms have been overwhelmingly male ideologies . . . in the way that national strength is defined so often as international potency and military power; men are treated as potential martyrs while women are mainly their mothers." From this general trait, it is interesting to note that Noble makes a case for Ewa, whose courage to prioritize her religion and national mandate over her own personal happiness becomes a model for Sung-yo and even Tong-sik. See Calhoun, *Nationalism*, 113–14.

62. Noble, *Ewa*, 307.

63. Ibid., 307.

64. Ibid., 316.

65. Ibid., 308. It might be argued that her sacrifice was influenced by the Christian idea of death and true reward in the spiritual world. See Betty Deberg, *Ungodly Women: Gender and the First Wave of American Fundamentalism* (Minneapolis: Fortress Press, 1990), 47–48.

66. Noble, *Ewa*, 304.

67. Ibid., 318.

68. Ibid., 354.

69. Ibid., 321.

70. Ibid., 320–21.

71. For a discussion of modern nationalist masculinity, see Vladimir Tikhonov, "Masculinizing the Nation: Gender Ideologies in Traditional Korea and in the 1890s–1900s Korean Enlightenment Discourse," *Journal of Asian Studies* 66, no. 4 (November 2007): 1029–65; and Sheila Miyoshi Jager, *Narratives of Nation Building in Korea: A Genealogy of Patriotism* (Armonk: M. E. Sharpe, 2003).

72. Ellasue Wagner was born in West Virginia in 1881. She graduated from Martha Washington College, 1895–96 (now united with Emory and Henry College), and later from Marion College, Virginia, 1899–AB (Lutheran College). She also received an MA degree from Scarritt College in 1936 and studied at the Teachers College, Columbia University, during her furloughs. Her publications include *At the Hermits Gate: A Presentation of Some Events of 1883–1884* (Seoul: The Korea Methodist News Service, 1934), *Kim Su Bang*

and Other Stories of Korea (Nashville: Publishing Home of the Methodist Episcopal Church, South, 1909), *Pokjumie* (Nashville: Publishing Home of the Methodist Episcopal Church, South, 1911), *Korea the Old and the New* (New York: Fleming H. Revell Company, 1934), *Kumokie (A Bride of Old Korea)* (Nashville: Publishing Home of the Methodist Episcopal Church, South, 1911), and *The Dawn of Tomorrow: True Stories from Old Korea* (Bristol, Tenn.: King Printing Co., 1948). See Mission Biographical Reference Files, GCAH.

73. Wagner, *The Dawn of Tomorrow*, 5–20.

74. For example, in her correspondence dated May 24, 1948, she talks about her forthcoming book, *Korea Calls*, which is an account of her first year in Songdo when "missionary work was real pioneering." In addition, she inquired into the possibility of republishing her book, *Kumokie (A Bride of Old Korea)*, and found that the Friendship Press was interested. However, since the book was published in 1911 by the publisher of the Methodist Episcopal Church, South, she was told she would need an approval from the Board (her letter, March 31, 1948). This request was not approved in the end (her letter, May 24, 1948). See Mission Biographical Reference Files, GCAH.

75. Among the photographs in Wagner's family collection, there is one of an American woman named Sue Wallace, who married a Korean man. This actual person might have been the inspiration for her story.

76. For an account of the dynamic cultural scene of colonial Korea, see Kim, *Sŏul e ttanshol ŭl hŏhara*, 202–43.

77. Deberg, *Ungodly Women*.

78. Wagner, *Korea the Old and the New*, 20–21; 83–84.

79. In her analysis of the ways in which Englishwomen represented the Indian *zenana*, Janaki Nair makes a cogent argument that "the idealized family as represented in the writings . . . served as a means not only to critique the colonized but emerged as a response to the 'threats' to the English family posed by the women's movement." See Janaki Nair, "Uncovering the Zenana: Visions of Indian Womanhood in Englishwomen's Writings, 1813–1940," *Journal of Women's History* 2, no. 1 (1990): 8–34.

80. This feature of gender discourse was shared by American missionaries in China. In her analysis of the changing gender discourse among missionaries in China, Gael Graham argues that "as the Chinese increasingly adopted certain external manifestations of Western culture, the missionaries, contrary to their prior practice, began to exhort the Chinese to distinguish between Christian and secular Western features and to keep the former but resist the encroachment of the latter." Graham, *Gender, Culture, and Christianity*, 90.

81. John C. Spurlock and Cynthia A. Magistro, *New and Improved: The Transformation of American Women's Emotional Culture* (New York: New York University Press, 1998).

82. In her analysis of American fundamentalism from 1880 to 1930, Betty Deberg takes gender as a central focus and examines the ways in which the fundamentalist crusaders reacted to the rapid changes and disruptions in gender ideology in the United States. Approaching fundamentalism not as a coherent

theology but rather as a rhetorically driven popular movement, she analyzes popular Christian literature and periodicals to reveal how the rhetoric strongly supported the Victorian ideology of the separate spheres and the glorification of motherhood. In this context, the New Woman and the Flapper of the 1920s became prime targets for criticism by fundamentalists. See Deberg, *Ungodly Women.*

83. I would like to express my appreciation to Yurie Hong Easton for drawing my attention to the significance of the character name Eva.

84. Ann L. Ardis, *New Women, New Novels: Feminism and Early Modernism* (New Brunswick, N.J.: Rutgers University Press, 1990), 1–28 (from 1–2)

85. Brown, *New Forces in Old China,* 125.

86. I: inserted page before page 7.

87. III: 5–6; X: 17. In citations of the novel, the chapter number will be given in Roman numerals, followed by page numbers. For example, "III: 5–6" means chapter 3, pages 5–6.

88. XIV: 1–11.

89. Susan L. Blake, "A Woman's Trek: What Difference Does Gender Make?" in *Western Women and Imperialism,* ed. Chaudhuri and Strobel, 19–34; Hunter, *The Gospel of Gentility;* Flemming, *Women's Work for Women;* Lewis, *Gendering Orientalism;* Chaudhuri and Strobel, eds., *Western Women and Imperialism;* Mills, *Discourses of Difference;* and Anne McClintock, *Imperial Leather: Race, Gender, and Sexuality in the Colonial Contest* (New York: Routledge, 1995).

90. I: 1.

91. Martha Banta, *Imaging American Women: Idea and Ideals in Cultural History* (New York: Columbia University Press, 1987), 92–139.

92. I: 3.

93. I:7, 12.

94. I: 4.

95. Peggy Pascoe, "Miscegenation Law, Court Cases, and Ideologies of 'Race' in Twentieth-Century America," in *Unequal Sisters: A Multicultural Reader in U.S. Women's History,* ed. Vicki L. Ruiz and Ellen Carol Dubois (New York: Routledge, 2000), 161–82.

96. Ellasue Wagner, *WMA* (January 1906): 249.

97. II: 4.

98. III: 11; X: 17.

99. XIII: 18.

100. For a discussion of the Confucian-patriarchal system in traditional Korea, see Deuchler, *The Confucian Transformation of Korea.*

101. Han Bong, "Singu kajŏng saenghwal ŭi changjjŏm kwa tanjjŏm" (Merits and Shortcomings of Old and New Family Life), *Pyŏlgŏn'gon* (December 1929). Reprinted in Kim, *Sŏul e ttansŭhol ŭl hŏhara,* 237–40. In this essay, Bong details his own story of how he married a woman selected for him by his parents when he was sixteen, but later fell in love with a New Woman. Unable to divorce the first wife because of his parents' strong opposition, he leads a

dual life in which he lives not with his legal first wife but with the second one, who is legally a concubine or, more simply, a lover. There are many reports and essays on this issue in the 1920s and 1930s. See, for example, Samch'ŏng dongin, "Yŏhakkyo rŭl cholŭphago ch'ŏp i toeŏ kanŭn saramdŭl" ("People Who Became a Concubine after Graduating from Girls' Schools"), Sin yŏsŏng (April 1924): 48–55; and the special issue "The Secondary Wife," Sin yŏsŏng (February 1933): 2–22.

102. Wagner, Korea, 84–87.

103. Robert, American Women in Mission, xvii. Annie Baird wrote frankly about the public's perception of missionaries in her book Inside Views of Mission Life (43–44). She wrote: "The traveling suits of Mrs. X—and the children represented the combined skill and ingenuity of the ladies of the station, but when they made their appearance in a large railway station in America, they were aware of a momentary suspension of business, and a sudden access of suppressed hilarity in the air. Finally a scrub-woman at work on the floor voiced the thought of all hearts when she asked, 'Whur'd you come frum?'"

104. XI: 8–14. Unmarried missionary women were often portrayed as lacking femininity and "refinement in table manners and in dress," but Wagner challenges that stereotypical image of single women missionaries. See Hunter, The Gospel of Gentility, 52–55.

105. XII: 9.

106. XII: 12–13.

CHAPTER 6

1. Yoo, "The 'New Woman' and the Politics of Love," 296.

2. Felski, The Gender of Modernity, 146; Angelique Richardson, "The Birth of National Hygiene and Efficiency: Women and Eugenics in Britain and America 1865–1915," in New Woman Hybridities, ed. Ann Heilmann and Margaret Beetham (London: Routledge, 2004), 243.

3. Felski, Doing Time, 15.

4. Ann Heilmann and Margaret Beetham, eds., New Woman Hybridities (London: Routledge, 2004).

5. Birgitte Søland, Becoming Modern: Young Women and the Reconstruction of Womanhood in the 1920s (Princeton, N.J.: Princeton University Press, 2000); Liz Conor, The Spectacular Modern Woman: Feminine Visibility in the 1920s (Bloomington: Indiana University Press, 2004); Mona L. Russell, Creating the New Egyptian Woman: Consumerism, Education, and National Identity, 1863–1922 (New York: Palgrave Macmillan, 2004); Hu Ying, Tales of Translation: Composing the New Woman in China, 1899–1918 (Stanford, Calif.: Stanford University Press, 2000); and Barbara Sato, The New Japanese Woman (Durham: Duke University Press, 2003).

6. Heilmann and Beetham, eds., New Woman Hybridities; Dina Lowy, The Japanese "New Woman": Images of Gender and Modernity (New Brunswick, N.J.: Rutgers University Press, 2007).

7. In 1912, the number of female students at high schools was merely 116. This tiny number expanded over the next few decades, reaching 1,100 in 1922, 4,770 in 1932, and 12,171 in 1942. Kim, *Yŏsŏng ŭi kŭndae, kŭndae ŭi yŏsŏng,* 283.

8. Yoo, *The Politics of Gender in Colonial Korea;* Shin and Robinson, eds., *Colonial Modernity in Korea;* and Michael E. Robinson, *Cultural Nationalism in Colonial Korea, 1920–1925* (Seattle: University of Washington Press, 1988).

9. Theresa Hyun, *Writing Women in Korea* (Honolulu: University of Hawai'i Press, 2004), 42–59.

10. Ibid., 56.

11. Kim Su-jin summarizes two major trends in defining New Women in Korea: one is to regard New Women as an actual, collective group, and the other is to focus on the discursive formation of New Women largely through print media. See Kim, "1920–30-yŏndae sin yŏsŏng," 1–19.

12. Yŏn'gu konggan suyu+nŏmŏ kŭndae maech'e yŏn'gu t'im, *Sin yŏsŏng: Maech'e ro pon kŭndae yŏsŏng p'ungsoksa* (New Women: The History of Modern Women and Their Lifestyle Reflected in the Media) (Seoul: Han'gyŏre sinmunsa, 2005), 13–51; Sin Yŏng-suk, "Ilche ha sin yŏsŏng ŭi yŏnae kyŏlhon munje" (Issues of Romance and Marriage among New Women under Japanese Colonial Rule), *Han'guk hakpo* 12, no. 4 (1986): 182–217.

13. P'albong sanin, "Sowi sin yŏsŏng naeŭmsae" (Scent of a So-Called New Woman), *Sin yŏsŏng* 2, no. 8 (1924): 20–21. Cited from Kim, *Yŏsŏng ŭi kŭndae, kŭndae ŭi yŏsŏng,* 52.

14. "Sin yŏja munje taeyahwahoe" (Big Night Conversation about New Women), *Sin yŏsŏng* 2, no. 12 (1924): 44–49 (from 47).

15. Sato, *The New Japanese Woman,* 49.

16. Ibid., 8.

17. Kenneth Wells points out that despite the explosion of debates on gender in the 1920s, "subsequent nationalist histories of the period" avoid such debates, which can be explained in part by male anxiety about being colonized, which resulted in the belittlement or complete exclusion of the first wave of feminist discourse in colonized Korea. See Wells, "The Price of Legitimacy," 193.

18. Hwang Sin-dŏk, "Chosŏn puin undong ŭn ŏttŏk'e chinaewanna," *Sin kajŏng* (April 1933): 22–23. Cited from Kim, *Yŏsŏng ŭi kŭndae, kŭndae ŭi yŏsŏng,* 74.

19. When members of Yŏja ch'inmokhoe (Friendship Association of Female Students in Japan) held a party to congratulate some of its members on their graduation, the ceremony had two Christian prayer sessions—one at the beginning and one at the end. At this gathering, Kim Maria offered the opening remark, and Na Hye-sŏk and Hŏ Yŏng-suk spoke as graduates. *Man'guk puin* 1 (1932): 21.

20. The disproportional representation of new women in Christian-related work spaces is well captured by an anonymous author who complained the "Christian-centered sphere of work" among the graduates of mission schools

possibly because of the main goal of those schools. "Odaehakbu ch'ul ŭi injae ŏn p'arettŭ," *Samch'ŏlli* 4, no. 2 (1932): 13–24.

21. "Oriental Women Students in America," *WW* 29, no. 6 (June 1914): 126–27.

22. Rosetta Sherwood Hall, MD, "One New Life in the Orient," *WMF* 28, no. 12 (June 1897): 342–43.

23. Blanche I. Stevens, "Contribution to the Christian Movement of Educational Work for Young Women," in *The Fiftieth Anniversary Celebration,* 145–54.

24. Han'guk yŏsŏngsa p'ŏnch'an wiwŏnhoe, *Han'guk yŏsŏngsa* 2, 512–17.

25. *Yŏnghwa 70-yŏnsa* (The Seventieth History of Yŏnghwa Girls' School) (Yŏnghwa yŏja chunghakkyo, 1963), 35.

26. Helen Kim, *Grace Sufficient: The Story of Helen Kim by Herself* (Nashville: The Upper Room, 1964), 21–28.

27. Ewha 100-yŏnsa p'yŏnch'an wiwŏnhoe, *Ewha 100-yŏnsa charyojip,* 255–56.

28. The other institution for women's higher education was Sookmyung Women's College, which offered a professional curriculum from 1938. Sookmyung began its history in 1906 as a girls' school, founded by Lady Ŏm as the first private Korean school for girls.

29. Yun Chŏng-nan, "1920-yŏndae kidokkyo yŏsŏngdŭl ŭi Kŭnuhoe ch'amyŏ kwajŏng kwa t'alt'oe paegyŏng e kwanhan yŏn'gu" (A Study of Christian Women's Particpation in and Withdrawal from Kŭnu in the 1920s), in *Yŏsŏng: Yŏksa wa hyŏnjae,* ed. Pak Yong-ok (Seoul: Kukhak charyowŏn, 2001), 208. See also Nancy Boyd, *Emissaries: The Overseas Work of the American YWCA 1895–1970* (New York: The Woman's Press, 1986).

30. Ch'ŏn, *Han'guk yŏsŏng kidokkyo sahoe undongsa,* 30.

31. *Tonga ilbo,* April 5, 1922. Korean Christian male leaders were also present at the meeting, including Sin Hŭng-u and Yi Sang-jae.

32. Ch'ŏn, *Han'guk yŏsŏng kidokkyo sahoe undongsa,* 33.

33. Kim, *Grace Sufficient,* 65–66.

34. Ch'ŏn, *Han'guk yŏsŏng kidokkyo sahoe undongsa,* 251.

35. Ibid., 95–96.

36. Ibid., 249–52.

37. Kim, *Grace Sufficient,* 63.

38. Ibid., 95–96.

39. For an example of one of her most representative speeches in her pro-Japanese activities, see Kim Hwal-lan, "Yŏsŏng ŭi mujang" (Armament of Women), *Tae tonga* 14, no. 3 (1942); Pak Sŏk-bun and Pak Ŭn-bong, *Kŭn hyŏndaesa sok ŭi yŏsŏng 30in ŭi sam ŭl t'onghae ponŭn inmul yŏsŏngsa* (The Character History of Thirty Women through Their Lives in Modern and Contemporary History) (Seoul: Saenal, 1994), 230–40.

40. In her article, Yi Hye-jŏng suggests that Kim Hwal-lan believed dedication to the "nation" was a way for women to exert themselves in the national sphere as equal partners to men and thus was a way to enhance the devel-

opment of the women's movement. See "Ilche malgi Kim Hwal-lan ŭi Ilche hyŏmnyŏk paegyŏng kwa nolli" (Kim Hwal-lan's Background and Rationale for Her Collaboration with the Japanese Imperial Power at the End of the Japanese Colonial Era), *Yŏsŏnghak nonjip* 21, no. 2 (2004): 58–61.

41. Kim Sŭng-t'ae, ed., *Han'guk kidokkyo wa sinsa ch'ambae munje* (Korean Christianity and the Issue of the Homage to Shinto Shrines) (Seoul: Han'guk kidokkyo yŏksa yŏn'guso, 1992).

42. Kim, *Grace Sufficient*, 98.

43. Horace Underwood, the president of Yŏnhŭi College, was also willing to collaborate with Japan in order to keep his college open even when other Presbyterian missionaries would rather close their schools than following Japan's demand for Homage to Shinto Shrines. See Yi, "Ilche malgi Kim Hwal-lan," 50–51.

44. "Uwŏl" was a name that Kim Hwal-lan used for herself.

45. *Han'gyŏre*, October 10, 1998.

46. Insook Kwon, "Feminists Navigating the Shoals of Nationalism and Collaboration: The Post-Colonial Korean Debate over How to Remember Kim Hwallan," *Frontiers* 27, no. 1 (2006): 39–66.

47. "Miss H. K. Kim spoke in behalf of women in Korea," in *The Christian Life and Message in Relation to Non-Christian Systems: Report of the Jerusalem Meeting of the International Missionary Council*, vol. 1 (London: Oxford University Press, 1928), 372.

48. Kim Hwal-lan, "Yŏsŏng ŭi mujang" (The Militarization of Women), *Tae tonga* 14, no. 3 (March 1942): 94–97.

49. Sheldon Garon, "Women's Groups and the Japanese State: Contending Approaches to Political Integration, 1890–1945," *Journal of Japanese Studies* 19, no. 1 (winter 1993): 5–41.

50. Kwok, "Chinese Women and Protestant Christianity," 200.

51. Cited from Pak and Pak, *Kŭn hyŏndaesa sok ŭi yŏsŏng 30in*, 175.

52. Pak Yong-ok, *Kim Maria* (Seoul: Hongsŏngsa, 2003), 339.

53. "Sin yŏsŏng ch'onggwan 2: Paekhwa ranman ŭi kimi yŏingun" (Overview of New Women 2: Splendid Women of the Year 1919), *Samch'ŏlli* 16 (June 1931): 22–23.

54. Kim Sŭng-t'ae and Pak Hye-jin, comp., *Naehan sŏn'gyosa ch'ongnam, 1884–1984* (A Comprehensive Survey of Missionaries in Korea) (Seoul: Han'guk kidokkyo yŏksa yŏn'guso, 1994), 232.

55. Pak, *Kim Maria*, 227–29.

56. Ibid., 271–98.

57. Ibid., 324.

58. Ibid., 342–49.

59. Ibid., 376–77.

60. Ibid., 467–69.

61. "Yukkaeguk ŭl manyu hago toraon Pak In-dŏk yŏsa pangmun'gi" (A Visit to Ms. Pak Indŏk upon her Return from a Trip to Six Countries), *Sin yŏsŏng* 5, no. 10 (1931): 48–51 (from 48).

62. Pil Ley Choi, "The Development of Korean Women during the Past Ten Years," *KMF* 18, no. 4 (1923): 222.

63. Pahk, *September Monkey*, 75.

64. Ibid., 78–79.

65. Ibid., 80.

66. Ibid., 88–91, 97.

67. Ibid., 118–19.

68. Ibid., 122.

69. Ibid., 128.

70. "Yukkaeguk ŭl manyu hago," 48–51.

71. Pahk, *September Monkey*, 164–65.

72. Ibid., 162–63.

73. Ken Wells, "Expanding Their Realm: Women and Public Agency in Colonial Korea," in *Women's Suffrage in Asia*, ed. Louise Edwards and Mina Roces, 152–69 (London: Routledge Curzon, 2004) (from 160).

74. "Ihon ŭi tosi Sŏul" (City of Divorce, Seoul), *Samch'ŏlli* 3, no. 11 (1931): 35.

75. "Pak In-dŏk konggaechang: Ihon sodong e kwanhayŏ" (An Open Letter to Pak In-dŏk Regarding the Fiasco of Her Divorce), *Sin yŏsŏng* 5, no. 11 (1931): 30–35.

76. "Chosŏn ŭi Nora ro inhyŏng ŭi chip ŭl naon Pak In-dŏk ssi" (Pahk Induk, Korea's Nora, Has Left a Doll's House," *Samch'ŏlli* 5, no. 1 (1933): 73–74. For the stage appearance of Ibsen's *A Doll's House* in Korea, see Jung-Soon Shim, "Recasting the National Motherhood: Transactions of Western Feminisms in Korean Theatre," *Theatre Research International* 29, no. 2 (2004): 143–54. In her article, Shim describes the male reaction to the play at one theater as follows: "Regarding the audience response, the critic Na records with certain sensitivity and sympathy for women: 'At Nora's last dialogue, rolling applause broke out from the ladies' seats, whereas the sound "hush, hush" rose among the gentlemen seats.' This critic further records the following exchange of conversation between male spectators: A: Isn't that rolling applause among the ladies' seats an indication that the women desire to liberate themselves from men's oppression? B: It's just a simple demonstration that 'we sympathize.' Their ulterior motive, however, is something else. In their minds, they want to marry a rich man and to live a comfortable life, even though it is a doll's house. C: Nora's leaving home is not natural. Her action lacks convincing motivation, and it isn't based on a firm belief. It seems she acted on the spur of the moment" (from 145).

77. "Chosŏn ŭi Nora," 74.

78. Wang, *Women in the Chinese Enlightenment*, 50; Bardsley, *The Blue-stockings of Japan*, 3; Phyllis Birnbaum, *Modern Girls, Shining Stars, the Skies of Tokyo* (New York: Columbia University Press, 1999), 26–30.

79. Yu Wu-sang, "Yŏsŏng ŭi hyŏksin saenghwal: Ipssen ŭi yŏsŏngjuŭi," *Sin yŏsŏng* 4, no. 1 (1926): 61–68.

80. Pak, *Han'guk kŭndae chŏngch'i sasangsa yŏn'gu*, 217–23.

81. "Hagi hyuga e kwihyang hanŭn Kyŏngsŏng yŏhakkyo haksaeng ŭi

p'obu" (A Wish List of Girl Students Returning Home from Seoul for Summer Vacation), *Sin yŏsŏng* 3, no. 8 (1925): 12–16.

82. Pahk Induk, "Work among Rural Women," *KMF* 29, no. 7 (1933): 136–37.

83. Ibid.

84. Pahk Induk, "T'aep'yŏngyang ŭl tasi kŏnnŭmyŏ" (Crossing the Pacific Ocean Again), *Samch'ŏlli* 8, no. 1 (1936): 74–78.

85. Pahk, *September Monkey*, 181–93.

86. Ibid., 187–88.

87. Ibid., 198–99.

88. Pahk Induk, "Agyo ŭi yŏhaksaeng kunsa kyoryŏnan" (Proposal for Military Training of Girl Students at Our School), *Samch'ŏlli* 14, no. 1 (1942): 102–5.

89. Haruko Taya Cook, "Women's Deaths as Weapons of War in Japan's 'Final Battle,'" in *Gendering Modern Japanese History*, ed. Barbara Molony and Kathleen Uno (Cambridge, Mass.: Harvard University Press, 2005), 326–56.

90. Pahk Induk, "Sŭngjŏn ŭi kil ŭn yŏgi itta" (This Is the Way to Win the War), *Samch'ŏlli* 13, no. 11 (November 1941): 35–38, 45.

91. *Tae tonga* 14, no. 3 (1942): 90–92.

92. Cemil Aydin, *The Politics of Anti-Westernism in Asia: Visions of World Order in Pan-Islamic and Pan-Asian Thought* (New York: Columbia University Press, 2007), 161–89.

93. Pahk, *September Monkey*, 9.

94. Ibid., 201.

95. Ibid., 199.

96. "Korean Author Plans School," *The Christian Science Monitor*, March 14, 1955.

97. "Oriental Women Students in America," *WW* 29, no. 6 (June 1914): 126–27.

98. Kim Ir-yŏp, *Chaet pit chŏksam e sarang ŭl mutko* (Burying Love under the Ash-Colored Jacket), ed. Kim Sang-bae (Seoul: Sol moe, 1982), 42–43.

99. Ibid., 43–45.

100. Ibid., 38–46, 118–21, 206–12, 244–46.

101. Na Hye-sŏk, "Isang chŏk puin" (Ideal Woman), *Hak chi kwang* (1914). Cited from Yi, *Na Hye-sŏk chŏnjip*, 183–85.

102. The only women's magazine that was founded by women for women readers was *Chasŏn puinhoe chapchi*, whose main purpose was to encourage charity activities by women. With slight differences in emphasis, this magazine also shared a large project that promoted the discourse of "civilization and enlightenment" and envisioned what role women should take in that project. The statement of the magazine's president captures this general mission: "This is the era of the survival of the fittest. If we do not act, we are likely to be turned into the subject of benevolence, let alone being benefactor. If this is the case, we not only cannot wash out the shame of the past but will make our future generation of women relegated to the miserable situation. Therefore,

we should not miss this opportunity. . . . From now on, we should work hard, encouraging education and charity activities. Then women's civilization is going to be better and better, and our future generation of every young women will be civilized." *Chasŏn puinhoe chapchi* 1 (1908), in *Han'guk yŏsŏng kwan'gye charyojip: Han mal yŏsŏngji*, ed. Ewha yŏja taehakkyo Han'guk yŏsŏng yŏn'guso (Seoul: Ewha yŏja taehakkyo ch'ulp'anbu, 1981), 98–101.

103. Yu Chin-wŏl, "'Sin yŏja' e nat'anan kŭndae yŏsŏngdŭl ŭi kŭl ssŭgi yangsang mit t'ŭksŏng yŏn'gu" (Patterns and Characteristics of Writing of Modern Women Reflected in Sin yŏja), *Yŏsŏng munhak yŏn'gu* 14 (2005): 147–73.

104. Yi, *In'gan ŭro salgo sipta*, 183.

105. Kim recalled that Pang Chŏng-hwan and Yu Kwang-yŏl supported her idea of creating a women's magazine and acted as advisers. See Kim, *Chaet pit chŏksam e sarang ŭl mutko*, 59.

106. One exception was Mr. Yang U-ch'on, who served as an adviser. Yu, "'Sin yŏja' e nat'anan kŭndae yŏsŏngdŭl," 150.

107. Kim and Pak, comp., *Naehan sŏn'gyosa ch'ongnam*, 166–67; Mun, *Sin yŏsŏng*, 55.

108. "T'ugo hwanyŏng" (Inviting Submissions), *Sin yŏja* 2 (April 1920).

109. Ibid.; Yu, "'Sin yŏja' e nat'anan kŭndae yŏsŏngdŭl," 148.

110. "A New Magazine—The New Woman," *KMF* 16, no. 10 (October 1920): 203, 213.

111. *Sin yŏja* 1 (1920): 2–3.

112. Kim, *Chaet pit chŏksam e sarang ŭl mutko*, 216–20.

113. Kathleen Canning, "Feminist History after the Linguistic Turn: Historicizing Discourse and Experience," *Signs* 19, no. 2 (winter 1994): 368–404. Canning notes that the discourse of sexually emancipated New Women was "one of the most profound ruptures in postwar culture" (385).

114. Hiroko Tomida, *Hiratsuka Raichō and Early Japanese Feminism* (Leiden: Brill, 2004), 144.

115. Pauline C. Reich, "Japan's Literary Feminists: The 'Seito' Group," *Signs* 2, no. 1 (autumn 1976): 280–91.

116. Yu, "'Sin yŏja' e nat'anan kŭndae yŏsŏngdŭl," 165.

117. In the beginning of the magazine, Kim Wŏn-ju secured financial support from her first husband, Yi No-ik, a professor at Yŏnhŭi College (presently Yonsei University) and Mrs. Bliss Billings, an American Methodist missionary wife whose husband was also a professor at Yŏnhŭi College. Mrs. Billings served as the publisher, and her involvement may be related to the fact that both her husband and Kim's were colleagues at Yŏnhŭi, and thus the two women might have had a chance to share the idea of starting a magazine.

118. After the closure of *Sin yŏja*, a number of women's magazines appeared, including *Sin kajŏng* (New Family, founded in 1921), *Puin* (Married Women, 1922), *Sin yŏsŏng* (New Women, 1923), *Puin chi kwang* (Light of Married Women, 1924), *Punyŏ segye* (Women's World, 1927), and *Kŭnu* (Friends of Rose of Sharon, 1929). These magazines, each with a different set of goals and

agendas, were important sites for women writers to engage in debates on new womanhood with other women, and men as well. A wide range of topics were discussed in the pages. Some of the arguments were in line with the discourse of "civilization and enlightenment," while others broke new ground by questioning enduring taboos related to womanly virtues and ideals. Sensational debates took place in the magazines, covering issues concerning women's quest for self and individual desire for happiness. The notion of the enlightenment project for a Korean nation-state with women being instrumental to nation-building was challenged by new women, who dared to transgress traditional sexual mores and family norms and assert new freedom and independence. See Yi Ok-jin, "Yŏja chapchi rŭl t'onghae pon yŏkwŏn sinjang" (A Study of the Enhancement of Women's Rights through Women's Magazines). (MA thesis, Ewha Womans University, 1979).

119. Kim Ir-yŏp, "Sinbul kwa na ŭi kajŏng" (Buddhist Faith and My Family), *Sin tonga* (December 1931). Cited from Kim, *Chaet pit chŏksam e sarang ŭl mutko*, 275–76.

120. Ibid., 275.

121. *Samch'ŏlli* 5, no. 9 (1933): 21; Kim, *Chaet pit chŏksam e sarang ŭl mutko*, 312.

122. *Kaebyŏk* (January 1935): 12–17.

123. Yi, *In'gan ŭro salgo sipta*, 50–56.

124. Sheldon Garon, "Women's Groups and the Japanese State: Contending Approaches to Political Integration, 1890–1945," *Journal of Japanese Studies* 19, no. 1 (winter 1993): 5–41. See also, Barbara Rose, *Tsuda Umeko and Women's Education in Japan* (New Haven, Conn.: Yale University Press, 1992), 52; Kathleen Uno, "Womanhood, War, and Empire: Transmutations of 'Good Wife, Wise Mother' before 1931," in *Gendering Modern Japanese History*, ed. Molony and Uno, 493–519.

125. Na Hye-sŏk, "Isang chŏk puin" (Ideal Woman), *Hak chi kwang* (1914). Cited from Yi, *Na Hye-sŏk chŏnjip*, 184.

126. Ibid., 183–85.

127. Kim Wŏn-ju, "Uri yŏja ŭi yogu wa chujang," *Sin yŏja* 2 (1920), in *Chaet pit chŏksam e sarang ŭl mutko*, 204–5.

128. Na Hye-sŏk married Kim U-yŏng, a lawyer trained at Kyoto Imperial University. Their Western-style wedding ceremony held in Chŏngdong Church in 1920 was widely publicized. Yi, *In'gan ŭro salgo sipda*, 190–91.

129. "Mo toen kamsanggi" (Reflections on Becoming a Mother), in Yi, *Na Hye-sŏk chŏnjip*, 217–34 (from 219).

130. Ibid., 219.

131. Ibid., 220.

132. Ibid., 221, 224.

133. Ibid., 230–31.

134. Ibid., 232.

135. Japanese feminists' debate over "motherhood-protection" focused on political, economic and moral issues. However, Na's discourse on motherhood

never went beyond the personal and philosophical. For the debate over motherhood-protection, see Tomida, *Hiratsuka Raichō and Early Japanese Feminism*, especially chapter 5; Lowy, *The Japanese "New Woman,"* 127–28; Kim Hwa-yŏng, "Kŭndae wa 'yŏsŏng' ŭi munje" (Modernity and the "Woman" Question), *Ilbonŏ munhak* 39 (2007): 275–94.

136. Paekkyŏl saeng, "Kwannyŏm ŭi namlu rŭl pŏsŭn piae: Na Hye-sŏk yŏsa ŭi 'Mo toen kamsanggi' rŭl pogo" (Tragedy after the Liberation from Old Fixed Ideas: A Comment on Na Hye-sŏk's essay "Reflections on Becoming a Mother"), in Yi, *Na Hye-sŏk chŏnjip*, 670–77 (from 673).

137. Na Hye-sŏk, "Kyŏng-hŭi," *Yŏjagye* (March 1918). From Yi, *Na Hye-sŏk chŏnjip*, 79–104; Kim, "Creating New Paradigms of Womanhood," 1–60.

138. Yi, *Na Hye-sŏk chŏnjip*, 689.

139. Na Hye-sŏk and her husband had a tour to Europe and the United States from June 1927 to March 1929. While Na was in Paris studying painting, her husband went to Germany to study law. It was during this time that Na encountered Ch'oe Rin.

140. Na Hye-sŏk, "Ihon kobaekchang" (Confession about Divorce) in Yi, *Na Hye-sŏk chŏnjip*, 397–427.

141. Ibid., 410.

142. Ibid., 412.

143. Ibid., 424–25.

144. Na Hye-sŏk, "Chapgam" (Micellaneous Thoughts), in Yi, *Na Hye-sŏk chŏnjip*, 188.

145. Na Hye-sŏk, "Sin saeghwal e tŭlmyŏnsŏ" (Beginning a New Life), in Yi, *Na Hye-sŏk chŏnjip*, 428–39.

146. Ibid., 438.

147. Ibid., 430.

148. Ibid., 432–33.

149. Ellen Key, *Love and Marriage* (New York: G. P. Putnam's Sons, 1911), 12. See also Hyun, *Writing Women in Korea*, 53–54.

150. Yi, *In'gan ŭro salgo sipta*.

151. Sally Ledger, *The New Woman: Fiction and Feminism at the Fin de siècle* (Manchester: Manchester University Press, 1977).

CHAPTER 7

1. Judith M. Bennett, "Feminism and History," *Gender and History* 1, no. 3 (Autumn 1989): 251–72.

2. Ellasue Wagner, "Then and Now Founders' Day at Holston Institute May 15th, 1940," *KMF* 36, no. 8 (1940): 133–35 (from 134).

3. Pak, *Kŭndae yŏsŏng*, 183–229. Yi, "Mosŏng chungsim ŭi yŏja kyoyuk," 19–20.

4. One can detect some influence of Christianity on Na Hye-sŏk and Kim Wŏn-ju in their earlier writings. For example, Na's short story "Kyŏng-hŭi," published in 1918, reaches its climax when the title character prays to God in

an exhilarated yearning for the free and independent life ahead of her. Her empowerment by the discovery of the self is closely interwoven with the power of God. Kim Wŏn-ju also wrote a short piece, "Kyesi" (Revelation), published in 1920, that is highly religious in content. See "Kyŏng-hŭi" in Yi, *Na Hye-sŏk chŏnjip*, 79–104; "Kyesi" in *Chaet pit chŏksam e sarang ŭl mutko*, 118–21.

5. As recent scholarship demonstrates, "feminine virtues" such as piety, morality, and domesticity could be a powerful source of influence that goes beyond the private. See Mary Kelly, "Beyond the Boundaries," *Journal of the Early Republic* 21, no. 1 (2001): 73–78.

6. Best, "Fifty Years of Women's Work," 83–92.

7. Moneta Troxel, "Women's Work Section," in *Fifty Years of Light*, 109.

8. Ibid., 110.

9. Emily G. Kemp, *The Face of Manchuria, Korea, Russian Turkestan* (London, Chatto & Windus, 1910), 76.

10. Central Election Management Committee, "Summary of Election for National Assembly," Korean Statistical Information Service, http://www.kosis.kr/eng/index.html.

11. Elaine H. Kim, "Men's Talk: A Korean American View of South Korean Constructions of Women, Gender, and Masculinity," in *Dangerous Women: Gender and Korean Nationalism*, eds. Elaine H. Kim and Chungmoo Choi (New York: Routledge, 1998), 67–117.

12. Hong Se-hwa, "Namsŏng chungsim ŭi sahoe" (A Men-Centered Society), *Han'gyŏre*, June 4, 2000.

13. Rey Chow, *Woman and Chinese Modernity: The Politics of Reading between West and East* (Minnesota: University of Minnesota Press, 1991), xi. See also Kwok Pui-lan, *Postcolonial Imagination and Feminist Theology* (Louisville: Westminster John Knox Press, 2005).

14. A feminist theologian, Nam-Soon Kang, assesses that "Christianity in Korea did not . . . shake the deep dimension of Confucian patriarchy. Rather, the patriarchal elements in Christianity came to be combined with the patriarchal value system of Confucianism." She further argues that the Korean church has been resistant to the idea of gender equality, with strong antagonism against feminism. See Nam-Soon Kang, "Creating 'Dangerous Memory': Challenges for Asian and Korean Feminist Theology," *The Ecumenical Review* 47, no. 1 (1995): 21–31 (from 26).

Bibliography

KOREAN NEWSPAPERS AND JOURNALS

Chasŏn puinhoe chapchi
Cheguk sinmun
Hak chi kwang
Han'gyŏre sinmun
Hwangsŏng sinmun
The Independent
Kaebyŏk
Kajŏng chapchī
Man'guk puin
Pyŏlgŏn'gon
Samch'ŏlli
Sin kajŏng
Sin yŏja
Sin yŏsŏng
T'aegŭk hakpo
Taehan maeil sinbo
Tae tonga
Tonga ilbo
Tonggwang
Tongnip sinmun
Yŏja chinam

MISSIONARY JOURNALS

The Gospel in All Lands
The Heathen Woman's Friend
The Korea Magazine
The Korea Methodist
The Korea Mission Field

The Korean Repository
The Korea Review
The Missionary Voice
Woman's Missionary Advocate
Woman's Missionary Friend
Woman's Work
Woman's Work for Woman

MISSION ARCHIVAL DOCUMENTS

For a list of the major archival sources used in this book, including reports, correspondence, and personnel files, see the Abbreviations, pp. 185–86.

BOOKS AND ARTICLES

Abu-Lughod, Lila, ed. *Remaking Women: Feminism and Modernity in the Middle East*. Princeton, N.J.: Princeton University Press, 1998.

An Kuk-sŏn. "*Kŭmsu hoeŭirok*" (Record of the Animals' Assembly). In *Han'guk sosŏl munhak taegye* (A Series of Korean Novels). Vol. 1, *Sin sosŏl* (New Fiction), 443–70. Seoul: Tusan tonga, 1995.

An Pyŏng-ju. "Yugyo ŭi iron powan: P'eminijŭm ŭi suyong kwa kwallyŏn hayŏ" (Complementing Confucian Theories: In Relation to the Accommodation of Feminism). *Yugyo sasang yŏn'gu* 12 (1999): 7–19.

Apple, Michael W., ed. *Cultural and Economic Reproduction in Education*. London: Routledge & Kegan Paul, 1982.

Ardis, Ann L. *New Women, New Novels: Feminism and Early Modernism*. New Brunswick, N.J.: Rutgers University Press, 1990.

Asad, Talal. *Formations of the Secular: Christianity, Islam, Modernity*. Stanford, Calif.: Stanford University Press, 2003.

Aydin, Cemil. *The Politics of Anti-Westernism in Asia: Visions of World Order in Pan-Islamic and Pan-Asian Thought*. New York: Columbia University Press, 2007.

Baird, Annie. *Daybreak in Korea: A Tale of Transformation in the Far East*. New York: Fleming H. Revell Company, 1909.

———. *Inside Views of Mission Life*. Philadelphia: Westminster Press, 1913.

Baird, Richard. *William Baird of Korea*. Oakland, Calif.: Baird, 1968.

Baker, Donald. "Christianity 'Koreanized.'" In *Nationalism and the Construction of Korean Identity*, edited by Hyung Il Pai and Timothy R. Tangherlini, 108–25. Institute of East Asian Studies, University of California, Berkeley, 1998.

Baker, Paula. *The Moral Frameworks of Public Life: Gender, Politics, and the State in Rural New York, 1870–1930*. New York: Oxford University Press, 1991.

Banta, Martha. *Imaging American Women: Idea and Ideals in Cultural History*. New York: Columbia University Press, 1987.

Barclay, Wade Crawford. *The Methodist Episcopal Church 1845–1939*. Vol. 3, *Widening Horizons 1845–95*. New York: The Board of Missions of the Methodist Church, 1957.

Barsley, Jan. *The Bluestockings of Japan: New Woman Essays and Fiction from Seitō, 1911–16*. Ann Arbor: Center for Japanese Studies, The University of Michigan, 2007.

Basu, Aparna. "Feminism and Nationalism in India, 1917–1947." *Journal of Women's History* 7, no. 4 (winter 1995): 95–107.

Bays, Daniel, ed. *Christianity in China: From the Eighteenth Century to the Present*. Stanford, Calif.: Stanford University Press, 1996.

Beaver, Pierce R. *American Protestant Women in World Mission: A History of the First Feminist Movement in North America*. Grand Rapids, Mich.: William B. Eerdmans, 1980.

Beger, Nicole J. *Present Theories, Past Realities: Feminist Historiography Meets Poststructuralisms*. Frankfurt: Viademica-Verlag, 1997.

Bendroth, Margaret L. "Women and Missions: Conflict and Changing Roles in the Presbyterian Church in the United States of America, 1870–1935." *American Presbyterians* 65, no. 1 (spring 1987): 49–59.

Benhabib, Seyla. *Situating the Self: Gender, Community, and Postmodernism in Contemporary Ethics*. New York: Routledge, 1992.

Bennett, Adrian A. "Doing More Than They Intended." In *Women in New Worlds*. Vol 2, edited by Rosemary Skinner Keller, Louise L. Queen, and Hilah F. Thomas, 249–67. Nashville: Abingdon, 1981.

Bennett, Judith M. "Feminism and History." *Gender and History* 1, no. 3 (autumn 1989): 251–72.

Bhattacharya, Nandini. *Reading the Splendid Body: Gender and Consumerism in Eighteenth-Century British Writing on India*. Newark: University of Delaware Press, 1998.

Birnbaum, Phyllis. *Modern Girls, Shining Stars, the Skies of Tokyo*. New York: Columbia University Press, 1999.

Bishop, Isabella Bird. *Korea and Her Neighbors: A Narrative of Travel, with an Account of the Recent Vicissitudes and Present Position of the Country*. New York: Fleming H. Revell Company, 1897.

Blair, William Newton. *Gold in Korea*. Topeka, Kans.: H. M. Ives & Sons, Inc., 1957.

Blake, Susan L. "A Woman's Trek: What Difference does Gender Make?" In *Western Women and Imperialism: Complicity and Resistance*, edited by Nupur Chaudhuri and Margaret Strobel, 19–34. Bloomington: Indiana University Press, 1992.

Boyd, Nancy. *Emissaries: The Overseas Work of the American YWCA 1895–1970*. New York: The Woman's Press, 1986.

Brannan, Emora T. "A Partnership of Equality." In *Women in New Worlds*. Vol. 2, edited by Rosemary Skinner Keller, Louise L. Queen, and Hilah F. Thomas, 132–47. Nashville: Abingdon, 1982.

Brouwer, Ruth Compton. *Modern Women Modernizing Men: The Chang-*

ing Missions of Three Professional Women in Asia and Africa, 1902–69. Vancouver: University of British Columbia Press, 2002.

Brown, Arthur. New Forces in Old China: An Unwelcome but Inevitable Awakening. New York: Fleming H. Revell Company, 1904.

———. One Hundred Years: A History of the Foreign Missionary Work of the Presbyterian Church in the USA. New York: Fleming H. Revell Company, 1936.

———. Report on a Second Visit to China, Japan and Korea 1909 (with a Discussion of Some Problems of Mission Work). New York: To the Board and the Missions of the Presbyterian Church in the USA, 1909.

Buckland, Augustus R. Women in the Mission Field: Pioneers and Martyrs. New York: Thomas Whittaker, 1895.

Bulbeck, Chilla. Re-Orienting Western Feminisms: Women's Diversity in a Postcolonial World. Cambridge: Cambridge University Press, 1998.

Burman, Barbara, and Carole Turbin. "Material Strategies Engendered." Gender and History 14, no. 3 (November 2002): 371–81.

Burton, Antoinette. "Thinking beyond the Boundaries: Empire, Feminism, and the Domains of History." Social History 26, no. 1 (January 2001): 60–71.

———. "Who Needs the Nation?: Interrogating 'British' History." In Cultures of Empire: Colonizers in Britain and the Empire in the Nineteenth and Twentieth Centuries: A Reader, edited by Catherine Hall, 137–53. New York: Routledge, 2000.

Buswell, Robert, and Timothy Lee, eds. Christianity in Korea. Honolulu: University of Hawai'i Press, 2006.

Calhoun, Craig. Nationalism. Minneapolis: University of Minnesota Press, 1997.

———, ed. Social Theory and the Politics of Identity. Oxford: Blackwell, 1994.

Canning, Kathleen. "Feminist History after the Linguistic Turn: Historicizing Discourse and Experience." Signs 19, no. 2 (winter 1994): 368–404.

Casanova, José. "Rethinking Religion, Secularization, and Secularism." Paper presented at the conference "Conflicts at the Border of Religions and the Secular: Alternative Modernities," Arizona State University, April 23, 2004.

Certeau, Michel de. The Writing of History. Translated by Tom Conley. New York: Columbia University Press, 1988.

Cha, Jae-ho, Chung Bom-Mo, and Lee Sung-Jin. "Boy Preference Reflected in Korean Folklore." In Virtues in Conflict, edited by Sandra Mattielli, 113–27. Seoul: The Royal Asiatic Society Korea Branch 1977.

Chai, Alice. "Integrative Feminist Politics in the Republic of Korea." In Feminist Nationalism, edited by Lois West, 169–86. New York: Routledge, 1997.

Chakrabarty, Dipesh. Provincializing Europe: Postcolonial Thought and Historical Difference. Princeton, N.J.: Princeton University Press, 2000.

Chan, Ching-kiu Stephen. "The Language of Despair: Ideological Representations of the 'New Women' by May Fourth Writers." Modern Chinese Literature 4, no. 1–2 (1988): 19–38.

Chang Byung-wook. *Han'guk kamnigyo yŏsŏngsa* (The History of Methodist Women in Korea). Seoul: Sung Kwang Publishing Co., 1979.

Chang Myŏng-hak. "Tongnip sinmun sasŏl e nat'anan kŭndaehwa kihoek" (The Project of Modernity Reflected in the Editorials of Tongnip Sinmun). *Yŏksa wa sahoe* 3, no. 30 (2003): 1–15.

Chaudhuri, Nupur, and Margaret Strobel, eds. *Western Women and Imperialism: Complicity and Resistance.* Bloomington: Indiana University Press, 1992.

Ch'oe Hye-sil. *Sin yŏsŏngdŭl ŭn muŏt ŭl kkum kkuŏnnŭn'ga* (What Did New Women Dream?). Seoul: Saenggak ŭi namu, 2000.

Ch'oe Yŏng-jin. "Yugyo wa p'eminijŭm, kŭ chŏpchŏm ŭi mosaek" (Confucianism and Feminism: Exploring Their Intersections). *Yugyo sasang yŏn'gu* 14 (2000): 115–31.

Choi, Hyaeweol. "An American Concubine in Old Korea: Missionary Discourse on Gender, Race, and Modernity." *Frontiers: A Journal of Women Studies* 25, no. 3 (2004): 134–61.

———. "Christian Modernity in Missionary Discourse from Korea, 1905–1910." *East Asian History* 29 (June 2005): 39–68.

———. "(En)Gendering a New Nation in Missionary Discourse: An Analysis of W. Arthur Noble's *Ewa.*" *Korea Journal* 46, no. 1 (spring 2006): 139–69.

———. "Missionary Zeal in a Transformed Melodrama: Gendered Evangelicalism in Korea." *The Asian Journal of Women's Studies* 7, no. 1 (2001): 7–39.

———. "A New Moral Order: Gender Equality in Korean Christianity." In *Religions of Korea in Practice*, edited by Robert Buswell, 409–20. Princeton, N.J.: Princeton University Press, 2006.

———. "Women's Literacy and New Womanhood in Late Choson Korea." *The Asian Journal of Women's Studies* 6, no. 1 (2000): 88–115.

———. "Women's Work for 'Heathen Sisters': American Women Missionaries and Their Educational Work in Korea." *Acta Koreana* 2 (July 1999): 1–22.

Choi, Kyeong-Hee. "Neither Colonial nor National: The Making of the "New Woman" in Pak Wansŏ's 'Mother's Stake 1.'" In *Colonial Modernity in Korea*, edited by Gi-Wook Shin and Michael Robinson, 221–47. Cambridge, Mass.: Harvard University Press, 1999.

Chŏn Ŏn-hu. "Ilche sigi yŏhaksaeng ŭisik ŭi pyŏnhwa" (Change of Consciousness among Girl Students during the Japanese Colonial Era). MA thesis, Ewha Womans University, 2000.

Chŏn Sin-yong, ed. *Han'guk ŭi kyubang munhwa* (The Domestic Culture of Korea). Seoul: Pagijŏng, 2005.

Chŏn T'aek-bu. *In'gan Sin Hŭng-u.* Seoul: Taehan kidokkyosŏhoe, 1971.

Chŏng Chi-yŏng. "Chosŏn sidae punyŏ ŭi noch'ul kwa oech'ul: Kyuje wa t'ŭmsae" (Escaping the Inner Room: Women between Regulation and Resistance in the Chosŏn Dynasty). *Yŏsŏng kwa yŏksa* 2 (June 2005): 149–81.

Chŏng Chin-sŏng. "Minjok mit minjokchuŭi e kwanhan Han'guk yŏsŏnghak ŭi nonŭi: Ilbon kun wianbu munje rŭl chungsim ŭro" (A Debate on Nation and Nationalism in Korean Feminism: The Issue of Comfort Women during the Japanese Colonial Era). *Han'guk yŏsŏnghak* 15, no. 2 (1999): 29–53

Chŏng Hyŏn-baek. "Chendŏ, minjok, kukka: Minjokchuŭi wa p'eminijŭm" (Gender, Nation, and the State: Nationalism and Feminism). *P'eminijŭm yŏn'gu* 1 (2001): 9–52.

Ch'ŏn Hwa-suk. *Han'guk yŏsŏng kidokkyo sahoe undongsa* (History of the Social Movement of Korean Christian Women). Seoul: Hyean, 2000.

Chow, Kai-wing, Kevin M. Doak, and Poshek Fu, eds. *Constructing Nationhood in Modern East Asia.* Ann Arbor: University of Michigan Press, 2001.

Chow, Rey. *Woman and Chinese Modernity: The Politics of Reading between West and East.* Minnesota: University of Minnesota Press, 1991.

Christian Life and Message in Relation to Non-Christian Systems: Report of the Jerusalem Meeting of the International Missionary Council. Vol. 1. London: Oxford University Press, 1928.

Chung, David. *Syncretism: The Religious Context of Christian Beginnings in Korea,* edited by Kang-nam Oh. Albany: SUNY Press, 2001.

Chung Yong-Hwa. "The Modern Transformation of Korean Identity: Enlightenment and Orientalism." *Korea Journal* 46, no. 1 (spring 2006): 109–38.

Clark, Allen D. *A History of the Church in Korea.* Seoul: The Christian Literature Society of Korea, 1971.

Clark, Donald N. *Christianity in Modern Korea.* Lanham. Md.: University Press of America, 1986.

——. *Living Dangerously in Korea: The Western Experience 1900–1950* (Norwalk, Conn.: EastBridge, 2003.

Clement, Ernest W. "The New Woman in Japan." *American Journal of Sociology* 8, no. 5 (March 1903): 693–98.

Cohn, Bernard S. *Colonialism and Its Forms of Knowledge.* Princeton, N.J.: Princeton University Press, 1996.

Committee for the Compilation of the History of Korean Women. *Women of Korea: A History from Ancient Times to 1945.* Edited and translated by Yung-Chung Kim. Seoul: Ewha Womans University Press, 1979.

Conor, Liz. *The Spectacular Modern Woman: Feminine Visibility in the 1920s.* Bloomington: Indiana University Press, 2004.

Cook, Haruko Taya. "Women's Deaths as Weapons of War in Japan's 'Final Battle.'" In *Gendering Modern Japanese History,* edited by Barbara Molony and Kathleen Uno, 326–56. Cambridge, Mass.: Harvard University Press, 2005.

Copplestone, J. Tremayne. *History of Methodist Missions.* Vol. 4, *Twentieth-Century Perspectives (The Methodist Episcopal Church, 1896–1939).* New York: The Board of Global Ministries, The United Methodist Church, 1973.

Cross, Barbara. *The Educated Woman in America: Selected Writings of Catharine Beecher, Margaret Fuller, and M. Carey Thomas.* New York: Teachers College Press, 1965.

Curtis, Susan. *A Consuming Faith: The Social Gospel and Modern American Culture.* Baltimore: The Johns Hopkins University Press, 1991.

Dallmayr, Fred. "Confucianism and the Public Sphere: Five Relationships Plus One?" In *The Politics of Affective Relations,* edited by Hahm Chaihark and Daniel A. Bell, 41–60. Lanham, Md.: Lexington Books, 2004.

Davidoff, Leonore. "Gender and the 'Great Divide': Public and Private in British Gender History." *Journal of Women's History* 15, no. 1 (spring 2003): 11–27.

Davidoff, Leonore, and Catherine Hall. *Family Fortunes: Men and Women of the English Middle Class, 1780–1850.* Chicago: University of Chicago Press, 1987.

Deberg, Betty. *Ungodly Women: Gender and the First Wave of American Fundamentalism.* Minneapolis: Fortress Press, 1990.

DeSmither, Carol Marie. "From Calling to Career: Work and Professional Identity among American Women Missionaries to China, 1900–1950." PhD diss., University of Oregon, 1987.

Deuchler, Martina. *The Confucian Transformation of Korea.* Cambridge, Mass.: Harvard University Press, 1992.

———. Preface to *Korean Women: View from the Inner Rooms,* edited by Laurel Kendall and Mark Peterson, 1–3. New Haven, Conn.: East Rock Press, Inc., 1983.

———. "Propagating Female Virtues in Chosŏn Korea." In *Women and Confucian Cultures in Premodern China, Korea, and Japan,* edited by Dorothy Ko, JaHyun Kim Haboush, and Joan Piggott, 142–69. Berkeley and Los Angeles: University of California Press, 2003.

Dirks, Nicholas B., ed. *Colonialism and Culture.* Ann Arbor: University of Michigan Press, 1992.

Donaldson, Laura E. *Decolonizing Feminisms: Race, Gender and Empire-Building.* Chapel Hill: University of North Carolina Press, 1992.

Donaldson, Laura E., and Kwok Pui-lan, eds. *Postcolonialism, Feminism, and Religious Discourse.* New York: Routledge, 2002.

Duara, Prasenjit. "The Discourse of Civilization and Pan-Asianism." *Journal of World History* 12, no. 1 (2001): 99–130.

DuBois, Ellen Carol. *Feminism and Suffrage: The Emergence of an Independent Women's Movement in America 1848–1869.* Ithaca: Cornell University Press, 1978.

Duncan, John. "The *Naehun* and the Politics of Gender." In *Creative Women of Korea: The Fifteenth through the Twentieth Centuries,* edited by Young-Key Kim-Renaud, 26–57. Armonk, N.Y.: M. E. Sharpe, 2004.

Duus, Peter. "The Takeoff Point of Japanese Imperialism." In *Japan Examined: Perspectives on Modern Japanese History,* edited by Harry Wray and Hilary Conroy, 153–57. Honolulu: University of Hawai'i Press, 1983.

Eckert, Carter J. "Epilogue: Exorcising Hegel's Ghosts: Toward a Postnationalist Historiography of Korea." In *Colonial Modernity in Korea,* edited by Gi-Wook Shin and Michael Robinson, 363–78. Cambridge, Mass.: Harvard University Press, 1999.

Elias, Norbert. *The Civilizing Process: The History of Manners*. Translated by Edmund Jephcott. New York: Urizen Books, 1978.

Ewha 100-yŏnsa p'yŏnch'an wiwŏnhoe. *Ewha 100-yŏnsa* (The Hundredth History of Ewha Womans University). Seoul: Ewha yŏja taehakkyo ch'ulp'anbu, 1994.

———. *Ewha 100-yŏnsa charyojip* (Sources of the Hundredth History of Ewha Womans University). Seoul: Ewha yŏja taehakkyo ch'ulp'anbu, 1994.

Ewha yŏja taehakkyo Han'guk yŏsŏng yŏn'guso, ed. *Han'guk yŏsŏng kwan'gye charyojip* (Sourcebook of Korean Women). Seoul: Ewha yŏja taehakkyo ch'ulp'anbu, 1981.

Felski, Rita. *Doing Time: Feminist Theory and Postmodern Culture*. New York: New York University Press, 2000.

———. *The Gender of Modernity*. Cambridge, Mass.: Harvard University Press, 1995.

Feng, Jin. *The New Woman in Early-Twentieth-Century Chinese Fiction*. West Lafayette, Ind.: Purdue University Press, 2004.

Fessenden, Tracy. "Gendering Religion." *Journal of Women's History* 14, no. 1 (2002): 163–69.

Fiftieth Anniversary Celebration of the Korea Mission of the Presbyterian Church in the U.S.A, June 30–July 3, 1934. Rpt., Han'guk kidokkyo yŏksa yŏn'guso, 2000.

Fifty Years of Light. Prepared by Missionaries of the Woman's Foreign Missionary Society of the Methodist Episcopal Church in Commemoration of the Completion of Fifty Years of Work in Korea. Seoul, 1938.

Flemming, Leslie A., ed. *Women's Work for Women: Missionaries and Social Change in Asia*. Boulder: Westview Press, 1989.

Foucault, Michel. *The Archaeology of Knowledge and the Discourse on Language*. New York: Pantheon Books, 1972.

———. "Nietzsche, Genealogy, History." In *The Foucault Reader*, edited by Paul Rabinow, 76–100. New York: Pantheon Books, 1984.

Fraser, Nancy. *Unruly Practices: Power, Discourse, and Gender in Contemporary Social Theory*. Minneapolis: University of Minnesota Press, 1989.

Freedman, Estelle. "Separatism as Strategy: Female Institution Building and American Feminism, 1870–1930." *Feminist Studies* 5, no. 3 (fall 1979): 512–29.

Gale, James. *Korea in Transition*. New York: Educational Department, The Board of Foreign Missions of the Presbyterian Church in the U.S.A., 1909.

Gaonkar, Dilip Parameshwar, ed. *Alternative Modernities*. Durham: Duke University Press, 2001.

Garon, Sheldon. "Women's Groups and the Japanese State: Contending Approaches to Political Integration, 1890–1945." *Journal of Japanese Studies* 19, no. 1 (winter 1993): 5–41.

Garrett, Shirley S. "Sisters All: Feminism and the American Women's Missionary Movement." In *Missionary Ideologies in the Imperialist Era: 1880–*

1920, edited by Torben Christensen and William Hutchison, 221–30. Aarhus: Forlaget Aros, 1982.

Geldhof, Joris. "'Cogitor Ergo Sum': On the Meaning and Relevance of Baader's Theological Critique of Descartes." *Modern Theology* 21, no. 2 (April 2005): 237–51.

Gewurtz, Margo S. "'Their Names May Not Shine': Narrating Chinese Christian Converts." In *Canadian Missionaries, Indigenous People*, edited by Alvyn Austin and Jamie S. Scott, 134–51. Toronto: University of Toronto Press, 2005.

Gifford, Daniel. *Every-Day Life in Korea: A Collection of Studies and Stories.* Translated by Sim Hyŏn-nyŏ. Seoul: The Institute for Korean Christian History, 1995.

Gilmore, George. *Korea from Its Capital.* Philadelphia: The Presbyterian Board of Publication, 1892.

Gong, Gerrit W. *The Standard of 'Civilization' in International Society.* Oxford: Clarendon Press, 1984.

Graham, Gael. *Gender, Culture, and Christianity: American Protestant Mission Schools in China 1880–1930.* New York: Peter Lang, 1995.

Grayson, James. *Early Buddhism and Christianity in Korea: A Study in the Emplantation of Religion.* Leiden: E. J. Brill, 1985.

———. "A Quarter-Millennium of Christianity in Korea." In *Christianity in Korea*, edited by Robert Buswell and Timothy Lee, 7–25. Honolulu: University of Hawai'i Press, 2006.

Grewal, Inderpal, and Caren Kaplan, eds. *Scattered Hegemonies: Postmodernity and Transnational Feminist Practice.* Minneapolis: University of Minnesota Press, 1994.

Ha Hŭi-jŏng. "Ch'ogi chŏndo puin ŭi sinang kwa sinhak" (The Belief and Theology of Early Bible Women). *Han'guk kiddokkyo yŏn'guso sosik* 34 (1999): 11–24.

Haboush, JaHyun Kim. "Versions and Subversions: Patriarchy and Polygamy in Korean Narratives." In *Women and Confucian Cultures in Premodern China, Korea, and Japan*, edited by Dorothy Ko, JaHyun Kim Haboush, and Joan Piggott, 279–303. Berkeley and Los Angeles: University of California Press, 2003.

Haggis, Jane. "'A Heart That Has Felt the Love of God and Longs for Others to Know It': Conventions of Gender, Tensions of Self, and Constructions of Difference in Offering to Be a Lady Missionary." *Women's History Review* 7, no. 2 (1998): 171–92.

Hall, Catherine, ed. *Cultures of Empire: Colonizers in Britain and the Empire in the Nineteenth and Twentieth Centuries: A Reader.* New York: Routledge, 2000.

Hall, Sherwood. *With Stethoscope in Asia: Korea.* McLean, Va.: MCL Associate, 1978.

Hall, Stuart, ed. *Representation: Cultural Representations and Signifying Practices.* London: Sage, 1997.

Hanan, Patrick. "The Missionary Novels of Nineteenth-Century China." *Harvard Journal of Asiatic Studies* 60, no. 2 (December 2000): 413–43.

Han'guk kidokkyo yŏksa yŏn'guso yŏsŏngsa yŏn'guhoe. *Han'guk kyohoe chŏndo puin charyojip* (A Sourcebook on Bible Women in the Korean Christian Church). Seoul: Han'guk kidokkyo yŏksa yŏn'guso, 1999.

Han'guk yŏsŏngsa p'yŏnch'an wiwŏnhoe. *Han'guk yŏsŏngsa* 2 (History of Korean Women). Seoul: Ewha yŏja taehakkyo ch'ulp'anbu, 1972.

———. *Han'guk yŏsŏngsa, purok* (History of Korean Women, Appendix). Seoul: Ewha yŏja taehakkyo ch'ulp'anbu, 1972.

Hayakawa, Noriyo. "Feminism and Nationalism in Japan, 1868–1945." *Journal of Women's History* 7, no. 4 (winter 1995): 108–19.

Henning, Joseph M. *Outposts of Civilization: Race, Religion, and the Formative Years of American-Japanese Relations.* New York: New York University Press, 2000.

Hershatter, Gail. *Women in China's Long Twentieth Century.* Berkeley and Los Angeles: Global, Area, and International Archive / University of California Press, 2007.

Hevia, James. "Leaving a Brand on China: Missionary Discourse in the Wake of the Boxer Movement." *Modern China* 18, no. 3 (July 1992): 304–32.

Hill, Patricia R. *The World Their Household: The American Woman's Foreign Mission Movement and Cultural Transformation, 1870–1920.* Ann Arbor: The University of Michigan Press, 1985.

Hopper, Helen. *A New Woman of Japan: A Political Biography of Katô Shidzue.* Boulder: Westview Press, 1996.

Hu Ying, *Tales of Translation.* Stanford, Calif.: Stanford University Press, 2000.

Huber, Mary Taylor, and Nancy Lutkehaus, eds. *Gendered Missions: Women and Men in Missionary Discourse and Practice.* Ann Arbor: University of Michigan Press, 1999.

Hulbert, Homer. *History of Korea.* Edited by Clarence Norwood Weems. New York: Hillary House Publishers Ltd., 1962. First published 1905 by the Methodist Publishing House.

———. *The Passing of Korea.* New York: Doubleday, Page and Company, 1906.

Hunt, Michael H. *Ideology and U.S. Foreign Policy.* New Haven, Conn.: Yale University Press, 1987.

Hunter, Jane. *The Gospel of Gentility: American Women Missionaries in Turn-of-the-Century China.* New Haven, Conn.: Yale University Press, 1984.

Huntley, Martha. *Caring, Growing, Changing: A History of the Protestant Mission in Korea.* New York: Friendship Press, 1984.

———. "Presbyterian Women's Work and Rights in the Korea Mission." *American Presbyterians* 65, no. 1 (1987): 37–48.

Hutchison, William R. "Modernism and Missions: The Liberal Search for an Exportable Christianity, 1875–1935." In *The Missionary Enterprise in China and America*, edited by John K. Fairbank, 110–31. Cambridge: Harvard University Press, 1974.

———. "A Moral Equivalent for Imperialism: Americans and the Promotion of 'Christian Civilization,' 1880–1910." In *Missionary Ideologies in the Imperial Era: 1880–1920,* edited by Torben Christensen and William R. Hutchison, 167–77. Aarhus: Forlaget Aros, 1982.

Hwang, Kyung Moon. "Country or State? Reconceptualizing *Kukka* in the Korean Enlightenment Period, 1896–1910." *Korean Studies* 24 (2000): 1–24.

Hyun, Theresa. *Writing Women in Korea.* Honolulu: University of Hawai'i Press, 2004.

Im Chi-hyŏn. *Minjokchuŭi nŭn panyŏk ida* (Nationalism Is Treason). Seoul: Sonamu, 1999.

Jager, Sheila Miyoshi. *Narratives of Nation Building in Korea: A Genealogy of Patriotism.* Armonk, N.Y.: M. E. Sharpe, 2003.

Jakobsen, Janet, with Ann Pellegrini. "World Secularisms at the Millennium." *Social Text* 64, no. 3 (fall 2000): 1–27.

Jang Sukman. "Protestantism in the Name of Modern Civilization." *Korea Journal* 39, no. 4 (winter 1999): 187–204.

Jayawardena, Kumari. *Feminism and Nationalism in the Third World.* London: Zed Books Ltd, 1986.

Jones, George Heber. *The Bible in Korea; or, The Transformation of a Nation.* New York: American Bible Society, 1916.

Judge, Joan. "Citizens or Mothers of Citizens? Gender and Meaning of Modern Chinese Citizenship." In *Changing Meanings of Citizenship in Modern China,* edited by Merle Goldman and Elizabeth J. Perry, 23–43. Cambridge, Mass.: Harvard University Press, 2002.

———. "Talent, Virtue, and the Nation: Chinese Nationalisms and Female Subjectivities in the Early Twentieth Century." *American Historical Review* 106, no. 3 (June 2001): 765–803.

Jung-Kim, Jennifer. "Gender and Modernity in Colonial Korea." PhD diss., UCLA, 2005.

Kang, Nam-Soon. "Creating "Dangerous Memory": Challenges for Asian and Korean Feminist Theology." *The Ecumenical Review* 47, no. 1 (1995): 21–31.

Kang Sŏn-mi. "Chosŏn p'agyŏn yŏ sŏn'gyosa wa (kidok) yŏsŏng ŭi yŏsŏngjuŭi ŭisik hyŏngsŏng" (Women Missionaries Sent to Korea and the Formation of Feminist Consciousness among Christian Women). PhD diss., Ewha Womans University, 2003.

Kang, Wi-Jo. *Christ and Caesar in Modern Korea: A History of Christianity and Politics.* Albany: SUNY Press, 1997.

Kaplan, Steven, ed. *Indigenous Responses to Western Christianity.* New York: New York University Press, 1995.

Keller, Rosemary Skinner. "Creating A Sphere For Women." In *Women in New Worlds: Historical Perspectives on the Wesleyan Tradition,* edited by Hilah F. Thomas and Rosemary Skinner Keller, 246–60. Nashville: Abingdon, 1981.

Kelly, Mary. "Beyond the Boundaries." *Journal of the Early Republic* 21, no. 1 (2001): 73–78.

Kemp, Emily G. *The Face of Manchuria, Korea and Russian Turkestan.* London, Chatto & Windus, 1910.

Kendall, Laurel, ed. *Under Construction: The Gendering of Modernity, Class, and Consumption in the Republic of Korea.* Honolulu: University of Hawai'i Press, 2002.

Kendall, Laurel, and Mark Peterson, eds. *Korean Women: View from the Inner Room.* New Haven, Conn.: East Rock Press, Inc., 1983.

Kennedy, Dane. "Imperial History and Post-Colonial Theory." *The Journal of Imperial and Commonwealth History* 24, no. 3 (September 1996): 345–63.

Key, Ellen. *Love and Marriage.* New York: G. P. Putnam's Sons, 1911.

Kijŏn 70-yŏnsa (The Seventieth History of Kijŏn). Chŏnju: Kijŏn 70-yŏnsa p'yŏnch'an wiwŏnhoe, 1974.

Kim Chin-myŏng. "Kabujang tamnon kwa yŏsŏng ŏgap: Naehunsŏ mit Ŭiryesŏ ŭi punsŏk ŭl chungsim ŭro" (Patriarchal Discourse and the Oppression of Women Focusing on Naehunsŏ and Ŭiryesŏ). *Asea yŏsŏng yŏn'gu* 33 (1994): 61–94.

Kim Chin-song. *Sŏul e ttansŭhol ŭl hŏhara* (Permit Dance Halls in Seoul). Seoul: Hyŏnsil munhwa yŏn'gu, 1999.

Kim, Dong-uk. "Women's Literary Achievements." *Korea Journal* 3, no. 11 (November 1963): 33–36, 39.

Kim, Elaine H. "Men's Talk: A Korean American View of South Korean Constructions of Women, Gender, and Masculinity." In *Dangerous Women: Gender and Korean Nationalism,* edited by Elaine H. Kim and Chungmoo Choi, 67–117. New York: Routledge, 1998.

Kim, Helen. *Grace Sufficient: The Story of Helen Kim by Herself.* Nashville: The Upper Room, 1964.

———. "Methodism and the Development of Korean Womanhood." In *Within the Gate,* edited by Charles A. Sauer, 76–83. Seoul: The Korea Methodist News Service, 1934.

Kim Hwa-yŏng, "Kŭndae wa 'yŏsŏng' ŭi munje" (Modernity and the "Woman" Question). *Ilbonŏ munhak* 39 (2007): 275–94.

Kim, Hyung-chan. *Letters in Exile: The Life and Times of Yun Ch'i-ho.* Covington, Ga.: Rhoades Printing Company, 1980.

Kim In-uk. "Hanmal yŏsŏng kyemong undong e taehan il yŏn'gu: 'Cheguk sinmun' ŭi yŏkhal ŭl chungsim ŭro" (A Study of the Enlightenment Movement for Women in Late Chosŏn Dynasty with a Special Focus on Cheguk Sinmun). MA thesis, Hanyang University, 1985.

Kim Ir-yŏp. *Chaet pit chŏksam e sarang ŭl mutko* (Burying Love under the Ash-Colored Jacket). Edited by Kim Sang-bae. Seoul: Sol moe, 1982.

Kim Kap-ch'ŏn. "Pak Yŏng-hyo ŭi kŏnbaeksŏ" (Pak Yŏng-hyo's Memorial to the King). *Han'guk chŏngch'i yŏn'gu* 2 (1990): 245–92.

Kim, Key-Hiuk. *The Last Phase of the East Asian World Order: Korea, Japan, and the Chinese Empire, 1860–1882.* Berkeley and Los Angeles: University of California Press, 1980.

Kim, Kichung. "Hŏ Nansŏrhŏn and 'Shakespeare's Sister.'" In *Creative Women of Korea*, edited by Young-Key Kim-Renaud, 78–95. Armonk, N.Y.: M. E. Sharpe, 2004.

Kim Kyŏng-ae. "Tonghak ŭi yŏsŏnggwan e taehan chae goch'al" (A Reexamination of the Views on Women in Tonghak). *Han'guk sasang sahak* 20 (2003): 83–111.

Kim Kyŏng-il. *Yŏsŏng ŭi kŭndae, kŭndae ŭi yŏsŏng* (Modernity of Women, Women of Modernity). Seoul: P'urŭn yŏksa, 2004.

Kim Mi-jŏng. "Chosŏn sidae saramdŭl ŭi p'aesyŏn kamgak" (The Fashion Sense of Chosŏn People). In *Chosŏn sidae saramdŭl ŭn ŏttŏk'e sarassŭlkka* 2, edited by Han'guk yŏksa yŏn'guhoe, 199–211. Seoul: Ch'ongnyŏnsa, 1996.

Kim Pong-hŭi. *Han'guk kidokkyo munsŏ kanhaengsa yŏn'gu* (A Study of the History of Publications on Christian Tracts in Korea). Seoul: Ewha yŏja taehakkyo ch'ulp'anbu, 1987.

Kim Su-jin. "1920–30-yŏndae sin yŏsŏng tamnon kwa sangjing ŭi kusŏng" (Excess of the Modern: Three Archetypes of the New Woman and Colonial Identity in Korea, 1920s to 1930s). PhD diss., Seoul National University, 2005.

———. "'Sin yŏsŏng,' yŏlyŏ innŭn kwagŏ, mŏjŏ innŭn hyŏnjae rosŏ ŭi yŏksa ssŭgi" ("New Woman," Writing History as the Open Past and Stagnant Present). *Yŏsŏng kwa sahoe* 11 (2000): 6–28.

Kim Suk-ja. "Tongnip sinmun e nat'anan yŏsŏng kaehwa ŭi ŭiji" (The Goals for Enlightening Women Reflected in Tongnip Sinmun). *Han'guksa yŏn'gu* 54 (1986): 59–74.

Kim Sŭng-t'ae, ed. *Han'guk kidokkyo wa sinsa ch'ambae munje* (Korean Christianity and the Issue of the Homage to Shinto Shrines). Seoul: Han'guk kidokkyo yŏksa yŏn'guso, 1992.

Kim Sŭng-t'ae and Pak Hye-jin, comp. *Naehan sŏn'gyosa ch'ongnam, 1884–1984* (A Comprehensive Survey of Missionaries in Korea). Seoul: Han'guk kidokkyo yŏksa yŏn'guso, 1994.

Kim, Susie Jie Young. "The Ambivalence of 'Modernity': Articulation of New Subjectivities in Turn of the Century Korea." PhD diss., UCLA, 2002.

Kim Tong-ch'un. *Kŭndae ŭi kŭnŭl* (Shadow of Modernity). Seoul: Tangdae, 2000.

Kim Ŭn-sil. "Minjokchuŭi tamnon kwa yŏsŏng: Munhwa, kwŏllyŏk, chuch'e e kwanhan pip'anjŏk ilkki rŭl wihayŏ" (Women and the Discourse of Nationalism: Toward a Critical Reading of Culture, Power, and Subjectivity). *Han'guk yŏsŏnghak* 10 (1994): 18–52.

Kim Yŏng-ok, ed. *"Kŭndae," yŏsŏng i kaji anŭn kil* ("Modernity," A Path Not Open to Women). Seoul: Tto hana ŭi munhwa, 2001.

Kim Yong-suk. *Han'guk yŏsoksa* (The History of Women's Customs in Korea). Seoul: Minŭmsa, 1990,

Kim, Yung-Hee. "Creating New Paradigms of Womanhood in Modern Korean Literature: Na Hye-sŏk's 'Kyŏnghŭi.'" *Korean Studies* 26, no. 1 (2002): 1–60.

———. "From Subservience to Autonomy: Kim Wŏnju's '"Awakening.'" *Korean Studies* 21 (1997): 1–21.

———. "Under the Mandate of Nationalism: Development of Feminist Enterprises in Modern Korea, 1860–1910." *Journal of Women's History* 7, no. 4 (1995): 120–36.

Kim, Yun-sung. "The Predicament of Modern Discourses on Gender and Religion in Korean Society." *Korea Journal* 41, no. 1 (spring 2001): 114–36.

King, Ross. "Nationalism and Language Reform in Korea: The *Questione della Lingua* in Precolonial Korea." In *Nationalism and the Construction of Korean Identity*, edited by Hyung Il Pai and Timothy R. Tangherlini, 33–72. Institute of East Asian Studies, University of California, Berkeley, 1998.

———. "Western Protestant Missionaries and the Origins of Korean Language Modernization." *Journal of International and Area Studies* 11, no. 3 (2004): 7–38.

Ko, Dorothy. *Teachers of the Inner Chambers: Women and Culture in Seventeenth-Century China*. Stanford, Calif.: Stanford University Press, 1994.

Kwok Pui-lan. *Chinese Women and Christianity 1860–1927*. Atlanta: Scholars Press, 1992.

———. "Chinese Women and Protestant Christianity at the Turn of the Twentieth Century." In *Christianity in China*, edited by Daniel Bays, 194–208. Stanford, Calif.: Stanford University Press, 1996.

———. *Postcolonial Imagination and Feminist Theology*. Louisville: Westminster John Knox Press, 2005.

Kwon, Insook. "Feminists Navigating the Shoals of Nationalism and Collaboration: The Post-Colonial Korean Debate over How to Remember Kim Hwallan." *Frontiers* 27, no. 1 (2006): 39–66.

———. "'The New Women's Movement' in 1920s Korea: Rethinking the Relationship between Imperialism and Women." *Gender and History* 10, no. 3 (November 1998): 381–405.

Lan, Hua R., and Vanessa L. Fong, eds. *Women in Republican China: A Sourcebook*. Armonk, N.Y.: M. E. Sharpe, 1999.

Landes, Joan B. "Further Thoughts on the Public/Private Distinction." *Journal of Women's History* 15, no. 2 (summer 2003): 28–39.

Ledger, Sally. *The New Woman: Fiction and Feminism at the Fin de siècle*. Manchester: Manchester University Press, 1977.

Lee, Hoon K. "Korean Migrants in Manchuria." *Geographical Review* 22, no. 2 (April 1932): 196–204.

Lee, Hyo-chae. "Protestant Missionary Work and Enlightenment of Korean Women." *Korea Journal* 17, no. 11 (November 1977): 33–50.

Lee, Ki-baik. *A New History of Korea*. Seoul: Ilchogak, 1984.

Lee, Peter, ed. *Sourcebook of Korean Civilization*. Volume 2, *From the Seventeenth Century to the Modern Period*. New York: Columbia University Press, 1996.

Lee, Timothy. "Born-Again in Korea: The Rise and Character of Revivalism in (South) Korea, 1885–1988." PhD diss., University of Chicago, 1996.

———. "A Political Factor in the Rise of Protestantism in Korea: Protestantism and the 1919 March First Movement." *Church History* 69, no. 1 (March 2000): 116–42.

Lewis, Reina. *Gendering Orientalism*. London: Routledge, 1996.

Liu, Judith, and Donald P. Kelly. "'An Oasis in a Heathen Land': St. Hilda's School for Girls, Wuchang, 1928–1937." In *Christianity in China: From the Eighteenth Century to the Present*, edited by Daniel Bays, 228–42. Stanford, Calif.: Stanford University Press, 1996.

Liu, Lydia. *Translingual Practice: Literature, National Culture, and Translated Modernity*. Stanford, Calif.: Stanford University Press, 1995.

Lodwick, Kathleen. *Educating the Women of Hainan: The Career of Margaret Moninger in China 1915–1942*. Lexington: University Press of Kentucky, 1995.

Loomba, Ania. *Colonialism/Postcolonialism*. London: Routledge, 1998.

Lowy, Dina. *The Japanese "New Woman": Images of Gender and Modernity*. New Brunswick, N.J.: Rutgers University Press, 2007.

Makdisi, Ussama. "Reclaiming the Land of the Bible: Missionaries, Secularism, and Evangelical Modernity." *American Historical Review* 102, no. 3 (June 1997): 680–713.

Mann, Susan. *Precious Records: Women in China's Long Eighteenth Century*. Stanford, Calif.: Stanford University Press, 1997.

McClintock, Anne. *Imperial Leather: Race, Gender, and Sexuality in the Colonial Contest*. New York: Routledge, 1995.

Mcdannell, Colleen. *The Christian Home in Victorian America, 1840–1900*. Bloomington: Indiana University Press, 1986.

Mills, Sara. *Discourses of Difference: An Analysis of Women's Travel Writing and Colonialism*. London: Routledge, 1991.

Mitchell, Timothy, ed. *Questions of Modernity*. Minneapolis: University of Minnesota Press, 2000.

Mun Ok-p'yo. "Chosŏn kwa Ilbon ŭi sin yŏsŏng" (New Women of Korea and Japan). In *Sin yŏsŏng*, edited by Mun Ok-p'yo, 245–82. Seoul: Ch'ŏngnyŏnsa, 2003.

———, ed. *Sin yŏsŏng* (New Women). Seoul: Ch'ŏngnyŏnsa, 2003.

Nair, Janaki. "Uncovering the Zenana: Visions of Indian Womanhood in Englishwomen's Writings, 1813–1940." *Journal of Women's History* 2, no. 1 (1990): 8–34.

Najita, Tetsuo. "Presidential Address: Reflections on Modernity and Modernization." *Journal of Asian Studies* 52, no. 4 (November 1993): 845–53.

Ninkovich, Frank, "Theodore Roosevelt: Civilization as Ideology." *Diplomatic History* 10 (summer 1986): 221–45.

No Ch'i-jun, *Ilcheha Han'guk kidokkyo minjok undong yŏn'gu* (A Study of the Korean Christian Nationalist Movement under Japanese Rule). Seoul: Han'guk kidokkyo yŏksa yŏn'guso, 1993.

Noble, Mattie, ed. *Victorious Lives of Early Christians in Korea: The First Book of Biographies and Autobiographies of Early Christians in the Prot-*

estant Church in Korea (Sŭngni ŭi saenghwal). Seoul: The Christian Literature Society, 1927.

Noble, W. Arthur. *Ewa: A Tale of Korea.* New York: Eaton & Mains, 1906.

Oak Sung-Deuk. "Ch'ogi Han'guk kaesin'gyo yebaedang ŭi palchŏn kwajŏng kwa t'ŭksŏng: Kidokkyo kŭndaesŏng kwa t'och'akhwa ŭi munje, 1895–1912" (Spacial Characteristics of the Early Protestant Churches in Korea: Christian Modernity and Indigenization, 1895–1912). *Tongbang hakchi* 141 (March 2008): 267–321.

———. "Ch'ogi Han'guk kyohoe ŭi ilbudach'ŏje nonjaeng" (Debates on Polygamy in the Early Korean Church). *Han'guk kidokkyo wa yŏksa* 16 (2002): 7–34.

———. "The Indigenization of Christianity in Korea: North American Missionaries' Attitudes towards Korean Religions, 1884–1910." ThD diss., Boston University, 2002.

———. *Sources of Korean Christianity, 1832–1945.* Seoul: Han'guk kidokkyo yŏksa yŏn'guso, 2004.

Paehwa 60-yŏnsa (The Sixtieth History of Paehwa). Seoul: Paehwa chunggodŭng hakkyo, 1958.

Pahk, Induk. *September Monkey.* New York: Harper & Brothers, 1954.

Paik, L. George. *The History of Protestant Missions in Korea 1832–1910.* 4th edition. Seoul: Yonsei University Press, 1987. First published 1929 by the Union Christian College Press.

Pak Ch'an-sŭng. *Han'guk kŭndae chŏngch'i sasangsa yŏn'gu* (A Study of the History of Modern Political Thought in Korea). Seoul: Yŏksa pip'yongsa, 1993.

Pak Sŏk-bun and Pak Ŭn-bong. *Kŭn hyŏndaesa sok ŭi yŏsŏng 30 in ŭi sam ŭl t'onghae ponŭn inmul yŏsŏngsa* (The Character History of Thirty Women through Their Lives in Modern and Contemporary History). Seoul: Saenal, 1994.

Pak Sŏn-mi. *Kŭndae yŏsŏng cheguk ŭl kŏch'ŏ Chosŏn ŭro hoeyu hada* (Modern Women Return to Korea via Empire). Seoul: Ch'angbi, 2007.

Pak Yong-ok. "1896–1910 punyŏ tanch'e ŭi yŏn'gu" (A Study of Women's Organizations 1896–1910). *Han'guksa yŏn'gu* 6 (1971): 103–35.

———. "A History of Korean Women." *Koreana* 4, no. 2 (1990): 34–45.

———. *Kim Maria: Na nŭn taehan ŭi tongnip kwa kyŏlhon hayŏtta* (Kim Maria: I Married Korea's Independence). Seoul: Hongsŏngsa, 2003.

Palais, James. *Confucian Statecraft and Korean Institutions: Yu Hyŏngwŏn and the Late Chosŏn Dynasty.* Seattle: University of Washington Press, 1996.

Park, Chung-shin. *Protestantism and Politics in Korea.* Seattle: University of Washington Press, 2003.

Park, Hyun Ok. "Korean Manchuria: The Racial Politics of Territorial Osmosis." *The South Atlantic Quarterly* 99, no. 1 (winter 2000): 193–215.

Parker, Alison M. "'Hearts Uplifted and Minds Refreshed': The Woman's Christian Temperance Union and the Production of Pure Culture in the

United States, 1880–1930." *Journal of Women's History* 11, no. 2 (1999): 135–58.

Pascoe, Peggy. "Miscegenation Law, Court Cases, and Ideologies of 'Race' in Twentieth-Century America." In *Unequal Sisters: A Multicultural Reader in U.S. Women's History*, edited by Vicki L. Ruiz and Ellen Carol Dubois, 161–82. New York: Routledge, 2000.

Peirce, Leslie. *The Imperial Harem: Women and Sovereignty in the Ottoman Empire*. Oxford: Oxford University Press, 1993.

Peterson, Mark. "The Sejong Sillok." In *King Sejong the Great*, edited by Young-Key Kim-Renaud, 15–18. International Circle of Korean Linguistics, 1992.

———. "Women without Sons: A Measure of Social Change in Yi Dynasty Korea." In *Korean Women: View from the Inner Room*, edited by Laurel Kendall and Mark Peterson, 33–44. New Haven, Conn.: East Rock Press, Inc., 1983.

Phillips, Clifton J. "The Student Volunteer Movement and Its Role in China Missions, 1886–1920." In *The Missionary Enterprise in China and America*, edited by John K. Fairbank, 91–109. Cambridge, Mass.: Harvard University Press, 1974.

Porter, Andrew. "'Cultural Imperialism' and Protestant Missionary Enterprise, 1780–1914." *The Journal of Imperial and Commonwealth History* 25, no. 3 (September 1997): 367–91.

Prakash, Gyan. "Subaltern Studies as Postcolonial Criticism." *The American Historical Review* 99, no. 5 (December 1994): 1475–90.

Pratt, Mary Louise. *Imperial Eyes: Travel Writing and Transculturation*. London: Routledge, 1992.

Ramusack, Barbara N. "Cultural Missionaries, Maternal Imperialists, Feminist Allies: British Women Activists in India, 1865–1945." In *Western Women and Imperialism*, edited by Nupur Chaudhuri and Margaret Strobel, 119–36. Bloomington: Indiana University Press, 1992.

Ravindiran, V. "Discourses of Empowerment: Missionary Orientalism in the Development of Dravidian Nationalism." In *Nation Work: Asian Elites and National Identities*, edited by Timothy Brook and Andre Schmid, 51–81. Ann Arbor: University of Michigan Press, 2000.

Reich, Pauline C. "Japan's Literary Feminists: The 'Seito' Group." *Signs* 2, no. 1 (autumn 1976): 280–91.

Richardson, Angelique. "The Birth of National Hygiene and Efficiency: Women and Eugenics in Britain and America 1865–1915." In *New Woman Hybridities*, edited by Ann Heilmann and Margaret Beetham, 240–62. London: Routledge, 2004.

Robert, Dana. *American Women in Mission: A Social History of Their Thought and Practice*. Macon, Ga.: Mercer University Press, 1996.

Robinson, Michael E. *Cultural Nationalism in Colonial Korea, 1920–1925*. Seattle: University of Washington Press, 1988.

Rose, Barbara. *Tsuda Umeko and Women's Education in Japan.* New Haven, Conn.: Yale University Press, 1992.

Ross, Heidi A. "'Cradle of Female Talent': The McTyeire Home and School for Girls, 1892–1937." In *Christianity in China: From the Eighteenth Century to the Present,* edited by Daniel Bays, 209–27. Stanford, Calif.: Stanford University Press, 1996.

Rothman, Sheila. *Woman's Proper Place: A History of Changing Ideals and Practices, 1870 to the Present.* New York: Basic Books, 1978.

Russell, Mona L. *Creating the New Egyptian Woman: Consumerism, Education, and National Identity, 1863–1922.* New York: Palgrave Macmillan, 2004.

Ryan, Mary. "The Public and the Private Good: Across the Great Divide in Women's History." *Journal of Women's History* 15, no. 2 (summer 2003): 10–27.

Ryu Tae-yŏng. *Ch'ogi Miguk sŏn'gyosa yŏn'gu: 1884–1910* (Early American Missionaries in Korea: 1884–1910). Seoul: Han'guk kidokkyo yŏksa yŏn'guso, 2001.

———. *Kaehwagi Chosŏn kwa Miguk sŏn'gyosa* (Chosŏn of the Enlightenment Era and American Missionaries). Seoul: Han'guk kidokkyo yŏksa yŏn'guso, 2004.

Sato, Barbara. *The New Japanese Woman.* Durham: Duke University Press, 2003.

Schlereth, Thomas. *Victorian America: Transformations in Everyday Life, 1876–1915.* New York: HarperCollins, 1991.

Schmid, Andre. *Korea between Empires, 1895–1919.* New York: Columbia University Press, 2002.

Shim, Jung-Soon. "Recasting the National Motherhood: Transactions of Western Feminisms in Korean Theatre." *Theatre Research International* 29, no. 2 (2004): 143–54.

Shin, Gi-Wook, and Michael Robinson, eds. *Colonial Modernity in Korea.* Cambridge, Mass.: Harvard University Press, 1999.

Shin, Yong-ha. *Formation and Development of Modern Korean Nationalism.* Seoul: Dae kwang munhwasa, 1989.

Showalter, Elaine. *Sexual Anarchy: Gender and Culture at the* Fin de siècle. New York: Viking, 1990.

Sievers, Sharon L. *Flowers in Salt: The Beginnings of Feminist Consciousness in Modern Japan.* Stanford, Calif.: Stanford University Press, 1983.

Silva, David J. "Western Attitudes toward the Korean Language: An Overview of Late-Nineteenth- and Early-Twentieth-Century Mission Literature." *Korean Studies* 26, no. 2 (2002): 270–86.

Sin Yŏng-suk. "Ilche ha sin yŏsŏng ŭi yŏnae kyŏlhon munje" (Issues of Romance and Marriage among New Women under Japanese Colonial Rule). *Han'guk hakpo* 12, no. 4 (1986): 182–217.

Smart, Barry. "Modernity, Postmodernity, and the Present." In *Theories of*

Modernity and Postmodernity, edited by Bryan S. Turner, 14–30. London: Sage, 1990.

Smith, Lillie Reed. *Korea Aflame for Christ*. Abilene, Tx.: privately printed, n.d.

Snyder, Louis L., ed. *The Imperialism Reader*. New York: D. Van Nostrand Company, Inc., 1962.

So Chae-yŏng and Kim Kyŏng-wan, eds. *Kaehwagi sosŏl* (Novels from the Period of Enlightenment). Seoul: Sungsil taehakkyo ch'ulp'ansa, 1999.

Sŏ Kwang-sŏn. "Han'guk yŏsŏng kwa chonggyo" (Korean Women and Religion). In *Han'guk yŏsŏngsa* 2 (History of Korean Women), edited by Han'guk yŏsŏngsa p'yŏnch'an wiwŏnhoe, 492–531. Seoul: Ewha yŏja taehakkyo ch'ulp'anbu, 1972.

Sohye Wanghu Han ssi. *Ŏje naehun*. 1475. Rpt., Seoul: Hongmungak, 1990.

Søland, Birgitte. *Becoming Modern: Young Women and the Reconstruction of Womanhood in the 1920s*. Princeton, N.J.: Princeton University Press, 2000.

Son Yŏn-ok. "Chosŏn 'sin yŏsŏng' ŭi naesyŏnŏllijŭm kwa chendŏ" (Nationalism and Gender in Chosŏn New Women). In *Sin yŏsŏng*, edited by Mun Ok-p'yo, 83–117. Seoul: Ch'ŏngnyŏnsa, 2003.

Spurlock, John C., and Cynthia A. Magistro. *New and Improved: The Transformation of American Women's Emotional Culture*. New York: New York University Press, 1998.

Stanton, Elizabeth Cady, and the Revising Committee. *The Woman's Bible*. New York: European Publishing Company, 1895. Rpt., New York: Arno Press, 1974.

Strong, Josiah. *Our Country*. 17th edition. Cambridge, Mass.: The Belknap Press of Harvard University Press, 1963. First published 1885 by The American Home Missionary Society.

Sungŭi yŏja chung kodŭng hakkyo. *Sungŭi 60-yŏnsa* (History of Sungŭi for the Past Sixty Years). Seoul: Sungŭi yŏja chung kodŭng hakkyo, 1963.

Taylor, Charles. "Modern Social Imaginaries." *Public Culture* 14, no. 1 (2002): 91–124.

———. *Modern Social Imaginaries*. Durham: Duke University Press, 2004.

———. "Two Theories of Modernity." In *Alternative Modernities*, edited by Dilip Parameshwar Gaonkar, 172–96. Durham: Duke University Press, 2001.

Taylor, Sandra. "Abby M. Colby: The Christian Response to a Sexist Society." *New England Quarterly* 52, no. 1 (March 1979): 68–79.

Thompson, Elizabeth. "Public and Private in Middle Eastern Women's History." *Journal of Women's History* 15, no. 1 (spring 2003): 52–69.

Thorne, Susan. *Congregational Missions and the Making of an Imperial Culture in Nineteenth-Century England*. Stanford, Calif.: Stanford University Press, 1999.

———. "Missionary-Imperial Feminism." In *Gendered Missions: Women and Men in Missionary Discourse and Practice*, edited by Mary Taylor Huber and Nancy Lutkehaus, 39–65. Ann Arbor: University of Michigan Press, 1999.

Tikhonov, Vladimir, "Masculinizing the Nation: Gender Ideologies in Traditional Korea and in the 1890s–1900s Korean Enlightenment Discourse." *Journal of Asian Studies* 66, no. 4 (November 2007): 1029–65.

Tocco, Martha. "Made in Japan: Meiji Women's Education." In *Gendering Modern Japanese History*, edited by Barbara Molony and Kathleen Uno, 39–60. Cambridge, Mass.: Harvard University Press, 2005.

Tomida, Hiroko. *Hiratsuka Raichō and Early Japanese Feminism*. Leiden: Brill, 2004.

Underwood, Elizabeth. *Challenged Identities: North American Missionaries in Korea, 1884–1934*. Seoul : Royal Asiatic Society—Korea Branch, 2004.

Underwood, Horace H. *The Call of Korea*. New York: Fleming H. Revell Company, 1908.

Underwood, Lillias H. *With Tommy Tompkins in Korea*. New York: Fleming H. Revell Company, 1905.

United Methodist Women's Oral History Project: Maud Keister Jensen, Six interviews, 1984, GCAH.

Uno, Kathleen. "Womanhood, War, and Empire: Transmutations of 'Good Wife, Wise Mother' before 1931." In *Gendering Modern Japanese History*, edited by Barbara Molony and Kathleen Uno, 493–519. Cambridge, Mass.: Harvard University Press, 2005.

van der Veer, Peter. *Imperial Encounters: Religion and Modernity in India and Britain*. Princeton, N.J.: Princeton University Press, 2001.

Vicinus, Martha, ed. *A Widening Sphere: Changing Roles of Victorian Women*. Bloomington: Indiana University Press, 1977.

Vickery, Amanda. "Golden Age to Separate Spheres? A Review of the Categories and Chronology of English Women's History." *The Historical Journal* 36, no. 2 (1993): 383–414.

Wagner, Ellasue. *Children of Korea*. London: Oliphants Ltd., 1911. Translated by Sin Pongryong as *Han'guk ŭi adong saenghwal*. Seoul: Chipmundang, 1999.

———. *The Concubine*. Unpublished manuscript, GCAH.

———. *The Dawn of Tomorrow: True Stories from Old Korea*. Bristol, Tenn.: King Printing Co., 1948.

———. *Korea the Old and the New*. New York: Fleming H. Revell Company, 1934.

Walkowitz, Judith. *City of Dreadful Delight: Narratives of Sexual Danger in Late-Victorian London*. London: Virago Press, 1992.

Wang Zheng. *Women in the Chinese Enlightenment: Oral and Textual Histories*. Berkeley and Los Angeles: University of California Press, 1999.

Weems, Clarence Norwood. "Profile of Homer B. Hulbert." In *History of Korea*, edited by Clarence Norwood Weems, ED 23–62. New York: Hillary House Publishers Ltd., 1962. First published 1905 by the Methodist Publishing House.

Wells, Kenneth M. "Expanding Their Realm: Women and Public Agency in Colonial Korea." In *Women's Suffrage in Asia: Gender, Nationalism, and*

Democracy, edited by Louise Edwards and Mina Roces, 152–69. London: RoutledgeCurzon, 2004.

———. *New God, New Nation: Protestants and Self-Reconstruction Nationalism in Korea, 1896–1937*. Honolulu: University of Hawai'i Press, 1990.

———. "The Price of Legitimacy: Women and the Kǔnuhoe Movement, 1927–1931." In *Colonial Modernity in Korea*, edited by Gi-Wook Shin and Michael Robinson, 191–220. Cambridge, Mass.: Harvard University Press, 1999.

Welter, Barbara. "The Cult of True Womanhood: 1820–1860." *American Quarterly* 18, no. 2 (summer 1966): 151–74.

———. "She Hath Done What She Could: Protestant Women's Missionary Careers in Nineteenth-Century America." *American Quarterly* 30 (winter 1978): 624–38.

White, Ann. "Counting the Cost of Faith: America's Early Female Missionaries." *Church History* 57, no. 1 (March 1988): 19–30.

Widmer, Ellen. "Foreign Travel through a Woman's Eyes: Shan Shili's *Guimao lüxing ji* in Local and Global Perspective." *Journal of Asian Studies* 65, no. 4 (November 2006): 763–91.

———. "The Rhetoric of Retrospection: May Fourth Literary History and the Ming-Qing Woman Writer." In *The Appropriation of Cultural Capital: China's May Fourth Project*, edited by Milena Doleželová-Velingerová and Oldřich Král, 193–225. Cambridge, Mass.: Harvard University Press, 2001.

Yang Hyǒn-hye. "Han'guk kaesin'gyo ǔi sǒng ch'abyǒl kujo wa yǒsǒng undong" (The Structure of Sex Discrimination in Korean Protestant Christianity and the Women's Movement). In *Han'guk yǒsǒng kwa kyohoeron*, edited by Ewha yǒja taehakkyo yǒsǒng sinhak yǒn'guso, 200–48. Seoul: Taehan kidokkyosǒhoe, 1998.

Yang Mi-gang. "Ch'amyǒ wa paeje ǔi kwanchǒm esǒ pon chǒndo puin e kwanhan yǒn'gu: 1910-yǒn-1930-yǒndae rǔl chungsim ǔro" (A Study of Bible Women in Terms of Participation and Exclusion: From the 1910s to the 1930s). *Han'guk kidokkyo wa yǒksa* 6 (1997): 139–79.

———. "Ch'ogi chǒndo puin ǔi sinang kwa hwaltong" (The Faith and Activities of Early Bible Women). *Han'guk kidokkyo wa yǒksa* 2 (1992): 91–109.

Yi Hǔi-gyǒng. "1920-yǒndae 'yǒhaksaeng' ǔi sahoe chǒk p'yǒsang" (The Social Representation of "Schoolgirl" in the 1920s). *Han'gǔl kyoyuk yǒn'gu* 10, no. 1 (2004): 55–79.

Yi Hye-jǒng. "Ilche malgi Kim Hwal-lan ǔi Ilche hyǒmnyǒk paegyǒng kwa nolli" (Kim Hwal-lan's Background and Rationale for Her Collaboration with the Japanese Imperial Power at the End of the Japanese Colonial Era). *Yǒsǒnghak nonjip* 21, no. 2 (2004): 58–61.

Yi Hye-sun and Chǒng Ha-yǒng, trans. and eds. *Han'guk kojǒn yǒsǒng munhak ǔi segye* (The World of Women's Classical Literature in Korea). Seoul: Ewha yǒja taehakkyo ch'ulp'anbu, 2003.

Yi Kwang-nin. *Han'guk kaehwasa yǒn'gu* (Study of the History of Korean Enlightenment). Seoul: Ilchogak, 1981.

———. *Kaehwap'a wa kaehwa sasang yŏn'gu* (Study of the Enlightenment Group and Its Thoughts). Seoul: Ilchogak, 1989.

———. "Sŏ Chae-p'il ŭi 'Tongnip sinmun' kanhaeng e taehayŏ" (About the Founding of "Tongnip Sinmun" by Sŏ Chae-p'il). *Chindan Hakpo* 39 (1975): 71–104.

Yi Man-yŏl. *Han'guk kidokkyo wa minjok ŭisik* (Korean Christianity and National Consciousness). Seoul: Chisik sanŏpsa, 1991.

Yi Nŭng-hwa. *Chosŏn yŏsokko* (Investigation of Women's Customs in Korea). Translated by Kim Sang-ŏk. Seoul: Tongmunsŏn, 1990.

Yi Ok-jin. "Yŏja chapchi rŭl t'onghae pon yŏkwŏn sinjang" (A Study of the Enhancement of Women's Rights through Women's Magazines). MA thesis, Ewha Womans University, 1979.

Yi Pae-yong. "19-segi kaehwa sasang e nat'anan yŏsŏnggwan" (Viewpoints on Women Represented in the Enlightenment Thought of the Nineteenth Century). *Han'guk sasang sahak* 20 (2003): 127–34.

Yi Pae-yong et al. *Uri nara yŏsŏngdŭl ŭn ŏttŏk'e sarassŭlkka* 1 (How Did Korean Women Live). Seoul: Ch'ŏngnyŏnsa, 1999.

Yi Pae-yong in cooperation with Son Sŭng-hŭi, Mun Suk-chae, and Cho Kyŏng-wŏn. "Han'guk kidokkyo yŏsong kyoyuk ŭi sŏnggwa wa chŏnmang— Ewha yŏja taehakkyo rŭl chungsim ŭro" (Accomplishment and Prospect of Korean Christian Education for Women—With Focus on Ewha Womans University"), *Ewha sahak yŏn'gu* 27 (2000): 9–36.

Yi Sang-gyŏng. *In'gan ŭro salgo sipta* (I Want to Live as a Human Being). Seoul: Han'gilsa, 2000.

———, ed. *Na Hyesŏk chŏnjip* (Anthology of the Works of Na Hye-sŏk). Seoul: T'aehaksa, 2000.

Yi, Sŏng-mi. "Sin Saimdang: The Foremost Woman Painter of the Chosŏn Dynasty." In *Creative Women of Korea: The Fifteenth Through the Twentieth Centuries*, edited by Young-Key Kim-Renaud, 58–77. Armonk, N.Y.: M. E. Sharpe, 2004.

Yi Sug-in. "Kaehwagi (1894–1910) yuhakchadŭl ŭi hwaltong kwa sidae insik" (Activities and Perspectives of Confucian Scholars during the Enlightenment Era, 1894–1910). *Tongyang ch'ŏlhak yŏn'gu* 37 (2004): 8–42.

———. "Yugyo ŭi kwan'gye yulli e taehan yŏsŏngjuŭi chŏk haesŏk" (Feminist Interpretations of Relational Ethics in Confucianism). *Han'guk yŏsŏnghak* 15, no. 1 (1999): 39–69.

Yi T'aek-hwi et al. *Sŏ Chae-p'il*. Seoul: Minŭmsa, 1993.

Yi Tŏk-chu. *Ch'ogi Han'guk kidokkyosa yŏn'gu* (Study of the Early History of Christianity in Korea). Seoul: Han'guk kidokkyo yŏksa yŏn'guso, 1995.

———. *Han'guk kyohoe ch'ŏŭm yŏsŏngdŭl* (Early Christian Women in Korea: Life Stories of 28 Women Who Loved Christ and Their Nation). Seoul: Kidokkyomunsa, 1990.

Yi U-jin. "Sŏ Chae-p'il ŭi chaeMi hwaltong" (Sŏ Chae-p'il's Activities in the United States). In *Sŏ Chae-p'il*, edited by Yi T'aek-hwi, 259–301. Seoul: Minŭmsa, 1993.

Yip, Ka-che. "The Anti-Christian Movement in China, 1922–1927, with Special Reference to the Experience of the Protestant Missions." PhD diss., Columibia University, 1970.

Yŏksa hakhoe, ed. *Nobi, nongno, noye: Yesokmin ŭi pigyosa* (Nobi, Serfs, and Slaves: Comparative History of Bonded Servitude). Seoul: Ilchogak, 1998.

Yŏnghwa 70-yŏnsa (The Seventieth History of Yŏnghwa Girls' School). Inch'ŏn: Yŏnghwa yŏja chunghakkyo, 1963).

Yŏn'gu konggan suyu+nŏmŏ kŭndae maech'e yŏn'gu t'im. *Sin yŏsŏng: Maech'e ro pon kŭndae yŏsŏng p'ungsoksa* (New Women: The History of Modern Women and Their Lifestyle Reflected in the Media). Seoul: Han'gyŏre sinmunsa, 2005.

Yoo, Theodore Jun. "The 'New Woman' and the Politics of Love, Marriage, and Divorce in Colonial Korea." *Gender and History* 17, no. 2 (August 2005): 295–324.

———. *The Politics of Gender in Colonial Korea: Education, Labor, and Health, 1910–1945.* Berkeley and Los Angeles: University of California Press, 2008.

Young, Rorbert. *Colonial Desire: Hybridity in Theory, Culture and Race.* London: Routledge, 1995.

———. *White Mythologies: Writing History and the West.* London: Routledge, 1990.

Yu, Chai-shin, ed. *Korea and Christianity.* Seoul, Berkeley: Korean Scholar Press, 1996.

Yu Chin-wŏl. "'Sin yŏja' e nat'anan kŭndae yŏsŏngdŭl ŭi kŭl ssŭgi yangsang mit t'ŭksŏng yŏn'gu" (Patterns and Characteristics of Writing of Modern Women Reflected in Sinyŏja). *Yŏsŏng munhak yŏn'gu* 14 (2005): 147–73.

Yu Kil-chun. *Sŏyu kyŏnmun* (Observations from My Travels in the West), translated by Hŏ Kyŏng-jin. Seoul: Hanyang ch'ulp'an, 1995.

Yu Su-gyŏng. *Han'guk yŏsŏng yangjang pyŏnch'ŏnsa* (A History of the Adoption of Western Dress among Korean Women). Seoul: Ilchisa, 1990.

Yu Tong-sik. *Han'guk chonggyo wa kidokkyo* (Korean Religions and Christianity). Seoul: Taehan kidokkyosŏhoe, 1965.

Yun Ch'i-ho. *Yun Ch'i-ho ilgi* (The Diaries of Yun Ch'i-ho). Available online, http://db.history.go.kr/.

Yun Chŏng-nan. "1920-yŏndae kidokkyo yŏsŏngdŭl ŭi Kŭnuhoe ch'amyŏ kwajŏng kwa t'alt'oe paegyŏng e kwanhan yŏn'gu" (A Study of Christian Women's Particpation in and Withdrawal from Kŭnu in the 1920s). In *Yŏsŏng: Yŏksa wa hyŏnjae*, edited by Pak Yong-ok, 187–215. Seoul: Kukhak charyowŏn, 2001.

Yun Ka-hyŏn. "Sŏng kwa sŏng ŭisik ŭi pyŏnhwa" (Sexuality and the Change in Sexual Consciousness). In *Chŏnt'ong kwa sŏgu ŭi ch'ungdol* (Clash between Tradition and the West), edited by Yŏksa munje yŏn'guso, 53–72. Seoul: Yŏksa pip'yŏngsa, 2001.

Yun T'aeng-nim. "Minjokchuŭi tamnon kwa yŏsŏng: Yŏsŏngjuŭi yŏksahak e taehan siron" (Women and the Discourse of Nationalism: A Thought on Feminist Historiography). *Han'guk yŏsŏnghak* 10 (1994): 86–119.

Index

tem in, 80; proactive role of women in, 40–41, 101; reform of, 31
Conrow, Marion, 120
contact zone, 17, 47
conversion, 24–25, 122, 127–28, 132, 136
Cook, Maude Hemphill, 57
Cooper, Kate, 66
Cram, Rosella, 95
cult of true womanhood, 13, 137–38
Cultural Rule, 146
Cutler, Mary, 54, 68

Dallmayr, Fred, 43
Davidoff, Leonore, 46, 50
Dawn of Tomorrow, The, 136
Daybreak in Korea, 48, 122–29
Dean, Lillian, 156
Denmark, 161
Deuchler, Martina, ix, 41, 46, 80
domestic science, 53, 102–3
domesticity: as wedge for political influence, 46; Christian, 8, 13, 38, 44, 97–107, 119–20, 166, 178, 179; modern, 84; Victorian notions of, 170
Doty, Susan, 29
Duara, Prasenjit, 11
Dubois, Thomas, 134
Duncan, John, 40, 46
Duus, Peter, 9

East Asia: Christianity and modern womanhood in, 5–8; new women's movement in, 146, 161
East Wind, West Wind, 136
education: for girls and women, x, 2, 3, 8, 14, 19, 32–33, 36–37, 39, 41, 42, 55, 76, 78, 86; higher education for women, 1, 55, 92, 100, 149; in East Asia, 8. *See also* mission schools
Ellers, Annie, 55
enlightenment *[kaehwa]*: Chinese, 8–9; Korean, 8–9, 31–32, 35–36, 38–39, 104, 124, 131, 135, 148, 167, 170; western, 8, 11, 21
Epworth League, 70

Estey, Ethel, 62
Europe, 159
Ewa, 122–35
Ewha haktang (Ewha Girls' School), 3, 24, 33, 51, 70, 78, 87–92, 98–99, 106, 109, 117, 149, 223n21
Ewha Womans University, 33, 152

Felski, Rita, 4, 16, 145
Feng, Jin, 104
Fifty Helps for the Beginner in the Use of the Korean Language, 123
Fifty Years of Light, 1
flapper, 137
Fleming H. Revell Company, 122
foreign mission organizations: American, 11; gender hierarchy in, 189n12; male leadership in, 58; prestige of the profession, 58; romanticized image of, 121
Freedman, Estelle, 62
Frey, Lulu, 54, 65, 69, 70, 71, 78, 91, 93, 97, 111, 120, 125, 149
Fukuzawa Yukichi, 33

Gale, James, 53, 60, 112, 123
Garon, Sheldon, 153
gender: as a category of analysis, ix–x, 192n28; discrimination, 3, 157; inferiority, 13; and modernity, 4, 16, 19–20; re-orienting, 1, 18
gender equality: as new moral order, 19, 21–44, 132; in Christian doctrines, 2, 13; missionary rhetoric of, 22–25, 188n10; or equality of purpose, 25, 30
genealogy: of modern woman, x, 5, 20, 177
Gibson girl, 140
Gifford, Daniel, 65
Gilmore, George, 47, 48, 53, 64, 115
girl student: problems of, 103, 104, 106, 225n93
Gospel for All Lands, The, 166
Gospel of Gentility, The, 17
Goucher, John F., 87
Goucher Women's College, 87

LaVergne, TN USA
11 November 2009
163746LV00004B/44/P